LEWIS AND CLARK

ORIGINALLY PUBLISHED AS THE NATIONAL SURVEY OF
HISTORIC SITES AND BUILDINGS • VOLUME XIII

Lewis and Clark

**Historic Places Associated with Their
Transcontinental Exploration (1804-06)**

ROBERT G. FERRIS
Series Editor

UNITED STATES DEPARTMENT OF THE INTERIOR
NATIONAL PARK SERVICE

Washington, D.C. 1975

ASSOCIATE DIRECTOR, PROFESSIONAL SERVICES
ERNEST ALLEN CONNALLY

ASSISTANT DIRECTOR, ARCHEOLOGY AND
HISTORIC PRESERVATION
A. RUSSELL MORTENSEN

DIVISION OF HISTORIC AND ARCHITECTURAL SURVEYS
CORNELIUS W. HEINE, *CHIEF*

HISTORIC SITES SURVEY
HORACE J. SHEELY, JR., *CHIEF*

This volume was prepared by:
Roy E. Appleman

with the collaboration of the Series Editor and
the research assistance of James H. Charleton

Assistant Editor: Richard E. Morris
Designer: Gary Gore

Incorporated in this book are survey and evaluation reports prepared by the following National Park Service historians and archeologists: Roy E. Appleman, Paul L. Beaubine, Chester L. Brooks, Daniel F. Burroughs, William C. Everhart, John A. Hussey, Alfred C. Kuehl, Andrew M. Loveless, Merrill J. Mattes, Ray H. Mattison, Frank B. Sarles, Jr., Charles W. Snell, and Erwin N. Thompson. These reports were reviewed by the Advisory Board on the National Parks, Historic Sites, Buildings, and Monuments and the Consulting Committee for the National Survey of Historic Sites and Buildings.

Library of Congress Cataloging in Publication Data
United States. National Park Service.
  Lewis and Clark: historic places associated with their transcontinental exploration
(1804-06)
  (The national survey of historic sites and buildings, v. 13)
  Bibliography: p.
  1. Lewis and Clark Expedition. 2. Lewis, Meriwether, 1774-1809. 3. Clark, William,
1770-1838. 4. Historic sites-The West. I. Title. II. Series.
F592.7.U56 1975   917.8'04'20922 [B]   73-20144

ISBN# 0-931056-09-8
Fourth Edtion, 2003

**JEFFERSON
NATIONAL PARKS
ASSOCIATION**

714 North Second Street, St. Louis, MO 63102-2519
Cover Design: Christina Watkins

FOREWORD

I first met this wonderful book by Roy Appleman in the gift shop at the Jefferson National Expansion Memorial in the early 1980s, one of the happiest coincidences of my life. Although I didn't know much about the subject at the time, I had decided -- more out of whim than long term planning -- to retrace the route of Lewis and Clark and see what a modern explorer might find in their footsteps.

That trip led to a magazine article, which led to a book, *Out West*, which led to a deeper passion about the Corps of Discovery's story, which led to a documentary film for PBS, which led to...Well, you get the idea. Lewis and Clark have become as intertwined with my own life's journey as they are with the nation's. And this book, along with Bernard De Veto's classic one-volume edition of the expedition journals, got me started down the long trail.

Its first half provides as succinct, yet satisfying, a treatment of the Lewis and Clark expedition as you're likely to find -- from Thomas Jefferson's dream of discovering a Northwest Passage to the post-expedition fates of the hardy explorers, with all the important milestones in between. Many other authors, myself included, have written full-length books about the Corps of Discovery and have struggled with what needs to be left in at all costs and what has to be dropped in the interest of space. Roy Appleman met that challenge, got the job done, and still had half a book left to devote to an equally valuable survey of historic sites along the trail. Believe me, that's a remarkable achievement.

In the quarter century since Appleman completed his work, the library of Lewis and Clark material has expanded and branched into many worthwhile directions. The entire journals, all 13 volumes of them, have been magnificently re-edited and published; scholars have written books devoted to every possible single aspect of the expedition, from its relations with Indians to its contributions to geography and science, from the medicine it practiced (and sometimes malpracticed) to stirring biographies of its members. Likewise, excellent volumes have since come out devoted solely to advise on which highway to follow and what sleeping accommodations are available for today's travelers who follow Lewis and Clark in station wagons instead of keelboats. With the expedition's bicentennial just around the corner, that library is destined to bulge even more. But Roy Appleman's *Lewis and Clark* still has a proud and special place on the shelf.

Especially if you're just getting started with the Corps of Discovery and want to travel light, I couldn't recommend a better single volume to stuff in your backpack. For recounting the history of America's first "road trip" *and* for telling you how to find its most significant locations all in one, this is the book.

Once you've got some miles behind you, you may decide you're ready for a weightier load. Whatever your more particular interest, there will be plenty of books to add to your supplies. In the meantime, let this volume be your guide -- always clear, always trustworthy, always to the point. If it starts you down a road anything like the one it led me to, you're in for the journey of a lifetime.

Dayton Duncan

Dayton Duncan is the author of *Out West: American Journey Along the Lewis and Clark Trail* and, with Ken Burns, *Lewis & Clark: The Journey of the Corps of Discovery*, the companion book to their PBS documentary film of the same name.

Contents

All photographs are indexed.

Maps

PART ONE

Lewis and Clark:
Historical Background

THE Lewis and Clark Expedition was one of the most dramatic and significant episodes in the history of the United States. In 1804–6 it carried the destiny as well as the flag of our young Nation westward from the Mississippi across thousands of miles of mostly unknown land—up the Missouri, over the Rocky Mountains, and on to the Pacific. This epic feat not only sparked national pride, but it also fired the imagination of the American people and made them feel for the first time the full sweep of the continent on which they lived. Equally as important, the political and economic ramifications of the trek vitally affected the subsequent course and growth of the Nation.

In its scope and achievements, the expedition towers among the major explorations of the North American Continent and the world. Its members included the first U.S. citizens to cross the continent; the first individuals to traverse it within the area of the present United States; and the first white men to explore the Upper Missouri area and a large part of the Columbia Basin as well as to pass over the Continental Divide within the drainage area of the two rivers.[1]

Before Lewis and Clark, the trans-Mississippi West was largely a virgin land. British, Spanish, and French explorers and traders had barely penetrated it. Apart from a tiny fringe of French-American settlement in the St. Louis area and elsewhere along the Mississippi and small Spanish colonies in the Rio Grande Valley of New Mexico and in California, the region was virtually uninhabited by whites. For the most part enveloped in rumor, fantasy, and mystery, it was almost as strange as outer space would be to the later generation that was first to orbit the earth and put a man on the moon.

The men of the expedition made their way through this vast land, living mainly off its resources and superbly adapting themselves to the new conditions it imposed. They encountered alien tribes and menacing animals. On foot, on horseback, and by boat, they pushed over jagged mountain ranges, across seemingly endless plains, through

3

tangled forests, against powerful currents and raging waters. Under two determined captains and three hardy sergeants, the explorers met danger as a matter of course and suffered hunger, fatigue, privation, and sickness.

Despite all these obstacles, the project was brilliantly managed and executed. Few, if any, comparable explorations have been so free of blunders, miscalculations, and tragedy. Its leaders were masters of every situation. Only one individual lost his life, but of a disease that could not have been cured in the best hospitals of the day. Clashes with the Indians were limited to two unavoidable instances—with the Teton Sioux and a small party of Blackfeet—but in both cases Lewis and Clark triumphed and their firmness won the respect of the natives.

Considering the frequent stress and their close association over a long period of time, relations between the two captains were remarkably harmonious. This was also true of their party, which when fully assembled consisted of a mixture of white, black, and Indian from various sections of the country and Canada.

Not many explorers in the history of the world have provided such exhaustive and accurate information on the regions they probed. Assigning high priority to the quest for knowledge, Lewis and Clark laboriously recorded in their journals and notebooks observations about the characteristics, inhabitants, and resources of the country through which they passed. All told, they amassed far more reliable data on the West than had ever been acquired before.

The expedition was as astutely conceived as it was efficiently conducted. President Thomas Jefferson organized it in 1802 because he foresaw the continental destiny of the Nation. At that time, the United States had been independent from Britain for only 19 years and depended to a large extent for its very survival on the conflicts generated by imperial rivalry among Britain, Spain, and France. Furthermore, the Union consisted of only 16 States, the Original Thirteen plus Vermont, Kentucky, and Tennessee. Although some settlers had reached the Mississippi, most parts of the western portion of the national domain were not settled at all and most of the remainder was but sparsely populated. In 1803 Ohio came into the Union, and the United States purchased from France the Louisiana Territory, a huge and ill-defined block of territory west of the Mississippi.

The purchase represented the replacement of French interests by those of the United States in the eastern part of the trans-Mississippi

President Thomas Jefferson, progenitor of the Lewis and Clark Expedition and architect of U.S. westward expansion.

West, all of which had long been a sort of international no-man's land by virtue of the undulating fortunes of global politics. The power of Spain was waning there, but she as well as Britain still claimed parts of the territory beyond the purchase. Jefferson recognized the need to explore and affirm U.S. control of the Louisiana Territory, and the purchase spurred his earlier determination to enter the struggle for the empire to its west and lay the basis for a claim.

In a broad sense, too, Jefferson was continuing the centuries-long search for a Northwest Passage to the riches of the Orient—an all-water or nearly all-water route from the Atlantic to the Pacific through or around northern North America that would obviate the need for U.S. and European ships to make the long voyages around South America and Africa. In 1778 the English explorer Capt. James Cook had made an inconclusive search for the passage along the Pacific coast of the continent, but in 1792–94 the Vancouver Expedition had demonstrated that for all practical purposes an all-water route through the continent did not exist. Jefferson hoped that the Lewis and Clark Expedition might still find a nearly all-water passage, but it made no such discovery.[2] As a matter of fact, the pathway it charted was not even economically feasible because of the long portages required and serious navigational problems.

Significance of the expedition

If Lewis and Clark did not discover the Northwest Passage or a practicable transcontinental channel of commerce, their other accomplishments were formidable. The significance of their exploration extends over a broad and interrelated gamut—in geopolitics, westward expansion, and scientific knowledge. From the standpoint of international politics, the expedition basically altered the imperial struggle for control of the North American Continent, particularly the present northwestern United States, to which the U.S. claim was substantially strengthened.

THE westward expansion that ensued in the wake of Lewis and Clark would provide substance to that claim. The wealth of detailed information they acquired about the climate, terrain, native peoples, plants, animals, and other resources of the princely domain they had trodden represented an invitation to occupy and settle it. In their footsteps, came other explorers, as well as trappers, traders, hunters, adventurers, prospectors, homesteaders, ranchers, soldiers, missionaries, Indian agents, and businessmen. They filled in the map, blazed the trails, traded in furs, mined the depths of the earth, tilled the soil, grazed stock, constructed railroads and roads, created towns, founded industries, and formed Territories and States. Ever moving westward, they conquered the land and carried civilization to the shores of the Pacific.

Many of these people followed for part of the way the Missouri River route that Lewis and Clark had pioneered—a waterway that became one of the major westward routes, though the complications of traveling it by steamboat restricted the flow of traffic to its lower reaches and rendered it less useful than the major overland trails.

THE initial spur to westward expansion was the news the explorers brought back about the rich potentialities of the western fur trade, which were concentrated in the Upper Missouri-Yellowstone River-Rocky Mountain area. This trade was the first means of exploiting the resources of the newly discovered land. Trappers and traders were the first to penetrate it in detail, and these mountain men laid the groundwork for the miners and settlers who followed.[3]

Reacting to newspaper and word-of-mouth accounts of the reports of Lewis and Clark to Jefferson and others of the wealth in furs and a natural all-water route of access, the Missouri, adventurers and trappers flocked to St. Louis in the winter and spring of 1806–7. But, as in the later days of the mining rushes, most of those who chose to operate independently were to meet frustration. They were forced to confine their activities to the Lower Missouri or join one of the large and well-organized companies that soon sprang up and monopolized the Rocky Mountain fur trade. Only they possessed the necessary capital to finance the long journeys necessary to reach the hunting grounds and send out parties of sufficient size to ward off Indian attacks.

BUT such hostilities, mainly limited to spasmodic outbreaks of the Teton Sioux, Arikaras, and Blackfeet, were undoubtedly far less severe than they might have been were it not for the reservoir of goodwill the expedition had left with nearly all the western tribes. This reservoir, which Clark deepened during his long and distinguished post-expedition career as Superintendent of Indian Affairs

William Clark.

Meriwether Lewis.

Reacting to the reports of Lewis and Clark on the abundance of fur-bearing animals they had discovered, trappers and traders soon pushed up the Missouri and Yellowstone Rivers. Beaver were the major lure.

in St. Louis, contributed to the success of the early westward movement.

Blending fairness, honesty, and strength with patience, respect, and understanding, Lewis and Clark recognized the personal dignity of the Indians, honored their religion and culture, sincerely proffered aid from the U.S. Government, and tried to establish intertribal peace. Masters of primitive psychology, they instinctively and unerringly always seemed to make the right decision and rarely offended the natives.

Tragically, this heritage of friendliness was not to prevail for more than a few decades. As the westward advance of the Nation burgeoned in the 1840's, the two civilizations clashed. Frontiersmen, eager for land and gold, considered the Indians as "uncivilized" obstacles in their path. The decency and integrity demonstrated by Lewis and Clark in their dealings with them gave way to disrespect and dishonor. In the Government's attitude, honesty too often yielded to deception and altruism to self-interest. Mortal conflict ensued that crushed the Indian way of life [see *Soldier and Brave* (New Edition), Vol. XII in this series].

THE Lewis and Clark Expedition also made major contributions to the fields of geography-cartography, ethnography, and natural history.[4] Scientists were kept busy for a long time digesting the mass of raw information, studying plant and animal specimens, analyzing descriptions and translating them into the appropriate technical language, and classifying and correlating data.

Neither of the two leaders were trained scientists by the standards of their day. Many of their geographic calculations were faulty because they often relied on dead reckoning and did not properly adjust their chronometer and other instruments. Their descriptions of plants and animals lacked professional nomenclature and polish. But, considering the time in which they lived and the circumstances they faced in the field, they demonstrated remarkable competence.

Except in cartography, Lewis was primarily responsible for most of the scientific contributions. He was better educated than Clark and during 2 years of residence with President Jefferson prior to the expedition had enjoyed access to his fine library and been able to draw on his extensive knowledge of zoology and botany. Lewis had also enjoyed the benefit of a cram course in science at Philadelphia and Lancaster that Jefferson arranged for him.

THE geographical findings were in themselves of outstanding significance. Lewis and Clark determined the true course of the Upper Missouri and its major tributaries. They discovered that a long, instead of short, portage separated it from the Columbia, which proved to be a majestic stream rivaling the Missouri itself rather than a short coastal river. Neither the Missouri nor the Columbia was found to be navigable to its source, as many had believed. The explorers also learned that, instead of a narrow and easily traversed mountain range, two broad north-south systems, the Rockies and the Cascades, represented major barriers.

Passing for the most part through country that no Americans and few white men had ever seen, the two captains dotted the map with names of streams and natural features. Some of the designations that have survived to this day include the Jefferson, Madison, Gallatin, Milk, Marias, and Judith Rivers, Beaverhead Rock, Rattlesnake Cliffs, White Bear Islands, York Canyon, and Baptiste Creek. Unfortunately, many other names that were bestowed have faded out of existence.

Clark made his scientific mark primarily in the field of cartography, for which his training consisted mainly of some experience in practical surveying and a limited amount of Army mapping. Yet his relatively crude maps, prepared under field conditions, enriched geographical knowledge and stimulated cartographical advances.[5]

Of particular importance were the three progressively improved maps Clark drew between 1804 and 1810 of the Western United States and lower Canada.[6] These were mainly based on the observations of the two captains, data provided by the Indians, earlier maps of the West, and the journals of preceding explorers. According to historical cartographer Carl I. Wheat, the last of the three (ca. 1809) was of "towering significance" and was "one of the most influential ever drawn" of the United States. Although deficient in its nonexpedition data, provided to Clark by others, for three decades it represented some of the best knowledge available about the West and practically all other maps were based on or influenced by it. Also valuable to geographers and cartographers were the detailed local and regional maps that Clark sketched in his journals or on separate sheets of paper.[7] They provided valuable information on hydrography and relief.

THE second scientific field on which the Lewis and Clark Expedition exerted a major impact was ethnography. Although the two captains' comprehensive descriptions of the natives and their way of life contained some errors and misconceptions, as a whole they were so astonishingly accurate and complete that they provided a basic document for western ethnologists.

Previously, almost nothing had been known of the Indians westward from the Mandan villages, in present North Dakota, to the Upper Columbia. Native groups residing in that area, whom the explorers were undoubtedly the first white men to encounter and describe, included the Northern Shoshoni, Flatheads, Nez Perces, Cayuses, Yakimas, and Walla Wallas. Although the expedition did not meet any Crows, their presence was noted.

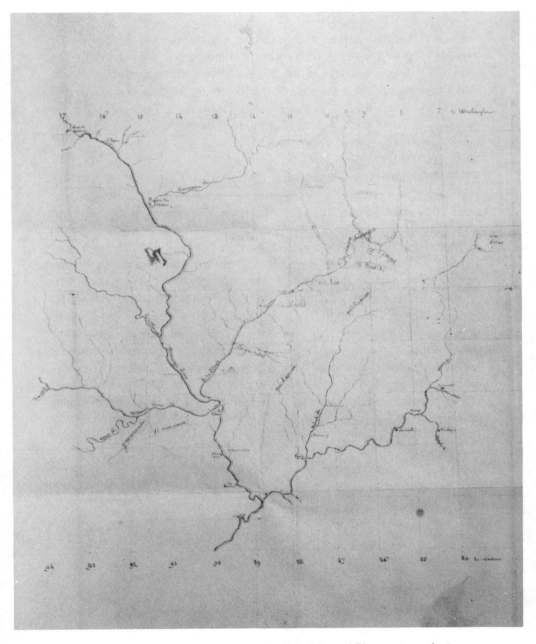

This map is based on early French drawings of the Missouri River system prior to the departure of Lewis and Clark. It is Map #1 of Volume VIII of the Rueben Gold Thwaites edition of the Lewis & Clark Journals, originally published in 1904-5. Contemporary editions of the Journals (e.g. Dr. Gary Moulton, University of Nebraska Press, partially funded by the Lewis & Clark Trail Heritage Foundation) often include a separate volume of maps. One of the most significant features of the Lewis & Clark Expedition was the accuracy of their mapping.

Even for those tribes that traders had contacted and casually reported on—those on the Lower Missouri from St. Louis to the Mandan villages and those at the mouth of the Columbia—Lewis and Clark furnished a far more complete body of data than had ever before been recorded. They also sent back from Fort Mandan, in present North Dakota, or brought back to Washington, D.C., a number of ethnological specimens.[8]

THE final category of scientific knowledge that the exploration enriched was natural history.[9] Usually based on their own observations but sometimes on Indian information, the two captains described hundreds of species of fishes, reptiles, amphibians, mammals, birds, plants, trees, and shrubs. Some were completely new to the world of science; others had never previously been encountered in North America; or earlier descriptions were sketchy and inadequate. In these categories, among mammals alone, are the pronghorn (antelope), bighorn sheep, mountain beaver, black-tailed prairie dog, white weasel, mountain goat, grizzly bear, coyote, and various species of deer, rabbit, squirrel, fox, and wolf. In addition to their descriptions, Lewis and Clark also sent back a large number of zoological specimens, including a few live ones as well as skins, bones, skeletons, teeth, talons, and horns, and in addition a diversity of botanical items.[10]

*   *   *

Augur of exploration

Late on the night of March 5, 1801, a young Army captain named Meriwether Lewis, paymaster of the 1st Infantry Regiment, arrived back at his base in Pittsburgh following a trip on military business to Detroit. It was not unlike many others he had made to posts on the Ohio and Michigan frontier. He did not realize it would be his last.

Apparently the next morning his friend Tarleton Bates, a young Pittsburgh businessman, delivered to him a letter that contained exciting news. It was to change the course of his life radically—and that of his Nation.[11] Dated February 23 and sent by the newly elected and soon to be inaugurated President Jefferson, the communication offered Lewis a position as his secretary-aide. It said: "Your knolege of the Western country, of the army and of all it's interests & relations has rendered it desireable for public as well as private purposes that you should be engaged in that office."

Because of the reference to Lewis' knowledge of the "Western country," even at this early stage Jefferson may have already decided to send out another expedition to explore the West, as he had tried to do on various preceding occasions, and had tentatively decided on Lewis as its leader. Some 8 years earlier, the latter had sought Jefferson's permission to join one of the explorations. And others available for the secretary-aide position were as well as or better qualified.

Whatever Jefferson's aims, Lewis realized that the job offered opportunities and challenges that few 27-year-old Army officers ever enjoyed. He would be on detached duty from the Army, retain his rank, and receive room and board with the Jefferson family as well as a salary of $500, somewhat more than his remuneration as a captain. On March 10 he notified Jefferson of his acceptance.

THE two men were fellow Virginians. Jefferson had long known the Lewis family, who were neighbors at his Monticello estate. The well-bred Lewis, of Welsh and English descent, carried his mother's maiden name as his first name.[12] Like Jefferson, he had been raised in Albemarle County in the shadow of the Blue Ridge Mountains. He was born in 1774 at Locust Hill, a plantation of more than 1,000 acres along Ivy Creek, about 9 miles west of Monticello and 7 miles west of Charlottesville. The second child, he had an elder sister named Jane; and a younger brother, Reuben.

In 1779, when Meriwether was only about 5 years old, his father, William, a reasonably prosperous planter-slaveholder who was then serving as a lieutenant in the Continental Army, died while on leave. The very next year, his widow, Lucy, married another military man, Capt. John Marks, by whom she was to bear a son and daughter. Young Lewis loved to roam the surrounding hills, woods, and fields hunting with his dog. But, a student of books as well as the outdoors, he attended a common day school and learned reading, writing, and arithmetic.

Not long after the War for Independence, in 1784, the family moved to frontier Georgia, where Marks was lured by possible wealth in land. The lad stayed there only 3 years, however, and returned to Albemarle County to continue his education. Under the supervision of one of his uncles, who acted as his guardian, he studied with the local gentry at private Latin schools. In 1792, the year after Marks died, Lucy came back to Locust Hill with her other offspring and Lewis joined them.

Two years later, when Meriwether was 20 years of age, President George Washington called for 13,000 militiamen from Virginia, Maryland, New Jersey, and Pennsylvania to help suppress the Whisky Rebellion, an insurrection in western Pennsylvania. The youth enlisted as a private in the Virginia militia under Gen. Daniel Morgan and served principally in the Pittsburgh area. In a matter of months, he rose to ensign, the equivalent of a modern second lieutenant.

Liking military life, in 1795 Lewis transferred to the 2d Sublegion of the Regular Army. Probably late that year or early the next, likely at Fort Greenville, Ohio, for a few months he served in a rifle company commanded by Lt. William Clark—who would one day join him in exploring the North American Continent and be a lifelong friend. In 1796 the 2d Sublegion became the 1st Infantry Regiment. Three years later, Lewis rose to first lieutenant, and the following year, at the age of 26, to captain. During this span of time, he saw little action but learned much about military life and discipline, the problems of command, Indian character, and frontier conditions— all of which would aid him as presidential secretary and as an explorer.

ON March 10, as soon as he had written Jefferson notifying him of his acceptance of the proffered position, Lewis made the necessary arrangements with his commanding officer and intensified preparations to leave Pittsburgh. Likely within a day or two, he set out for Washington with all his baggage packed on three horses. Because spring rains had turned the roads and trails into a sea of mud and one of his horses went lame, he did not reach Washington until April 1.

For 2 years, Lewis was to live with Jefferson at the White House and Monticello. In addition to the seasoning he gained in governmental and congressional affairs as presidential secretary, he met many prominent politicians, statesmen, and scientists who visited Jefferson. The two men also undoubtedly carried on innumerable conversations on the subject of western exploration. It was a subject dear to both of their hearts, but particularly to Jefferson, who had been immersed in it since boyhood.

Antecedents of exploration

Like many momentous events in history, the Lewis and Clark Expedition was the culmination of the thoughts and desires of many men over a long period of time and the outgrowth of previous abortive attempts to accomplish the same thing. In the case of the Lewis and Clark exploration, the antecedents are traceable principally to one man, Jefferson.

Jefferson was born in 1743 on the Virginia frontier, and his eyes naturally turned westward. His father, Peter, was a civil engineer and surveyor who was attracted to cartography and western exploration. One of the executors of his will, who must have considerably influenced young Jefferson, was Dr. Thomas Walker, surveyor, land speculator, and explorer. He was the first white man known to have entered Kentucky from Virginia and he discovered Cumberland Gap. The year after Peter's death, Walker undoubtedly persuaded Thomas to attend the school of Rev. James Maury, an ardent proponent of westward expansion.

BUILDING on this foundation, quite early in his political career Jefferson became an advocate of western exploration. In December 1783, the year the War for Independence ended by treaty and while he was serving in the Continental Congress, he wrote from Annapolis to his old friend retired Gen. George Rogers Clark, who had been instrumental in winning the old Northwest for the Colonies. Jefferson knew of his interest in the frontier, and they shared a love of natural history and archaeology.

Jefferson had learned that a large amount of money had been subscribed in Britain to send an expedition into the trans-Mississippi West. He feared that the subscribers were using the pretext of promoting knowledge—one he would later employ to justify the Lewis and Clark Expedition—as a guise for intentions to colonize.

Although Jefferson doubted that funds could be raised and was vague about whether the auspices would be private or governmental, he suggested to Clark that he lead an expedition into the trans-Mississippi West. The next February, replying from Richmond, the general stated that the poor condition of his finances would prevent him from doing so. He offered his support of the enterprise, however, and suggested that it be limited to three or four men so as not to alarm the Indians.

Nothing further came of this proposal, but it is significant because the concern expressed by Jefferson over British penetration of the West indicates that he was thinking continentally and geopolitically as early as 1783.

JEFFERSON'S second involvement with planned western exploration—albeit more indirectly—occurred 2 years later while he was serving in Paris as the Confederation's Minister to France. There he first met and encouraged John Ledyard, part genius and part stargazer, in his astounding plan to proceed to the northwestern coast of North America and cross and explore the continent on foot.[13] This plan had become merged in Ledyard's mind with his other major obsession, U.S. participation in the northwest trade.

Ledyard, a Connecticut-born sailor, had seen the trade's potentialities while serving as a corporal of marines in the Royal Navy on Capt. James Cook's third and highly significant round-the-world expedition (1776–80). It was commanded by various subordinate officers after the natives killed Cook in 1779 while he was visiting the Sandwich (Hawaiian) Islands, which he had discovered the previous year. A major unplanned consequence of the voyage was discovery of the fabulous market for sea otter skins, which the sailors had acquired along the North American coast, when the boats reached Canton, China, near the end of 1779.

This discovery was in time to lead to the founding of the triangular northwest trade. It would revolutionize British and American trading patterns, bring a new era to the Pacific, and complicate British, American, Russian, and Spanish diplomatic relations for decades. British, American, and other seamen bartered their trinkets and other goods to coastal Indians for sea otter furs, which they carried to China and traded for Chinese products, transported to home ports and sold at high profits.

Americans did not begin to take part in the trade until 1788, or

3 years later than the English. The belated U.S. participation was no fault of Ledyard, though his widely read book, published at Hartford in 1783, pointing out the immense possibilities of the trade, was the basic stimulus.[14] He was the first American to see clearly the tremendous advantages of the trade and to propose it.

Ledyard had arrived back in the United States in 1782, at what should have been a propitious time to interest shippers in the project. At the end of the War for Independence, they lost their commerce with the British West Indies. Nearly ruined, they were forced to seek new markets, especially in the Pacific. Yet Ledyard was unable to obtain financial backers for his visionary scheme. Disappointed but undeterred, in 1784 he continued his search for capital in Paris and London, where he mingled with the social and scientific elite and lived on their largesse. But all his proposed exploration and trade ventures came to naught.

In 1785, at Paris, Ledyard made the acquaintance of Jefferson, discussed with him the significance of the northwest trade, and broached to him his plan to cross and explore North America from west to east—conceived years before Lewis and Clark were to accomplish the feat in the opposite direction. Jefferson, enthused about Ledyard's plan but recognizing his failure to obtain passage by ship to the northwest coast, suggested that he proceed overland to the Siberian coast and cross the Pacific in a Russian fur boat. Ledyard subsequently returned to London. After at least one more failure to arrange for travel by ship, Ledyard finally acted on Jefferson's suggestion.

Late in 1786—with scant funds, without a passport, and accompanied only by two dogs—Ledyard set out from London. Traveling by boat and land, usually relying for a ride on the generosity of travelers and shippers, he proceeded via Hamburg, Copenhagen, Sweden, and present Finland to St. Petersburg (later Leningrad). There, where he stayed between March and June 1787, the German scientist Peter Simon Pallas, a member of the faculty of the Russian Academy of Sciences, provided him with a passport. Often riding on a three-horse *kibitka*, in September he reached Yakutsk, in eastern Siberia, where difficulty in making travel arrangements under winter conditions to Okhotsk delayed him for months.

In February 1788 Russian officials, possibly because they distrusted Ledyard's interest in their Alaskan colony and its fur trade, arrested

Prior to the Lewis & Clark Expedition, various legends regarding the Rocky Mountains were told and often misunderstood. Even after the publication of the Journals, the extent and magnitude of the mountains was not appreciated fully. It must have been a remarkable experience for co-Captains Lewis and Clark as they sighted this incredible range of peaks through and over which they knew they must lead their men safely.

him. The next month, after a rapid return trip, he was deported across the Polish border. A year later, he died in Cairo while on another exotic expedition, to interior Africa. At the time of his death, Ledyard was still expressing interest in exploring the North American Continent, this time in an east-to-west direction from Kentucky—a plan he explained to Jefferson, who approved.

Jefferson's relations with Ledyard undoubtedly whetted his interest in the West. Equally as important, he learned of the economic significance of the northwest trade—the furtherance of which was to be a major factor in his sponsorship of the Lewis and Clark Expedition.

SOME years elapsed after Jefferson encouraged Ledyard before he became associated for a third time with proposed western exploration. In this case, however, it was a more tangible and practical enterprise, but like the Ledyard project it ultimately came to naught because of the involvement of a foreign nation.

In 1793, while Secretary of State, Jefferson worked through Philadelphia's American Philosophical Society, in which he was a prominent member. Acting on his proposal, the society raised funds by subscription to send French botanist André Michaux on a scientific exploration from the Mississippi to the Pacific. He had been in North America since 1785 and had traveled extensively in the Eastern United States. Interestingly enough, young Meriwether Lewis, only about 18 years old at the time, requested but failed to obtain Jefferson's permission to accompany the explorer.

Michaux's instructions, written by Jefferson, were very similar to those he was to provide Lewis a decade later. They also reveal how early he had precisely formulated his goals in western exploration. He urged Michaux to explore and give "unquestioned preference" to the Missouri River, which he said probably interlocked with the Columbia, while finding "the shortest & most convenient route of communication between the U.S. & the Pacific ocean, within the temperate latitudes, & to learn such particulars as can be obtained of the country through which it passes, it's productions, inhabitants & other interesting circumstances." Michaux was also directed to learn what he could about the mammoth and "whether the Lama, or Paca of Peru is found in those parts of this continent, or how far North they come."

The instructions contain no references to the means of travel, the size of the party, or the type of equipment to be employed, all of which were presumably left to the discretion of the leader. He was, however, directed to proceed to Kaskaskia in Illinois country, cross the Mississippi, and en route overland to the Missouri to skirt the "Spanish settlements" to "avoid the risk of being stopped."

IN this regard, it is probable that Jefferson was influenced by knowledge that fear of Spanish reaction had apparently deterred a proposed exploration in 1790 by Lt. John Armstrong of the Missouri and its southern tributaries in relationship to the Rio Grande.[15] In any event, the very existence of this plan is significant as a precursor of that of the Lewis and Clark Expedition. And, coming as it did in 1790, only 2 years after ratification of the Constitution, it demonstrates early national interest in exploration.

In proposing the ambitious project to Gen. Josiah Harmar, headquartered at Cincinnati, Secretary of War Henry Knox, aware that penetration of Spanish territory was anticipated, stressed the need for secrecy with everyone except for Arthur St. Clair, Governor of Northwest Territory. Knox felt that two separate parties should accomplish the exploration so that at least one might succeed if the other failed. He suggested that each consist of an "enterprizing" officer and a noncommissioned officer, disguised as Indians, and four or five "hardy" and loyal Indians. The major equipment necessary would be a pocket compass and pencils and paper for taking notes. Canoes would be a good mode of transportation.

The man Harmar chose for the task was Lt. John Armstrong. In February 1790 he proceeded from Cincinnati to Fort Kaskaskia, the post nearest to the Missouri, in present Illinois some distance below St. Louis; and then traveled to Cahokia, opposite St. Louis. Seeking information and possibly traveling incognito, he crossed the Mississippi, visited the Spanish cities of Ste. Genevieve and St. Louis, and obtained a map of the Missouri area as well as other information. Nevertheless, in May St. Clair decided that the expedition was impractical. Adverse factors were its difficulty and the nonavailability of Indian participants because of intertribal warfare. Another problem, implied by St. Clair, was Spanish opposition. He and Armstrong advocated that the mission later be assigned to someone traveling in the guise of a trader.

MICHAUX did not even get as far as Armstrong. If the interest of the American Philosophical Society in his expedition was scientific, it soon became apparent that Michaux entertained strong political motives. As a secret French agent, working under Citizen Edmond C. Genêt, France's Minister to the United States, he merged intelligence operations with scientific exploration—if, indeed, he intended to accomplish any of the latter at all.

Genêt arrived in the United States in April 1793. Flagrantly ignoring Washington's Proclamation of Neutrality and straining even Jefferson's Francophilism, he unleashed a series of wild anti-British and anti-Spanish schemes, including the recruitment of Americans to take part in them. According to one plan, a force of newly recruited westerners, who had a long list of grievances against the Spaniards, would strike down the Mississippi Valley, win the aid of French settlers there, and seize Spanish Louisiana. William Clark's brother, George Rogers, embittered over the financial disaster he had suffered during the War for Independence and the failure of Virginia to compensate him for his personal expenditures, became involved in this plan. Genêt commissioned him as a major general in the French Army to help carry it out.[16]

Supposedly to pursue the American Philosophical Society's project, Michaux set out from Philadelphia and traveled to the Louisville area. He consulted there with Clark, probably more about the proposed anti-Spanish expedition than the flora and fauna of the West. But, by this time, President Washington had grown weary of Genêt's machinations and demanded that the French Government recall him. This also brought about termination of the journey of Michaux, whose association with Genêt was clear by this time.

Many years were to pass before Jefferson enjoyed another opportunity to realize his old dream of western exploration.

Lack of knowledge about the West

Meantime, the French, Spanish, and British had obtained some knowledge about the trans-Mississippi West, including the Missouri country, but most of it was wrapped in surmise and conjecture. The initial penetration of the Missouri area, as far north as present North Dakota, was accomplished by the French from the Mississippi and Canada in the period 1719–62. In the latter year, France ceded Western Louisiana to Spain.

Spanish strength in the New World, however, was beginning to wane, and her colonies in New Mexico and California were underpopulated. As a result, administration of Western Louisiana had to be entrusted to a handful of officials. They presided over a population consisting of tiny clusters of Frenchmen from present Canada and New Orleans who had settled at a few points along or near the Mississippi. Beyond, to the west lay a vast land inhabited mostly by unknown tribes. Into their midst, only a few traders, mostly Frenchmen operating under the Spanish flag, dared to venture.

During the first three decades of her control of Western Louisiana, Spain made virtually no advance up the Missouri, and not many traders passed the mouth of the Platte. She was finally prodded to act by aggressive British traders of the North West Company and the Hudson's Bay Company. Beginning in the mid-1780's, they pushed southward into Spanish territory from Canadian posts along the Assiniboine and its southern tributary, the Souris. From a base at the Mandan villages, near present Bismarck, N. Dak., they began to trade with the tribes in the area.

The Spaniards realized that they must either control the fur trade there or lose it permanently and with it possibly that part of the country. Indicative of their lack of geographical knowledge and the inadequacy of their intelligence gathering, they also feared the British would invade New Mexico by land or water. For all these reasons, plus interest in finding a route to the Pacific, in 1793 Spanish authorities subsidized and granted a monopoly of trade on the Upper Missouri, above the Ponca tribe, to a company of St. Louis entrepreneurs who already controlled trade along its lower stretches.[17] The first expedition, in 1794–95, was under Jean Baptiste Truteau, who reached the Arikara villages, in present South Dakota.

The company's most successful venture was that conducted in 1795–97 by James Mackay and John Evans, accompanied by about 30 men with four pirogues full of merchandise.[18] Among the Omaha tribe, they established a trading post, Fort Charles, intended as the first of a string extending to the Pacific coast. While seeking a route to the Pacific, Evans spent the winter of 1796–97 at the Mandan villages, where Jacques d'Eglise had preceded him on a solo venture in 1792. On his arrival, Evans took possession of a British "fort" and raised the Spanish flag.

In March, however, René Jessaume of the North West Company

put in an appearance. Failing to persuade the Indians to do so, he tried to murder Evans, who was saved only by the quick action of his interpreter. In the spring Evans, unable to replenish his small— and inferior—stock of trade goods, trekked back to St. Louis, as had Mackay earlier. This ended the Spanish role along the Upper Missouri. After that, in the years before Lewis and Clark, trade from the St. Louis area was restricted almost entirely to the river's lower reaches.

Thus by 1803, when Jefferson launched the expedition, traders and explorers of other countries had gained a reasonably good knowledge of the Missouri as far as the Platte River, about 600 river miles from its mouth, and a lesser acquaintanceship with the next 1,000 miles, to the Mandan villages. Yet, almost nothing was known of the Upper Missouri and the river's major tributaries: the Yellowstone, Kansas, and Platte.

All along the stream, Indian opposition was strong, particularly from the Omahas, Teton Sioux, and Arikaras. These tribes and a few others pillaged, blackmailed, and killed traders at will; anyone who tried to ascend the river took his life in his hands. The idea that a dozen men could make the journey safely, as Jefferson and Lewis thought, hardly conformed to the facts. These were not well known in the East, and Lewis was not to learn of them until he reached St. Louis late in 1803.

Apart from some data obtained from the Indians, mainly the Minitaris at the Mandan villages, almost nothing reliable was known about the region to the west of them. It was a mélange of rumor and speculation. Two rivers were known to exist on its western and eastern peripheries, the Columbia and Missouri. The former, the "Great River of the West" or "Oregon," had been a matter of myth and assumption until Capt. Robert Gray discovered and named it in 1792. Geographers speculated that it was a short coastal stream, and knew absolutely nothing about its tributaries.

It was believed that the Columbia and Missouri were navigable to their sources and that they possibly interlocked. They were probably separated only by a single, short portage of 20–100 miles, perhaps but a day's travel. This portage-divide was usually pictured as a pyramidal height of land, a level upland, or a high plateau that might be the source of many North American rivers.

The Rockies—the "Stoney Mountains" or "Shining Mountains"—

were only mistily envisioned. In most quarters, their nature as a Continental Divide was not understood. Usually they were thought of as a single chain of ridges or hills fairly close to the Pacific that afforded no substantial barrier. Although intellectuals of the day knew that late in the 18th century Mackenzie had traversed the Rockies to the north and that the Spanish had crossed them to the south much earlier, the most common belief was that a gap divided the cordillera in the middle.

As far as the nature and resources of the trans-Mississippi West as a whole were concerned, only a few Americans held any sort of conception of them and these were conjectural.

Jefferson makes overtures to the Spanish

Near the close of 1802, the year after he assumed the Presidency, Jefferson took preliminary official action to lay the groundwork for the Lewis and Clark Expedition. Late in November, aware that the Spaniards still administered Louisiana Territory, though they had retroceded it to France in the Treaty of San Ildefonso (1800), he met in Washington, D.C., with Spanish Ambassador Don Carlos Martínez, Marqués de Casa Yrujo.

Jefferson frankly explained that, should Congress approve, he proposed to send a small party up the Missouri River and on to the Pacific Ocean. He sought approval of the Spaniards on behalf of France to pass through Louisiana Territory, and ignored their claim to the territory beyond. He said the exploration's real purpose would be only "literary," or the expansion of geographical knowledge, though seemingly it would be examining commercial potentialities— the only constitutional basis on which congressional approval could be made.

Reflecting the persistent position of Spanish officialdom, which had itself long been interested in similar exploration and was wary of U.S. expansion beyond the Mississippi Valley, Yrujo objected. Jefferson said he could not understand such a position inasmuch as his object would only be "observation" of the territory between 40° and 60°N. latitude from the mouth of the Missouri to the Pacific. The purpose would be to unite any findings with those of Mackenzie in 1793 and determine whether or not there could be established in the region a "continual communication or little interrupted, by water as far as the South Sea." Yrujo, exaggerating the facts, insisted that

Don Carlos Martínez, Marqués de Casa Yrujo, Spanish Ambassador to the United States. He and his government opposed Jefferson's proposal to send an expedition to the Pacific.

Spanish and British explorers had already determined during the previous two centuries that such a Northwest Passage did not exist.

In his report to the Spanish Minister of Foreign Affairs, Yrujo characterized Jefferson as a "lover of glory," and warned that he might try to "perpetuate the fame of his administration" not only by his "frugality and economy" but also by "discovering or attempting at least to discover the way by which the Americans may some day extend their population and their influence up the coasts of the South Sea." Yrujo said, too, that should Congress approve Jefferson's proposal, he would immediately notify his Government and await further orders.

Jefferson obtains congressional approval

About the time of Jefferson's meeting with Yrujo, Lewis submitted to the former an estimate of $2,500 to cover the cost of a 10–12 man expedition. Jefferson submitted the estimate unchanged to Congress in a special and confidential message on January 18, 1803.[19] He first asked approval for continuance of the act that had established Indian trading houses.[20] But, after reviewing the need for extending the act and making recommendations for the conduct of Indian affairs within the U.S. boundaries, he came around to his prime purpose. Reversing what he had told the Spanish ambassador about the pursuit of knowledge as the goal of western exploration, he stressed the possible benefits of trade beyond the national boundaries to U.S. citizens.

Jefferson pointed out that not much was known of the Indians along the Missouri, who "furnish great supplies of fur & peltry to the trade of another nation [present Canada] carried on in a high latitude, through an infinite number of portages and lakes, shut up by ice through a long season." He continued:

> The commerce on that line could bear no competition with that of the Missouri, traversing a moderate climate, offering according to the best accounts a continued navigation from it's source, and, possibly with a single portage, from the Western ocean, and finding to the Atlantic a choice of channels through the Illinois or Wabash, the Lakes and Hudson, through the Ohio and Susquehanna or Potomac or James rivers, and through the Tennessee and Savannah rivers.

At this point, Jefferson proposed sending an expedition up the Missouri:

An intelligent officer with ten or twelve chosen men, fit for the enter-
prize and willing to undertake it, taken from our posts, where they
may be spared without inconvenience, might explore the whole line,
even to the Western ocean, have conferences with the natives on the
subject of commercial intercourse, get admission among them for our
traders as others are admitted, agree on convenient deposits for an
interchange of articles, and return with the information acquired in
the course of two summers.

Jefferson emphasized that the modest cost of $2,500 for this
exploration of the "only line of easy communication across the continent, and so directly traversing our own part of it" could easily be
justified on the basis of "extending the external commerce of the
U.S." and would avoid any obstructions placed by "interested individuals." Additionally, the expedition would enhance geographical
knowledge of "our own continent," a factor that would cause the
"nation claiming the territory [France]" not to be disposed to "view
it with jealousy, even if the expiring state of it's interest there did
not render it a matter of indifference."

In other words, about 6 months before Jefferson learned of the
Louisiana Purchase, he was virtually ignoring French ownership of
Louisiana Territory as well as Spanish claims to the area west of it
and blandly proposing exploration of the entire region. At the same
time, he was encouraging a U.S. takeover of the British fur trade
in the interior of North America.

Somehow, the Spanish Ambassador learned of the contents of
Jefferson's confidential message and reported it to his Government
on January 31, but he explained that the Senate would not pass the
measure for fear it "might offend one of the European nations."
Congress nevertheless appropriated funds for the expedition on
February 28, 1803.

Logistical arrangements and scientific indoctrination

About this time, Lewis intensified his planning and logistical preparations. About the middle of March, he set out from Washington
for Lancaster and Philadelphia by way of the U.S. armory at Harpers
Ferry. At the latter place, he ordered or checked on the status of
manufacture of 15 advance, or prototype, specimens of the first
regulation U.S. Army rifle, the Harpers Ferry Model 1803, which
was on the verge of being put into full production.[21] The armory
also was to supply tomahawks and knives.

Lewis was delayed about a month beyond his expectations at Harpers Ferry because of problems associated with the manufacture of a light iron framework for a boat, which was to be assembled and covered with hides along the Upper Missouri and be named the "Experiment." He wanted to be sure the workmen fully understood the framework's design, and he needed to experiment with the dimensions. The frame, when later finished, weighed only 44 pounds and could support a burden of 1,770 pounds.

Because of the time lost at Harpers Ferry, Lewis did not reach Lancaster until April 19. He stayed there until about May 7, studying procedures for celestial observations with astronomer-surveyor Andrew Ellicott. He was one of a group of eminent scientists, the rest at the University of Pennsylvania in Philadelphia, whom Jefferson had written to in late February and early March requesting that they indoctrinate the would-be explorer.

Either at Lancaster or Harpers Ferry, Lewis wrote to Maj. William McRae, commanding the Army post at South West Point, Tenn., and the commanders of two forts in present Illinois, Massac and Kaskaskia, and a projected post at Cahokia. These officers were requested to help recruit volunteers for the exploration. At this point, Lewis planned to proceed overland from Washington to Nashville, stopping at South West Point to pick up recruits, and then move by boat down the Cumberland River to the Ohio-Mississippi and gather volunteers at the Illinois posts. He had written Dr. William Dickson at Nashville and authorized him to contract confidentially for the construction of a boat, according to specifications furnished, and to purchase a light wooden canoe.

At about this same time, by mail Lewis also hired as an interpreter a man named John Conner, who was living at an Indian village near present Muncie, Ind., and who had offered his services. Describing the mission and cautioning secrecy, Lewis requested him to recruit two Indians with appropriate qualifications and join the expedition at one of the Illinois forts. As it turned out, for some reason Conner decided not to do so.

About May 7 Lewis proceeded from Lancaster to Philadelphia, where he had arrived by May 10. There he was even busier than he had been at the two earlier stops. One of his principal activities was study with the university scientists: naturalist-physician Benjamin S. Barton, anatomist Dr. Caspar Wistar, physician Dr. Benjamin

Rush, and mathematician Robert Patterson. They instructed Lewis in the use of scientific instruments, including those employed to determine latitude and longitude; surveying; methodology of celestial observations; medicine; natural history; and Indian ethnology and history. Thus, he acquired rudimentary outlines of virtually every branch of natural and physical science considered to be important in conducting the exploration. The experts also recommended scientific instruments that should be taken along, provided instructions in collecting and preserving specimens, furnished guidance on the general types of information that should be sought, and supplied lists of specific questions that should be answered if possible.

The academic instruction was intensive enough, but another major problem occupied Lewis' attention: procurement of basic supplies and equipment to sustain a 2-year expedition. He purchased or obtained these from the Schuylkill Arsenal, merchants, and public stores. Scientific devices included a quadrant, mariners' compass, pocket telescope, sextant, chronometer, magnet, and pole chains. Other categories were some food items, including 193 pounds of "portable soup" in 32 canisters; tents and camp equipment; clothing and blankets; medicines and a few basic surgical instruments; cutlery and tools; various types of armament, gunpowder, and weapon accessories; and such odds and ends as writing paper, tobacco, soap, and fishing equipment.

Indian trade goods and presents obviously ranked high in the procurement and included:

> 4,600 assorted needles
> 2,800 assorted fishhooks
> 1,152 moccasin awls
>   500 brooches
>   180 scissors
>   180 pewter looking glasses
>   130 pigtails of tobacco
>   122 handkerchiefs
>   73 bundles of assorted beads
>   72 pieces of striped ribbon
>   48 calico ruffled shirts
>   12 pipe tomahawks
>   11½ pounds of beads
>   1 quart of vermilion

Meriwether Lewis learned the rudiments of several scientific disciplines from Benjamin Rush, Caspar Wistar, Benjamin Barton, Andrew Ellicott, and Robert Patterson. Lewis and his men had to adapt to a new environment. The essential task of the expedition was to capture as much knowledge as possible and bring it back for scientists and future explorers. Lewis is shown here in frontier dress.

With his own funds, apparently as a novelty or to impress the Indians, Lewis also purchased an air gun.[22]

In addition to the Indian goods, a large supply of silver and copper Indian peace medals were obtained. On one side, they bore the likeness of Washington or Jefferson; and, on the other, various inscriptions.[23] Also procured was a good supply of printed certificates for issuance to Indian leaders. These documents, which contained a blank to be filled in with the names of chiefs and their tribes, certified the status of the chiefs, asserted the sovereignty of the United States, and guaranteed its protection.

Lewis recruits Clark

After the frantic month in Philadelphia, Lewis returned to Washington, probably arriving there on June 17. By this time, he had decided to take steps to recruit a cocommander. On June 19, with Jefferson's consent, he wrote and offered the assignment to his friend and former commanding officer, William Clark, who was living with his brother George Rogers at Clarksville, Indiana Territory.[24]

Explaining the mission of the expedition, Lewis warned that it should be kept "inviolably secret." Near the end of the letter, he said:

> If therefore there is anything under those circumstances, in this enterprise, which would induce you to participate with me in it's fatiegues, it's dangers and it's honors, believe me there is no man on earth with whom I should feel equal pleasure in sharing them as with yourself; I make this communication to you with the privity of the President, who expresses an anxious wish that you would consent to join me in this enterprise . . . .

Clark was also informed that the President would grant him a captaincy and that he would receive land warrants equal to Lewis' own. Assistance was asked in recruiting personnel, who should be "good hunters, stout, healthy, unmarried men, accustomed to the woods, and capable of bearing bodily fatigue in a pretty considerable degree."

By this stage, Lewis had drastically changed his proposed itinerary, probably because of the possibility that Clark would join the expedition at the Falls of the Ohio and because word from the commander of South West Point indicated that he could recruit few qualified volunteers. Now, instead of moving via South West Point and Nashville, Lewis planned to travel to Pittsburgh and descend the Ohio by keelboat.

BY June 20, the day after Lewis wrote Clark, preparations were far advanced. On that date, Lt. Col. Thomas H. Cushing, adjutant and inspector of the 2d Infantry Regiment, stationed at Fredericktown (present Frederick), Md., did his part to set the wheels in motion. He directed Lt. William A. Murray, who was apparently recruiting men at Carlisle, Pa., for his artillery company at Fort Mifflin near Philadelphia, to dispatch eight of the best men in his party to Pittsburgh. They were to meet Lewis there, help him downriver with the keelboat, and then proceed to Fort Adams in Mississippi Territory, where the artillery company was scheduled to be reassigned.

Jefferson's instructions to Lewis

Also on June 20, Lewis received final instructions from Jefferson, who had coordinated them with his Cabinet. Late in April Jefferson had also sent a draft of them to Lewis in Philadelphia, and he had discussed it with the scientists at the University of Pennsylvania.

After briefly treating supply procedures for the 10–12 man expedition, the instructions stated that they applied to the period "after your departure from the United states"; prior to that, "occasional communications" would be most effective. The directive explained that the Governments of Spain, France, and Britain had been notified of the expedition and that French and British passports had been obtained; the latter one was intended for use with any traders who might be encountered.

Jefferson continued:

> The object of your mission is to explore the Missouri river, & such principal stream of it, as, by it's course and communication with the waters of the Pacific ocean, whether the Columbia, Oregan, Colorado or any other river may offer the most direct & practicable water communication across this continent for the purposes of commerce. . . . The interesting points of the portage between the heads of the Missouri, & of the water offering the best communication with the Pacific ocean, should also be fixed by observation, & the course of that water to the ocean, in the same manner as that of the Missouri.

Special investigation was to be made of the possibility of a transcontinental tieup with the northwest trade:

> Should you reach the Pacific ocean inform yourself of the circumstances which may decide whether the furs of those parts may not be collected as advantageously at the head of the Missouri (convenient

as is supposed to the waters of the Colorado & Oregan or Columbia) as at Nootka sound, or any other point of that coast; and that trade be consequently conducted through the Missouri & U.S. more beneficially than by the circumnavigation now practised.

Latitude and longitude and compass variations were to be calculated at key places, and river courses were to be traced. Careful observations were to be made of topography, soils, crops, flora and fauna, extinct or rare remains, mineral resources, volcanic activity, climate, and weather.

Considerable space was devoted to the Indians, who were to be treated kindly:

> In all your intercourse with the natives, treat them in the most friendly & conciliatory manner which their own conduct will admit; allay all jealousies as to the object of your journey, satisfy them of it's innocence, make them acquainted with the position, extent, character, peaceable & commercial dispositions of the U.S., of our wish to be neighborly, friendly & useful to them; & of our dispositions to a commercial intercourse with them; confer with them on the points most convenient as mutual emporiums, and the articles of most desireable interchange for them & us.

Lewis was also directed to try to arrange for influential chiefs to come to Washington, D.C.; and to tell the tribes that, if they so desired, arrangements would be made to rear their young people among Americans and teach them useful arts.

Everything possible was to be learned about the natives: tribal names, population, and boundaries; intertribal relations; way of life, languages, traditions, and monuments; occupations and associated tools and implements; armament; food and clothing; domestic accommodations; diseases and remedies applied; and laws, customs, morality, and religion. If a superior force of Indians proved to be hostile, it was preferable not to engage them, so that the knowledge the explorers had gained would not run the risk of being lost.

Although the route was to be along the Missouri, inquiries were to be made about its tributaries, especially the southern ones, and population and topography along them. Any knowledge that could be gained about the northern tributaries would be interesting, but the instructions stated the British had already learned much about them.

Lewis was to send back letters and reports to Cahokia or Kaskaskia with traders or Indians and to utilize a cipher that had been set up

Dear Sir   Washington, US. of America. July 4, 1803

In the journey which you are about to undertake for the discovery of the course and source of the Missouri, and of the most convenient water communication from thence to the Pacific ocean, your party being small, it is to be expected that you will encounter considerable dangers from the Indian inhabitants. should you escape those dangers and reach the Pacific ocean, you may find it imprudent to hazard a return the same way, and be forced to seek a passage by sea, in such vessels as you may find on the Western coast. but you will be without money, without clothes, & other necessaries, as a sufficient supply cannot be carried with you from hence. your resource in that case can only be in the credit of the US. for which purpose I hereby authorise you to draw on the Secretaries of State, of the Treasury, of War & of the Navy of the US., according as you may find your draughts will be most negociable, for the purpose of obtaining money or necessaries for yourself & your men: and I solemnly pledge the faith of the United States that these draughts shall be paid punctually at the date they are made payable. I also ask of the Consuls, agents, merchants & citizens of any nation with which we have intercourse or amity to furnish you in those supplies which your necessaries may call for, assuring them of honorable and prompt retribution, and our own Consuls in foreign ports where you may happen to be, are hereby instructed & required to be aiding & assisting to you in whatsoever may be necessary for procuring your return back to the United States. And to give more entire satisfaction & confidence to those who may be disposed to aid you, I Thomas Jefferson, President of the United States of American, have written this letter of general credit for you with my own hand, and signed it with my name.

Th:Jefferson

To Capt. Meriwether Lewis.

Jefferson furnished Lewis with a special letter of credit. The text of this letter of credit, backed by the "faith of the United States," is above. The letter itself is in the Clark Papers of the Missouri Historical Society, St. Louis, Missouri. Every attempt has been made to follow the spelling, capitalization, and punctuation as used in the letter, typical of late eighteenth and early nineteenth centuries.

for the expedition for any secret information. On arrival at the Pacific coast, should that be attained, two trusted men were to be sent back to the United States with a copy of the expedition's notes on the vessel of a northwest trader or other ship. The same mode of transportation could be utilized for the entire party if it were deemed better not to return by the westbound route. For such purposes, a letter of credit drawn on the U.S. Government was to be provided. At the end of the instructions, Jefferson expressed a *"sincere prayer for your safe return."* [25]

IT seems clear not only that Jefferson clarified and modified these instructions verbally to Lewis, but that he also gave him additional ones—particularly on internationally sensitive subjects or those that were to be altered by the subsequent news of the Louisiana Purchase.

For instance, the intense interest that Lewis and Clark were to reveal in the northern tributaries of the Missouri, whose importance was augmented by the vague northern boundaries of the purchase, is at variance with the instructions, which emphasized the southern tributaries. It is likely, however, that Jefferson privately told Lewis to investigate the northern tributaries before he learned of the purchase.

In commenting on the draft instructions, as far back as April 13, Secretary of the Treasury Albert Gallatin had granted that knowledge of the southern tributaries of the Missouri was desirable vis-a-vis Spanish interests and claims. He further said, however, that special efforts should be made to determine the northern extent of the Missouri drainage basin; of British communications with that river from Canada; and of the best places to occupy immediately, if necessary, to prevent British interests from taking over any part of the Missouri country. Gallatin summed up his point by stating:

> . . . the future destinies of the Missouri country are of vast importance to the United States, it being perhaps the only large tract of country, and certainly the *first* which lying out of the boundaries of the Union will be settled by the people of the U. States.

Secretary of State James Madison, though striking a less imperialistic chord, recommended that emphasis be placed on the commercial goals of the expedition to repel "criticism of illicit principal objects of the measure." Certainly such comments by two of his Cabinet members imply that Jefferson probably shared their sentiments.

Jefferson's motivations

Jefferson's motivations basically reflected his political acumen and interest in science. Particularly revealing are the attitudes he manifested toward western exploration over a period of two decades, his dealings with the Spanish Ambassador, his message to Congress on January 18, 1803, his communications with his Cabinet, and his instructions to Lewis.

The primary motivation was in the realm of geopolitics and economic nationalism. Jefferson envisioned the Nation's ultimate expansion all the way to the Pacific, as it had already pushed westward to the Mississippi. Sending as he was an expedition to investigate a water route suitable for U.S. commerce across territory held or claimed by foreign powers, he could hardly have believed it would long remain in their hands—or at least he hoped it would not.

As a minimum, Jefferson intended that the United States would play a key role in the commerce of the region, whose inhabitants and resources he instructed Lewis to investigate carefully. All the information he obtained would be useful to settlers. And in 1803 the United States, whose President dreamed of a utopian agrarian republic, was an agricultural Nation that in time would presumably need more lands for expansion. Living, too, at the dawn of the canal era, before the advent of railroads, he undoubtedly hoped to create a transcontinental water route.

A successful exploration would also link up with and strengthen the basis for a U.S. claim to the Columbia Basin that Capt. Robert Gray had provided in May 1792 by discovering the mouth of the Columbia, strategic key to the hinterland of Northwest America. As Jefferson well knew, that claim—still untested against those of Spain, Britain, and Russia—had been challenged only 5 months later by the Royal Navy's Lt. William R. Broughton. One of the officers of the Vancouver Expedition (1791–95), he entered the Columbia estuary in the *Chatham*, and then in smaller boats he and some of his crew voyaged about 100 miles upriver, almost to the unnavigable Cascades. He took possession of the country for his King. Obviously, if a U.S. overland expedition could descend the Columbia and explore the bordering lands, U.S. rights would be improved.

Taking advantage of French, Spanish, British, and Russian failure to explore fully or effectively settle the trans-Mississippi West, Jefferson also hoped to discover any unrevealed riches before European

The Lewis & Clark Expedition brought back a great deal of information which encouraged the fur trade. The two contemporary National Park Service fur trade reenactors shown here are on the banks of the Missouri, upstream from where the Yellowstone River joins it. They are standing just outside the gate of Fort Union Trading Post, the major Upper Missouri operation of the American Fur Company and now a National Park area. The American Fur Company was started by John Jacob Astor shortly after Lewis & Clark returned from their explorations. Operated out of St. Louis, it and its competitors furthered the exploration and opening of the West through business and commercial enterprises.

powers did and gain an early commercial ascendancy. That would enhance the possibility of political control, a future basis for which would obviously be bolstered by initial exploration.

Jefferson was particularly interested in advancing U.S. participation in the fur trade—the major economic enterprise of the day and one of the principal forces that had generated the longtime imperial rivalries for control of North America. By 1803 U.S. northwest traders had gained dominance over the British in the triangular maritime trade. But New England shippers, lacking a river route to the Pacific, were forced to make long, time-consuming, and hazardous voyages around Cape Horn. Jefferson believed that a short, single portage existed between the Missouri and the Columbia. A Missouri-Columbia route, if feasible, would immeasurably stimulate the northwest trade and, if U.S.-controlled, would be relatively safe from naval blockades and privateers. 'Additionally, it would foster further economic penetration; provide lines of communications; and, if political hegemony could be achieved, settlement. In the process, an inland fur trade, as much an object of interest to Jefferson as the maritime, could be established.

Jefferson was well aware of the extension of British authority in present Canada through the continued westward push of fur traders. If the United States did not take steps to counter this penetration, the British might win complete control. Jefferson hoped to learn of fur resources and create trade channels with the Indians along the route of the expedition.

RIVALRY between the Hudson's Bay Company and the North West Company in Canada had produced in 1791–93 the British predecessor of the Lewis and Clark Expedition: Alexander Mackenzie's daring crossing, from Fort Chipewyan on Lake Athabaska, of the North American Continent. He was the first white man to accomplish this heroic feat north of Spanish Mexico. In one of the most stirring passages in the annals of North American exploration, he later described his small party's arrival at the Pacific, north of Vancouver Island at the mouth of the Bella Coola River:

> I now mixed up some vermillion in melted grease, and inscribed, in large characters, on the South-East face of the rock on which we had slept last night, this brief memorial—"Alexander Mackenzie, from Canada, by land, the twenty-second of July, one thousand seven hundred and ninety-three." [26]

Tremendous though his achievement was, the North West Company's Mackenzie had found no navigable all-water, or nearly all-water, route to the Pacific. On the basis of Indian reports of a big river that ran into the Pacific, he did discover the Fraser River, which he called the Tacoutche Tesse. But he was unable to navigate it to its mouth and was forced to descend the Bella Coola. He and everyone else, until Lewis and Clark demonstrated otherwise, assumed that the Tacoutche Tesse was the Columbia, which Gray had earlier discovered.

Mackenzie was subsequently disillusioned by his company's failure to find a Pacific outlet for the inland fur trade and to counter American advances in the northwest maritime trade. In 1799 he withdraw from the company and went to England, where he proposed to the Government and private industry an aggressive and anti-American policy of trade imperialism. He outlined it, as well as his exploratory experiences, in *Voyages from Montreal* . . . (late 1801), which Jefferson read and Lewis and Clark probably carried with them on their expedition.

The book proposed unification of the British fur trade in present Canada and advocated a transcontinental operation that would insure dominance of the fur trade and fisheries from 48° to the North Pole except in Russian America. Specifically recommended were the relaxation of East India Company restrictions on British northwest traders at Canton so they could better compete with the Americans; merger of the Hudson's Bay Company and the North West Company; establishment of a firm trade stance on the northwestern coast of North America; and the attainment of British sovereignty over the Columbia River, which Mackenzie believed would become the major western artery for the fur trade.

THESE daring proposals by one of the major figures in the Canadian fur trade for intensified competition with the United States spurred Jefferson to evolve plans that were almost as militant. He hoped that Lewis and Clark could find a northern tributary of the Missouri that would permit much of the Canadian trade east of the Rockies, particularly that along the Saskatchewan River, to be diverted to what he hoped would become U.S. waterways and even U.S. control. He recognized that the existing Canadian route to Montreal was laborious and inconvenient because of the many portages required and

When the Hudson's Bay Company and the North West Company merged in 1821 at the direction of the British parliament, George Simpson was 29 years old. He was elected deputy governor of the merged Hudson's Bay Company and put in charge of all field operations in what was then called Rupert's Land, now called Canada, the Western District of which included the land west of the Rocky Mountain divide and north of California, plus all the land drained by the Columbia River. Five years later, in 1826, Sir George Simpson was elected a governor of the Company. Shown here in the fullness of his title, Simpson had to deal with the growing American presence in the Rocky Mountains and along the Pacific coast, especially after the publication of the journals of the Lewis & Clark Expedition.

its closure by ice during the long winters. Unaware that the Upper Missouri and its tributaries also froze over, he felt that the southern route would provide a faster and cheaper year-round outlet.

Jefferson's final motivation was in science, a personal field of interest. For years he had been collecting information about the West and had made various unsuccessful attempts to send an expedition to explore it. He was anxious to know all he possibly could about the natives, plants, and animals, and was intrigued by the notion that prehistoric creatures might be roaming over the vast unexplored spaces on the map.

News of the Louisiana Purchase

Shortly before Lewis left Washington on July 5, President Jefferson confirmed to him some momentous news, completion of negotiations for the Louisiana Purchase. Based on advance information, both of them had been expecting the event to occur.[27] In one of the most resounding diplomatic triumphs in U.S. history, representatives at Paris had purchased from Napoleon for roughly $15 million not only the isle of Orleans, as they had hoped to do, but also all of Louisiana west of the Mississippi.[28] The impact on the course of U.S., as well as world, history was to be immeasurable.

The purchase, the largest single accession of territory in the history of the Nation, doubled its size. Added to it, though the boundaries of the acquisition were poorly defined at the time, were the rich resources of more than 820,000 square miles—essentially the western drainage of the Mississippi, extending approximately from the Gulf of Mexico to the present Canadian border and from the Mississippi to the Rocky Mountains (Continental Divide).[29]

The purchase not only resolved some serious international and domestic problems of Jefferson that affected the Lewis and Clark Expedition but also intensified its importance and gave it a clearer rationale. Amazingly little was known of the area and its native population, even in high Government circles. The available information consisted essentially of much of that which had been obtained or surmised by the French, Spanish, and British through their exploration and trading activities, as well as advice they had received from the Indians—mingled with a body of speculation by U.S. journalists and geographers. The need for accurate knowledge about the new domain was urgent; fortunately, the means to gather it, the Lewis and Clark Expedition, had already been organized.

A second ramification of the purchase for the expedition was in the realm of diplomacy. The United States would now need to assert its jurisdiction over and pacify the native tribes. This was specially desirable because in the event of war with Britain the warlike Sioux and other pro-British groups might overwhelm frontier settlements. Until the purchase, in all their preparations Jefferson and Lewis had acted on the assumption that the entire extent of their exploration, including the Missouri River country, would be foreign land. The sudden turn of events meant that the Indians along the river could be told that their Great White Father was Jefferson rather than the Spanish and French rulers. Attempts could be made to further peace among the tribes and impress them with U.S. strength. The British traders known to be active around the Mandan villages could be notified they were operating in U.S. territory.

Thirdly, representing as it did a major advancement in the Nation's westward expansion, the purchase stimulated interest in the area that was to be probed by the Lewis and Clark Expedition to the west of its boundaries. Indeed, the western limits were so ill understood that in effect the area acquired could not be distinctly delineated from the lands to the west. Ultimate acquisition of the westernmost of the two areas was to be facilitated in part by the adverse effect of the purchase on British, French, and Spanish imperial ambitions in North America.

Until not long before he sold Louisiana to the United States, Napoleon had hoped to restore the French Empire in North America through occupation of Western Louisiana, which Spain had secretively retroceded to him in the Treaty of San Ildefonso (October 1800) along with the isle of Orleans. The U.S. Government learned of this action in the spring of 1801, though Spanish officials continued their lethargic administration of the region pending Napoleon's takeover. This possibility, by a ruler with global ambitions, was sufficient to cause Anglophobe Jefferson to consider an alliance with Britain.

But Napoleon's proposed occupation of Louisiana failed because of costly reverses he suffered in attempting to quell a native uprising in Santo Domingo (Hispaniola). Heavy losses, from yellow fever as much as combat action, forced him to divert there the force scheduled to move into Louisiana. Defenseless in America, he faced the loss of Louisiana to his seafaring enemy Britain. To replenish his treasury and to finance the renewed wars he planned in Europe, as well as to deny Louisiana to Britain, he decided to sell it to the

WASHINGTON CITY

MONDAY, JULY 4.

OFFICIAL.

The Executive have received official information that a Treaty was signed on the 30th of April, between the Ministers Plenipotentiary and Extraordinary of the United States and the Minister plenipotentiary of the French government, by which the United States have obtained the full right to and sovereignty over New Orleans, and the whole of Louisiana, as Spain possessed the same.

This item in the *National Intelligencer* (Washington, D.C.), July 4, 1803, not only broadened the importance of the Lewis and Clark Expedition, but also carried momentous news for the Nation.

United States. At the same time, he created a barrier to British expansion in North America.

The purchase also resolved a major domestic crisis by pacifying the westerners. Most of them resided along the Ohio River and its tributaries in Kentucky and Tennessee. They had become highly agitated in October 1802 when Spanish officials, taking advantage of the pending formal transfer of Louisiana to France, in effect closed the port of New Orleans and thus the Mississippi to American trade, a policy that most Americans felt Napoleon would continue. This crippled the marketing of trans-Appalachian farm produce— nearly half the national total. It flowed down the Ohio and Mississippi, the only effective outlet in the absence of a good cross-mountain road system.

This weakened the bonds of the West with the young National Government. Many westerners had agitated for separation from the Union and sought an attachment to Spain, France, or Britain, or else the establishment of an independent republic that would negotiate suitable arrangements with any of those countries. They all encouraged and abetted the ferment in the West, for they clearly recognized that the U.S. frontier would not stop at the Mississippi, to whose banks the vanguard of migration had already reached.

Separation was one thing. Even worse was the possibility that the westerners, to achieve control of the Mississippi, might use armed force to seize New Orleans, or possibly parts of Louisiana. This would result in war with Spain, which because of the international turmoil at the time might in turn make the United States vulnerable to French or British attack.

To avoid war and settle the Mississippi question once and for all, in 1802 Jefferson directed the U.S. Minister to France, Robert R. Livingston, to attempt to buy New Orleans. The next January, some 3 months after the Spanish closed it to navigation, Jefferson attempted to convince the West that diplomacy promised better results than force by appointing a special plenipotentiary, James Monroe, to join forces with Livingston. By the time he arrived in Paris, in April, Napoleon had already decided to sell all of Louisiana to the United States.

The purchase helped cement the West to the Union and bring about a national consolidation that insured the occupation of Louisiana and increased the probability of ultimate acquisition of the lands beyond all the way to the Pacific. More immediately, the Lewis and Clark Expedition, which had been projected as an interesting scientific exploration, albeit with imperialist overtones, was converted partly into an assertion of control over and pragmatic investigation of possessed territory—lands that the previous owners had never been able to explore fully.

Most of these factors were apparent to Lewis as he prepared to leave Washington and augmented his sense of urgency to launch the expedition. Little did he know how many delays lay ahead.

Lewis sets out from Washington

Lewis left Washington on July 5 and arrived that evening at Fredericktown (present Frederick), Md. He learned that the wagon carrying supplies from Philadelphia had already passed by en route to Harpers Ferry to pick up the weapons and other equipment but on its arrival there on June 28 the driver had decided not to take any part of them because he felt his team could not haul the whole augmented load. At Fredericktown, Lewis arranged with another teamster to transport the supplies, but he did not show up at the arsenal. Neither had the replacement wagon Lewis hired by the time he set out from Harpers Ferry on the afternoon of July 8.

Delay and frustration at Pittsburgh

Lewis was to spend far more time at Pittsburgh than he had hoped. The planned week stretched out to six—from July 15 to August 31. The delay was attributable to the failure of the boatbuilder to complete the keelboat by July 20, the date specified in his contract, which had been negotiated by mail or courier. Otherwise, departure would have been possible about July 22 or 23. On the former date, the wagon from Harpers Ferry arrived. By then, 7 of the 8 soldiers from Carlisle, Pa., one of whom had deserted en route, had put in their appearance. The wagon from Philadelphia had already been on hand when Lewis arrived.

A BIT of good news was the receipt on July 29 of a letter from Clark accepting the assignment as cocommander. He had replied on July 18, the day after getting Lewis' letter of June 19, which had taken about a month in the mails. Meantime, because of the delayed reply, the uncertainty of a positive response, and the urgent need

One of the earliest depictions (ca. 1803–6) of Harpers Ferry. The large building in the lower center is the main arsenal, where weapons were stored. The edifice on the slope of the hill is the Harper House, a tavern. At the lower left, the main structure is the armory, where manufacturing took place.

to get underway, Lewis had persuaded Lt. Moses Hooke, a 26-year-old officer in his own regiment with a fine background, to take Clark's place in case he had not replied or declined by the time everything was in readiness to leave Pittsburgh. Lewis believed that Hooke was as qualified "as any other officer in the Army" to fulfill the responsibilities.[30] But, when Clark accepted, Hooke lost his chance to gain a niche in the Nation's annals.

Clark was enthusiastic about the project and stated, "The enterprise &c. is Such as I have long anticipated and am much pleased with." He went on to say that he would cheerfully partake of the "dangers, difficulties, and fatigue" of the expedition as well as the "honors and awards" if it were successful. He said he knew it was an undertaking "fraited with many difficulties," but in an affirmation of friendship asserted, "My friend I do assure you that no man lives with whome I would perfur to undertake Such a Trip &c. as your self." [31] On August 3 Lewis notified Clark that he was gratified by his decision.

PENDING completion of the keelboat, Lewis purchased in Pittsburgh or its environs a pirogue, a type of flat-bottomed dugout commonly used on inland waters. He also recruited or welcomed three prospective members of the expedition, one of whom was probably George Shannon, a 17- or 18-year-old youth from Ohio. Around this time or earlier, Lewis paid $20 for a dog that he named Scannon. It was a Newfoundland, a large and powerful black breed.

NONE of the progress assuaged the commander's exasperation at the vexsome delay in keelboat construction. Daily visits to the builder, who was sick when he was not drunk or fighting with his crew, had slight effect, though he was convinced to hire more hands. One of his series of excuses was the problem of obtaining timber, but he kept saying the boat would soon be ready. Cajolery, threats, or entreaties were to no avail with him, or even his work crew. But such was the scarcity of boatbuilders that no other could be found. At one point, Lewis considered purchasing two additional pirogues and proceeding downriver hoping to buy a keelboat there, but local authorities told him that this would be impossible. Finally, at 7:00 a.m. on August 31, the keelboat was finished.

Apparently built according to specifications earlier forwarded to the builder, the craft was 55 feet in length and a little over 8 feet wide in the central part. It was capable of carrying a cargo of about 10 tons, and had a shallow draft, like other keelboats used on western rivers.[32] Its 32-foot-high mast, jointed near the base so that it could be lowered, supported a large, square sail and a foresail. A 10-foot-long deck at the bow, provided a forecastle; an elevated deck of similar length at the stern accommodated a cabin. The hold was about 31 feet in length.[33]

As soon as the boat was finished, it was hurriedly loaded with the assembled supplies. This work was probably done under Lewis' supervision by the seven soldiers, three prospective recruits, and possibly other personnel assigned by Pittsburgh military authorities. To lighten the keelboat, as much as possible was loaded in the pirogue. And arrangements were made for a wagon to haul a load of supplies to Wheeling, where they would be picked up. These actions were necessary because the Ohio was not only at a seasonal low, but the unusually dry summer had also shrunk it to a depth far below that in most previous years. Even the warnings of oldtimers that it was impractical to descend the river with the keelboat did not deter Lewis, for at this point he hoped to move 200 or 300 miles up the Missouri before establishing winter quarters.

Down the Ohio to the Falls

Only 3 hours after the keelboat was finished, at 10:00 a.m. on August 31, 1803, Lewis set out from Pittsburgh.[34] Accompanying him were at least 11 men, consisting of a pilot he had hired to guide the group as far as the Falls of the Ohio, the seven soldiers, and the three prospective expedition members. In the party, however, were possibly one or more additional hands, who were employed and discharged at various points all along the way.

The exceptionally low water level, in some places no more than 6 inches deep, created trouble. The boats averaged only about 12 miles a day, sometimes as few as 4 or 5. The major problems were riffles, wide bars of small stones often mingled with driftwood, or shoals that blocked the channel. On some days, as many as five of them were encountered. Each time, it was necessary to unload the keelboat's cargo temporarily. When the party, getting into the water, could not lift the empty boat over an obstruction, horses and oxen were hired from riverside farms to drag it over.

On the positive side, the downriver current smoothed the way. When the wind was favorable and the water deep enough, the sail of the keelboat was employed. At other times, oars and poles were probably used to propel it, as well as the pirogues and canoes.[35] On September 4, at Georgetown, Pa., Lewis hired a canoe, as he was to do at different times later; many of them proved to be leaky. Anyway, supplies often got wet and guns rusted. Frequent stops were required to unload, dry, and repack the cargo.

The party paused at Wheeling, in present West Virginia, on September 7–9 and picked up the wagonload of supplies from Pittsburgh. To accommodate them, a second pirogue was purchased, apparently smaller than the one that had been acquired in the

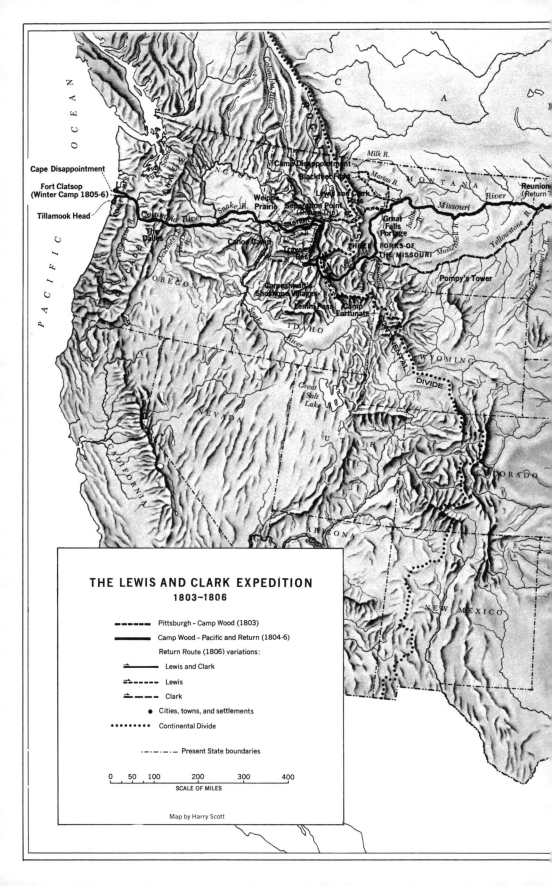

OCEAN

Columbia River

Cape Disappointment

Fort Clatsop
(Winter Camp 1805-6)

Tillamook Head

PACIFIC

WASHINGTON

Weippe
Prairie

The Dalles

Canoe Camp

OREGON

Snake R.

Columbia River

Snake
River

Great
Salt
Lake

NEVADA

CALIFORNIA

UTAH

ARIZONA

Camp Disappointment

Blackfeet Fight

Lewis and Clark
Pass

Separation Point
(Return Trip)

Travelers
Rest

CHIEF

Cameahwait's
Shoshone Village

Lemhi Pass

Camp
Fortunate

IDAHO

Milk R.

Marias R.

MONTANA

Missouri

River

Reunion
(Return

Great
Falls
Portage

Judith

Mussellshell R.

Yellowstone R.

FORKS OF
THE MISSOURI

Pompy's Tower

CONTINENTAL
DIVIDE

WYOMING

COLORADO

NEW MEXICO

THE LEWIS AND CLARK EXPEDITION
1803–1806

------- Pittsburgh – Camp Wood (1803)

——— Camp Wood – Pacific and Return (1804-6)

Return Route (1806) variations:

⇉——— Lewis and Clark

⇉------ Lewis

⇉— — — Clark

● Cities, towns, and settlements

•••••••• Continental Divide

—·—·—·— Present State boundaries

0 50 100   200   300   400
SCALE OF MILES

Map by Harry Scott

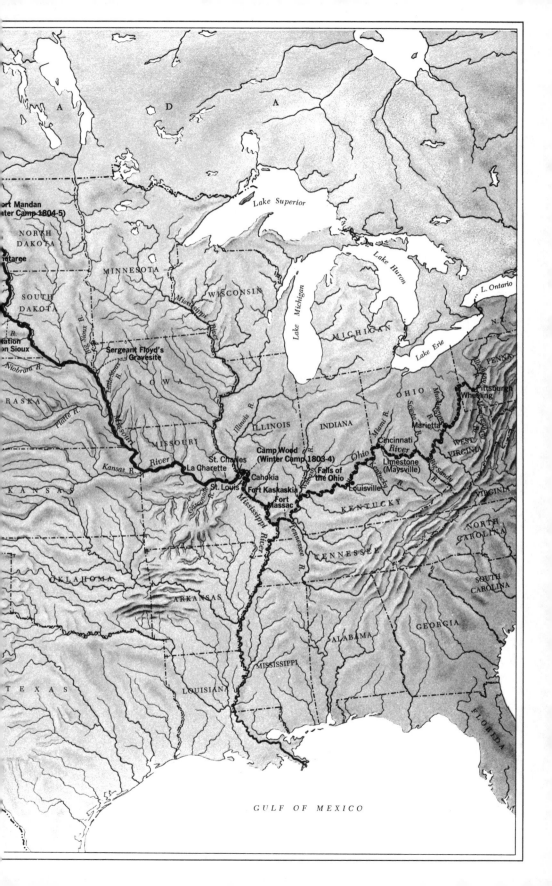

Fort Mandan
(Winter Camp 1804-5)

NORTH
DAKOTA

Mandaree

SOUTH
DAKOTA

R.

Station
on Sioux

Niobrara R.

RASKA

Platte R.

Kansas R.

KANSAS

OKLAHOMA

TEXAS

CANADA

Lake Superior

MINNESOTA

WISCONSIN

Mississippi River

Big Sioux R.

Little Sioux R.

Sergeant Floyd's
Gravesite

IOWA

Missouri River

MISSOURI

La Charette
St. Charles

Gasconade R.

St. Louis

Cahokia
Fort Kaskaskia

Fort
Massac

Mississippi River

ARKANSAS

LOUISIANA

MISSISSIPPI

Illinois R.

ILLINOIS

Camp Wood
(Winter Camp 1803-4)

Lake Michigan

MICHIGAN

Lake Huron

L. Ontario

N.Y.

Lake Erie

OHIO

Muskingum R.

Miami R.

Scioto R.

PENNA.

Pittsburgh
Wheeling

Marietta

Cincinnati
River

Limestone
(Maysville)

Falls of
the Ohio

Louisville

Ohio

Wabash R.

Kentucky R.

Tennessee R.

INDIANA

KENTUCKY

TENNESSEE

ALABAMA

GEORGIA

Big Sandy R.

WEST
VIRGINIA

VIRGINIA

NORTH
CAROLINA

SOUTH
CAROLINA

FLORIDA

GULF OF MEXICO

Pittsburgh area.[36] By this time, after the delay at Pittsburgh and the subsequent navigational problems, Lewis was impatient to move on—so much so that he lost the chance to gain a doctor for the expedition. When Lewis arrived at Wheeling, he had met Dr. William E. Patterson, son of the mathematician he had obtained instructions from in Philadelphia. Young Patterson expressed a desire to join the expedition, but when he was not ready by 3 o'clock on the 9th as agreed, it pushed on without him.

In the 100-mile stretch between Wheeling and Marietta the water level improved; horses and oxen were needed only twice to drag the keelboat over riffles. On September 13 the party reached Marietta, at the mouth of the Muskingum River. Founded in 1788, it was the oldest permanent settlement in Ohio; 2 years earlier, Fort Harmar had been built on the opposite, or west, bank of the Muskingum. The departure date was apparently the 14th.[37]

Lewis made a comparatively long stop in the Cincinnati area, between September 28 and October 4 or 5, to rest his men, take on provisions, and visit an archeological site. By this time, one or possibly two of the three prospective recruits who had joined at Pittsburgh had either been dismissed or departed of his own volition. The two who remained were George Shannon and probably John Colter.[38] According to family tradition, the latter had set out from the family farm near Staunton, Va., and intercepted Lewis at Old Limestone (modern Maysville, Ky.).

Apparently at Jefferson's urging as well as to satisfy his own curiosity, Lewis visited Big Bone Lick, Ky., about 17 air miles southwest of Cincinnati on the south bank of the Ohio. Earlier in the year, Dr. William Goforth had found there the bones of a mammoth. Lewis sent Jefferson a detailed report on the site, forwarded him specimens, and called on Goforth in Cincinnati.[39]

By this time, Lewis had become quite alarmed at the delays he had encountered. Fearing adverse congressional reaction, he conceived a plan for a side expedition during the coming winter that he hoped would demonstrate some action to Congress. He would undertake a solo horseback ride for "some hundred miles through the most interesting portion of the country adjoining my winter establishment" on the "South side of the Missouri," possibly toward Santa Fe. If Clark were available, he, too, might be able to undertake a "similar excurtion through some other portion of the country."

Lewis apparently did not give much consideration to the impact on the expedition of the absence of its two leaders. He also demonstrated political naivete vis-a-vis the danger of conflict with Spanish officials. His proposals further strikingly reveal how little anyone knew about the geography of the trans-Mississippi West.

Jefferson's reply on November 16, to Lewis' letter of October 3 outlining the plan, minced no words. The captain was directed to forgo any such excursions—"more dangerous than the main expedition up the Missouri." The missive stated emphatically, "The object of your mission is single, the direct water communication from sea to sea formed by the bed of the Missouri & perhaps the Oregon."

Personnel gains

A key stopping point on the downriver trek was at the Falls of the Ohio. Beside their western end, on the south bank, was located Louisville, Ky.; and, on the north, Clarksville, Indiana Territory. The falls, a serious handicap to navigation, were actually a long rapids created by a 24-foot drop of the river over a 2-mile long series of irregular limestone ledges.[40] The best passage followed the north bank of the river. Lewis and his party arrived at the falls on October 14.[41] Probably the next day, aided by local pilots, they took their boats through the dangerous channel and tied up at Clarksville.

William Clark lived there with his older brother, George Rogers, and Lewis likely stayed with them.[42] The reunion of the two younger men must have been a happy one. They undoubtedly reminisced about old Army days, and George Rogers probably joined them in discussing all aspects of the momentous expedition that lay ahead. He likely provided valuable information, for no one else knew as much as he about personages and conditions in the West. And his younger brother, though he had been a civilian for 7 years, had extensive Army experience on the frontier, including an acquaintance with some of the Spanish authorities in Western Louisiana.

RED-HAIRED William, like Lewis, stood 6 feet tall and had a strong physique, but he was 4 years older, aged 33. He had been born in 1770 of Scottish descent on a farm in Caroline County, Va.[43] His father, John, had inherited it from a bachelor uncle and brought his family there sometime after 1754, probably in 1755, from a log cabin at the present northeastern edge of Charlottesville—where they had known the Jeffersons.

St. Louis was founded by Pierre Laclede and Auguste Chouteau in 1763-64. The Chouteau family was interested in the fur trade and its management throughout the West. It would be difficult to over-state the presence of the Chouteau family, or the importance of Auguste Chouteau, in the opening of the West as information came back from the Lewis and Clark Expedition. In addition, because these French trappers had already been throughout much of the Missouri River drainage, they helped the expedition get started with information and supplies. They also assisted the later Pike, Long, Schoolcraft, and Fremont expeditions.

William was the youngest of six sons and the ninth child in a family of ten children. All his older brothers fought in the War for Independence; and four of the six sons, including William, became general officers. The father made his own more direct contribution to the war in the form of large amounts of personal funds he provided his son George Rogers to support his army, but which at the end of the war the State of Virginia refused to reimburse.

Hoping to mend his fortune, in 1784, when William was only 14 years of age, John set out with his family for the Kentucky country. After an icebound winter on the Monongahela near Pittsburgh, in the spring they floated down the Ohio with other westbound emigrants to Louisville. It had grown up around a fort that George Rogers had founded in 1778–79 as a headquarters during his campaign against the British.

John settled along Bear Grass Creek, 3 miles south of the site of his son's fort, and soon built Mulberry Hill. There, on the frontier, William rapidly matured and grew to manhood. He received limited formal schooling. But he was interested in Indians and worshipped George Rogers, who probably taught him something about soldiering, woodcraft, and the Indians. By the time he was 19, the youth had joined the militia, where he soon gained a captaincy.

In 1791 Clark transferred to the Regular Army as an ensign and quickly won a reputation for bravery. In March 1792 he became a lieutenant and in September was assigned to the 4th Sublegion of Gen. "Mad Anthony" Wayne's western army. For 4 years he lived the life of the typical officer in the field in present Indiana and Ohio. It was not all combat action. Drilling and disciplining his troops occupied much of his time. He also became adept at living in the wilderness, gained a good knowledge of Indian character, and learned the practical principles of military engineering, construction, and cartography.

On one occasion, Clark was commanding a group of 60 to 70 men who were escorting a supply packtrain of 700 horses. After some hard fighting, he drove off a superior force of Indians and won the general's commendation. Clark also took part with him in the decisive Battle of Fallen Timbers (1794), which destroyed the power of the Indians in Ohio.

Wayne was so impressed with the young officer that he twice sent him with small parties on undercover, intelligence-gathering missions down the Ohio. In 1793 he traveled to the Chickasaw villages, near some Spanish posts in the Cumberland and Tennessee Valleys; he apparently sought to determine what aid the tribe might provide the Americans in the event war broke out with Spain. The other mission occurred 2 years later. Carefully studying Spanish fortifications and military activities all along the way, Clark proceeded down the Mississippi as far as the vicinity of New Madrid, in present Missouri. In a meeting with Spanish officials, he protested their occupation of the Chickasaw Bluffs (present Memphis), in U.S. territory, on the east bank of the river. They considered him an "enterprising youth of extraordinary activity."

Clark liked these adventurous episodes and enjoyed military life. But because he was suffering from a temporary bout with ill health and his family was urging him to come home to help out with business affairs, in July 1796 he resigned his lieutenant's commission and returned to Mulberry Hill. There he began an activity that was to occupy him on and off for many years—trying to straighten out the tangled affairs of his bachelor brother George Rogers. No longer a national hero and his petitions for monetary aid to Congress unheeded, disappointed in love, in poor health, financially insolvent, and deeply depressed, he had turned to drink. William spent long hours dealing with creditors and made trips on associated matters to present Illinois and New Orleans.

In 1799 John Clark died, the year after his wife. For some reason, William instead of the eldest son, Jonathan, inherited Mulberry Hill, most of its slaves, and assorted debts. In 1803, subsequent to his decision to join Lewis, William sold the residence to Jonathan for use by his son. George Rogers built a small, two-story log cabin at Clarksville, across the river from Louisville on Clark's Point, and William took up residence with him.

CLARK was to prove to be the right choice as joint leader of the expedition and to fulfill all the promise indicated by his previous record. In capability and background, he and Lewis shared much in common. They were relatively young, intelligent, adventurous, resourceful, and courageous. Both were natives of Virginia and came from good families. Born leaders, experienced woodsmen-frontiersmen, and seasoned Army officers with previous militia experience, they were cool in crises and quick to make a decision.

On the other hand, in temperament they were opposites, and each supplied to the partnership what the other lacked. Lewis was introverted, melancholic, and moody; Clark, extroverted, even-tempered, and gregarious. The better-educated and more refined Lewis, who was equipped with a philosophical, romantic, and speculative mind, was at home with abstract ideas; Clark, of a pragmatic mold, was more of a practical man of action.

Yet the relationship ranks high in the realm of notable human associations—a rare example of two noble men of heart and conscience sharing responsibility for the conduct of a dangerous enterprise without ever losing the other's respect or loyalty. Despite the frequent stress, hardships, and other conditions that could easily breed jealousy, mistrust, or contempt, they proved to be self-effacing brothers in command and leadership. During their long journey, as well as their subsequent careers, there is not a single trace of a serious quarrel or dispute.

ACCOMPANYING Clark from Clarksville was his servant York, a black man of exceptional size and strength who had served the family as a slave since birth, as had also his father "old York" and his mother. About the same age as Clark or possibly younger, York, who was married to a girl named "Rose," had been his lifelong companion and had been bequeathed to him by his father. Although not an official member of the expedition, York was to share in its dangers and contribute considerably to its success. Especially because of curiosity about his blackness and interest in his physical prowess on the part of the Indians, his presence did much to smooth relations with them.

NINE men, some of whom Lewis and Clark probably knew previously, were inducted into the Army at the Falls of the Ohio—the first permanent members of the party except for the two leaders.[44] John Colter and George Shannon arrived with Lewis. Clark, possibly with the help of George Rogers, had recruited and assembled the other seven: William Bratton, Joseph and Reuben Field, Charles Floyd, George Gibson, Nathaniel H. Pryor, and John Shields, plus others who were rejected. Shannon was a resident of Ohio and Colter of Virginia at the time they joined the expedition. All the others were likely living in Kentucky, but some had earlier emigrated there from Virginia, Pennsylvania, Tennessee, and possibly other Eastern States.

They were all handpicked frontiersmen, hunters, and woodsmen. Most of them, especially Colter and the Field brothers, were to distinguish themselves during the exploration and participate in some of the most dangerous episodes. Floyd was a member of a family already famous in the history of Kentucky and was the son of Capt. Charles Floyd, who had soldiered with George Rogers Clark. The younger Floyd and his cousin, Pryor, became sergeants. Shields proved to be the most skillful blacksmith-gunsmith of the entire complement. Shannon, Gibson, and Bratton, on the other hand, made no special mark.[45]

Navigating the Lower Ohio

After spending almost 2 weeks at Clarksville, the party set out on October 26.[46] It consisted of the two leaders, York, the nine new permanent members, and the seven temporarily assigned soldiers. By this time, navigation was no special problem.

On November 11 the group arrived at Fort Massac, which had been founded in 1794 near present Metropolis, Ill., on the north bank of the Ohio about 35 miles from its junction with the Mississippi. The commander was Capt. Daniel Bissell of the 1st Infantry Regiment. That same day, Lewis and Clark tentatively engaged as an interpreter a man who was apparently a civilian employee at the post.[47] His name was George Drouillard, and he was to prove to be the most indispensable man in the expedition after Lewis and Clark themselves.[48] He may have been born in or near Detroit. His father, Pierre, was a French-Canadian; his mother, a Shawnee Indian.[49] The younger Drouillard was a skilled frontiersman, hunter-trapper, scout, master of sign language, interpreter, and expert in Indian ways.

Disappointed not to find at Fort Massac a group of volunteers awaiting them from South West Point, Tenn., Lewis and Clark dispatched Drouillard on the long overland journey to that post to bring the men.[50] The two captains were further dismayed to learn that Captain Bissell had not yet been able to procure many qualified volunteers for the exploration; only Joseph Whitehouse and possibly John Newman joined at this point. According to original plans, the seven soldiers who were temporarily assigned to the party to help it down the Ohio apparently remained behind at the fort, where they may have rejoined Lieutenant Murray before proceeding to Fort Adams, in Mississippi Territory.

The two captains bade farewell to Bissell on the afternoon of November 13, and the next evening reached the mouth of the Ohio and camped on its bank. They spent a week measuring the width of the rivers, examining the land on both sides of the Mississippi, and making celestial observations. Delaware and Shawnee Indians were found to be occupying the west bank. One of the latter took a fancy to Scannon, but Lewis rejected his offer of three beaver pelts for the dog.

Up the Mississippi

On November 20, 1803, Lewis and Clark moved up the Mississippi, making observations on population and topography as they went. About a week later, they reached Fort Kaskaskia, established as an American post the year before in present Illinois about 50 air miles below St. Louis. The next day, while Lewis remained behind to confer on personnel and supply needs with Capt. Russell Bissell, commanding the company of the 1st Infantry Regiment assigned to the post, Clark proceeded with the boat party.

That night, camp was made on the Illinois side of the river opposite the site of the old city of Ste. Genevieve, which had been abandoned in 1784–91 because of floods. Clark waited there until about December 3, when he apparently received a message from Lewis to continue on to Cahokia, a few miles below St. Louis on the opposite bank of the river, where they would rendezvous.

Meantime, Lewis had made arrangements for some volunteers to join the party and issued requisitions to the Army contractor for the delivery of supplies to Cahokia. He also undoubtedly took advantage of the opportunity to visit with his old friend, Capt. Amos Stoddard of the Corps of Artillerists, who was commanding a company temporarily based at the fort. The latter's original assignment had been to erect a post at Cahokia. In July, however, the War Department, reacting to news of the Louisiana Purchase, rescinded these instructions and ordered him to stay at Fort Kaskaskia until the transfer of Upper Louisiana could be effected and then establish a military headquarters at St. Louis.

On December 5 Lewis departed on horseback and apparently arrived at Cahokia the following day. He immediately introduced

The Bolduc house in Ste. Genevieve, Missouri, is an example of French Colonial architecture, such as Lewis & Clark saw in St. Louis in 1803-4.

himself to John Hay, U.S. postmaster and trader-merchant, and Nicholas Jarrot, a French fur trader. Because of their fluency in French, Lewis persuaded them to cross over with him to St. Louis and serve as interpreters at a conference with Spanish authorities, still in control of Upper Louisiana on behalf of France.

Lewis meets with Spanish authorities

The next day, December 7, the three met with Col. Carlos Dehault Delassus, Lieutenant Governor of Upper Louisiana. Lewis presented his French and English passports as well as a communication from President Jefferson, explained his purpose, and asked for permission to pass up the Missouri River. Delassus was polite but rejected his request and suggested he wait at Cahokia until spring. By then Delassus said he would have instructions from his Government on the matter and Upper Louisiana would have been transferred to the United States. Acquiescing, Lewis indicated he would probably establish winter camp at the mouth of the Wood River (River Dubois), above St. Louis and opposite the mouth of the Missouri, a site George Rogers Clark might have recommended.

Had Lewis received Spanish permission, he doubtless would have gone some distance up the Missouri before camping for the winter— probably at La Charette, the last white settlement. Long before, prior to arrival at the Falls of the Ohio, he had relinquished the idea of proceeding up the Missouri for 200 or 300 miles.

The opposition of Spanish officials to the expedition reveals that the Louisiana Purchase did not reduce their interest in it. Indeed, if anything, the purchase made the project more important to their role in western America. They were aware that Louisiana's northern and western boundaries were especially vague. Anyway, beyond its western extent, the expedition would be crossing through territory claimed by Spain. Finally, the Spaniards feared that the headwaters of the Missouri might be close to those of the Rio Grande not far north of Santa Fe, the capital of their New Mexican domain.

Two days after the meeting, Delassus reported to his superiors in New Orleans that Lewis enjoyed a reputation for being "a very well educated man and of many talents" and that his mission had "no other object than to discover the Pacific Ocean, following the Missouri." Humorously, he and his colleagues, experiencing difficulty in rendering the American name "Meriwether," called him "Capt. Merry," "Merry," "Merry Lewis," and "Capt. Merry Weather."

Throughout the winter, the Spaniards observed the movements of Lewis and Clark and the activities at Camp Wood. And, as it turned out, they took belated steps to intercept the expedition. For that purpose, in the fall of 1804 and again in 1805—long after it had moved upriver—the Governor of New Mexico sent out two abortive expeditions under Pedro Vial, a Frenchman in the service of Spain.[51] The Spaniards may also have sent out a third expedition.

ON December 8, after his meeting with Delassus, Lewis returned to Cahokia, where Clark and the boat party had tied up the day before. On December 10 the reunited party moved upstream a few miles and early the next morning rowed over to St. Louis. Lewis, planning to handle logistical arrangements and gather intelligence, temporarily took leave of his comrades there.

Clark establishes Camp Wood (1803–4)

Clark departed with the boats at 11 o'clock and continued upriver. The next day, December 12, about 17½ miles from St. Louis according to his calculations, he reached his destination, the mouth of the Wood River (River Dubois), a small stream that flowed into the Mississippi from the northeast directly across from the mouth of the Missouri.

Reconnaissance of the area and reports of hunters, who spotted some bear and abundant turkey, raccoon, and deer, confirmed Clark's judgment that it would be a good one for winter quarters. Close to the mouth of the Wood River on its south bank along a well-timbered bottom 1 to 3 miles wide, on December 13 he selected a site for what came to be known as Camp Wood (Camp Dubois).[52] He immediately put everyone to work clearing land and cutting logs for huts, which probably numbered 8–10 and were finished by Christmas Eve. The next day, the men celebrated by firing their weapons, hunting, and frolicking—marred by some drunkenness and fighting.

Earlier, an opening had been cut for a road about 1½ miles long that ran to the nearby prairie. This undulating and stream-laced plain ran parallel with the Mississippi from about 3 miles above Camp Wood to Kaskaskia and extended in width from 3 to 7 miles. Because settlers occupied its edge from Cahokia to a point about 3 miles below Camp Wood, it was known as the "American bottom."

Clark readies supplies and personnel

Once the camp was established, Clark could turn his attention to the formidable array of tasks necessary to prepare for the arduous journey ahead. They included receiving, selecting, training, and disciplining personnel; modifying the keelboat; providing it and the two pirogues with armament; and the assembling and packing of supplies.

A KEY aspect of the preparation was final determination of the number of personnel who would be required and their selection. By the time they arrived in the St. Louis area, Lewis and Clark realized they would need at least twice the number of 10 or 12 men originally planned. As veteran traders there knew, that number would not be sufficient to take the keelboat upriver, let alone fend off any hostile Indians. Although Clark's calculations for personnel requirements in relation to boat space and logistical support fluctuated throughout the winter between 25 and 50, the figure finally chosen for the permanent party, in addition to the two leaders, was 29: Drouillard, York, and 27 enlisted men. In addition, about seven Army personnel would be assigned to a temporary detachment that would travel only as far as the Mandan villages and then return with the keelboat to St. Louis.

Clark probably reached Camp Wood with roughly half of the per-

manent party. With him were York and the nine men from Clarksville; [53] Joseph Whitehouse and possibly John Newman, from Fort
Massac; and perhaps John Ordway, John G. Robertson, and Alexander H. Willard. If the latter three men did not arrive at the camp
with Clark, they undoubtedly did so soon thereafter.

More volunteers flowed in during December, and a few probably
later in the winter. On December 22 Drouillard arrived from South
West Point, Tenn., with eight men from Capt. John Campbell's company of the 2d Infantry Regiment. Other personnel came from the
1st Infantry Regiment, either from Capt. Daniel Bissell's company
at Fort Massac or from Capt. Russell Bissell's unit at Fort Kaskaskia;
or from Capt. Amos Stoddard's artillery company at Fort Kaskaskia.[54]

Making the final selections was a difficult task for Lewis and Clark,
and they probably chose some men who lacked the temperament and
qualifications they would have preferred. For example, they were
especially dissatisfied with the group of eight men from South West
Point, noting that not even one of them was a hunter, yet four of
the party were accepted. Others were rejected for various reasons,
or chose not to join the expedition.

On April 1 Clark issued a detachment order listing the permanent
party "for the Expedition through the interior of the Continent of
North America." Charles Floyd, John Ordway, and Nathaniel H.
Pryor were designated as sergeants; in the case of Ordway, this was
simply a confirmation of rank, for he had held it when he joined the
expedition. The following 22 privates were listed: William E. Bratton,
John Collins, John Colter, Joseph Field, Reuben Field, Patrick Gass,
George Gibson, Silas Goodrich, Hugh Hall, Thomas P. Howard, Hugh
McNeal, John Newman, John Potts, Moses B. Reed, George Shannon,
John Shields, John B. Thompson, William Werner, Joseph White-
house, Alexander H. Willard, Richard Windsor, and Peter M. Wiser.
Two more privates were to be added to this group at St. Charles.

The order also stated that Cpl. Richard Warfington and Pvts. John
Boley, Robert Frazer, and John G. Robertson were to be "retained
in service." These personnel, plus apparently Pvts. John Dame,
Ebenezer Tuttle, and Isaac White, were ultimately assigned to the
special detachment that only went as far as the Mandan villages.

NOT much is known about these men individually. Collectively, they
represented diverse origins, backgrounds, qualifications, and experi-

View toward the southwest from the north bank of the old (1804) channel of the Wood River at its present junction with the Mississippi in Illinois. Camp Wood, Ill., was located on the south bank of the Wood near its mouth. Because of changes in the Mississippi, Missouri, and Wood Rivers over the years, the campsite is now in Missouri along the west bank of the Mississippi about ⅝ of a mile to the southwest of the present mouth of the old Wood River channel. Today, the Wood River empties into the Mississippi in a new manmade channel north of the one shown in this photograph.

ences. They were natives of such present States as Indiana, Kentucky, Maryland, Massachusetts, New Hampshire, North Carolina, Pennsylvania, Vermont, and Virginia. One man, Potts, had been born in Germany; Wiser was probably of similar descent. Gass was of Irish extraction. Most were single but at least one, Shields, and possibly others, including Pryor, may have been married. The majority were young. Shannon, aged 18 or 19, was probably the youngest; Shields, likely the oldest, followed by Clark and Gass. A few, Ordway and Shannon for example, were well educated, but most had little formal schooling. Some were illiterate.

On the other hand, the bulk of them had gained worthwhile practical experience on the frontier. A large number possessed special skills. Chief carpenter Gass, also a boatbuilder, was assisted by Joseph Field. Another individual with boatbuilding skills was Shields, who served as the head blacksmith, gunsmith, and general repairman. Willard and possibly one or two others assisted him. Some of the personnel specialized as cooks, hunters, or boatmen.

On December 23, the day after Drouillard returned from South West Point, he told Clark he had decided to accompany the expedition, but that he first wanted to settle his affairs at Fort Massac.[55] When or if he ever did so is not clear, but on December 30 he left for Cahokia with Sergeant Ordway. And, during the rest of the winter, he was absent from Camp Wood most of the time, carrying out special missions—for which his reliability, expert woodsmanship, and excellent knowledge of the frontier country admirably suited him.

ONCE the final personnel complement was selected, it needed to be forged into a closely knit and well-motivated team. The primary requirement was the establishment of discipline—imperative for a small group undertaking such a dangerous mission. Otherwise, the lives of all its members would be jeopardized. Most of the newly inducted frontiersmen and some of the soldiers transferred from frontier garrisons of the Regular Army—young and hardy and no doubt anxious to enjoy a last fling before heading into the wilderness—not only demonstrated a strong liking for whisky and brawling but also resented military control. They inevitably would test their new leaders to see what they could get away with.

At one time or another, practically all the men in camp engaged in some wrongdoing. Yet some of the rowdiest and most undisciplined, such as Colter and Reuben Field, were later to number among the most reliable in the command. Whisky peddlers from Cahokia and St. Louis set up shop near camp or came by frequently selling their wares. The drinking inevitably led to fights. Other offenses were insubordination, general disorder, absence-without-leave (AWOL), refusal to mount guard duty or obey orders, and theft of Government property. Many of these violations occurred when Sergeant Ordway was in charge during Clark's absence.

But this pattern was not new to an experienced Army officer such as Clark, and he did not intend to tolerate any form of insubordination or misbehavior. He dealt harshly with all infractions of the rules. The guilty were restricted to camp, reprimanded, or if necessary court-martialed. As a positive step, Clark tried to keep the men busy. He awarded extra whisky rations to winners of marksmanship drills and those distinguishing themselves in work parties. By the end of the winter, he had tightened up discipline considerably, though a few scattered problems were to arise on the way up the Missouri.

One problem for Clark was that for much of the winter he was sick. This may have originated when he got wet and cold one time and froze his feet. Lewis brought a doctor to treat him at least once. Pryor and a few others also suffered from illness.

ANOTHER major activity was modifying the interior of the keelboat to allow for better loading, protection of supplies, and military defense. After Clark drew a sketch of the boat with proposed modifications and made estimates of needed materials, he started a party whipsawing planks. The blacksmiths set to work making iron hinges and other fixtures.

Lockers were constructed along the sides of the hold, between the bow and stern decks. These were 2½-feet wide and 1½-feet deep. Other lockers, 3 feet wide and 3 feet deep, were built on both sides of the elevated cabin on the stern. Cleverly devised, the locker lids could be raised to form a breastwork, or shield, around the outside of the boat and behind which the crew could fight in the event of attack. When the locker tops were down, they protected baggage from the elements and prevented inspection by Indians, as well as provided catwalks, or "passe-avants," for passage from the forecastle to the stern cabin deck. Crosswise between the lockers 11 benches were built, each 3 feet long for use by two oarsmen. At Camp Wood,

This drawing of the departure from Camp Wood (Camp Dubois) on May 14, 1804, depicts the Corps of Discovery under Co-Captain William Clark crossing the Mississippi and making its way into the mouth of the Missouri River. Like other drawings made for the National Park Service about various episodes of the Lewis and Clark expedition, it was meant for the Museum of Westward Expansion under the Gateway Arch on the St. Louis Riverfront. A National Park Service area, Jefferson National Expansion Memorial tells the story of Westward Expansion during the nineteenth century. When Clark and his men left Camp Wood, they were heading for St. Charles and a rendezvous with Co-Captain Meriwether Lewis who left by a land route from St. Louis for St. Charles on the Missouri River. The party left Camp Wood at 4:00 p.m. and traveled two hours before camping. Known as a "Hudson's Bay start," anything inadvertently forgotten would be noticed at the first camp stop and could be retrieved quickly since only a two hour trip had been taken. From the beginning, the Corps of Discovery followed the frontiersmen's and trappers' way of moving into the unknown. The St. Charles Riverfront has a developing historic area and a Lewis & Clark center.

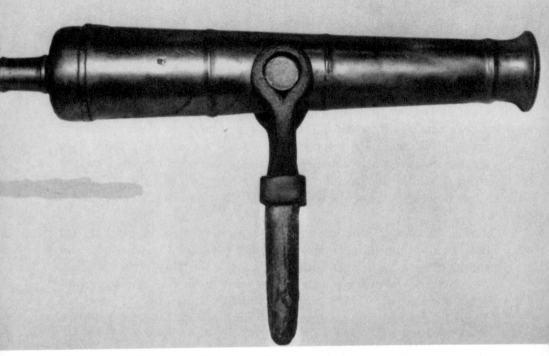

Bronze swivel gun, a small cannon of Spanish manufacture, probably similar to the one Lewis and Clark carried with them. This weapon, captured during the Philippine Insurrection (1899–1902) and displayed by the U.S. Army at the 1905 St. Louis World's Fair, is now in the John M. Browning Memorial Museum, Rock Island, Ill.

if not at Pittsburgh, oarlocks were provided along the sides of the vessel.

Another substantive modification was erection over the hold of three removable ridgepoles, resting on center supports that were forked at the top. These poles held up the center of an awning, which was lashed to the sides of the boat. A similar ridgepole awning also apparently covered the cabin deck.

The two pirogues, obtained in the Pittsburgh or St. Louis areas, were apparently not altered except for the placing of waystrips along the gunwales of the six-oared, smaller one, called the white pirogue because of its color. The other vessel, equipped with seven oars, was known as the "red" pirogue. Neither of them was decked.

Finally, the keelboat and pirogues were provided with armament. On the bow of the large boat a small cannon was mounted on a swivel so it could be turned and fired in any direction. Apparently of Spanish or French manufacture, it was probably similar to those used at Spanish forts in Upper Louisiana, and Lewis likely obtained it in the St. Louis area. Representing the expedition's heaviest armament and at the time the largest weapon ever taken up the Missouri, it was capable of delivering a deadly discharge at close range and would be valuable for persuasion or defense among the natives. Two smaller swivel guns, probably blunderbusses, were mounted on the stern of the keelboat, and one each on the two pirogues. The two types of weapons could be loaded with balls, scrap iron, or buckshot.[56]

A THIRD major function was the repacking of supplies that had been brought down the Ohio, receipt and packing of other goods, and the loading of all of them into the boats. John Hay, who had once been a trader with the North West Company in Canada, was probably more helpful than anyone in the St. Louis area. He assisted Lewis in numerous ways and advised him on supplies that would be

The keelboat was armed with a number of swivel guns, one of which was apparently a small-bore cannon. The others may have been blunderbusses or pieces similar to the Spanish Miquelet that is illustrated here and is presently exhibited at the Springfield (Mass.) Armory Museum.

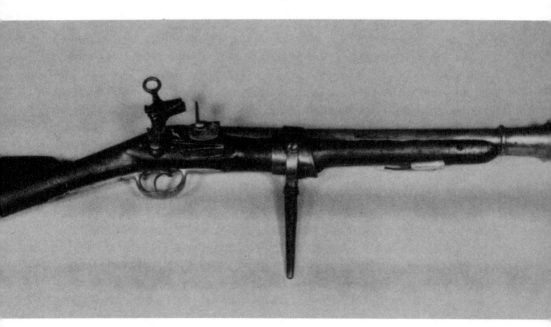

needed. On several occasions, including the period April 26–May 2, he also came up from Cahokia to Camp Wood to help with the packing, which required special care because no other basic supplies could be procured in the wilderness ahead.

At Hay's suggestion, the Indian trade goods and presents were packed into 14 bales and one box, each containing a portion of the various items. This allowed the opening of only one container at a time, insured that a variety of goods would then be accessible, and guaranteed the availability of a diversity of goods in the event some of the containers should be lost or damaged. Essential supplies, such as clothing, tools, flints, locks, and powder were packed in a similar manner, in seven bales and one box. Gunpowder was ingeniously sealed in lead kegs that when emptied could be melted down and molded into bullets.

Except mainly for 32 canisters (193 pounds) of dried soup, 2 pounds of Hyson tea, and some wine that had been purchased in Philadelphia, apparently most of the basic food supplies were procured in the St. Louis-Cahokia area through requisitions drawn on Maj. Nathan Rumsey at Cahokia, agent for Elijah G. Galusha, the Army contractor. Because all the necessary food could not be transported and the expedition would need to live off the land as much as possible or barter for food with the Indians, provisions were restricted to staple items.

Wagons or boats, often accompanied by Major Rumsey, brought most of the food from Cahokia. The month of April was an especially busy one in receiving, processing, and packing it. The men parched corn and packed it into bags. Other food supplies consisted of kegs, half-barrels, and barrels of flour and salt pork, as well as barrels and bags of biscuits. In smaller quantities were salt, coffee, sugar, and dried apples. As early as April, on hand were 4,175 complete rations, 5,555 of flour, and 4,000 of pork, as well as 100 gallons of whisky.

THERE were respites from the hard work. Visitors were numerous, and social exchanges often relieved the tedium. Passing boatmen dropped by. Neighboring Indians—Kickapoos, Sauks, and Delawares —appeared at the camp almost daily, sometimes trading game to the expedition's members. In other instances, they merely sought provisions, which Clark liberally supplied, as well as whisky and tobacco. Local settlers, including some from along the Missouri in Louisiana

Territory, gratuitously furnished or bartered to the party corn, vegetables, butter, milk, and other produce. Members with a sweet tooth enjoyed the honey some of the men obtained in the woods. Another welcome dietary change were fish, caught in the river.

Also breaking the humdrum were occasional visits by Lewis, and Clark made several trips to St. Louis. On one occasion, the two of them traveled up the Missouri to St. Charles to procure supplies. The soldiers welcomed the opportunity afforded to get away from camp for awhile when Clark sent them with messages to Lewis or others at St. Louis and Cahokia. Shooting matches with local settlers afforded another enjoyable pastime. The settlers won the first one, early in January, but none after that. On May 6 Clark wrote as follows: "Several of the Countrey people in Camp Shooting with the party   all git beet and lose their money."

Lewis' activities in the St. Louis area

While Clark was wrestling with personnel and supply problems at Camp Wood, Lewis was busy in St. Louis, Cahokia, and Kaskaskia. He arranged for and expedited the shipment to the camp of food and other supplies. He also sought to obtain maximum data about Louisiana Territory for Jefferson, as well as all possible intelligence on the expedition's route and conditions along the way.

AN invaluable source of assistance to Lewis were prominent St. Louis citizens and French fur traders Auguste Chouteau, Sr., his half-brother Pierre, Sr., and their brother-in-law Charles Gratiot. Their cooperation probably stemmed at least in part from their recognition of the political realities associated with the newly won U.S. control of Louisiana Territory—which would have a substantial impact on their business. When he was in St. Louis, Lewis usually stayed with Auguste, as Clark also likely did when he visited the city.

Considering Lewis' close relations with the Chouteaus, it is not surprising that he had little to do with Spanish fur trader Manuel Lisa, who anyway could only converse poorly in French and English. He had arrived in St. Louis about 1798 and won the enmity of the Chouteaus for his attempts to muscle into the Missouri fur trade, which they had controlled since the establishment of St. Louis in 1764. But Lewis had his own reason for disliking Lisa, whom he suspected of circulating a petition critical of him.

Manuel Lisa settled in St. Louis in 1798-99. Born in New Orleans in the early 1770s, he started numerous fur companies working out of St. Louis. His partners included members of the Chouteau family as well as William Clark after he returned from the great expedition. Many of Lisa's men, such as Colter and Drouillard, were veterans from that expedition. Many of the early fur trading posts on the Missouri and Yellowstone Rivers were placed and built by Lisa and his men, including Fort Manuel and Fort Raymond. Of Spanish descent, Lisa challenged the established French fur traders and their new American rivals. Manuel Lisa had a major role in the establishment of the Missouri River trading practices after the return of Lewis and Clark.

Nevertheless, as the trader who in 1807–8 would lead the first organized fur-gathering party up the Missouri in the wake of the Lewis and Clark Expedition, Lisa must have been closely interested in its activities in the St. Louis area during the winter of 1803–4. He visited Camp Wood at least once, but probably received a cold reception, for Clark was aware of Lewis' animus toward him.

JEFFERSON was interested in anything Lewis could learn about Louisiana Territory—its population, resources, location of settlements, state of agriculture, national origins of its inhabitants, and the nature of land claims and holdings. But not much could be found out about any of these subjects, especially because of the reticence of French residents of St. Louis, who seemed afraid of the Spanish officials.

The most cooperative, though still cautious, was Antoine Soulard, a Frenchman who was surveyor-general of Upper Louisiana for Spanish authorities and who made available census information to Lewis. It recorded a population of about 10,000 persons. About 2,000 of them were "people of colour" and slaves, mainly owned by Frenchmen. Two-thirds of the remainder had immigrated from the United States. Virtually all the balance, except for an insignificant number of Spaniards, were French or French-Canadian. Almost all of the latter two groups made their living from the Indian trade. Lewis felt that the overall population and the number of U.S. immigrants were greater than the census indicated.

LEWIS was more successful in obtaining data useful to the expedition. Soulard granted him permission to copy a local merchant's map that included a portion of the Mississippi and the Missouri to the mouth of the Osage River and the entire extent of that river. Soulard, too, apparently made available a general map of Upper Louisiana. Lewis received through Clark, from William Henry Harrison, Governor of Indiana Territory, a copy of James Mackay's map of the Missouri River from its mouth to the Mandan villages; and, from Jefferson, John Evans' delineation of the same area.

Lewis also obtained copies of the latter two men's journals describing their trip up the Missouri in 1795–97, and Hay translated them from French into English.[57] In addition, the latter, who was familiar with the Indian trade and English policy in Canada, provided Lewis with much information and probably let him read the journal he had prepared years before describing his round trip from Michilimackinac to the Assiniboine River in Canada.

These documents, some or all of which Lewis made available to Clark for estimating distance and cartographic planning, represented virtually everything that was known to white men of the Missouri country as far as the Mandan villages and some Indian information about the lands to their west.[58]

A HIGHLIGHT of Lewis' stay in St. Louis was his attendance, with Clark, at the long-delayed ceremonies formally transferring Upper Louisiana to the United States.[59] Their old friend and the principal U.S. representative, Capt. Amos Stoddard, had invited them. Lewis served as the chief official witness. On hand for the ceremony was a detachment of the 1st Infantry Regiment from Fort Kaskaskia under Lt. Stephen Worrell, Corps of Artillerists. It had reached Cahokia on February 29, 1804, but ice prevented it from crossing the river until March 8.

The next day, in front of Government House, which had served as Spanish headquarters for the government of Upper Louisiana, the transfer was made from Spain to France. Colonel Delassus presided for Spain, and Stoddard acted as agent-commissioner for France. The following day, March 10, to the salute of guns and cheers from the audience, the French Tricolor was lowered and the Stars and Stripes were raised, the documents were signed, and congratulatory speeches were presented. Most of the population of St. Louis, including a sizable number of Americans, were in attendance. Stoddard assumed the position of military-civil Governor of Upper Louisiana pending its reorganization by Congress. After the ceremonies, Lewis and Clark accompanied him on an inspection tour of the Spanish defenses of the city.

About a month later, on Saturday evening, April 7, Clark again came down from Camp Wood and he and Lewis went to a party given by Stoddard to demonstrate his appreciation of the courtesies shown to him by the St. Louis citizenry. About 50 gentlemen enjoyed a dinner, which was followed by a ball that lasted until 9 o'clock in the morning.

After the transfer ceremonies, many Indians arrived at St. Louis to visit their new "father" and obtain the customary presents. Stoddard furnished them with provisions, and Lewis gave them tobacco and whisky. During the later part of his stay in St. Louis, Lewis also assisted Pierre Chouteau get underway on his trip to Washington, D.C., with a delegation of Osage chiefs, whose tribe he had visited and arranged for a call on President Jefferson. Because of delays in arrival of the chiefs at St. Louis and supply problems, Lewis may have moved the expedition's departure date from Camp Wood back from April until May. Chouteau apparently left in the middle of the latter month, and Lewis provided him with letters of introduction for use along the way.

Final preparations at Camp Wood

In March, April, and the first 2 weeks in May the tempo of preparations at the camp accelerated. One major action was checking and readying personal weapons, which would be a critical factor in the expedition's chance for success.[60] They would not only provide defense against hostile Indians and wild beasts but also furnish game for food.

Lewis and Clark and 13 of their men were probably armed with the Model 1803 rifles that had been obtained at the Harpers Ferry Arsenal. These were short, .54 calibre rifles. The volunteers from South West Point and Forts Massac and Kaskaskia probably brought their arms with them. These undoubtedly were either the regulation U.S. Flintlock Musket, Model 1795, a Revolutionary War type of gun, or a "Pennsylvania" or "Kentucky" handmade rifle of the type the Army purchased under contract after 1792.

The musket, reasonably accurate for only a short distance, shot a single heavy ball or, to provide a scatter load for small game, buckshot or birdshot. The long-barreled "Pennsylvania" or "Kentucky" rifles discharged bullets of .40 or .44 calibre, and were accurate at long distances when expertly handled. The nine men inducted into the Army at Clarksville, as well as Drouillard, probably brought with them this kind of rifle, the typical arm of frontiersmen at the time.

The blunderbusses carried by the expedition, all of which may have been placed on swivels in the boats, were short-barreled weapons with flared muzzles that delivered a scattering charge for short-range effect. In addition to their rifles, Lewis and Clark were each armed with a pistol and an espontoon, a type of spear or halbert becoming obsolete as a military arm but possibly useful in the wilderness.

Examples of weapons similar to those carried on the Lewis and Clark Expedition

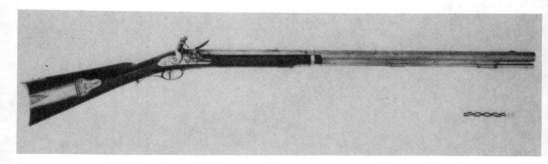

Harpers Ferry Model 1803, .54 caliber, the first regulation U.S. Army rifle. This example, now in the Smithsonian Institution, was manufactured in 1804, one of the earliest made in regular production. Lewis and Clark utilized 15 of the prototypes.

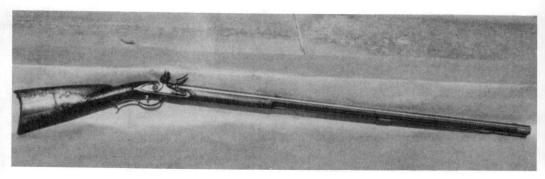

Kentucky flintlock .45 caliber rifle of the War for Independence period, now in the Claude Fuller Collection at Chickamauga and Chattanooga National Military Park, Ga.-Tenn.

Flintlock blunderbuss, with a Harpers Ferry lock dated 1808 and trigger guard of the 1795 type. Today, this weapon is in the Claude Fuller Collection at Chickamauga and Chattanooga National Military Park, Ga.-Tenn.

Clark wore a sword at least part of the time. In addition to firearms, every member of the permanent party carried a tomahawk and knife on his belt.[61]

DURING the last hectic days at Camp Wood, Clark had to swallow a bitter pill. On May 6 Lewis sent him a note from St. Louis enclosing his commission as a second lieutenant in the Corps of Artillerists and expressing deep regret at the War Department's failure to provide the expected captaincy in the Corps of Engineers.[62] The trouble was that in the small peacetime Army at the time vacancies were scarce and much sought after, and a position was available only in the Corps of Artillerists. Although sorely disappointed, Clark carried on. This was made somewhat easier by Lewis' insistence that they keep the actual rank secret. Thus equality of command became a fact. To the men of the expedition, they were the two captains and so they have come down in history.

ON May 7 the party loaded the keelboat. The following day, Clark and 20 oarsmen took it for a ride in the Mississippi to check its balance in the water. Subsequently, the loading was adjusted. On May 10 Clark ordered every man to have 100 balls for his rifle or 2 pounds of buckshot for his musket. The next day, Drouillard brought to camp seven *engagées*, or French boatmen, whom the Chouteaus had helped recruit in Cahokia, Kaskaskia, and Ste. Genevieve.[63] Experts in river navigation, they resided in those towns when they were not off on some trading venture. They were to return with the keelboat from the Mandan villages.

Finally, on the evening of May 13, everything was in readiness for departure the next morning. The plan was that Lewis, after he completed his business at St. Louis, would join the others at St. Charles. Clark decided to proceed leisurely to that point, studying the boatloading en route, and on arrival to make any necessary adjustments while waiting for Lewis.

The great adventure begins

The morning of Monday, May 14, 1804, broke cloudy, and rain later delayed departure until 4 o'clock. Elatedly taking leave of their home for 5 months and 2 days, Clark and about 42 men bade goodbye to the group of settlers who came to wish them *bon voyage*.[64] A round fired from the cannon saluted the well-wishers. The two pirogues and the keelboat, pushed by a light breeze, crossed the Mississippi and headed up the Missouri. A stop for the night was made at the first island, a small one only about 4 miles from Camp Wood. The westward trek—which had been the object of everyone's thoughts and labors for so many months—was finally underway.

At noon 2 days later, May 16, the boats docked at St. Charles, frontier outpost for traders who dealt with the Indians along the Missouri. Dating from about 1769, the town was the first permanent white settlement on the Missouri River and one of the first in the present State of Missouri. It consisted of about 100 houses that stretched along the north bank of the river for a mile at the foot

Clark's journal entry for Sunday, May 13, 1804, at Camp Wood, the day before heading up the Missouri. Part of the entry reads as follows: "...River a Dubois opposit the mouth of the Missourie River *Sunday* May the 13th 1804 — I despatched an express this morning to Capt Lewis at S. Louis, all our provisions goods and equipage on Board of a Boat of 22 oars, a large Perogue of 7 oars a second Perogue of 6 oars, complete with Sails...."

On Sunday, September 21, 1806, the Lewis & Clark Expedition returned to St. Charles from which they had departed 2 years and 4 months earlier.

of a hill. On hand to furnish greetings were many of the 450 inhabitants, mostly of French descent; some Indians; and a few new members of the expedition.

The latter consisted of two permanent personnel, Pvts. Pierre Cruzatte and François Labiche, and one or more additional temporary boatmen.[65] Cruzatte, skilled in sign language, was the son of a French father and an Omaha Indian mother. Labiche spoke several native tongues and was fluent in French and English. Both had traded and wintered among tribes several hundred miles up the Missouri. Although primarily recruited as boatmen, they were also to serve as interpreters.

The next day, Clark counciled with a group of Kickapoos, who paid him a visit, and welcomed Drouillard, who had been absent from Camp Wood at the time of the departure from there. The following day, however, Clark sent him with a message to Lewis in St. Louis; he returned the next day. Pending the arrival of Lewis, Clark took advantage of the opportunity to rearrange the loading of the boats for better balance, procure last-minute supplies, send out hunting parties, and make other final preparations.

But social activities broke up the routine. Friendly villagers, entertained aboard the boats, reciprocated by furnishing vegetables and holding festive balls, at which the men enjoyed dancing with the ladies. Some individuals celebrated their last fling too much for their own good, and made Clark realize that discipline was still a problem. John Collins, a chronic troublemaker, was court-martialed under the Articles of War and received 50 lashes for being absent without leave (AWOL), misbehaving at a ball, and using disrespectful language to Clark. William Werner and Hugh Hall were also found guilty of being AWOL, but Clark remitted their sentences of 25 lashes. Other personnel, of a religious bent, were more inclined to say last-minute prayers than to misbehave. About 20 attended a Mass offered by a local priest on Sunday, May 20, the day before the upriver voyage resumed.

About 6:30 p.m. that same evening Lewis arrived, rounding out the manpower complement. He had started out by carriage or horseback at 10:00 a.m. from St. Louis on the 24-mile road and ferry journey, but had been delayed en route by a severe thunderstorm. Accompanying him to see him off was a group of prominent St. Louis citizens: Capt. Amos Stoddard, Lts. Stephen Worrell and Clarence Milford, Dr. Antoine F. Saugrain, and Messrs. Auguste Chouteau, David Delaunay, Charles Gratiot, Sylvestre Labbadie, and James Rankin.

The night of the 20th and part of the next day, Lewis and Clark made final arrangements. At 3:30 o'clock in the afternoon, May 21, to the sound of "three cheers" from the audience lining the riverbank, the Corps of Discovery—about 48 strong—set out in earnest up the Missouri.[66]

The second night out of St. Charles, the party bivouacked near a group of Kickapoo Indians, whose gift of four deer was reciprocated with two quarts of whisky. The next day, the 23d, a stop was made at Femme Osage to pick up two men who had been sent ahead to purchase corn and butter. Near this village of 30–40 families, on the north bank, lived the aged Daniel Boone, noted frontiersman of another day. If he were present, he may have watched with moist eyes and a yearning heart as the band of his countrymen passed out of sight upstream. Two nights later, camp was again established on the north bank just above La Charette, a tiny cluster of seven cottages that had probably been founded about 1766.[67]

Encounters with St. Louis-bound traders

La Charette was the last outpost of white civilization on the Missouri, but there were soon reminders that lines of communication had extended westward. Before June 15, the expedition was to meet eight parties of traders, sometimes accompanied by Indians, coming downriver with rafts and canoes loaded with pelts that represented the fruit of a winter's trading with the Sioux, Oto, Pawnee, Osage, Omaha, and other tribes.

The first trader encountered, at the camp near La Charette, was Régis Loisel, returning from his post at Cedar Island in present central South Dakota. He gave Lewis and Clark valuable information about the land and tribes that lay ahead. He said he had met no Indians below the Poncas.

Another meeting, on June 12, was with a party of Loisel's employees, guiding two rafts laden with peltry and buffalo tallow. With them was an old French trader named Pierre Dorion, who had lived for about two decades among the Sioux Indians. Lewis and Clark purchased some tallow from the traders, and managed to persuade Old Dorion to turn back with them to serve as an interpreter. More importantly, they hoped he might be able to influence some of the Sioux chiefs to journey to Washington, D.C., for the purpose of visiting President Jefferson. Apparently one nameless member of the expedition, probably from Warfington's detachment and possibly John G. Robertson, went back to St. Louis with the Loisel party.[68]

Initiating a routine

By the time Old Dorion was recruited, as the days and miles melded, a general routine was being established that would be employed all the way to the Pacific and back. In May and June the party usually traveled as much as 14 to 20 miles a day, sometimes even 26 or 27 miles, or as few as 4 or 5. Camp was made at the most convenient and accessible spots: along the banks of the river, on sandbars, and whenever possible on islands, which offered special protection from any unwelcome visitors—animal or man. Guarded by sentries, the men slept in the boats or in tents.

Some days, Lewis and Clark stopped to rest the complement,

Clark carried this compass, now in the Smithsonian Institution, with him to the Pacific and return. The instrument is embedded in walnut, and the carrying case is of leather.

repair equipment, or reload the cargo and straighten the boats; or else they took advantage of the opportunity to do so when summer rains and storms held the group in camp. With minor exceptions, the permanent personnel rode in the keelboat, Warfington's detachment in the white pirogue, and the French boatmen in the red pirogue.

The military organization, which had been initiated at Camp Wood, was refined. Lewis and Clark commanded through the three sergeants, who rotated in performing key duties on the keelboat. Ordway, in effect the First Sergeant, issued provisions and appointed guard details. All the sergeants maintained duty rosters for the assignment of chores to their squads. The cooks and a few others with special assignments were exempted from guard duty, pitching tents, collecting firewood, and making fires.

No cooking was done during the day's travel. Daily provisions were ordinarily issued and cooked in the evening, a portion being reserved for consumption during the next day. The entire party was divided into messes for cooking and eating. Their composition and number varied from time to time, but en route to the Mandan villages they usually numbered three. One accommodated permanent enlisted personnel, another Warfington's detachment, and the other the French boatmen. Lewis, Clark, York, and Drouillard ate with one or the other of the messes.

To maintain a maximum supply of preserved provisions for possible future emergencies, the expedition lived off the land as much as possible. For this reason, no salt pork was issued when fresh meat was available; and, when feasible, excess venison was jerked—cut in long, thin slices—and dried in the sun to carry along.

A well-defined hunting procedure was inaugurated immediately upon leaving St. Charles. Two men were left behind there to bring up two horses, brought from St. Louis to the south bank of the river. Hunters rode them, and when game was killed some distance from the river they packed the meat to the riverbank, where the boats picked it up. The number of horses, which at one time totaled four, changed from time to time as one or more were lost or strays were found.

Usually the hunters set out from camp in the morning and rejoined the main party in the evening. Drouillard, a master woodsman, was the principal hunter. An important assistant was Reuben Field. Aiding them were Joseph Field and, as time went on, John Colter and young George Shannon, sometimes supplemented by one or two others. On occasion, Lewis and Clark themselves lent a hand.

Clark, more the riverman, usually stayed on the keelboat, while Lewis often walked along shore and observed flora and fauna. Both of them, alert and interested in the new country they were passing through, avidly filled their journals, usually at day's end, with accurate and detailed descriptions of topography, plant and wildlife, drainage, and mineral resources. They also recorded distances and directions traveled, temperature, weather conditions, and latitude and longitude. To determine latitude, celestial observations were made with the sextant and quadrant; for longitude, the chronometer was used. But dead reckoning was a major means of navigation. Clark did the mapping.

Special display of the original Lewis and Clark journals, arranged through the courtesy of the American Philosophical Society. Clark drew the sketch of the fish.

Lewis, who had served as President Jefferson's secretary and was better educated, wrote in a more literate and usually lengthier fashion than Clark, whose English was rough but no less colorful. The latter in particular, and Lewis to a lesser degree, employed spelling and punctuation that would not meet modern standards. But they were essentially frontiersmen who lived in a day when the educational level was lower and there was less concern with spelling and grammar. Grammatical merit aside, Lewis and Clark wrote with an enthusiasm, breadth of mind, and lack of pretension or boastfulness that makes a reading of their journals an unforgettable experience.

Marias R.

Breaks of the Missouri

Mouth of Marias ×

Teton R.

Buffalo Jump

Sun R.

Missouri River

Milk R.

River

Souris R.

× Great Falls Portage

Gates of the Rocky Mountains ×

Judith R.

Musselshell R.

M O N T A N A

Yellowstone R.

Little Missouri R.

Mandan and Minnetaree Villages ×

Fort Man (Wint 180

Knife R.

Missouri R.

Three Forks of the Missouri

Jefferson R.

Madison R.

Gallatin R.

Bighorn R.

Powder R.

Tongue R.

Heart R.

Slant Village ×

Cannonball R.

Beaverhead Rock ×

Lemhi Pass ×

Rattlesnake Cliffs ×
Camp Fortunate

Grand R.

Arikara Villages

Moreau R.

C A N A D A

N O R T DAKOT

I D A H O

CONTINENTAL DIVIDE

Snake R.

W Y O M I N G

Cheyenne R.

Confrontation with Teton Sioux

Bad R.

S O U T H DAKOT

W

Niobra

Great Salt Lake

U T A H

N E B R

C O L O R A D O

K

UP THE MISSOURI

CAMP WOOD — CAMP FORTUNATE

MAY 1804 – AUGUST 1805

⟵ Route
× Sites
● Cities, towns, and settlements
•••••• Continental Divide
— · — Present State boundaries

0   50   100   150
SCALE OF MILES

Map by Harry Scott

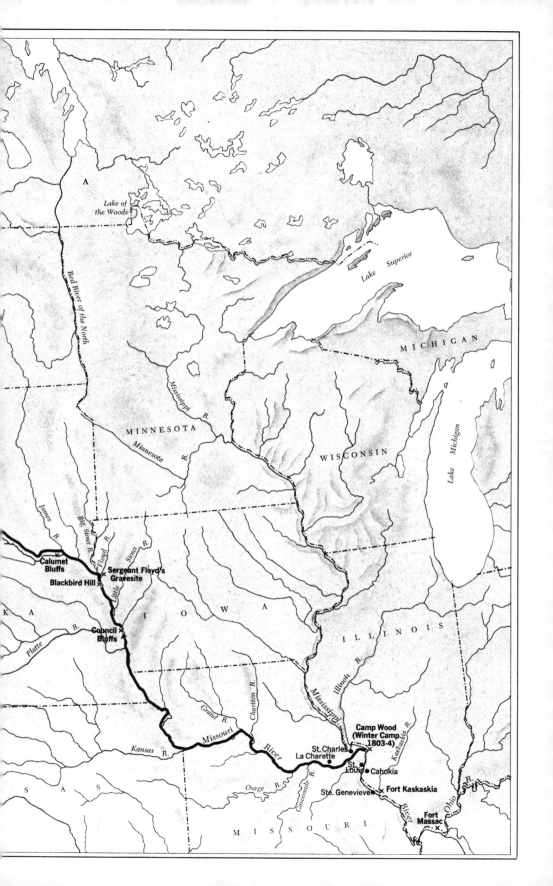

Journal of Sgt. John Ordway, Vol. I, now held by the American Philosophical Society.

A lush and beautiful land

The well-timbered country along the Lower Missouri, not too dissimilar from that the men had known in the East, was resplendent in its summer beauty. Wildflowers bloomed everywhere, and the profusion of wildlife was astounding. A hunter's paradise, the rich land of rolling hills teemed with game: deer, bear, squirrel, rabbit, turkey, duck, and geese. Clark commented, "Deer to be Seen in every direction and their tracks are as plenty as Hogs on a farm."

Bear, rarely eaten, were a valuable source of cooking grease. Supplementing the provisions brought from Camp Wood and fresh meat were various wild-growing greens, berries, grapes, plums, cherries, currants, as well as all kinds of fish—mainly catfish but also such species as pike, bass, silver fish, perch, redhorse, and buffalo fish. Sometimes hundreds were caught at one time.

Conquering the Missouri

Food was plentiful and the scenery attractive, but life was far from serene. The river led the list of aggravations. More treacherous than in the present day, when it is controlled by dams and dikes, it was often a curse. Its powerful 4 to 5 mile-an-hour current, sometimes intensified by encroaching bluffs, islands, sandbars, and narrow channels, provided a constant deterrent. The high and turbulent water, created by spring and early summer rains and runoff of mountain snows, crumbled and caved in riverbanks, which menaced any travelers caught near or under them. Vicious obstructions were often invisible just below the surface of the turbid water. Sawyers, or trees imbedded in the river bottom and projecting above or near the surface, and mats of driftwood scraped and threatened to gouge holes in the hulls of the boats or even overturn them. Sometimes, to help dodge obstacles, the crews had to rush to one side or the other.

Branches, even whole trees, which had toppled into the water when banks caved in, swirled dangerously by. Often partially submerged sandbars, shifting regularly with the strong current, blocked channels. The boats ground into them, and sometimes much effort was required to set them free. At times, sudden violent squalls, whipping the river into a furious sea of whitecaps, drove the craft toward banks or islands with such force that only frantic struggle kept them from being smashed to bits.

Three, and possibly four, means were available to propel the keelboat and four for the two pirogues. All were used at different times, alone or in conjunction with the others depending on the circumstances. When the wind was favorable, sails were used, and some days were all that was necessary. On others, oars offered the only means to make headway. Sometimes, towropes offered the only means of propulsion, particularly for the keelboat. The expedition's members pulled them from the shore or the shallow water at stream's edge. Slipping and sliding on the muddy bottom knee or waist deep in water and crashing their way through brush and over rocks and trees, they struggled slowly forward. Where water depth permitted, setting poles were probably employed, at least for the pirogues and perhaps for the keelboat.[69]

This replica of the Lewis & Clark Expedition keelboat was built by volunteers at Lewis and Clark State Park near Onowa, Iowa, with the leadership of the state park professionals and members of Iowa chapters of the Lewis and Clark Trail Heritage Foundation. The national Foundation supported this effort and many national members and officers took part. In addition to the keelboat, the two pirogues have been reproduced as well. These replica boats are all kept in Blue Lake, an oxbow of the Missouri River, which is the central feature of Lewis and Clark State Park. Visitors are welcome to photograph and board the replica, upon advance request to the park staff. The adjacent camp ground and picnic facilities make this one of the excellent stops along the Lewis and Clark Trail.

The boats were kept out of the main current wherever possible, but this meant crossing and recrossing the river, cutting off the big bends but intensifying the problem of warding off floating debris. The pilots experienced difficulty identifying crossings, the points at which channels moved to the opposite sides, just downstream from which were shoal waters covering sandbars.

Yet, though the men did not know it at the time, they were traversing the easiest part of the river. Despite all their problems, they could sail for long periods. In the middle and upper river, the bends and crossings were to be far more numerous and rapids were to require more exhausting use of towropes, setting poles, and oars. On the other

The location of Fort Osage was selected by William Clark as the expedition returned to St. Louis. When it was built in 1808, it overlooked much of the great bend of the Missouri River. On the edge of what is now Sibley, Missouri, the fort was rebuilt by fur trade era students and is managed by the Jackson County Parks Department. Its visitor center and museum conveys a great amount of information about the Missouri River frontier in the first years of the nineteenth century.

hand, in that sparsely timbered, grass-covered region, the navigation threats caused by floating trees and limbs decreased to the point they presented almost no problem. And, in the upper river, sandbars caused fewer difficulties.

Other tribulations

The annoyances, discomforts, and problems were not confined to navigation. The summer heat was sometimes unbearable. Drenching rains lowered morale. The two captains, utilizing the contents of their medical kits, spent a good deal of their time treating a variety of ills: boils, abcesses, callouses, bunions, sore feet and backs, sunstroke, dysentery, fatigue, injuries, colds, fevers, snakebites, toothaches, headaches, inflamed throats, colic, pleurisy, and rheumatism. The medical knowledge of the two captains was limited to a blend of frontier lore and the sort of elementary skills possessed by Army officers of that day. When necessary, the commanders bled their patients or applied poultices. Sometimes serious accidents were barely avoided. On May 23 Lewis almost fell from a 300-foot-high pinnacle of rocks. On June 20 York nearly suffered serious eye damage when one of the men threw sand at him in fun.

Ranking high among the pests were snakes, ticks, gnats, and mosquitoes. The latter, which were to prove to be a plague throughout the expedition, were sometimes as large as flies and flew in thick swarms. The men, who often could not keep them out of their eyes, noses, ears, and throats, tried to drive them away with pieces of brush, made fires, coated their bodies with cooking (bear) grease, sought shelter in their mosquito nets, or hoped for breezy days. Scannon, the dog, sometimes yowled in agony.

Another problem continued to be discipline. Once again, Collins and Hall were the culprits. On June 29, 1804, while guarding the whisky barrel, Collins became intoxicated and allowed Hall to take a supply. A court-martial decreed 100 lashes for Collins and 50 for Hall. On July 12 Willard received 100 lashes for sleeping on guard duty.

A turn to the north—signs of Indians

Meantime, on June 26, the expedition completed its almost due-west trek of nearly 400 river miles across the present State of Missouri and arrived at the mouth of the Kansas River, the site of Westport Landing, Mo., and later Kansas City. Camp was made there for 4 days. At this point, in a sweeping big bend, the river switched its course almost directly to the north. Clark commented that the Kansas Indians were not at their two villages, located 20 and 40 leagues upriver, but were out on the plains hunting buffalo. The party celebrated Independence Day, July 4, near the site of Atchison, Kans., with the discharge of the cannon and an extra issue of whisky. The day before, the first beaver had been seen.

On July 21, some 600 miles and 69 days upstream from Camp Wood, the expedition reached the mouth of the Platte River. Indicative of their lack of knowledge about the course of the Missouri west of the Mandan villages, traders considered the Platte to be the dividing point between the Upper and Lower Missouri. Lewis and Clark knew this was Indian country from Mackay's map and from Labiche, Cruzatte, and several of the French boatmen who were familiar with the area. In particular, it was known that Pawnees and Otos lived along the south bank of the Platte. The leaders and six men traveled up the river about a mile but met no Indians. As a matter of fact, to this point, though the expedition had discovered traces of Indian camps—Sauk, Iowa, Missouri, Osage, Sioux, Kansas—it had encountered no natives since the Kickapoos near St. Charles.

Beyond the Platte, considerable evidence was seen of Indians, mainly abandoned Oto and Iowa villages. On July 28 Drouillard returned from hunting with a Missouri. One of the few remaining of that nation, he said he lived at a small camp of 20 lodges of Otos about 4 miles from the river and that the bulk of them were away hunting buffalo on the plains.

The next day, Lewis and Clark sent boatman La Liberté (Jo Barter) with the Indian to the Oto camp to invite them to come to the river for a council. The following day, the 30th, about 50 miles north of the mouth of the Platte, the decision was made to stop to await the return of La Liberté. Selecting a campsite on a smooth stretch of bottomland along the west, or south, bank of the river, Lewis and Clark called it "Councile Bluff or Handsom Prarie."[70] They estimated it was about 25 days away from Santa Fe, and recognized that it was a natural place for a post to trade with the Indians on the Platte River and surrounding area—Otos, Missouris, Pawnees, and Omahas—and that it was convenient to the Sioux hunting country.

The first Indian council

At sunset on August 2 a party of Otos and a few Missouris as well as a trader named "Mr. Fairfong"—minus La Liberté—arrived at camp. Six were chiefs, but not principal chiefs. The two captains, exchanging gifts with them, asked them and other representatives of their tribes to attend a council the next day. The expedition was also put on the alert, for it was learned that the Otos and Missouris numbered about 250 men, about a third of whom were Missouris.

The council began right after breakfast under an awning formed by a sail. First came a "parade" by the soldiers, equipped with all their weaponry, that was probably designed to demonstrate U.S. military prowess. Lewis, or possibly Clark, then delivered a long speech explaining the changes in government of the area from Spain to France to the United States, of which the Indians probably understood little; describing the desire of the new Great White Father to learn more about his Indian children and how he could best cultivate their

Peace Medals were given to American Indians by the United States Government beginning with the presidency of George Washington. The medal illustrated here is from 1801 and the time of President Thomas Jefferson. Medals like this one were carried by the Lewis & Clark Expedition for distribution as the Corps of Discovery met native peoples while crossing the continent. A major collection of Indian Peace Medals of the eighteenth and nineteenth centuries is on permanent display in the Museum of Westward Expansion under the Gateway Arch on the St. Louis Riverfront.

friendship and protect them; stressing his desire for peace among the various tribes; advising the Otos and Missouris on how to conduct themselves; and explaining the purpose of the expedition.

The chiefs, in their speeches, approved the sentiments that had been expounded, promised to pursue the advice proferred, and expressed happiness to find that they could rely on the Great Father. The peace pipe was smoked. The captains distributed gifts, including flags, medals, clothing, ammunition, and a bottle of whisky. The principal chiefs, including those who were absent, were awarded printed certificates from the U.S. Government in which Lewis and Clark had filled in the names of the chiefs and tribes. These certificates attested to their status as leaders and guaranteed their protection by the United States, whose sovereignty over them was affirmed. The Indians were intrigued with Lewis' demonstration of his air gun.

THIS council set the pattern for many more that were to follow all the way to the Pacific and back. They all usually were amicable; included a parade; speeches by Lewis or Clark and the chiefs; smoking the pipe; awarding of medals and certificates to the Indians; the exchanging of gifts; and, to awe the natives, a technological display, involving such items as the air gun, magnet, spyglass, compass, and watch. The outstanding characteristic of these councils was the sincere recognition accorded by Lewis and Clark to the dignity of the Indians—a trait that was to be sorely lacking on the part of many later U.S. officials.

Desertion of La Liberté and Reed

On August 3, upon the conclusion of the council with the Otos and Missouris, the expedition pushed on upriver. En route the next day, Private Reed received permission to return to the last camp to find his knife, which he said he had left behind. This was likely a pretext, for it soon became apparent he had deserted—a cardinal offense. Still missing, too, was La Liberté, who had never come back from his mission to the Otos.

On August 7, by which time neither had reappeared, Lewis dispatched Drouillard, Reuben Field, Bratton, and Labiche to the Oto villages to apprehend them. Drouillard had authority to kill Reed if he did not return peaceably. He also was to invite some of the Oto chiefs to accompany the expedition in the hope that Lewis and Clark might help them make peace with the Sioux and Omahas. The latter, who lived just north of the Otos, had long plundered or levied tribute on Spanish and French traders from St. Louis and were considered to be treacherous.

Visiting Chief Blackbird's grave

The main body continued slowly onward. But it saw scant trace of the Omahas, who had been decimated by a smallpox epidemic in 1800 and their population reduced from about 700 to 300. On the 11th, however, Lewis and Clark and 10 men visited the grave of the notorious Omaha Chief Blackbird. On a high bluff along the river near present Macy, Nebr., it afforded a view of the wandering Missouri for 60 to 70 miles. The chief, feared by all the tribes in the area, had won ascendancy over them by his possession of arsenic, which he had apparently looted or obtained in tribute from the traders and used to threaten his enemies.

When Blackbird had died in the 1800 epidemic, his followers buried him, according to his wishes, sitting erect on a horse on top of a high hill overlooking the Missouri so that he might "watch" the traders as they ascended it. His grave was marked by a turfed mound of earth about 12 feet in diameter and 6 feet high on the top center of which was an 8-foot-high pole, to which were attached all the scalps the chief had taken. The visitors affixed to it a white flag bound with red, white, and blue.

As the main body moved forward, search parties were unable to contact the Omahas but found some traces of Sioux camps. Lewis and Clark set the prairie on fire, the usual signal, to lure any members of either tribe who were near, but none responded.

Punishment of Reed

On August 18 the Drouillard party, accompanied by three principal chiefs of the Otos and a few braves, brought in Reed. La Liberté, who had also been captured, had escaped. Reed was court-martialed on the spot. His punishment was harsh. Despite the entreaties of the chiefs for his pardon, he was forced to run the gauntlet four times between the assembled men while they flogged his bare back—a custom the Indians found strange and offensive. He was also officially discharged from the expedition, though he was carried along on suf-

Blackbird Hill in 1832, when it was still a landmark and the river bluffs and surrounding scenery had changed little from the days of Lewis and Clark. Chief Blackbird's grave marker may be seen on top of the hill, which is now obscured by dense brush and timber. The river has also moved a couple of miles to the east.

ferance until he could be sent back to St. Louis.[71] The day ended on a happier note. The men toasted Lewis' birthday with an extra gill of whisky and danced until almost midnight.

Death of Floyd

With the dawn, merriment turned to tragedy. Sergeant Floyd became violently ill and was unable to retain anything in his stomach. The alarmed captains diagnosed the disease as "Biliose Chorlick" (bilious colic), but modern medical authorities believe it was peritonitis, which resulted from an infected appendix that had perforated or ruptured. Floyd had been ill some weeks earlier of what Clark thought was a cold. On July 31 the former had written in his diary, "I am verry sick and has ben for Sometime but have Recovered my helth again." Now, he was stricken again, and nothing Lewis or Clark did seemed to help.

Meantime, the commanders had held a council with the three Oto chiefs similar to the one held earlier with other tribal leaders. The plan to take the three chiefs along to make peace with the Sioux and Omahas was abandoned for some reason, and they returned home the next morning.

Although Clark had stayed up most of the night ministering to Floyd, the upriver trek resumed. But, just before noon, it became obvious that the latter was near death, for no pulse could be detected. The boat was pulled up along the east bank of the river at the southern edge of present Sioux City, Iowa, so that a bath could be prepared to comfort him. Before this could be done, he whispered with composure to his commanders, "I am going away" and succumbed. He was the first U.S. soldier to die west of the Mississippi River, and the only member of the expedition to lose his life on the entire journey to the Pacific and back. And he died of an illness

This 1832 painting depicts Sergeant Floyd's hilltop grave, still probably marked by the same cedar post his comrades had erected.

that none of the finest doctors of the day could have cured.

The highest bluff in the vicinity, about a mile away, was selected for the grave. His comrades buried Floyd with the honors of war, Lewis reading the services. The spot was marked with a red cedar post carved with Floyd's name and the date. The bluff and a small stream lying not far to the north were named after him. Two days later, the enlisted men selected Pvt. Patrick Gass to replace Sergeant Floyd, and 4 days later Lewis appointed him to the position.[72]

Penetrating Sioux country—the friendly Yanktons

In the vicinity of present Sioux City, the river switched directions from north to northwest. Near the mouth of the James River, on August 27, the first Sioux, three Yanktons, were contacted. They explained that their village was not far up the James. Lewis and Clark sent Sergeant Pryor, a French boatman, and Old Dorion to invite the chiefs to a council. The next day, the main party made camp on the present Nebraska side of the river at the foot of Calumet Bluff, near present Gavins Point Dam and opposite the site of the city of Yankton, S. Dak.

Late the following day, the 29th, the Pryor party and Old Dorion's son, who was residing with the Yanktons, arrived on the opposite shore with five chiefs and about 70 men and boys. In the morning, the group was brought across the river in a pirogue. The grand council, under an oak tree near a high flag staff from which waved the Stars and Stripes, started at noon and lasted throughout the next day. Gifts to the grand chief included a U.S. flag and an Army officer's hat and coat.

The peaceably inclined Yanktons, one of the tribes that dealt with St. Louis traders rather than with the British upriver, accepted U.S. sovereignty and agreed to make peace with their neighbors. Lewis and Clark prevailed upon Old Dorion to take a small amount of trade goods and remain with them to help try to negotiate peace and to arrange for deputations of chiefs to call on President Jefferson in Washington. Departure from the campsite occurred on September 1.

About 2 miles above the mouth of the Niobrara River, 4 days later, Shields and Gibson visited a Ponca village, but because most of the tribe was out on the prairie hunting buffalo no further contact was made. Closely related to the Omahas and once united with them, the Poncas—along with the Omahas and some of the Sioux—had once

Elk were a valuable source of food and clothing for the expedition. Here is a group at the National Elk Refuge, Jackson, Wyo.

been the terror of the river to traders, but smallpox had reduced them, as well as the Omahas, to a remnant of their former strength.

Young Shannon's escapade

On September 11 everyone was relieved when young Shannon, nearly starved, rode down to the river and rejoined his comrades. Energetic and eager to learn though a poor shot, he had gone hunting with Drouillard but had become separated from him and had been lost for 16 days. On several occasions, Lewis and Clark, anxious because they realized hostile Sioux were probably in the vicinity, sent out Drouillard, the Field brothers, and Colter to search for the lost man, but they were unsuccessful. Colter—whose skill as a hunter was becoming apparent by this time and who was more and more being employed in that capacity rather than an oarsman—reported that Shannon had apparently been under the impression that he had fallen behind the boats and had ridden on ahead trying to catch up with them.

One of his two horses gave out, and Shannon abandoned it. Later, his supply of bullets exhausted, for 12 days all he had to eat was a rabbit and some grapes. Weakened, he had stopped at a favorable place near the river hoping he might meet a trading boat. He was overjoyed when he spotted the expedition's craft. This was not the last time he was to get lost, for which he seemed to have a propensity. But he did not fear the wilderness, and as the months passed he became an adept and seasoned woodsman.

The episode astounded Clark, who exclaimed, "thus a man had like to have Starved to death in a land of Plenty for the want of Bullitts or Something to kill his meat."

Changing terrain and wildlife—high Plains country

And a land of plenty it was. In the last week or so of August and the first 3 weeks of September—on the stretch of river between present Sioux City, Iowa, and Chamberlain, S. Dak.—the terrain changed drastically. It was unlike anything the men had seen in the East. The woodlands receded, tailed off into tall grass prairie, and finally gave way to the short grass of the drier high Plains—home of the buffalo.

Wildlife became even more abundant than downriver. Elk, some of which had been present before, now roamed in almost every copse of woods, as had deer all along. Buffalo, the first of which had been seen late in June near the mouth of the Kansas River, were becoming a common sight on the riverbanks and adjacent plains. On August 23, just below present Vermillion, S. Dak., Joseph Field killed the first one.

The men of the expedition were the first Americans to see some remarkable new species of animals. French, Spanish, and British trappers probably had seen most of them but, unlike the two captains, had not described them in the detail necessary for scientific purposes. On September 7, in present Boyd County, Nebr., everyone was intrigued upon discovering a village of prairie dogs, one of which was captured with considerable difficulty for specimen purposes. A week later, in present Lyman County, S. Dak., Clark shot a pronghorn (antelope), a species originally observed on September 6. On September 17, not far south of the site of Chamberlain, S. Dak.,

The explorers were among the first nonnatives to observe many kinds of animals. One of these was the mule, or black-tailed, deer, which is much larger than the eastern white-tailed variety. Lewis coined the name "mule deer" because of the species' large ears.

The black-tailed prairie dog was unknown to scientists until Lewis sent back a live specimen from Fort Mandan to President Jefferson in 1805. Today, the species, which once flourished in semiarid regions of the West, is virtually extinct.

Colter downed a mule deer, different than the species in the Eastern United States and on the lower river. The next day, Clark killed a coyote, the first one of which had been seen about 5 weeks earlier.

Skirting calamity—fending off the Teton Sioux

Wildlife was lush, but Lewis and Clark feared lurking enemies and tightened security. They were nearing the territory of the Teton Sioux, whom the Yanktons had said were located along the mouth of the Bad River. This aggressive tribe, one of the most powerful on the Upper Missouri, was pressuring others westward. It had long harassed and intimidated Spanish and French traders from St. Louis. Not only did the Tetons desire weapons and trade goods for themselves, but they also wanted to deny them to their enemies farther upriver—the Arikaras, Mandans, and Minitaris. If any of them were to obtain any goods or weapons, the Tetons wanted to be the suppliers, so as to control the quantity and reap the middleman's profit. The two captains had heard of their bad reputation way back in St. Louis, and knew that firmness would be required to assert U.S. sovereignty over them.

On the night of September 23 three Teton boys swam the river to the expedition's camp on the north side of the Missouri. They stated that two of their villages—one of 80 lodges and one of 60— lay not far ahead. Lewis and Clark, sending a gift of tobacco along for the chiefs, requested the boys to invite them to a council. The next day, the boats moved up 13 miles to the mouth of the Bad River, which Lewis and Clark called the Teton, and stopped at a spot almost directly opposite modern Pierre, S. Dak. As a defensive measure, the keelboat was anchored off the west, or south, bank. Two-thirds of the group slept on it, and the rest on shore.

Reflecting satisfaction with their progress, Lewis and Clark had called an island they passed Good Humored Island. But this mood soon changed. During the day, some Tetons had stolen the last hunting horse—an augur of trouble to come. The commanders learned that an Indian village was situated 2 miles up the Bad River. That evening, some chiefs arrived. At a conference they agreed to take part in a council the next day.

It began at noon near camp on a sandbar, in the mouth of the Bad River, where a U.S. flag had been placed. The Tetons were represented by their grand chief, Black Buffalo; second chief, The Partisan; third chief, Buffalo Medicine; and two lesser leaders. A special problem—one that was to complicate other relations with the Tetons in the days ahead—was translation. Old Dorion was sorely missed. Only two men in the complement knew any of the Sioux tongue and they did not know much of it. Finally, it was decided to utilize Cruzatte, who spoke Omaha, to translate through one of that tribe, apparently a prisoner, who was present and who knew the Sioux language.

After the council, Lewis and Clark took the three principal chiefs in a pirogue out to the keelboat to see the air gun and other curiosities. The Indians gulped down drinks of whiskey. The Partisan, pretending to be drunk, began to grow ugly. Clark and three men hurriedly took their guests to shore—where the expedition faced its first test. Three young warriors, among many lining the shore,

Although Spanish explorers had earlier seen pronghorn (antelope) in the present Southwestern United States, Lewis and Clark described them in detail and obtained skin and bone specimens. Vast herds then ranged over much of the West. In some places, the animals still roam there today.

grabbed the pirogue's towrope. The Partisan pushed into Clark, said the presents were cheap, and stated that the boats could go no farther. The situation was tense.

Although Clark realized he was badly outnumbered, he was determined not to be bullied and drew his sword. The braves on the bank, their bows already strung, pulled arrows from their quivers. Lewis, watching intently from the keelboat, ordered the entire complement to take up their rifles and directed that the large swivel gun at the bow be manned and pointed at the Indians. Black Buffalo, seeing that these white men were ready to fight, seized the towrope and ordered the warriors to let go.

Clark, hemmed in and seeing that any attempt on his part to get back to his pirogue would be interpreted as a retreat, ordered his

Coyotes, many of which the expedition encountered, still live in a wild state in various parts of the West. The two captains, who referred to the species as "prairie foxes" or "prairie wolves," sent a skin back to Jefferson from Fort Mandan.

three companions to take it to the keelboat to obtain reinforcements. There, a dozen well-armed men leaped aboard and returned to shore. They and Clark outfaced their adversaries, who backed off.

Clark acceded to the request of Black Buffalo, Buffalo Medicine, and two other Indians to be taken out to the keelboat to spend the night. All the boats then proceeded upstream about a mile and anchored off an island in the river that Clark, recognizing the sad turn of events with the Tetons, called Bad Humored Island. Although a heavy guard was posted, the captains slept fitfully.

In the morning, on the 26th, the craft traveled about 5 miles upriver and anchored along the south bank near an Indian village of at least 80 lodges. That day, tensions subsided somewhat as the Indians decided to play the role of hosts. Unsuccessful with their hostile actions the previous day, they were apparently turning either to diplomacy or to subterfuge, possibly awaiting another village to join them. Although they probably outnumbered the strangers 10 to 1, they had undoubtedly been awed by their courage, cannon and other superior weaponry, and keelboat.

In the afternoon, six Indians carried Lewis and Clark individually to the village on an elegant painted buffalo robe—a privilege ordinarily extended only to renowned chiefs. Adorning the council tent were two Spanish flags and the U.S. flag that had been given to Black Buffalo the day before.

As the council ended and dusk approached, the entertainment began. A dog, considered a delicacy by the Tetons, and pemmican were the principal items in a feast, which was followed by a scalp dance. The Indians displayed 65 scalps. Clark saw 25 women and boy prisoners of 48 the Tetons had captured during a recent raid to the south on the Omahas. During the clash, 75 of that tribe's men and "some boys and children" had died and 40 lodges had been destroyed. About midnight, Lewis and Clark returned to the boats, accompanied by four chiefs. Following what had become almost a fetish among the Indians, they stayed for the night on the keelboat. Everyone in the expedition kept on the alert.

During the next day, the 27th, Lewis and Clark separately revisited the Indian villages and presented more gifts and printed certificates to the chiefs, who entertained their visitors with another round of scalp dances. The Partisan and another Indian came back with Clark to pass the night on the keelboat. All the soldiers were apprehensive

In 1832 Catlin painted this huge Teton Sioux encampment of about 600 tipis near Fort Pierre, S. Dak., which is situated along the riverbank in the middle of the painting. This encampment, only a few miles downstream from the one where Lewis and Clark parleyed in 1804, probably resembled the latter.

for two reasons. First, the loss of the craft's anchor in an accident that day had necessitated bringing the boat along shore under a "falling bank" and exposed the party to hostile action. Secondly, that night some of the Omaha prisoners managed to warn Cruzatte that the Tetons were feigning a display of friendship for the whites while actually plotting their destruction.

Thus the decision was made to set out in the morning, the 28th. But any sighs of relief were premature. As the boats made ready to cast off, some of the 200 or so armed warriors along the bank grabbed the cable of the keelboat. Black Buffalo, who had by this time boarded it for a ride upstream, said his people wanted tobacco. Clark, by now a veteran of such harrassment, threatened the crowd with the large swivel gun. As a final gesture, he tossed some tobacco to the chief. He gave it to the men holding the cable, jerked the rope away from them, and handed it to the bowmen. Despite efforts of the Sioux to lure the boats to shore again, they held to the river and pushed onward.

The 4-day ordeal was over. Against weaker men, the Tetons would have triumphed. Only sleepless vigilance, excellent judgment, and bold determination had saved the day. For the time being at least, the two captains had gained much prestige and established U.S. authority over this stretch of the Missouri, which north of the Tetons switched from its previous northwest course once again to almost directly north all the way to the Mandan villages. The news spread rapidly up and down the river and promised a peaceful welcome for the explorers among the upriver tribes.

Stopoff at the Arikara villages

Such proved to be the case at the Arikara, or Ree, villages, in north central South Dakota, visited between October 8 and 12.[73] About 600 men and their families resided in a cluster of villages located just above the mouth of the Grand River along the Missouri. The lower village was situated in the center near the west, or south, side of a 3-mile-long island, whose lower end was 3 miles north of the Grand; the other two villages, about 2½ to 3 miles above the upper end of the island, were on the north bank only one-half mile apart.

The Arikaras lived in pole-and-brush framed octagonal earth-lodges with dome-shaped roofs. Basically an agricultural people, they cultivated extensive fields of corn, beans, tobacco, squash, and melons —a trade lure to other Plains tribes from several hundred miles around. As a matter of fact, at the time of the Lewis and Clark visit, some Cheyennes were at the villages. The Tetons, the nearest tribe downstream, persistently intimidated and pretty much dominated the Arikaras, who from time to time fought with their other neighbors. They were then warring with the Mandans, and one of the chiefs was to accompany the expedition to the Mandan villages in the hope that Lewis and Clark could arrange a peace.

Clark was surprised to find that the Arikaras, unlike the other tribes, had no thirst for whisky. But, as a result of their liberal sex practices and their numerous contacts with traders, venereal disease was rampant. From two of Régis Loisel's resident employees—Pierre

Near Bismarck, North Dakota, the rebuilt "On-A-Slant Village" location is cared for by the North Dakota Parks Department. It shows how earthen lodges looked on the Upper Missouri.

Antoine Tabeau and Joseph Gravelines—Lewis and Clark learned much about the surrounding country and its tribes. Lewis, seeing that Gravelines would be useful, hired him as an interpreter, and he later went along with the expedition to the Mandan villages. The councils with the Arikara leaders went smoothly. They seemed pleased with their gifts and expressed amazement at the air gun.

While the captains counciled, their command took advantage of the respite from the wearying journey upriver and the recent tension with the Tetons. Particularly diverting were the Arikara women. The giant York was tremendously popular with men, women, and children alike. Because they had never seen a black man, they excitedly flocked around him and examined him carefully from head to toe. Tongue in cheek, he told them he had been a wild animal until his master caught and tamed him. To "verify" his story, he displayed his unusual strength and roared at the children, who would flee screaming. Clark, fearing York was carrying his teasing too far, said he "made himself more turribal than we wished him to doe."

Another disciplinary problem

On October 13, the day after setting out from the Arikara villages, the captains were confronted with another disciplinary problem. A

On December 8, 1804, the men of the Lewis and Clark Expedition were building their winter compound near the Mandan and Hidatsa Villages, which they named Fort Mandan. The native Indian Village areas are now part of the Knife River Villages, a National Park Service area.

court-martial found John Newman guilty of "criminal and mutinous expressions" and sentenced him to 75 lashes and dismissal.[74] On a sandbar the next noon, he felt the slash of the whip—the last corporal punishment inflicted during the expedition. The Arikara chief accompanying the party cried aloud and explained his tribe never whipped anyone, even children. He said a man might be killed but never lashed, the worst possible disgrace. Until Newman could be returned to St. Louis, he was attached as a laboring hand to the red pirogue, occupied by the French boatmen, and stripped of his arms and equipment.

Winter's portents

By this time, almost into present North Dakota, Lewis and Clark were eager to reach the Mandan villages and set up winter quarters.

During the past month, on some days biting fall winds had been sweeping out of the north. Dense masses of gray clouds often moved overhead. Many of the nights were frigid, and frost painted the ground white. The men bundled themselves in heavier clothes.

Signs of the approach of the villages, too, soon became apparent. Near the mouth of the Cannonball River, 4 days after Newman's lashing, the party met two of Gravelines' trappers descending the river in a pirogue. They reported that the Mandans had stolen their traps. Lewis and Clark persuaded them to turn back with the expedition by promising help in obtaining redress.

Two nights later, on October 20, a stop was made just above the site of later Fort Abraham Lincoln, a few miles south of and across the river from present Bismarck, N. Dak. Above and below that camp, mostly on the west side of the river, a number of deserted Mandan villages were noted. The Sioux had forced their occupants to move northwestward. Mandan and Minitari hunting parties began to be encountered. On October 21 the first snow fell.

Arrival at the Mandan villages

On October 26, 1804, roughly 60 miles upstream from the site of Bismarck near the junction of the Knife and Missouri Rivers—1,600 miles from Camp Wood according to the leaders' estimates—they arrived at the relocated Mandan villages. There they were to build a fort to endure the icy blasts of winter on the northern Plains before they could set out westward.

The so-called "Mandan villages," five in number, were actually occupied by Minitaris and Amahamis as well as the Mandans. These three groups lived harmoniously together; joined forces against their principal enemy, the Sioux; and traded their agricultural products with other tribes in the region. The Minitaris, also known as "Minitaris of the South," Gros Ventres ("Big Bellies") of the Missouri, and later as Hidatsas, were close kin of the Crows, but had stayed behind when the latter emigrated westward. The Mandans lived in the lower two villages, along the Missouri south of the mouth of the Knife; the Amahamis, protected and absorbed by the ethnically related Minitaris, in the center one, at the mouth of the Knife; and the Minitaris in the upper two, farther up that river.

Lewis and Clark estimated that the population of the five villages, located within an 8 by 2 mile rectangle, totaled 4,400. About 1,400 of

Sheheke's Mandan village in 1832, as portrayed by Catlin. Lewis and Clark had visited there during the winter of 1804–5. The burial ground is on the river bottom beyond the village, about midway between its far edge and the distant bluffs. Note the bull boats on top of several of the earthlodges, and the varying manner in which the Indians used the roofs.

these were adult males, 700 Mandans, 650 Minitaris, and 50 Amahamis. This was clearly the largest concentration of Indian population on the Missouri River and probably in the upper Great Plains area. Rather well armed with white men's weapons and ammunition, the three tribes still were able to hold their own against the Teton Sioux, who had pressed far enough upriver by this time to harass them continually.

The Minitaris, Mandans, and Amahamis were agriculturists-hunters. They raised large quantities of corn, beans, squash, tobacco, and sunflowers; and hunted buffalo and other game on the surrounding plains. The Mandans specialized in raising crops; the Minitaris, in hunting. The latter, whose hunting and war parties ranged far to the west, also were less friendly than the other two groups and aroused some mistrust on the part of Lewis and Clark. The five villages, consisting of large, round, domed earthlodge houses, most accommodating several families, were surrounded by picket enclosures.

Building Fort Mandan (1804–5)

One of the first tasks of Lewis and Clark, particularly because of the onset of cold weather, was to survey the area to find a suitable spot for winter camp. Sites reconnoitered on October 28, or 2 days after arrival at the Mandan villages, and on October 30 were rejected because of lack of suitable timber or game or distance from the two rivers. On November 2 a place was selected. It was located on the east, or north, bank of the Missouri about 6 air miles below the mouth of the Knife on a point of low ground sheltered by bluffs. It was directly opposite the lower of the five Indian villages and 2 miles away from it.

George Catlin (1796-1872) was among the first artists to paint along the Upper Missouri. Although he traveled the area nearly 30 years after Lewis and Clark, he was able to record the lifestyle of the Upper Missouri village Indians before their virtual destruction due to epidemic disease.

The next day, watched by many Mandans who lived in the village across the river, the men set to work with their axes building a triangular-shaped structure named Fort Mandan. It apparently consisted of two rows of huts, or rooms. At the rear, they joined a small semicircular structure, the top of which provided a sentry post and the lower story of which consisted of one or two storerooms. At the front, or third, side, which probably faced the river, a palisade, or picket-type fence, equipped with a gate, connected the two rows of huts. Each of the rows contained four units, measuring individually 14 feet square. The roofs, built in shed fashion and providing a loft over the rows of huts, rose from the inner side of the rows to a height of about 18 feet on the outer side. The backs of the huts connected with the peak of the loft.

The fort was not finished until Christmas Day. But, the weather growing increasingly cold, on November 16 the men had moved into their quarters and 4 days later the two leaders into theirs. This was none too soon, for on the 13th ice had run in the river and it had snowed all day. The fort was strong enough to hold off any Indian war party. Fearful of Sioux raids and suspicious of the Minitaris, however, the two captains mounted the swivel cannon from the bow of the keelboat on the fort; refused Indians admittance after dark; kept a sentry on duty at all times; and subsequent to February 7 kept the gate locked at night.

Relations with the Mandans and Minitaris

Another matter that almost immediately occupied Lewis and Clark on their arrival at the villages was the establishment of good relations with the Mandans and Minitaris. On October 29, only 3 days after their arrival, the two captains held the most impressive council they had yet staged.[75] It was the first of many with the tribes.

Lewis and Clark managed to obtain redress for the stolen traps of the two French trappers who had joined them near the mouth of the Cannonball. More important, the commanders, working closely with Tabeau at the Arikara villages, arranged a peace they hoped would be lasting between the Arikaras and the Mandans and Minitaris. On November 2 a Mandan-Minitari delegation traveled to the Arikara villages with the Arikara chief who had accompanied the expedition to the Mandan villages. Four days later, Lewis and Clark sent Gravelines and French boatmen Baptiste La Jeunesse and Paul Primaut to help in the negotiations.

One of the few drawings made from life of an Indian identified in the Lewis and Clark journals. This painting (1832) by Catlin portrays Black Moccasin, a Minitari chief, who was then more than 100 years old.

Dealings with British traders

The Indian chiefs were not the only ones with whom Lewis and Clark had dealings during the long winter months. Upon their arrival, they found that various British and French-Canadian traders from posts in the Assiniboine River area in present Canada about 9 days north of the Mandan villages were well established with the natives.

As time went on, the traders came and went. Most of them represented the North West Company: René Jessaume, Toussaint Charbonneau, Hugh Heney, Hugh McCracken, François Antoine Larocque, Charles McKenzie, and Baptiste Lafrance. Two represented the Hudson's Bay Company: G. Henderson and George Bunch. The company affiliations, if any, of Baptiste Lepage and a man named Garrow cannot be determined.

A strange combination of animosity and friendliness characterized relations between Lewis and Clark and these traders. Despite the tension and suspicion that colored their associations and their basic differences, which they recognized, they exchanged friendly visits, performed favors for each other, and conducted frank discussions. The two captains gained considerable information about the nature and extent of the British fur trade, including the tribes involved. The traders tried to learn all they could of the motives of the expedition.

But all was not harmonious. The Britishers, recognizing that the visit of Lewis and Clark was probably a first step in the extension of U.S. authority and trade, tried to stir up trouble between the explorers and the Indians, made anti-American statements to them, and gave them British flags and medals. The two commanders warned the traders to cease these activities, made it clear that they were operating on U.S. soil, and hinted that the U.S. Government might establish a "factory" in the area for commerce with the Indians, who were under its jurisdiction. On the other hand, the captains said the British were free to conduct their business unless they violated U.S. regulations.

Lewis' interest in early asserting national sovereignty is revealed in his letter of October 31, sent the next day with McCracken, to Charles Chaboillez, head of the Department of the Assiniboine for the North West Company. This letter, with which was enclosed a copy of Lewis and Clark's British passport, explained their mission, stated their plans to winter at the Mandan villages, stressed that the U.S. Government would extend its protection to the British traders who were operating in its territory, and solicited any aid Chaboillez might extend. On December 16 Heney brought Chaboillez' cordial reply assuring his cooperation.

Personnel gains and losses

An unexpected dividend from the British traders was personnel. On October 27 Lewis and Clark temporarily hired Jessaume as an

interpreter with the Mandans. A week later, to replace Private Newman, they recruited Lepage into the permanent party. The next day,
November 4, Charbonneau applied for a job as interpreter with the
Minitaris. A 44-year-old French-Canadian from near Montreal, he had
been living and trading among them for 5 years and had been active
on the Upper Missouri since at least 1793. Lewis and Clark hired him
and eventually convinced him to accompany the expedition.[76]

Some manpower was also lost at the Mandan villages. On November 3 a group of the French boatmen, whose assignment ended at the
Mandan villages, began to build a pirogue for their homeward trip
to St. Louis.[77] Not long thereafter, part of them, after apparently
being paid in cash by Lewis, returned to St. Louis, but a few of them
stayed over the winter and two went back with Corporal Warfington's
party in the spring.[78]

Sacagawea joins the expedition

On November 11 two Indian women from one of the Minitari villages
visited Fort Mandan. One, named Sacagawea, was young and preg-
nant. A 16- or 17-year-old Shoshoni, she was one of two "wives" of
that tribe which Charbonneau had bought or won in a gambling
game from some Minitaris.[79] They had captured her about 5 years
earlier in a raid on her people in the foothills of the Rockies near the
Three Forks of the Missouri. She did not speak French or English,
but communicated with Charbonneau in Minitari. On February 11,
1805, she gave birth to her first child, a son named Jean Baptiste. To
ease her labor, Jessaume ground up in water some rattlesnake rattles,
obtained from Lewis, and administered them.

Lewis and Clark finally assented to Charbonneau's request that
Sacagawea be allowed to come with him. By this time, they knew
that the Shoshonis would be crucial to their success because they
could provide horses for the land traverse, of uncertain length, that
would need to be made from the Missouri to the Columbia watershed.
The Indian girl not only could help interpret in her native tongue,
but might also be a valuable intermediary with her tribe. Because
women, particularly those carrying a papoose, were not members of
war parties, she would also remove fear and ease the way with all the
natives.

Sacagawea, the only female member of the expedition, was never
the brilliant guide and inspirational force that her eulogistic biog-

This heroic bronze statue is located in Great Falls, Montana, near where the Sun River enters the Missouri. The Forest Service has a Lewis & Clark Trail Center nearby.

raphers have presented. Yet she exhibited courage and determination and aided in many important ways. She did smooth relations with the Shoshonis and other tribes, in places guided the group, served as interpreter on occasion, pointed out or collected herbs and roots that had food or medicinal value, and provided other valuable help.

This segment of Lewis' journal entry for May 20, 1805, is the most explicit original source on Sacagawea's name. Lines 8–10 state: "…this stream we called Sâh-câ-gee Me-âh or bird woman's River, after our interpreter the Snake woman." Later, someone lined through Lewis' handwriting and supplied the spelling "Sah ca gar wea."

A severe winter

Few of the men had ever experienced the sort of severe weather they endured at Fort Mandan. It began early in December. On the 10th, Clark saw large numbers of buffalo crossing the Missouri without breaking the ice. The temperature sometimes dropped as low as 45° below zero, and the river ice continually groaned. The cold was sometimes so bad that sentries needed to be replaced every half hour. Many of the complement suffered frostbite. The natives were no more immune; Lewis amputated the frozen toes of an Indian boy.

Hunting and other activities

Hunting was a major function. Plentiful game—antelope, deer, elk, buffalo—supplemented vegetables obtained from the Indians, but sometimes it was located many miles away and long sleigh hauls were necessary. At other times, animals came close to Fort Mandan, apparently seeking shelter along the river breaks from the cold winds of the Plains. Other chores were gathering firewood and making moccasins and clothes. To obtain corn from the Indians, Lewis and Clark set their blacksmiths to work on trade items. Utilizing a sheet iron stove that had been damaged, they made battleaxes, arrow points, and scrapers (used to separate flesh from buffalo hides before tanning).

But, during the long winter nights, the men found time to relax around the fire. Cruzatte's fiddle provided music for frequent dances.[80] Christmas and New Years were also celebrated with drinking and feasting. On the former occasion, a U.S. flag was hoisted and saluted with a shot from the keelboat cannon.

Some of the Mandans paid visits to the fort, where they were allowed during the day. On special occasions, Lewis and Clark authorized members of the party to visit their villages. Less friendly were the Minitaris, whose towns were farther away anyway. The Mandan women, as promiscuous as the Arikaras, passed on venereal disease to their paramours. York was again highly popular with the natives. Because none of them had seen a black man before, he elicited exceptional curiosity. The Minitari principal chief Le Borgne ("One-Eye"), who had heard reports about him, examined him closely. The astonished Le Borgne suspected a trick. Unable to rub off the "black paint" from York's body with his moistened fingers, he was only convinced

The Knife River Villages National Park Area is about one hour north of Bismarck, North Dakota. Its apparently smooth greenery masks undulations in the ground which show where thousands of people once lived.

that York was indeed black when he examined his scalp through his hair.

Any boredom was alleviated by recurring rumors of Sioux attacks on Fort Mandan. The Tetons did make raids in the area, but on only one occasion did the expedition's members become involved with them. In February Clark ranged far afield on a 9-day hunt. Killing more meat than he could transport, when he returned to the fort he dispatched Drouillard with three men and three horse-drawn sleighs to retrieve it. A large band of Sioux, numbering more than 100, jumped the party and stole two horses and the knives of two of the men. Lewis and 24 men later pursued the culprits without success. The only other Indians encountered were some Cheyennes, who traveled up from the Arikara to the Mandan villages; and bands of Assiniboins, who lived to the north of the Mandans and Minitaris and came to trade for corn.

Learning of the country to the west

Highly concerned as they were with their westward route in the spring and the nature of the land and its occupants, Lewis and Clark zealously questioned the Mandans and Minitaris on these subjects. The two leaders possessed only a rudimentary knowledge about them, based mostly on information they had obtained in St. Louis from people who had never visited the area.

The Minitaris had. Their war and hunting parties had ranged far to the west, some of them penetrating the Rocky Mountains. The tribe possessed an intimate knowledge of the terrain, drainage, and inhabitants of the Upper Missouri country all the way to the Three Forks, as well as good understanding of the area beyond up to the Bitterroot Mountains. Tracing stream courses with charcoal on animal hides or with a stick in the dirt and heaping up mounds of earth to show the main mountain ranges, the Minitaris provided Lewis and Clark with exceedingly valuable information about the region—much more probably than any white men had ever possessed before.

The Indians told of the Yellowstone and its tributaries and the Great Falls of the Missouri. They explained that the Missouri was navigable nearly to its source. They said that in the country west of the point that it branched into three forks (Three Forks) was a tribe (the Shoshonis) that possessed many horses. The northern-most fork of the three would lead to a route across the Rockies. Just west of the Continental Divide at the base of the mountains ran a big northward-flowing river (apparently the Lemhi-Salmon or Bitter-root Rivers or the combination of them). Lewis and Clark hypothe-sized this to be a south fork of the Columbia River, particularly because their native informants said that a tribe (the Flatheads) residing along this stream north of the westernmost area frequented by the Shoshonis lived principally on large fish, which the two cap-tains assumed to be salmon.

For the crossing of the Rockies, the Minitaris described two routes, both requiring a considerable amount of land travel: the easier one led west just beyond the Great Falls to the Bitterroot River; the second, far more difficult, continued up the Missouri from the Great Falls to the Three Forks, moved up the Jefferson and Beaverhead Rivers, crossed the divide to the Lemhi River, and then went down it to the Salmon River. For some reason, the two captains misunderstood the nature of the first of the routes, and apparently applied the information the Minitaris presented to the second. The captains were also to interpret incorrectly some of the other data presented by the Minitaris. Most of it, however, was essentially accurate, even on details.

One subject of special interest to Lewis and Clark in their queries to the Minitaris—the possible existence of a navigable tributary of the Missouri flowing into it from the north—involved a farsighted goal of President Jefferson in the realm of international geopolitics. Such a stream would be part of the Missouri drainage and the Mississippi system, whose farthest reaches he hoped would extend to at least 49° and hopefully to 50°, which he planned to propose to Great Britain as the northern boundary of the Louisiana Purchase. This boundary had not been defined at the time the United States acquired Louisiana from France in 1803 nor had a comparable boundary ever been specified in earlier treaties—Treaty of Utrecht (1713), Treaty of Paris (1763), Treaty of Paris (1783), and Jay's Treaty (1794)—transferring territory in North American between the major powers.

A second reason for the interest in a northern tributary of the Missouri, which the Minitaris said did exist, was Jefferson's feeling that such a river, even if a portage were involved, would provide an entree to the rich fur trade of present Canada and in time, hopefully, to U.S. control of it.

Advent of spring

Near the end of March, as the weather moderated, the ice broke up in the river and huge flocks of ducks and geese were seen winging their way northward. Also witnessed were the efforts of local Indians to replenish their food supply from buffalo that had become stranded on ice floes as they tried to cross the Missouri. The natives demonstrated extraordinary dexterity in jumping from one cake of ice to another. Others retrieved from the water dead bodies of the animals as they floated down. Clark noted that the plains near Fort Mandan on both sides of the river were on fire. The Indians set them to the torch early in the spring to bring green grass, which provided food for their horses and attracted buffalo.

Preparations for departure

The arrival of spring meant that the time was near to push on westward and that the necessary preparations had to be made.

Because the keelboat was considered too large for use farther upriver and was to return to St. Louis, one of the first tasks was to build six dugout canoes to supplement the two pirogues, which late in February were chopped out of the ice, along with the keelboat, and brought up on shore so they could be readied for the journey. The cottonwoods near Fort Mandan were not large enough for the canoes, so on February 28 Lewis and Clark sent Sergeant Gass and 16 men to locate some of desirable size and build the canoes. Large trees were found 5 miles to the north of Fort Mandan near the mouth of the Knife River. The canoes were completed in about 3 weeks, and on March 20 and 21 were carried a short distance to the Missouri and then paddled down to the fort. Before departure, the swivel cannon that had originally been mounted on the bow of the keelboat and removed to fortify Fort Mandan was dismounted and probably set up in one of the pirogues.

Another major effort preparatory to leaving Fort Mandan was numbering, labeling, and packing the extensive collection of zoological, botanical, and ethnological specimens and artifacts that had been obtained so far for dispatch to President Jefferson on the keelboat.[81] The shipment consisted of four boxes, one trunk, and three cages. The cages contained a live prairie dog, a sharp-tailed grouse, and four magpies. Included in the boxes and the trunk were the pelts, horns, and skeletons of various animals; dried plant, soil, mineral, and insect specimens; Mandan and Minitari artifacts and items such as plain and decorated buffalo robes, an earthen pot, bow and quiver of arrows, an ear of corn, and tobacco seed; and Arikara tobacco and tobacco seed.[82] Labels included the date and place obtained and brief description. All told, the collection consisted of a wealth of information about the flora and fauna and native peoples of the West.

Also sent back on the keelboat were various letters, reports, dispatches, and maps addressed to Jefferson and Secretary of War Henry Dearborn.[83] The major topics treated in the letters and reports were descriptions of Indian tribes that had already been encountered and those to the west of the Mandan villages, mainly based on Minitari data, as well as geographical information. The dispatches included a large, extensively annotated table prepared by Clark that represented the first summary of the trans-Mississippi tribes—an ethnological classic.[84] One of Clark's maps showed the detailed course

Henry Rowe Schoolcraft was once the Superintendent of Indian Affairs for nearly the entire northern part of the United States. He published this illustration showing "Shoshonee Implements" among his early reports to Congress. Lewis and Clark met their first Shoshoni when they were introduced to Charbonneau's wife, Sacagawea (Sakagawea) among the Mandan people. Later in the journey, her people helped the expedition. She returned with her husband to the Mandan Villages.

of the Missouri as far as Fort Mandan and a general map of the country west of there to the Pacific between the 34th and 54th parallels, based to a considerable extent on data provided by the Minitaris.[85]

Return of the keelboat

By April 5, 1805, the river was sufficiently clear of ice in both directions to allow for navigation, but final preparations consumed 2 more days. Late in the afternoon on April 7, at the same time, the keelboat under Corporal Warfington headed back to St. Louis and the expedition set out westward. Accompanying Warfington were Privates Boley, Dame, Tuttle, and White;[86] Privates Newman and Reed, who had been discharged; Gravelines, acting as pilot and interpreter; two of the French boatmen;[87] possibly two other French-Canadian traders;[88] and a lame Arikara chief returning to his village. Traveling along with the keelboat in a pirogue were the two trappers originally encountered near the mouth of the Cannonball River.

Coming on board at the Arikara villages were Antoine Tabeau and apparently four of his employees with a load of peltry, as well as Chief Ankedoucharo, who planned to visit President Jefferson. Gravelines acted as the chief's interpreter. On the way downriver, a large number of other chiefs, totaling 44, from among the Poncas, Sioux, Omahas, Otos, and Missouris augmented the party.[89] It arrived in St. Louis on May 20, 1805.

Breaching the unknown

As the main party pushed westward into the unknown that spring afternoon of April 7, 1805, Lewis walked along on shore for a few miles, probably as usual accompanied by Scannon. Some of the thoughts that must have flashed through his mind concerning the momentous nature of the exploration that lay ahead, he dramatically recorded in his journal that night:

> Our vessels consisted of six small canoes, and two large perogues. This little fleet altho' not quite so rispectable as those of Columbus or Capt. Cook, were still viewed by us with as much pleasure as those deservedly famed adventurers ever beheld theirs; and I dare say with quite as much anxiety for their safety and preservation. we were now about to penetrate a country at least two thousand miles in width, on which the foot of civilized man had never trodden; the good or evil it had in store for us was for experiment yet to determine, and these little vessells contained every article by which we were to expect to

Downstream view along the Missouri from the top of Crow High Butte, near Sanish, N. Dak., before Lake Sakakawea (Garrison Reservoir) engulfed the area. This scene was probably typical of the high Plains to members of the Lewis and Clark Expedition.

subsist or defend ourselves. however, as the state of mind in which we are, generally gives the colouring to events, when the immagination is suffered to wander into futurity, the picture which now presented itself to me was a most pleasing one. enterta[in]ing as I do, the most confident hope of succeeding in a voyage which had formed a da[r]ling project of mine for the last ten years, I could but esteem this moment of my departure as among the most happy of my life.

No one could guess what "futurity" held, but Lewis was certain the expedition could never reach the Pacific and get back to St. Louis that year. In a letter dated April 7, forwarded on the keelboat with Corporal Warfington, Lewis had told President Jefferson that by winter he expected to be able to return only to the "head of the Missouri" or possibly to Fort Mandan—a highly optimistic prediction.[90]

But Lewis was cheered by the calibre of his men, who were "zealously attatched to the enterprise, and anxious to proceed." They had passed through the shakedown period and been welded into a cohesive force. Their wits and nerves had been tempered by their experiences, such as those with the Teton Sioux. The unreliable had been weeded out; the youths had matured. Lewis could not detect "a whisper of discontent or murmur" among them and he found that they all acted in unison and "with the most perfect harmoney." Except for venereal complaints, they were in fine health.

Disciplinary problems had long since been brought under control. What was to prove to be the last court-martial had been conducted at Fort Mandan in February. Even that involved a minor offense and Lewis remitted the sentence.

Tried and true, the party consisted of 31 people, in addition to the two leaders: [91] Sergeants Ordway, Pryor, and Gass; interpreters Drouillard and Charbonneau; 23 privates; [92] Sacagawea with her infant son, Baptiste; and York. At this point, the principal long-range objective was contact with the Shoshonis somewhere between the Three Forks and the Continental Divide. It was hoped they would be friendly and provide horses and guides for the passage across the mountains to the Columbia River, which would afford a water route to the Pacific. But, to reach the Shoshonis, it would be necessary to traverse more than a thousand miles of unknown country, possibly peopled by hostile tribes, frequented by fierce animals, and characterized by rugged terrain.

Camping procedures remained essentially the same as before, except that special arrangements were necessary to accommodate some of the new members. Lewis and Clark, interpreters Drouillard and Charbonneau, Sacagawea, and her infant son slept in an Indian-style tent made of dressed buffalo skins sewn together and supported by poles.

Crossing the treeless Plains

Beyond Fort Mandan the rolling, treeless plains of present North Dakota unfolded endlessly. The nights remained frosty, water still froze readily, and sometimes snow fell. Game continued to be abundant. Deer, elk, buffalo, and antelope were visible in all directions, and hunters took some fine-looking beaver. Three unnamed French trappers, on their way to the Yellowstone River from the Mandan villages, were encountered on April 10 and they accompanied the expedition for 3 days. Had its members known that these white men were the last they would see for 16 months, the farewell might have been more poignant.

Only fragments have survived of the herds of buffalo that Lewis and Clark viewed — sometimes an estimated 10,000 in one sweep of the eye.

On April 15, only 8 days out of Fort Mandan, the farthest point upstream on the Missouri known by Lewis and Clark to have been reached by white men was passed. They were Lepage, now a member of the expedition, and another Frenchman, but the former was unable to indicate the exact spot. It was apparently a few miles above the creek across from the camp on the previous night that Lewis and Clark had named for Charbonneau, who had earlier camped at its mouth.

Signs of grizzlies

On the 14th, an exciting event occurred. Clark saw the first "white bear"—the huge, dreaded grizzly—in the distance passing over some hills. Talk and speculation about these creatures had been rampant. The Mandans, Minitaris, and traders at the Mandan villages had told many tales about the animals, which it was claimed feared neither man nor beast, and on meeting a human would more likely attack than flee.

The Indians called the species "white bear," though their hair varied in color from yellow-brown to white tipped. They were dreaded so much that they were never hunted except in parties of eight to 10, and even then one or more men were often lost. According to Lewis, before the natives set out in quest of a grizzly, they painted themselves and performed "all those supersticious rights commonly observed when they are about to make war uppon a neighboring nation."

Yet Lewis and Clark, confident their new Harpers Ferry rifles would take care of any animal they met, discounted the stories of the strength and ferocity of the grizzlies as grossly exaggerated. Almost daily their paw tracks were seen along the river's edge around the carcasses of buffalo, on which they had been feeding. Sometimes the bears themselves were visible in the distance. But, before the first direct encounter occurred, concern about wildlife turned to geographic amazement.

At the mouth of the Yellowstone

Sensing from the topography that the Yellowstone was near, at 11:00 a.m. on April 25 Lewis took four men and pushed ahead.[93] Within a matter of a few hours, they reached the river and set up camp. In the morning, Lewis sent Joseph Field on a day's excursion up the Yellowstone, while he and another man probed the region at the juncture of the two rivers. It was beautiful and teemed with all kinds of wildlife. At noon the main party arrived. That day, the first bighorn, or Rocky Mountain, sheep was seen—a species that was to be observed in large numbers all the way to the mouth of the Marias.[94] In the evening, happy to have reached this key spot and unmindful of tribulations to come, the group enjoyed a liquor ration and sang and danced to Cruzatte's fiddle.

Lewis and Clark designated the river the "Roche Jaune" (Yellow Rock or Yellow Stone), the name applied by French trappers in a literal translation of a Minitari word apparently describing the grayish-yellow rocks lining its banks. At least three French-Canadian traders had undoubtedly reached there before Lewis and Clark, but the latter were the first to provide firsthand documentary evidence.[95] Even before they arrived at the Yellowstone, back at Fort Mandan when the Mandans and Minitaris had told them about it, they had recognized its strategic importance and at that time recommended its mouth as a site for the establishment of a trading post.[96]

Skirmishes with grizzlies

On April 29, the day after the expedition moved upriver from the Yellowstone, the first grizzly was killed. Lewis and a companion wounded two of them. One escaped, and the other was taken. It was a young male, weighing only about 300 pounds. Clark and Drouillard killed the first full-size beast, a 500-600 pound male, on May 5, but had to expend 10 bullets to do so. Five days later, in present Dawson County, Mont., the men saw their first moose.[97]

May 14 was almost a Black Tuesday. Either of two episodes could have resulted in calamity. First, a huge grizzly almost made "mincemeat" of six men who went out to kill him after he was discovered lying on open ground along the river. They crept up unnoticed within 120 feet of him and concealed themselves behind a mound of earth. Four took careful aim and shot, two holding fire. All the shots hit their mark, two of them passing through the lungs. Oblivious to his wounds, the bear leaped to his feet and charged the group. The two men with loaded weapons shot and hit him, one bullet breaking his shoulder, but on he came. Everyone ran for his life.

The bear nearly overtook them before they reached the river. Two of the men jumped into a canoe, and the other four separated and hid in the willows. Reloading as fast as they could, they refired. But the bear nearly caught two of them before they threw away their guns in panic and dove off the 20-foot-high bank into the river. As the beast leaped into the river close on the heels of the second man, another on the bank fatally drilled the animal through the head. Examination showed he had eight bullets in him.

A nautical near-disaster

Potentially even more disastrous was an accident occurring that evening. While the boats were moving upriver, Lewis and Clark were both walking along the shore, an unusual thing. Charbonneau, who could not swim and was in Lewis' opinion "the most timid waterman in the world," was temporarily relieving Drouillard at the helm of the white pirogue, well offshore. It contained Lewis and Clark's papers, books, instruments, medicines, and many of the trade goods

Close calls with grizzlies, or "white bears," were numerous. At first, the explorers tended to discount Indian fear of this "king of beasts," but soon learned to treat them with the utmost respect. A few other Englishmen and Frenchmen had seen them before Lewis and Clark, but the two captains were the first to provide scientific descriptions.

—in Lewis' words, "almost every article indispensibly necessary to further the views, or insure the success of [our] enterpize."

A sudden wind squall hit the boat obliquely and turned it partially. The inept sailor Charbonneau swung the rudder around so as to bring the full force of the wind against the square sail. The sail brace, or rope, flew out of the hands of the person holding it, the pirogue turned over on its side, and water began pouring in. By the time the crew took in the sail and righted the boat, it was filled with water to within an inch of the gunwales. Charbonneau, still crying out to the Deity for succor, had not even recovered the rudder.

The alert Cruzatte saved the day. Threatening to shoot Charbonneau if he did not grasp the rudder and regain control, the former ordered two men to bail with kettles and directed the others to row toward shore. Meantime, Sacagawea, sitting in the rear of the boat up to her waist in water, had not lost her poise. She calmly leaned out and recovered most of the light articles as they floated past on the water—an act that later won Lewis' praise.

Lewis, viewing the spectacle from shore, was distraught. Recognizing the value of the cargo and forgetting himself for a moment, he threw down his gun and was in the act of unbuttoning his coat to jump into the river and swim the 300 yards to the boat when the folly of the idea struck him. Had he pursued it, he probably would have lost his life in the high waves and swift current.

It was a close call. The next 2 days were spent unpacking, drying, and repacking the soaked supplies, papers, and medicine that had remained in the boat or Sacagawea had retrieved. Losses, including unsalvageable items, consisted of some medicine and gunpowder, garden seeds apparently obtained from the Mandans, and culinary articles.[98]

New landscape and mounting navigational problems

By this time, the flat and barren plains of present North Dakota and far eastern Montana were giving way to rugged hills that gradually began to be covered with pine and cedar. The country also grew increasingly arid, and game thinned out. Navigation became a serious problem as the river grew more narrow and crooked and its current faster. Shoals, rapids, and treacherous currents caused anxiety and extra labor.

On May 18 Clark recorded that deerskins were beginning to be in demand for use in moccasins and leggings as the original clothing supply began to give out. The next day, he was astounded to see a grizzly he had shot through the heart run a quarter of a mile before dropping. Also, one of the men wounded a beaver. Scannon swam out into the water to retrieve it, but was bitten in the hind leg and suffered a severed artery. Only with considerable difficulty was Lewis able to stem the bleeding.

Entering the Breaks of the Missouri

Not long after passing the mouth of the Musselshell, where camp was made the night of May 20–21, the boats entered the badlands area known today as the Breaks of the Missouri—majestic geological formations and towering sandstone cliffs, spotted here and there with black and red layers and erosional remnants. For the next 2½ weeks, the frail craft were to be hemmed in by the walls of the breaks, whose crags were frequented by many bighorn sheep, which had first been seen on April 26. On May 25 Clark, Drouillard, and Bratton killed three. The only timber in the desert-like, rocky country were scattered patches of pine and spruce.

Shoals and rapids became more troublesome. Rock outcroppings were especially dangerous. If not straining at the towropes in water up to their armpits, the men were clambering along the bank, keeping a keen lookout for sharp rock fragments that had fallen from the cliffs above.

On the 26th Lewis and Clark separately labored up the sandstone bluffs and in the distance viewed snowy mountain crests, which like many another later traveler they mistakenly assumed were a chain in the main range of the Rockies.[99] Lewis' delight at finding himself so close to the head of the "heretofore conceived boundless Missouri" was sharply diminished by realization that crossing the Rockies would require much hardship.

Three days later, Clark named a large stream flowing in from the south the Judith River in honor of "Judith" (Julia) Hancock back in Fincastle, Va. Then but a girl of 13, within less than 3 years she would become Mrs. William Clark. The Judith was reconnoitered a short way.

Evidences of Blackfeet

Near the confluence of the two rivers, the first of two exciting discoveries was made—evidences of large Indian encampments, of 100

Part of the White Rocks Section of the Missouri River Breaks, Mont. The spectacular stone formations in this part of the river amazed and delighted the men. This view is from Citadel Bluff toward the southeast.

and 126 lodges, one vacated only 2 weeks earlier and the other 5 or 6 weeks before. Sacagawea, examining abandoned moccasins, judged that the inhabitants were Blackfeet, whom Lewis and Clark were later to learn were the enemy of all surrounding tribes and the scourge of the Upper Missouri.[100]

The second discovery was viewed that same day about 13 miles farther up the Missouri, according to the leaders' calculations, at the foot of a 120-foot cliff along the north side of the river. Stretched out at its base were about 100 putrefied carcasses of buffalo, probably driven over the cliff a few weeks earlier by the Indians who had been camped at the mouth of the Judith. It was a buffalo jump, which the Indians had told the explorers about, with the animals still in place—a sight no other American had likely ever seen. In the vicinity were large numbers of wolves, which had gorged them-

The North Dakota Badlands along the Little Missouri River present a wonderland of vistas and eroded landscapes best known as the later stomping ground of Theodore Roosevelt during his western years. The north unit of Theodore Roosevelt National Park is about 100 miles south of Fort Union Trading post near the Montana/North Dakota Border.

selves into extreme docility; Clark easily killed one with his espontoon, a steel-pointed pike, or staff. Lewis and Clark, the grisly sight still in their minds and the stench fresh in their nostrils, dubbed a small nearby stream "Slaughter Creek" (present Arrow Creek).

A natural wonderland

The scenery was startling. From the mouth of the Judith onward, the geological wonderland that had begun unfolding not long after passing the Musselshell River burst forth into unusual splendor. For 4 days, an enchanting panorama lured all eyes to the steep, often perpendicular, cliffs that sometimes rose 300 feet. Nature's sculptor-mason—centuries of wind, ice, rain, and snow—had etched picturesque and intriguing formations out of the stone. The fanciful and grotesque shapes resembled the ruins of cities and buildings, spires, statuary, toadstools—or whatever else the mind chose to identify.

Gradually the terrain changed. The bluffs diminished, the plains became more level and extensive, timber increased, and game grew more plentiful. Suddenly, on June 2, on arrival at a major fork in the river, geologic wonder yielded to geographic dilemma.

Dilemma at the mouth of the Marias

Lewis and Clark faced their first major navigational test and primary crucial decision. They needed to decide and decide correctly which fork was the Missouri, the river that would lead them to the Rockies, the Shoshonis, and horses. Two months of the travel season had already elapsed. If the wrong branch were followed, the loss of time in retracing their steps and returning to the other would dampen morale, deplete supplies, and undoubtedly prevent crossing the Rockies before winter set in. As a result, the Pacific could not be reached that year, and an ignominious retreat to St. Louis would likely be necessary. Worst of all, though the commanders did not know it at the time, if they had gone up the northwestern stream they would probably have eventually encountered hostile Blackfeet—with possibly calamitous results.

The information the Minitaris had provided the two captains, some of which they had misinterpreted or misunderstood, puzzled them. It did not place a key river flowing in from the north at this point. Unfortunately, on May 8 they had incorrectly determined that the Milk River was the "River That Scolds All the Others" that the Indians had described. Now what stream was the northwestern one? Or did the southwestern one flow into the northwestern?

Complicating the problem, the northwestern branch, gorged by spring runoff from the mountains, was much bigger than normal. And it had the same muddy color as the Missouri so far. The sparklingly clear southwestern fork, larger and with a faster current, passed over a rocky bed. Although the captains early surmised that the southwestern fork was the Missouri, the final decision was to take about a week.

Between June 4 and 8, Lewis and a party reconnoitered overland about 60 miles up the northwest branch (Marias).[101] On this trip, Lewis and Windsor almost fell off a precipice; the former was saved by his espontoon, which he usually carried when walking. Meantime, on June 4–6, Clark and another overland group explored the southwestern branch (Missouri) about 13 miles upriver to the site of present Fort Benton, Mont., then traveled northwestward to an upstream point on the Teton River. From a ridge, they could see

Modern junction of the Marias and Missouri, looking downstream and to the east. The former enters from the left center. In the foreground, is the narrower of the two Missouri channels in the area; the main channel runs on the far side of the island in the center of the picture. In 1804–6 the Marias ran closer to the bluff line, and the confluence of the two rivers was about 2½ miles downstream.

that the branch ran southwestward for a long stretch.[102] They turned back to camp.

Comparing notes, reevaluating the Minitari data, and utilizing maps they had brought from St. Louis, Lewis and Clark finally agreed beyond a doubt that the southwestern branch was the Missouri— though all the other men held the opposite to be true. The bigger southwestern stream ran in the expected direction, its current was swifter, and its clearness and rocky beds indicated that nearby mountains fed it. Because of the turbid nature and muddy bed of the northwestern fork, the leaders judged that it probably either did not penetrate the mountains or upon leaving them traveled a long

Packs of timber, or lobo, wolves were encountered at the confluence of the Judith and Missouri Rivers and at the Great Falls of the Missouri. Today, this predatorial species faces extinction.

distance over the plains. Lewis and Clark decided that this fork rose east of the Rockies and south of the Saskatchewan, the British river to which they oriented so many of their geographical judgments.

Not to be outdone by Clark's naming of the Judith, Lewis called the stream flowing in from the northwest "Maria's River" after Maria Wood, a cousin in Virginia. It was noble enough, though he felt that its troubled waters poorly comported with the "pure celestial virtues and amiable qualifications of that lovely fair one."

A majestic view: the Great Falls

If the right decision had been made, according to the Minitaris the Great Falls could not be far distant. Anxious to find out, on June 11—after the expedition had spent 9 days at the Marias— Lewis, Drouillard, Joseph Field, Gibson, and Goodrich set out from its mouth via land to make maximum speed. Clark and the main party followed the next day with all the boats except the red pirogue. It had been hidden on an island at the mouth of the Marias, where equipment and supplies had also been cached along the riverbank.

The Lewis group pushed westward across the mountain-defined plains. Before noon the second day, a tremendous roar was heard and in the distance spray could be seen rising like a column of smoke. The elated Lewis knew he had arrived at the falls, the true beginning of the Rocky Mountains. That day and the next, the 13th and 14th, he and his companions reconnoitered the falls all the way to the Sun River. Within a stretch of 10 miles, the Missouri dropped 400 feet, foaming over five cascade-like falls and a series of rapids. Lewis estimated the height of the highest of these falls, the one farthest downstream, at 87 feet.

Realizing that Clark was anxious to know whether or not the correct decision had been made at the Marias, at sunrise on the 14th Lewis sent Joseph Field back to tell him they had found the falls and to proceed only to their lower end, where the portage would begin, and wait there. The timber available, rare in the area, made it an especially desirable campsite.

On the 14th, while waiting for the main party and investigating the portage area, Lewis had his fill of adventure. Alone and dreamily contemplating a buffalo he had just shot, his rifle not reloaded, to his shock he suddenly saw a grizzly only 20 paces away lumbering toward him. Lewis attempted to avoid a charge by walking nonchalantly away. But the animal charged at full speed. Lewis bolted for the river, 80 yards away. Dashing into the water up to his waist, he suddenly whipped around and pointed his espontoon at the beast. For some strange reason, it stopped, turned, ran pellmell back across the prairie, and disappeared into some woods.

A short time later, Lewis suddenly saw a brownish-yellow, feline-like animal he could not identify about to pounce on him. His gun loaded this time, he fired but the beast disappeared into a burrow. The relieved Lewis rejoined his companions. The next morning, upon waking, he shot a large rattlesnake, coiled up about 10 feet away on the leaning trunk of the tree he had been sleeping under, and found it had 17 rattles. By this time, rattlers had become a serious threat and several men had experienced close calls with them.

Clark and the main party, which had been slowed by rapid currents and dangerous rocks, arrived at the lower end of the falls on the evening of June 15. They camped on the south, or east, bank of the river about a mile north, or below, of what they called "Portage Creek" (modern Belt Creek) at a spot that came to be known as

This photograph shows the Great Falls of the Missouri prior to the construction of dams to support the area's mining industry by providing electrical power. Meriwether Lewis first saw the Great Falls on June 13, 1805.

"lower portage camp." The next afternoon, they reunited with the Lewis detachment.

Illness of Sacagawea

Everyone was concerned about Sacagawea, who had been seriously ill for a week. Clark had bled her, applied poultices to her abdomen, and ministered all kinds of purges and other medicines. Feverish, she had a weak pulse and seemed near death, but neither of the captains could correctly diagnose her condition. Fortunately, water brought from a sulphur spring someone had discovered across the river proved to have a beneficial effect and she recovered in a few days.

The sulphur water saved the life of the Indian girl, but no such panacea was available for the staggering job of portaging around the Great Falls.

The grueling Great Falls portage

The Great Falls surpassed any obstacle previously encountered. On the river, 18 miles a day had often easily been attained; now

William Clark first saw Giant Spring on Tuesday, June 18, 1805. Today it is much like it was then, pouring hundreds of thousands of gallons a day into the Missouri. It is now a state park with a trout hatchery nearby. The Missouri waterfront in this area is quite attractive, making Great Falls, Montana, a delightful experience anytime of the year.

almost 2 weeks would be required to move the canoes and baggage roughly the same distance.

On the 16th, the day before Clark went on ahead to map out a portage route, the canoes were unloaded and moved over rapids and rocks about a mile up Belt Creek to a spot where ascent to the high plain was most convenient. Beginning the next day and lasting through the 20th, at the lower portage camp Lewis directed preparations for the move. The white pirogue, too big to move overland, was also unloaded, pulled ashore near the camp, and hidden in a grove of willows about a mile below the mouth of Belt Creek for possible use on the return trip; plans now called for assembly of the "Experiment" to replace it. Because the smaller craft would accommodate fewer goods and because supplies would be needed on the eastward trip, some equipment and food were cached.[103]

Lewis supervised the construction of two crude wagons to carry the canoes and baggage. Fortunately, a cottonwood tree was found that was large enough to supply crosscut disc wheels about 22 inches in diameter. The wood, soft and brittle but all that was available except for willow and box elder, was also fairly suitable for tongues, couplings, frames, and braces. The mast of the white pirogue supplied the axles.

Meantime, during the period June 17–20, Clark, a better topographer than Lewis, and five men had surveyed the terrain and on the south side of the river staked out a route measuring 18¼ miles long.[104] They also established a camp at the upper end of the portage about 2 miles south of the Sun River, opposite some small islands in the Missouri called the "White Bear Islands" because of the large number of grizzlies there. This camp was referred to as "upper portage camp" or "White Bear Islands camp."

The transfer began on June 21 and was not completed until July 2. Equipment was hand-carried about 2 miles from the lower portage camp to the point where the wagon portage began. Similarly, the canoes were borne about three-quarters of a mile to that place from the spot about a mile up Belt Creek where they had been brought. At the beginning of the wagon portage, the canoes were loaded one at a time on the bodyless wagons, filled with supplies, and pulled to the upper portage camp. Some equipment was hand-carried the entire route.

The men laboriously dragged the wagons over the uneven ground around gullies and ravines, up steep slopes, and around rocks. The primitive wagons, ill-fitted to travel over even a paved road, repeatedly broke down in the rugged terrain. Willow and box elder were utilized to replace the cottonwood parts.

Personnel took as much a beating as the wagons. Prickly pear thorns and dagger-sharp ridges of earth, created by the drying of buffalo-tramping grounds after recent rains, stabbed through thin moccasin soles, lacerated feet already sore, and caused infections and huge boils. The hardy men, forced to stop and rest often in the scorching summer heat, frequently dropped off into a deep sleep before staggering to their feet to limp onward once again. Sometimes agony and fatigue caused them to faint. Even Cruzatte's fiddle playing in the evening elicited less enthusiasm than usual.

Seeking to spare every possible step, Clark found a way to shorten the original 18¼-mile route by half a mile. The men also needed no prodding to take advantage of the two shortcuts available to walkers at the eastern end of the portage route. The only other surcease, a comic relief, was the occasion when someone hoisted the sail in one

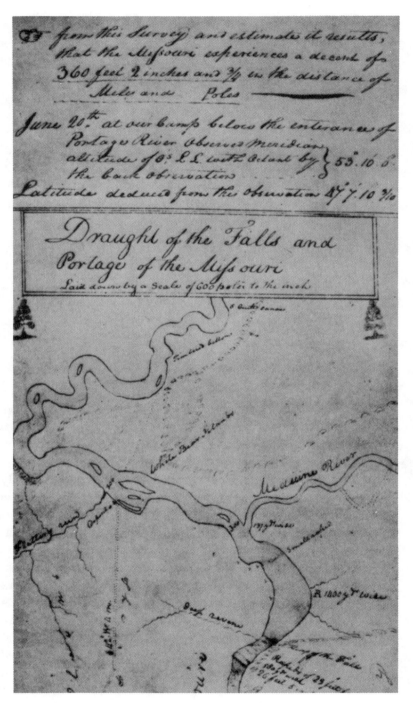

from this Survey, and estimate it results, that the Missouri experiences a decend of 360 feet 2 inches and 2/4 in the distance of _____ Miles and _____ Poles _____

June 20th at our camp below the entrance of Portage River observed meridian altitude of 0° L.L. with Octant by the back observation .... } 55. 10. 6

Latitude deduced from this observation 47. 7. 10 7/10

Draught of the Falls and Portage of the Missouri

Laid down by a Scale of 600 poles to the inch

Upper portion of Clark's map of the Great Falls and the portage route. Upstream is to the top of the map.

Where the land has been undisturbed, prickly pear cactus, which ripped the feet of members of the expedition, still flourishes in the Great Falls area.

of the canoes, and the wind helped move the wagon carrying it. "Saleing on Dry land in every sence of the word," Clark called it.

On June 29, an extremely hot day, a violent storm struck suddenly, unleashing torrents of rain and huge hailstones. Falling with incredible velocity, some of the stones bounced as high as 12 feet in the air. They felled one man three times, and bloodied the heads of several others. The storm caught Clark, York, Charbonneau, Sacagawea, and her baby at the river. To avoid being blown into it, they were forced to take shelter in a gully. Suddenly, a well of water deluged them. Clark was waist deep in it before he could start clambering up the steep slope. Pushing Sacagawea, carrying Baptiste in her arms, ahead of him, he was hardly able to move upward fast enough to avoid engulfment. In the narrow escape, he lost his knapsack, gun, tomahawk, umbrella, shot pouch, powderhorn, and the expedi-

The prickly pear cactus was quite a problem for the men of the Lewis & Clark Expedition as they portaged around the Great Falls area in the summer of 1805. The spines of this mountain cactus pierced the leather foot coverings worn by the explorers.

tion's only large compass. The only item recovered, the next day, was the compass—to Lewis' relief.

The weary toil and weather hazards were not the only sources of concern. Grizzlies were a menace. They were so numerous that the commanders found it imprudent to send a man alone on any errand that required passing through the brush. Scannon roamed the camp at night and barked when the bears were near, which was frequent. The men were ordered to sleep with their weapons close at hand. Everyone had learned by this time to accord the utmost respect to the huge beasts. Lewis confessed he would rather fight two Indians than one of them. Smaller, but equally as dangerous were the numerous rattlesnakes. Swarms of mosquitoes tried tempers.

But, on the positive side, food was plentiful. In one sweep of the eye, Clark estimated he could see 10,000 buffalo on the plain. He also saw floating down over the falls many carcasses of animals that had been pushed into the river by those behind them on the steep and narrow trails leading to it and drinking water. All the men were wearing deer and elk skin shirts and breeches by this time. And, anticipating that less game would be available in the mountains that lay ahead, they took advantage of the opportunity to stock up on leather clothing. Until the herds began to disappear early in July, pemmican was also made from buffalo meat.

Abandonment of the "Experiment"

While the portage was being made, progress was registered in another important preparation necessary before the journey could continue upriver. The iron-framed "Experiment," Lewis' pet project, which had been manufactured at Harpers Ferry for use on the Upper Missouri and brought all the way from Pittsburgh, had to be assembled and covered as a replacement for the white pirogue. The former was one of the first items portaged so that assembly work could begin. Taking Shields, Gass, and Joseph Field with him to the upper portage camp, Lewis on June 23 had eagerly begun work and, on July 2 when the move was completed, everyone pitched in to help. Two days later, July 4, was as usual cause for celebration; the last of the whisky was consumed. But at least the portage had been completed.

Once the 36-foot-long iron frame was assembled and timber struts put in place, they were covered with elk and buffalo skins that were sewn together. The method of caulking the seams posed a serious problem. No tar or pitch was available, so Lewis improvised with a mixture of pounded charcoal, buffalo tallow, and beeswax. Launched on the 9th, the boat floated like a "perfect cork," but by that night most of the caulking had separated from the skins, which left open seams. The "mortifyed" as well as depressed Lewis, because the season was late and most of the buffalo had departed, decided that any more caulking experiments would probably be useless and decided to abandon his "favorite boat." Failure to bring along suitable caulking material represented the one major error in logistical planning.

Abandonment of the "Experiment" necessitated the expenditure of 5 additional days to construct two dugout canoes to replace it and supplement the six other canoes. Between the 10th and the 14th, at a site about 8 miles by land or 23 miles by water above the upper portage camp, Clark and a crew of 10 men found cottonwoods of large enough size along the Missouri to build the canoes. Both were 3 feet wide, one 25 and the other 33 feet long. Meantime, the frame of the "Experiment" had been disassembled and buried near the upper portage camp, as well as the wagon wheels. Supplies that were cached

View from the north bank of the Missouri River looking toward the mouth of modern Belt Creek, known to the explorers as Portage Creek. They pulled their canoes about a mile up it, carried them to the high plains at the top of the bluffs, and then laboriously transported them on crude wagons to the upper portage area. The above scene has changed little over the years except that a number of upstream dams now seasonally restrict the water flow.

included all the plant specimens acquired since leaving Fort Mandan, a few bearskins, various papers, and some medicines.

On the 14th the rest of the expedition moved up to the canoe-building camp from the upper portage camp. The next morning, the entire complement set out once again.

BY this time, the two captains were becoming highly apprehensive about meeting the Shoshonis. The anxiety experienced even before arrival at the Great Falls had been compounded by the month required to portage around them and build the two canoes to replace the "Experiment." More than 3 months had elapsed since departure from Fort Mandan and the Rockies had barely been penetrated. How long it would take to reach the Pacific could not even be estimated, but it was certain that the trip there and back to Fort Mandan or even to the Great Falls could not be made that season.

The difficulties at the portage had already forced a change of plans. Lewis and Clark decided not to dispatch a detachment to St. Louis from the Great Falls as they had planned at Fort Mandan. The most perilous part of the journey lay ahead. The Shoshonis and other tribes might be hostile. The morale of those who would have to remain would be lowered. Every last man would be needed in the days that were to follow.

Heading for the Three Forks

Not far upstream from the Great Falls, the river, confined by steep cliffs in gorges, became increasingly narrow and swift and in some places shallow. Furious waters and rapids made navigation nerve-wracking. Except for the minimum number of oarsmen, everyone had to walk along the shore—an unpleasant alternative for men whose feet were already badly lacerated. Even worse was the frequent need for them to tow, a disagreeable enough task without the summer heat.

On July 17 the river entered long Missouri Canyon, hemmed in by mountain walls. It marked the beginning of a long stretch of spectacular river-mountain scenery where the river ran in a series of closely confined canyons. The visual delight afforded slight solace to the weary crew, who labored every mile of the way.

After breakfast on the morning of the 18th, seeking the Shoshonis or some trace of them, Clark, despite his torn feet, set out ahead of the boats overland with Joseph Field, John Potts, and York. Shortly thereafter, the boats reached a stream nearly as large as the Missouri that flowed into it from the north, or west, side. Lewis named it the Dearborn River in honor of Secretary of War Henry Dearborn. Unfortunately, the former did not realize it was the river the Minitaris had said would lead to an excellent shortcut across the Continental Divide to Lolo Creek, gateway to the crossing of the Bitterroot Mountains.

The next evening, the 19th, the boat party entered a stretch of "remarkable clifts" that soared perpendicularly to a height of 1,200 feet. For a distance of 5¾ miles the river ripped its way through

Entrance to Gates of the Mountains, Mont., date unknown. This feature, now in Helena National Forest, is the greatest canyon of the Missouri River, but in contrast to the stretch of river near the Great Falls does not have any falls or impassable rapids.

solid rock just the width of a channel about 150 yards wide. Spots where a man could step ashore were virtually nonexistent, so towing was impossible. The depth of the water precluded use of the setting poles. It was fortunate that, though the current was strong, rowing was feasible. Although the expedition had been in the Rocky Mountains since the Great Falls, Lewis called the area the "Gates of the Rocky Mountains."

The party left the gates on July 20, not far from present Helena. The river soon broadened out onto an untimbered valley plain, about 11 miles in width, bounded by two nearly parallel snow-topped ranges. Many islands were encountered. On July 22 Sacagawea recognized the country. She assured Lewis that her tribe lived on the river and said the Three Forks were not far ahead. That evening, Lewis reunited with Clark and his party of three. The next morning, however, Clark, Charbonneau, Frazer, and the Field brothers continued ahead again on land.

Decision at the Three Forks

On the morning of July 25, Clark and his four footsore companions reached the Three Forks of the Missouri—the first white men ever to visit there. Two days later, the boat party arrived. Reconnoitering the area to determine which fork to take and nursing the ill Clark, the group stayed there until July 30.

LEWIS termed the Three Forks "an essential point in the geography of this western part of the Continent." Within a short distance of each other, three rivers joined to form the Missouri almost 2,500 miles from its mouth.[105] On July 28 the two captains gave them the names they have retained ever since. The eastern fork was named the Gallatin after Secretary of the Treasury Albert Gallatin; the middle one, the Madison, for Secretary of State James Madison; and the western one, which they were to choose to take, the Jefferson "in honor of that illustrious personage Thomas Jefferson."

At this point, the captains faced their second geographical puzzle. As at the junction of the Marias and the Missouri, if they made the wrong decision, the success of the expedition might well be irretrievably compromised. The three streams that converged at the Three Forks discharged an almost equal amount of water and all ran with strong velocity, though the eastern fork (Gallatin) was more rapid but not as deep or wide as the other two. As it turned out, the decision was a far easier one than at the Marias. As a matter of fact, when the captains arrived separately at the Three Forks, each decided on his own almost at once that the western fork (the Jefferson) was probably the river they should follow.

WHEN Clark and his four companions reached the Three Forks on the morning of July 25, Clark left a note at the junction of the middle (Madison) and western (Jefferson) forks telling Lewis of his proposed reconnaissance route and requesting him to wait there. The Clark party proceeded up the Jefferson 20 miles and camped on the north, or west, bank. The next day, leaving Charbonneau and Joseph Field in camp suffering from battered feet and fatigue, Clark and the two other men climbed a mountain 12 miles farther to the west. Clark saw no evidence of Shoshonis or other Indians, but the topography convinced him that the stream he was on was the mainstream extension of the Missouri. The three men picked up the other two at camp and they all crossed the Jefferson and headed back to the Three Forks.

The next day, the 27th, though all five were suffering from blisters on their feet and punctures by prickly pears, they traveled eastward

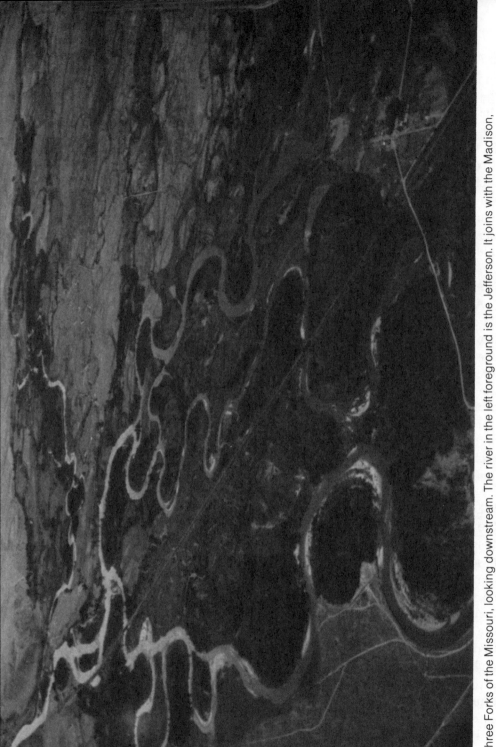

Three Forks of the Missouri, looking downstream. The river in the left foreground is the Jefferson. It joins with the Madison, which forks not far from its mouth, in the upper left center. Slightly farther downstream, they merge with the Gallatin, the smallest of the three rivers, to form the Missouri (far upper left).

This view, in Three Forks State Park, Montana, is taken near the confluence of the Jefferson, Gallatin, and Madison Rivers which form the Missouri River. The area includes stone work and eroded land forms which sheltered many different forms of fur-bearing animal life. The Blackfeet Indian nation claimed this land as their own and kept other natives as well as all European and American fur trappers out well into the 1830s.

and struck the Madison about 20 miles upstream. Following it downstream to its junction with the Jefferson, they rejoined Lewis and the main, or boat, party at their nearby camp on the Jefferson. By this time, Clark was feverish and totally exhausted.

THE Lewis contingent had arrived at the point where the Gallatin joined the Missouri at 9:00 a.m. that same morning and set up camp. Lewis proceeded up the former half a mile and ascended a high limestone cliff on the northeast side to obtain a view of the neighboring country. A panorama of mountains and plains filled his eyes. His careful study of the course of the three streams as far as he could see them convinced him that the Jefferson offered the best route to the west. He recommended the Three Forks as the location of a trading post, a judgment confirmed later in the day by observation of large numbers of beaver, otter, and other game.[106] After Lewis returned to camp, the party then moved up to the junction of the Madison and Jefferson, found Clark's note, and proceeded up the Jefferson a short distance beyond the junction before making camp on the south bank and awaiting Clark's return.

AT 3:00 p.m. that afternoon, the 27th, Clark arrived, feverishly ill. Lewis, recognizing the necessity to minister to him and the desirability of further reconnaissance, decided to stop for a couple of days. The next day, he dispatched two men up the Gallatin to investigate it. The commanders compared the information they brought back with what Clark had gained on his survey of the Jefferson and Madison, their celestial observations, and their interpretation of the information the Minitaris had given them. The captains agreed that only the Jefferson could lead anywhere near the headwaters of the Columbia; the others slanted in the wrong direction, to the south and east, to the vicinity of present Yellowstone National Park. The Jefferson appeared to have its origin in the snowclad mountains to the west and southwest. Again, as at the Marias, Lewis and Clark made the right deduction about which stream to follow.

Whither the Shoshonis?

Pushing southwestward up the Jefferson on July 30, the group faced a desperate situation. In fact, without the Shoshonis, it was lost. Indeed, not one Indian had been met since leaving the environs of Fort Mandan early in April. Many signs of them had been seen along the riverbank after leaving the Great Falls, and smoke signals had been sighted. Some of the abandoned campsites were old, probably dating from the previous autumn, but others appeared to have been vacated only a few days before. Indians had likely seen the intruders, but none made an appearance.

Although Sacagawea had recognized the country as they approached the Three Forks, on arrival she did not know which of the three streams led to the western mountains. She did recognize the campsite near the junction of the Jefferson and Madison as the spot where her village had been encamped 5 years earlier when the Minitaris attacked it. She also knew the place where she had been captured, about 4 miles farther up the Jefferson.

The expedition had moved only 3 days up that beaver-infested and island-studded stream when Clark celebrated his 35th birthday, on August 1. It was not a particularly joyous one, for his feet were still badly lacerated and a huge boil festered on one ankle. Confined to the canoes, he could not walk any distance.

In view of Clark's indisposition, that same morning Lewis, Drouillard, Charbonneau, and Sergeant Gass set out overland, scouting

Jefferson River, looking downstream to the northeast, from a point about 8 miles southwest of Three Forks of the Missouri, Mont. When the explorers passed through this area, they were eagerly seeking the Shoshonis, whom it was hoped would provide help in crossing the mountains to the west.

frantically for any sign of Shoshonis. Near the present city of Twin Bridges, Mont., the explorers came to a fork in the Jefferson and turned up the western one, the Big Hole River. Before long, realizing they were not on the main stream, they turned back and followed the other fork, the Beaverhead River, an extension of the Jefferson.

Meanwhile, Clark and the canoes had been struggling up the ever shallower and narrower Jefferson, which had become a mountain rather than a plains river. He was still barely able to walk. Everyone was worn out; sickness and despondence were common; game grew scarcer. In a misadventure on August 5–6 the group went up the same stream, the Big Hole, that Lewis had mistakenly taken a few days before. Unfortunately, a beaver had chewed down a pole to which Lewis had fastened a note directing Clark.

In a rapids one of the canoes upset and two others partially filled with water. Whitehouse was badly hurt; 20 pounds of powder were lost; many provisions were damaged and some were not recovered. After Drouillard found the astray men on the 6th and told them they were following the wrong stream, they retraced their way to the fork, proceeded up the Beaverhead, and reunited with the Lewis party. The next day, because of the reduction of the cargo, one of the canoes was hidden and left behind.

On August 8 Sacagawea created a stir of excitement when she recognized far in the distance on the west side of the river the features of Beaverhead Rock, usually known today as Point of Rocks and located 14 miles northeast of Dillon, Mont. She said it was not too distant from the summer retreat of her people, which was located on a westward-running river (Lemhi) beyond the mountains. She said her tribe would be on the Beaverhead River or on the river (Lemhi) immediately west of its source.

Intensifying the search for the Shoshonis

Lewis, excited, decided to make a second attempt to push on ahead on foot to find the Shoshonis. Anxiety about contacting this tribe had by now increased greatly. The next morning, at a point about 21 miles north of present Dillon, Lewis, Drouillard, Shields, and McNeal set out. Each of them was allowed to carry only one blanket and his weapons; their packs were filled with Indian trade goods.

The next day, the 10th, coming upon an Indian trail, the group followed it upstream. It led past high cliffs, on both sides of the river. Lewis named them Rattlesnake Cliffs (known locally today as Beaverhead Rock) because of the large number of rattlers in the vicinity. About 15 miles farther was a fork in the Beaverhead, into which flowed Horse Prairie Creek and the Red Rock River. The trail also forked at this point, one branch going up each stream. After some investigation, the party followed Horse Prairie Creek, the western fork leading toward the mountains, rather than the other, which flowed from the southeast. But, recognizing the insufficiency of water in both streams for navigation, Lewis left a note for Clark at the fork for him to stop and await his return. Five miles from the fork, the men made camp in a mountain cove, Shoshoni Cove.

Continuing on the next day, the party soon found that the Indian trail disappeared. Lewis sent Drouillard out on one flank and Shields on the other, but still within sight, and instructed them to watch for the trail as they advanced toward a pass (Lemhi) through the mountains (Beaverheads) they had seen to the west. They proceeded this way for about 5 miles. Lewis suddenly viewed about 2 miles ahead a lone horseman coming down the plain toward the group— the first Indian encountered since leaving the Mandan village area in April.

Scrutinizing the native with his spyglass, Lewis recognized that he belonged to a tribe the expedition had never seen. He was riding an "eligant" horse and was armed with a bow and a quiver with arrows. Lewis, overjoyed at the sight of this stranger, was certain

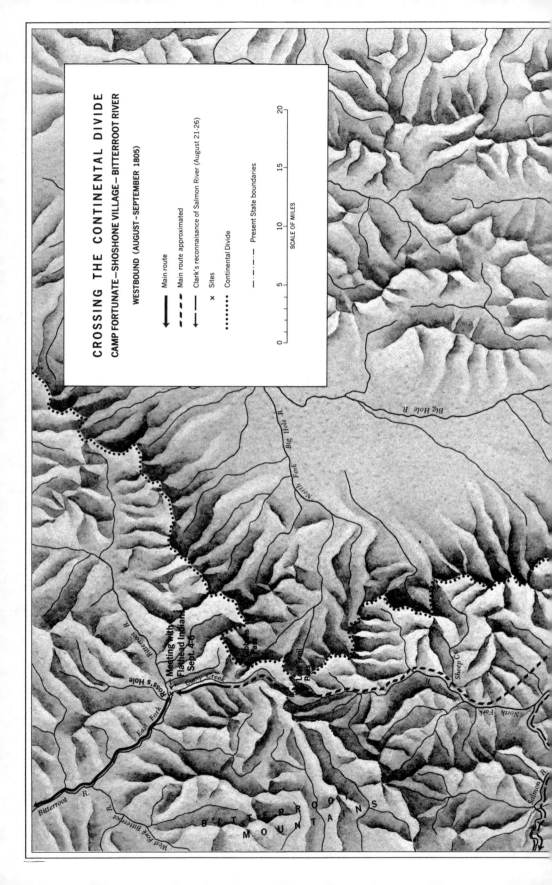

CROSSING THE CONTINENTAL DIVIDE
CAMP FORTUNATE—SHOSHONE VILLAGE—BITTERROOT RIVER

WESTBOUND (AUGUST–SEPTEMBER 1805)

Main route

Main route approximated

Clark's reconnaisance of Salmon River (August 21-26)

× Sites

Continental Divide

—··—··— Present State boundaries

SCALE OF MILES

0   5   10   15   20

Big Hole R.

Big Hole R.

North Fork

Bitterroot R.

Ross's Hole

East Fork

Bitterroot R.

West Fork Bitterroot R.

Bitterroot R.

Meeting with
Flathead Indians
Sept. 4–6

Camp Creek

Gibbons Pass

Lost Trail Pass

North Fork

Sheep Cr.

Salmon R.

BITTERROOT
MOUNTAINS

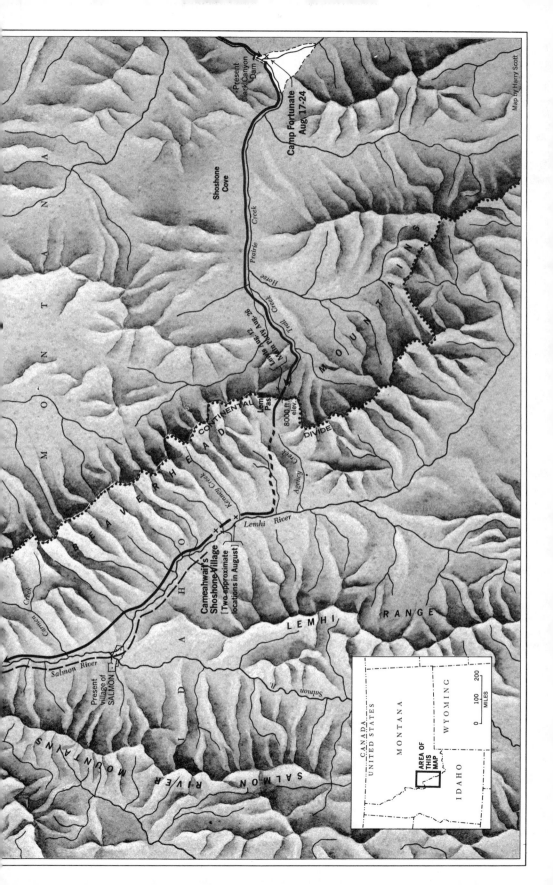

Map by Harry Scott

Present Black Canyon Dam

Camp Fortunate
Aug 17-24

Shoshone Cove

Prairie Creek

Horse Creek

Trail Creek

Lewis Party Aug 10-12

McNeal Aug 26-28

Lemhi Pass

CONTINENTAL

8000 ft. elev.

DIVIDE

Agency Creek

B E A V E R H E A D

M O U N T A I N S

M O N T A N A

Kenney Creek

Lemhi River

Cameahwait's
Shoshone Village
[Two-approximate
locations in August]

I D A H O

Cannon Creek

Salmon River

Present
village of
SALMON

Salmon R.

L E M H I   R A N G E

S A L M O N   R I V E R   M O U N T A I N S

CANADA
UNITED STATES

MONTANA

AREA OF
THIS
MAP

IDAHO

WYOMING

0   100   200
MILES

Shoshone Cove, Mont., looking westward. Horse Prairie Creek, rising in the distance near the Continental Divide, drains this region and empties into the Beaverhead River about 5 miles to the east, or rear, of the point from which this photograph was taken. In this cove, Lewis and his three companions saw their first Shoshoni, who when the four approached rode away to the west. Indian trails led across Lemhi Pass to the west side of the Continental Divide, where the long-sought Shoshonis were encountered.

he was a Shoshoni and was anxious to convince him they were white men and not the dreaded Blackfeet, who often preyed on the Shoshonis.

At a distance of about a mile, the Indian suddenly stopped. Lewis and McNeal immediately did likewise, the former spreading his blanket as a token of friendship. The Indian suspiciously watched the four men. Drouillard and Shields were still advancing on the flanks, so far out they could not hear Lewis when he called to them. Lewis feared if he signaled them he would alarm the native.

Lewis, laying down his gun and walking ahead of McNeal bearing gifts he had taken from his pack, approached within 200 paces of the Indian. Suddenly, the latter turned his horse and slowly edged away. Lewis called out the Shoshoni word "*tab-ba-bone*," which he mistakenly thought meant "white man" but which probably meant "enemy" or "foreigner." He then signaled Drouillard and Shields to halt. The former complied but the latter, not seeing the signal, kept advancing. The horseman stopped again and seemed to be waiting, wary of a trap because of Shields' advance. When Lewis was within 10 paces, the rider suddenly turned his horse, laid the whip to it, and plunged out of sight into some willow bushes. Deeply resenting failure when success seemed so near and irritated at Shields, Lewis found that his "pleasure and expectation" had turned to "mortification and disappointment."

A U.S. flag was affixed to a pole, which McNeal carried, and the men moved on toward the pass, tracking the Indian in the hope he would lead them to his camp. In several places, natives appeared to have been digging for roots. Elsewhere, fresh hoof prints of 8 to 10 horses were visible. The next day, the 12th, Drouillard followed the trail of the Indian westward into the mountains until it disappeared.

The search then turned toward any Indian trail. Evidences of a village and more digging for roots were noted. Near this point, a major trail leading to the southwest along Trail Creek was discovered and followed for several miles. Suddenly, it turned abruptly west toward the mountains. Two miles farther, McNeal "exultingly stood with a foot on each side of [a] little rivulet [Trail Creek] and thanked his god that he had lived to bestride the mighty & heretofore deemed endless Missouri."

At a point 2 miles more to the westward, the four men arrived at what they considered to be the source of the Missouri—in Lewis' words "the most distant fountain of the waters of the Mighty Missouri in surch of which we have spent so many toilsome days and wristless nights . . . one of those great objects on which my mind has been unalterably fixed for many years." [107] A short ways farther, they strode onto the Continental Divide—Lemhi Pass—the first Americans to reach it. Before them lay the land of the Columbia drainage, whose distant manifestation were immense ranges of snow-covered mountains. The journey up the Missouri had ended, and the portage to the Columbia system was soon to begin.

Descending the Beaverhead Mountains from Lemhi Pass along the Indian trail about three-quarters of a mile and at the same time moving from present Montana into Idaho, the party found a bold-running creek, one of the headwaters of the Lemhi River. From it, Lewis first tasted the water of the great Columbia system. Camp was made some miles down the mountain slope leading to the Lemhi Valley.

The next morning, August 13, the march continued along the trail. Near the valley floor, two women, a man, and some dogs came

Trail Creek, one of the sources of the Missouri, about 2 miles east of Lemhi Pass. Lewis said, "...McNeal had exultingly stood with a foot on each side of this rivulet and thanked his god that he had lived to bestride the mighty & heretofore deemed endless Missouri." Above, Roy Appleman, National Park Service, straddles the same stream at approximately the same place.

into view about a mile away. For a time, they watched the approaching white men. When the natives were about half a mile away, Lewis moved on ahead alone, carrying the flag. He cried out *"tab-ba-bone"* and walked toward them, but they disappeared when he came within 100 yards.

A fortuitous meeting

About a mile farther down the trail, now dusty and apparently recently traveled by men and horses, Lewis and his group suddenly came upon a native woman and two young girls, only 30 paces away. Until then, ravines had prevented the two parties from seeing each other. One of the girls immediately took flight, but her companions remained. Lewis laid down his gun and advanced toward them. Alarmed, they sat down, holding their heads "as if reconciled to die

Eastern approach to Lemhi Pass, looking eastward from the Continental Divide.

which the[y] expected no doubt would be their fate." Lewis walked up to them, took the older woman by the hand, raised her up, and repeated the expression *"tab-ba-bone."* At the same time, aware that the rest of his body was so tanned he resembled an Indian, he lifted his shirt sleeve to show his white skin and then passed out presents. These actions had a calming effect. Drouillard, McNeal, and Shields came up.

Lewis, fearful that the second young girl, who was watching from a distance, might leave and alarm her camp, directed Drouillard to tell the older woman in sign language to call back the younger one. She did this. Lewis gave the newcomer gifts, and used vermilion from his trade goods to paint the cheeks of all three—a practice Saca-gawea had said signified peace to the Shoshonis. Drouillard indicated to the woman and girls that Lewis wanted them to lead him to their village to see their chief. They readily assented and led the way down the trail along the Lemhi River.

When about 2 miles had been traversed, a band of 60 braves gal-loped up. They were responding to an alarm carried to the village by the first group of Indians that the Lewis complement had seen, and were riding out to meet what they thought was a Blackfeet war party. Lewis, putting down his gun and carrying the flag, advanced a short distance ahead of his group. Tension subsided as soon as the three women informed the chief, Cameahwait, of the friendliness of the white men, none of whom this band of Shoshonis had ever seen.[108]

Greetings were exchanged until Lewis grew "tired of the national hug." After the pipe was smoked, Lewis presented the chief with the flag and other gifts, and the Indians painted the four visitors. Everyone then moved to the Indian village, about 4 miles northward on the east bank of the Lemhi River. Lewis and his companions were made comfortable in a skin tipi. It was the only one in the village; the other lodges were also conical but constructed of willow brush. A gift of a piece of salmon from one of the natives that evening convinced Lewis beyond doubt that he was on waters leading to the Columbia.

Realizing mounts would be needed to reach navigable waters of that system, the next day Lewis carefully examined the large horseherd, which numbered around 700. He observed that most of the animals, some of which carried Spanish brands, were in good condition and would "make a figure on the South side of James River or the land of fine horses." The herd included about 20 mules, also of Spanish origin and highly valued by the Indians.

Despite their wealth in horses, the Shoshonis were near starvation, living on roots, berries, fish, and an occasional antelope or deer. Thus, despite the general hospitality extended to them, Lewis and his men had to eat their own limited rations, supplemented by berries and what game they could find.

Drouillard could communicate well with Cameahwait in sign language. Lewis experienced difficulty in persuading the chief to provide horses and return with him to the point where he planned to meet Clark and the boat party, at the junction of Horse Prairie Creek and the Red Rock River. Lewis was afraid that if he lost contact with the Indians he might not find them again. The Shoshonis mortally feared meeting the Blackfeet, who raided from as far away as present Canada, as well as the Minitaris. Only that spring a Blackfeet war party had attacked, killed, or captured 20 men; stole many horses; and destroyed all the skin tipis except the one Lewis and his men occupied. But at last, employing all the diplomacy at his command, including the questioning of Indian courage, Lewis convinced Cameahwait to make the crossing and bring along a group of his braves.

On August 15 the trek began back through Lemhi Pass to the planned rendezvous point with Clark, reached the next day. Lewis was alarmed to find that Clark and his party, who had been making only slow progress up the rugged Beaverhead, had not arrived yet. This presented a dilemma, for the Shoshonis suspected treachery. Lewis resorted to all sorts of stratagems. He turned over the party's guns to Cameahwait, tried to deceive him into believing that a note he had earlier left for Clark telling him to wait there was actually from Clark saying he was coming up, and promised to show him a black man. Everything, possibly even the success of the entire expedition, depended on Clark's arrival the next morning, particularly because Sacagawea was with him and she would reassure the Shoshonis.

When dawn did not bring Clark, the distraught Lewis dispatched Drouillard, accompanied by several mounted braves, with a note urging all haste. Two hours later, an Indian who had strayed a short way from camp, ran in and stated that the white men were coming in boats.

AT 7 o'clock that same morning Clark, his feet much improved and eager to contact Lewis or the Shoshonis, had set out ahead of the boat party with Charbonneau and Sacagawea. The latter, in her home country, was in the lead. They had not gone more than a mile when Clark saw her stop, dance with joy, signal to him, point to some mounted Indians approaching, and start sucking her fingers to signify that they were her own people. After greeting Drouillard and his companions, the entire party moved forward. About noon, as it approached the Lewis-Cameahwait camp, a young Indian woman ran out and embraced Sacagawea. As a child, she had been captured by the Minitaris at the same time as Sacagawea but had escaped.

The boat party had ended its last day of toil westward on the waters of the Missouri drainage. There were good reasons for the tardy arrival. Daily progress had finally averaged only 4 or 5 miles. It had been necessary literally to drag the canoes along the shallow, boulder-covered bed of the Upper Beaverhead, by this time no more than a large creek. Accidents and injuries were frequent. Clark ignored repeated entreaties to leave the canoes and proceed overland.

Upper Beaverhead River Valley, viewed to the south, or upstream, from the mouth of Clark Canyon. Since the time of this photograph, Clark Canyon Reservoir has swamped the entire valley. This caused relocation of the Union Pacific Railroad line and Highway U.S. 91, both shown here. Camp Fortunate was situated in the distance on the east side of the river near the point of high land rising from the river bottom at the upper left.

Establishment of Camp Fortunate

Reunited on August 17, the expedition established camp on the east, or south, bank of the Beaverhead, where it was formed by Horse Prairie Creek and the Red Rock River—3,096 miles from Camp Wood according to Clark's reckoning. This site, occupied until August 24, has become known in the Lewis and Clark literature as Camp Fortunate because of the crucial meeting with the Shoshonis in the vicinity.

The first order of business was a council with Cameahwait. Once the peace pipe had been smoked and the meeting was ready to begin, Sacagawea was brought in to help interpret. She sat down and was beginning to do so when she recognized Cameahwait as her brother.[109] Leaping up, she ran over, embraced him, threw her blanket over him, and wept profusely. She then resumed her translation duties, fre-

Upper Beaverhead River near Camp Fortunate, Mont. Clark Canyon Reservoir has inundated both this stretch of river and the site of the camp since this photograph was taken, at an unknown date.

quently interrupted by tears. She translated from Shoshoni into Minitari, Charbonneau into French, and Labiche into English.

Lewis and Clark explained to Cameahwait that his tribe as well as his band, which numbered about 300, was now under the jurisdiction of the powerful U.S. Government. It was peacefully disposed toward them, would defend them, and provide them with trade goods. The two leaders also explained that, because the purpose of their mission to the "western" ocean was to find a more direct way to bring goods to the Shoshonis, they should help in every possible way, especially by providing horses and a guide to cross the mountains (Bitterroots) in the event a river passage was impossible. Lewis and Clark presented peace medals and other gifts to the chiefs and the people. They were all intrigued with York and the air gun.

The Shoshonis gave assurance of their friendship, promised to provide horses and a guide, and said they would anxiously await establishment of the trading posts.

THE next day, the 18th, Lewis celebrated his 31st birthday. Shrugging aside his substantial achievements, which included a successful Army career, service as secretary to the President of the United

States, and leadership of a major national expedition, he introspectively and moodily philosophized about the need to improve himself:

> This day I completed my thirty first year, and conceived that I had in all human probability now existed about half the period which I am to remain in this Sublunary world. I reflected that I had as yet done but little, very little, indeed, to further the hapiness of the human race, or to advance the information of the succeeding generation. I viewed with regret the many hours I have spent in indolence, and now soarly feel the want of that information which those hours would have given me had they been judiciously expended. but since they are past and cannot be recalled, I dash from me the gloomy thought, and resolved in future, to redouble my exertions and at least indeavour to promote those two primary objects of human existence, by giving them the aid of that portion of talents which nature and fortune have bestoed on me; or in future, to live *for mankind,* as I have heretofore lived *for myself.*

Some fruitful councils

During their sojourn with the Shoshonis, Lewis and Clark learned much about their culture and obtained valuable information about the country to the west. Counting only three guns among the Indians, Lewis noted they were North West Company trade items and suspected they had been obtained from a friendly tribe to the east. He also observed that the tribe suffered from venereal disease.

The Shoshonis said they lived on the west side of the Continental Divide from about May until August or September, when salmon became scarce. In that area, though they nearly starved, they felt safe because the Blackfeet and Minitaris had never penetrated that far. Each summer's end the Shoshonis moved eastward across the Beaverhead Mountains to the Missouri River country—a journey they were now preparing for. There they joined friendly tribes such as the Flatheads for mutual protection against the Blackfeet and Minitaris and hunted buffalo on the edge of the plains until they obtained a supply of dried meat. Once this was accomplished, they hurried westward to their mountain fastnesses. They expressed an interest in obtaining guns to put them on an equal basis with their Blackfeet and Minitari enemies.

The Shoshonis told of two tribes to the north and west, the Flatheads and the Nez Perces. Lewis and Clark had apparently never heard of the latter before, but the Minitaris had told them of the Flatheads. Based partly on information they had obtained from the

Nez Perces, the Shoshonis said that a river (Salmon) into which the Lemhi flowed eventually led to the ocean, where there were white men, but that gigantic rapids and precipices rendered it impassable by land or water. Game was scarce along its shores, and the timber was not large enough to make canoes. Lewis and Clark assumed the stream must be the Columbia's south fork, which they had posited back at Fort Mandan. The Nez Perces, according to the Shoshonis, annually crossed the mountains (Bitterroots) to and from the Missouri River country over a heavily timbered and rocky road to the north, though they usually starved in the process because of the shortage of game. This road, which led to the Nez Perce buffalo hunting grounds in present Montana, later came to be known as the Lolo Trail.[110]

DESPITE the lateness of the season, the two captains decided that, though the road undoubtedly offered the best route, they would first reconnoiter the westward-flowing river to verify the Indian reports. Clark, his feet and ankle vastly improved and anxious to investigate the country ahead as Lewis had already done, would perform the reconnaissance and take along axes and other tools to build canoes should this prove to be feasible. Sacagawea and Charbonneau would travel with him to the Shoshoni village. They would hasten the return of the Indians with horses to Camp Fortunate to help Lewis, who would barter for more steeds and move the base camp westward over the mountains to the planned rendezvous point at the Shoshoni village.

Clark reconnoiters the Salmon River

On the morning of August 18, along with most of the Indians, the Clark contingent set out from Camp Fortunate. Besides Clark, it consisted of Sacagawea, Charbonneau, and 11 others.[111] Clark also took along two of three horses that Lewis had purchased from the natives earlier in the day; these were the only horses belonging to the expedition at the time except for one that some of the men had bought to transport their gear.

The party arrived at the Shoshoni village on the morning of the 20th.[112] Clark pleaded with the Indians to return with horses to Camp Fortunate to assist Lewis' crossing. According to plan, he left Sacagawea and Charbonneau to prod them along. Clark also recruited a

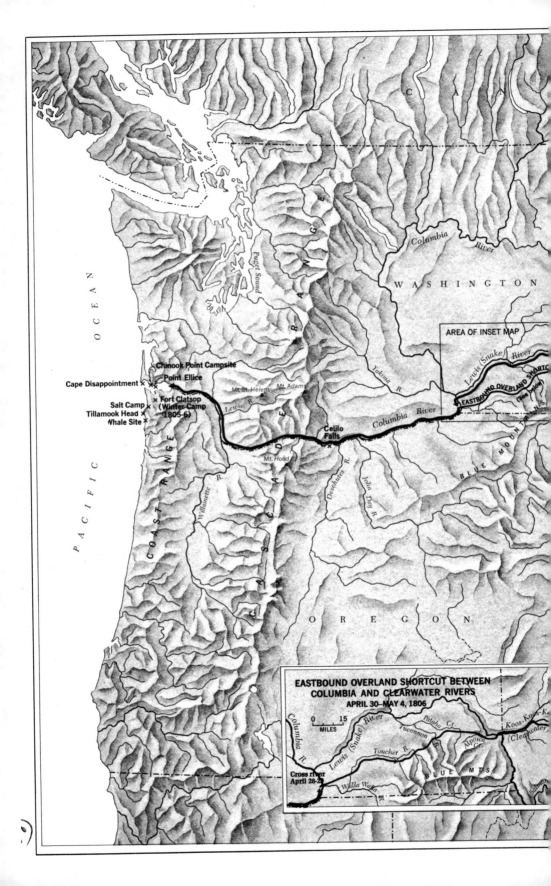

C A N A D A

Columbia River

WASHINGTON

AREA OF INSET MAP

Lewis (Snake) River

EASTBOUND OVERLAND SHORTCUT

(See below)

Puget Sound

Yakima R.

Chinook Point Campsite
Point Ellice
Cape Disappointment ×
× Fort Clatsop
Salt Camp × (Winter Camp
Tillamook Head × 1805-6)
Whale Site ×

Mt. St. Helens   Mt. Adams

Lewis R.

Columbia River

Celilo Falls

BLUE MOUNTAINS

Mt. Hood

Willamette R.

Deschutes R.

John Day R.

O R E G O N

PACIFIC OCEAN

COAST RANGE

CASCADE RANGE

EASTBOUND SHORTCUT BETWEEN COLUMBIA AND CLEARWATER RIVERS
APRIL 30–MAY 4, 1806

0   15
MILES

Columbia R.

Lewis (Snake) River

Tucannon R.

Pataha Cr.

Koos-Koos-Ke
(Clearwater)

Touchet R.

Alpowa Cr.

BLUE MTS

Salmon

Cross river
April 28-29

Walla Walla R.

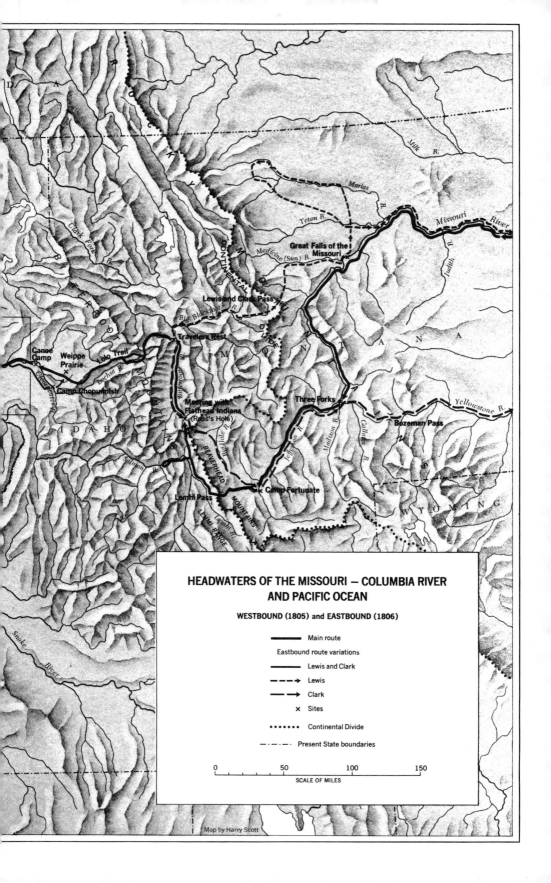

HEADWATERS OF THE MISSOURI — COLUMBIA RIVER
AND PACIFIC OCEAN

WESTBOUND (1805) and EASTBOUND (1806)

Main route

Eastbound route variations

Lewis and Clark

Lewis

Clark

× Sites

•••••• Continental Divide

—·—·— Present State boundaries

0   50   100   150

SCALE OF MILES

Map by Harry Scott

Modern float trip moving down the Salmon River through Salmon National Forest, Idaho. The lack of timber prevented Lewis and Clark from building boats, and they found the edge of the stream to be impassable on foot or horseback.

guide named Old Toby, who was familiar with the country to the north and west.

That same afternoon, the group set out northwestward down the Lemhi and made 8 miles before setting up camp. The next day, 5 miles farther, an Indian fishing camp was passed and after another 5 miles the junction of the Lemhi and Salmon, at present Salmon, Idaho. In the evening, Cruzatte, who had been left behind at the Shoshoni village to buy a third horse, rode into camp.

Clark named the present Salmon River after Lewis.[113] Between the 21st and 24th, Clark and his men explored the Salmon for about 52 miles from its junction with the Lemhi. From that junction, it ran north and slightly westward until a point near the mouth of the north fork, where the main branch veered almost directly westward.

Beyond the north fork, the farther the river was descended, the more impassable it became. As a matter of fact, at the point of Clark's farthest penetration he probably entered a stretch of the river that even today is known as the "River of No Return" and can only be navigated with specially built craft. He soon realized that boats could not be taken down the treacherous stream, whose powerful current foamed into vicious rapids that snaked their way through a boulder-filled bed. The banks were no more passable for an overland party, for precipitous and often perpendicular canyon walls allowed almost no room to travel along the sides. Finally, it became impossible for the horses to follow the rocky and steep river's edge, but Clark, Old Toby, and three men labored on foot along the river for an additional 20 miles or so.

Everything the Shoshonis had said was true. The river could not be negotiated, game was scarce, and the timber was unsuitable for building canoes. On August 23 Clark decided to turn back. Reuniting with the rest of his party the next day, he sent Colter with one of the horses carrying a message to Lewis advising him of the impassability of the river and encouraging him to procure the maximum number of horses for the trip over the Lolo Trail.

Reunion at the Shoshoni village

Meantime, Sacagawea and Charbonneau had been successful in their mission. On August 22, with Cameahwait, a substantial number of his people, and a herd of horses, they had arrived back at Camp Fortunate. Lewis had already cached part of the remaining supplies about three-quarters of a mile away and sunk the seven canoes in a nearby pond in the hope they could be raised on the eastbound trip.

Lewis briskly bartered with the Indians for additional horses. By the morning of August 24 he had acquired a total of nine and one mule, in addition to the two Clark was using, and was able to hire two additional mounts. All the baggage possible was loaded on them, as well as three Indian steeds, and Indian women shouldered the rest.

At noon of the 24th, the Lewis contingent and Cameahwait and his band set out for the Shoshoni village to reunite with Clark. The next day, Charbonneau, who apparently obtained the information from Sacagawea, told Lewis that Cameahwait had sent a messenger on ahead with instructions to his village to begin its annual eastward trek and meet him en route. This would mean the loss of the services of the three Indian horses and the Indian women porters, as well as obviating the possibility of purchasing more horses.

Alarmed, Lewis counciled with Cameahwait and his subordinate chiefs, who explained that such a step was critical because their people were starving. Nevertheless, Lewis, drawing on all his powers of persuasion, finally managed to convince Cameahwait to cancel his instructions and send a runner on ahead to hold the village where it was in the Lemhi Valley until his arrival. When the party reached there on August 26, it found Colter waiting with the message from Clark.[114] Lewis immediately set about trying to buy more horses, which the Shoshonis were reluctant to sell because the Minitaris had stolen a large number that spring and they needed all those on hand for the forthcoming hunt.

THAT same day, the Clark party arrived back at the Indian fishing camp about 5 miles up the Lemhi, which it had passed on the outbound trip, and spent the night there. The next morning, a message from Lewis told Clark to remain there until the main body came up that same noon. On the following morning, August 28, by which time Lewis had still not put in an appearance, Clark sent Gass back to the Shoshoni village, about 13 miles to the south, to see what had happened. He returned that night with a note from Lewis directing Clark to move back to the village the following day. He did so, leaving two men behind with the baggage.

Clark at once began helping Lewis barter for horses, for they agreed that the only feasible route was the Lolo Trail. By the morning of the 30th they had obtained a total of about 29 of them and a mule—to "Eate if necessary," said Clark.[115] These were far less than the number desired, and most of them had sore backs. In addition, some saddles, probably including a few of Spanish origin, were obtained from the Shoshonis, and the men of the expedition made others. Old Toby agreed to lead the party over the trail, though he said he had traversed it only once and that was many years earlier. Sacagawea decided to continue on rather than stay with her own people.

Pushing northward toward the Lolo Trail

By this time, autumn in the Rocky Mountains was well advanced. The sun was sinking on the horizon, and some nights were frosty.

This added to the worries of the two leaders. The Columbia had not yet been reached. Food supplies were low. Game had been scarce ever since meeting the Shoshonis, and would likely be even more so in the rugged and unknown mountains ahead.

On August 30 the expedition moved northward, while the Shoshonis headed eastward over the Beaverhead Mountains to the Missouri River area. At the fishing camp, the two men and the baggage Clark had left were picked up. Four of Old Toby's sons accompanied him at first, but on September 1 three of them turned back.

As the explorers moved down the Lemhi River and the Salmon and up its north fork along the eastern slopes of the Bitterroot Mountains, the hilly, broken country became progressively more rugged and mountainous. In many places the timber was so heavy that thickets had to be axed through. On the rocky slopes, often coated with sleet or wet from rain, several horses fell or slipped and were crippled. Others gave out from fatigue. A 2-inch snowfall on September 3 turned into rain and then sleet. The last of the salt pork brought from St. Louis was consumed.

The next day, the group climbed a high spur of the Bitterroot Range, moved through a pass, probably Lost Trail Pass, and reentered present Montana. After the descent, Camp Creek was followed to its junction with the present Bitterroot River, which Lewis named the Clark River.

Visit with the Flatheads

That same day, Flatheads, whom the Minitaris and Shoshonis had spoken of, were encountered. They had never seen white men before. Their village, numbering 33 lodges and populated by about 400 people, was situated at the base of the Bitterroot Mountains in a beautiful cove that later became known as Ross's Hole. The pipe was smoked and medals and gifts were presented to the chiefs. A Shoshoni boy living among the Flatheads who understood their language translated to Sacagawea. She rendered the words into Minitari for Charbonneau. He in turn translated them into French for Labiche, who passed them on in English to Lewis and Clark. They noted that the tribe spoke in a throaty, gurgling manner.

The Flatheads were not only friendly. Equally as important, they possessed a lot of horses, at least 500, which Clark said were "ellegant." Many of them they had undoubtedly stolen or obtained

View to the south into Idaho from the Montana side of Lost Trail Pass, likely crossed by the explorers on their westward journey. Guided by Old Toby, they passed through this morass of mountains and forest during a sleet- and snow-storm while en route from the Lemhi to the Bitterroot Valley.

from their Nez Perce neighbors across the mountains to the west. Thus the herd possibly included some of the spotted breed known today as the Appaloosa, which the Nez Perces may have developed from the Spanish-Arabian strain that had come into their possession and been selectively bred to become recognized far and wide as the finest owned by any North American Indians. Lewis and Clark bartered with the Flatheads for about 13 horses, including at least three colts, and exchanged seven that were worn out. This increased the horseherd to approximately 39 horses, three colts, and one mule— for riding, packing, or food.[116]

On September 6, goodbyes were said to the Flatheads, who set out for the Three Forks of the Missouri to meet their Shoshoni allies. Early in the afternoon, the expedition moved northward down along

The Lewis & Clark Expedition collected botanical specimens as it crossed the continent, many of which were lost in the wetness of the Pacific Northwest. When traveling the Trail today, it is a good idea to consult such books as *Lewis and Clark: Pioneering Naturalists*, by Paul R. Cutright, for information regarding new plants and animals the expedition brought to the science of the time.

the Bitterroot River, viewing the spectacular scenery of the Bitterroot Valley, dominated on the west by the saw-toothed Bitterroot Range. This area is one of the most beautiful intermountain areas in the entire Rocky Mountain region.

Sojourn at Travelers Rest

Three days later, about 10 miles south of present Missoula, the party reached a large creek flowing into the Bitterroot River from the west. Old Toby said it would be followed, along the Lolo Trail over the Bitterroots. Desiring to take advantage of the fine weather conditions to make celestial observations and anticipating an ordeal ahead, Lewis and Clark decided to stop and rest the men and horses for a day or two, put packs in order, and make final preparations for crossing the Bitterroots. The hunters were able to do little to augment the critically low food supply. Moving up the creek about 2 miles, the weary men camped along its south bank. The two captains called it Travelers Rest Creek (today's Lolo Creek), and so the campsite has come to be known as Travelers Rest.

As had the Minitaris and Shoshonis, Old Toby described an excellent shortcut overland from the Travelers Rest area to the Missouri that the Indians commonly used. He explained that not far to the north the Bitterroot joined a stream nearly as large as itself that rose in the mountains near the Missouri and passed over a broad prairie to the latter stream at a point about 30 miles downstream, or north, of the Gates of the Rocky Mountains.[117] By using the shortcut, Old Toby said the journey from the Missouri to Travelers Rest could be made by land in only 4 days—instead of the 53 days consumed between the same points by Lewis and Clark over land and water along the route they had followed. They had not recognized the Sun and Dearborn Rivers as access routes to the shortcut that they had first heard of from the Minitaris.

From Travelers Rest, the expedition reconnoitered a short way up Lolo Creek and about 10 miles down the Bitterroot River. While out hunting, Colter met three Flathead Indians, who explained they were pursuing some Shoshonis who had stolen 23 of their horses, and brought them back to camp. Two left to carry on the chase. One remained and joined the party as a guide. Old Toby could not understand him but communicated with sign language. The Flathead said that a related tribe lived 5 days distant over the mountains on a plain on the Columbia River, which he said was navigable to the sea. This was good news to Lewis and Clark and confirmed what the Shoshonis had told them. But 5 days to cross the mountains was not to prove to be accurate, at least for the expedition. Eleven days were to be consumed. For some reason, the journey was made without the newly recruited guide.

A harrowing mountain journey: the Lolo Trail

For more than a week, the men had been anxiously eyeing the lofty, snow-capped Bitterroots to the west. They knew from the Indians that crossing them over the Lolo Trail, which extended 155–165 miles from the Travelers Rest vicinity to present Weippe Prairie, was an ordeal.[118] But they could hardly have imagined that it would involve some of the worst terrain in the Rockies and prove to be the most agonizing part of their entire journey.

The nightmare began on September 12, the day after leaving

Present Lolo Creek, known to Lewis and Clark as Travelers Rest Creek, about 10 miles west of its mouth. The stream, along which the route of part of the Lolo Trail generally passes, drains the eastern side of the Bitterroot Mountains from the vicinity of Lolo Pass.

Travelers Rest along Lolo Creek on a clearly defined road. It not only turned into a mere trail, but in places fallen timber made it almost impassable. Pushing up the steep hills and rocky mountain slopes, struggling through deep gorges and hollows, and tearing through tangled forest choked with underbrush, drained the strength of man and beast.

The next day, the 13th, a stop was made at Lolo Hot Springs, whose waters Clark tasted. A few miles farther, skirting Lolo Pass a mile or so to its east and reentering present Idaho from Montana, the group traversed a fine glade, Packers Meadow. Two miles beyond, camp was established by Pack Creek—part of the Columbia drainage.

Lolo Hot Springs, in the mid-1850's before roads were built in the area. The men of the expedition bathed in these springs, which are in the upper reaches of Lolo Creek.

Snow fell on the following day. Old Toby, whose knowledge of the trail was weak, strayed from the main branch. He followed what turned out to be a fishing path. It led down to the Lochsa River, a branch of the Clearwater; Lewis and Clark called both streams the Koos-koos-kee. That night, camp was made opposite an island at the site of present Powell Ranger Station in Clearwater National Forest. Ever since leaving the Jefferson River, rations had been short. The food now all but gone and game practically nonexistent, a colt was killed and roasted. Gass called it "good eating." To mark the occasion, a nearby creek (modern White Sand Creek) was designated Killed Colt Creek.

The following morning, the 15th, the Lochsa was followed downstream, or westward, for about 4 miles before a turn was made to the north up steep Wendover Ridge. Some of the horses gave out and were left behind. Several others slipped and incurred minor injuries. A few rolled down the mountainside. Clark's field desk, carried by

Packers Meadow, Idaho, a short distance southeast of Lolo Pass. Camp was made at this place on September 13, 1805.

one of them, was broken. That evening, the main trail was reattained. It followed a high divide that sometimes reached more than 7,000 feet in height. In the rarefied air, the men gasped for breath.

Morale further sagged on September 16, one of the worst days. Just before dawn, a severe snowstorm began. By nightfall 6 to 8 inches had accumulated over the old snow. Through it all, the explorers, wet and cold and their hands and feet freezing, pushed on. In the blinding snow, they could barely distinguish the vague trail, sometimes defined only by low-hanging foliage that packs of Indian horses had earlier rubbed against. During the day, the landmark known as Indian Post Office, two rock cairns placed by the Indians, was probably passed.[119] This was the highest point on the trail, an elevation of 7,036 feet. Because the hunters found no game, supper consisted of another colt and some unpalatable canned and dried "portable soup," the Army experimental ration Lewis had obtained in Philadelphia.

Koos-Koos-Kee
(Clearwater) Riv.

Canoe Camp
Sept. 26–Oct.   1805

First encounter with Nez Perce
(Sept. 20, Clark;
Sept. 22, Main party)

W E I P P E

Nez Perce
villages

P R A I R I E

Hungry Cr.

(Lolo Cr.)

Collins Cr.

Commeash
June 10, 1806

CANADA
UNITED STATES

MONTANA

AREA OF
THIS MAP

IDAHO   WYOMING

0   100   200
MILES

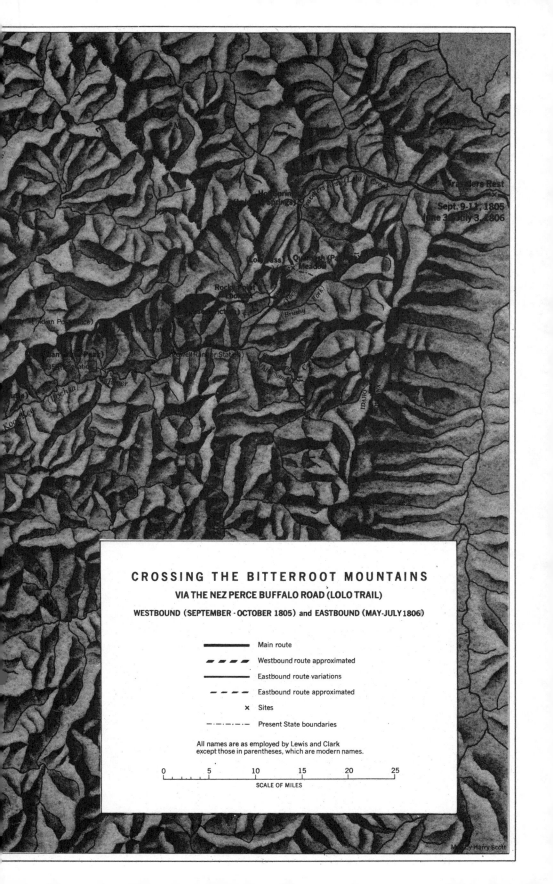

Travelers Rest
×
Sept. 9-11, 1805
June 30-July 3, 1806

(Lolo Hot
Springs)

(Lolo Pass)   Quamash (Packer)
× Meadow

Rock Fort
Camp

Brushy
Fork

(Indian Post Office)

(Powell Ranger Station)

IDAHO

(Tochan)

CROSSING THE BITTERROOT MOUNTAINS

VIA THE NEZ PERCE BUFFALO ROAD (LOLO TRAIL)

WESTBOUND (SEPTEMBER - OCTOBER 1805) and EASTBOUND (MAY-JULY 1806)

━━━━━━━ Main route

━ ━ ━ ━ Westbound route approximated

━━━━━━━ Eastbound route variations

─ ─ ─ ─ Eastbound route approximated

× Sites

─·─·─·─·─ Present State boundaries

All names are as employed by Lewis and Clark
except those in parentheses, which are modern names.

0   5   10   15   20   25
SCALE OF MILES

Map by Harry Scott

Lolo Trail, Idaho-Mont. The rugged mountainous terrain and heavy timber alone would have made the crossing difficult enough, but severe weather conditions further hampered progress.

About 10 more miles were covered on September 17. All that was visible in every direction was the jumble of the Bitterroot Mountains. That night, the last colt was consumed. The two captains conferred on their desperate plight and decided they would need to separate to get through the mountains.

In the morning, Clark and six hunters pushed ahead. From a high mountain, Sherman Peak, they saw miles ahead an extensive plain, bounded by mountains. Later, describing the food situation, Clark named a stream Hungry Creek (present Obia Creek). Progress for the day totaled 32 miles. A stray Indian horse encountered the following day, a heartening indication that Indians were probably in the vicinity, provided a meal. The remainder was hung up for the main party, which found it the next day.

Contacting the Nez Perces

Meantime, Clark had pressed on ahead. On September 20, he came out onto the beautiful, pine-bordered plain he had viewed earlier. It

Lochsa River at modern White Sand Creek, known to the explorers as Killed Colt Creek. On the night of September 14, 1805, they camped opposite an island in the river, at the present site of the Powell Ranger Station of Clearwater National Forest, and killed a colt for food.

was modern Weippe Prairie, which the two captains referred to variously as the "quawmash ground," "quawmash flats," and "camas flats." Clark encountered some hospitable Nez Perces residing in two villages, separated by a distance of 2 miles. They were probably an even more welcome sight than the Shoshonis had been. The seven hungry men voraciously consumed a meal of dried salmon, berries, and cakes of camas roots. The Indians said in sign language that their highest chiefs were away on a war expedition and that the ranking one on hand was Twisted Hair, who was fishing at a camp about 20 miles to the northwest on the Clearwater.

Late the next day, the 21st, Clark set out for the fishing camp.

Rock cairns on the Lolo Trail near Indian Post Office, Idaho. These markers, erected by the Indians and probably rebuilt several times during the past century, may have had some religious significance.

From the westernmost of the two villages, he sent back Reuben Field and a Nez Perce with some dried salmon, berries, and camas roots he had obtained by barter to meet Lewis and the main party. Clark did not reach the camp until about 11:00 p.m., but held a long conference with Twisted Hair. In the morning, they returned to the villages, where late in the day the Lewis party staggered into the eastern village. Earlier, in the foothills 8 miles away, it had met Field and his Indian companion.

On September 23, at the first village, Lewis and Clark held a council with Twisted Hair and other secondary chiefs. Neither Old Toby, his son, nor Sacagawea could speak Nez Perce, so communication was with signs. After passing out medals and gifts, Lewis and Clark explained their mission and requested assistance in building canoes so that they could proceed by water, which was feasible according to the chiefs. In the evening, the expedition traveled with Twisted Hair to the western village, his place of residence. The leaders were anxious to get to the Clearwater to build canoes.

Sherman Saddle, looking toward the northwest. At this place, the present Lolo Trail departs from the one Lewis and Clark followed and proceeds to the west and northwest.

The next day, the explorers and some Indians, apparently including Twisted Hair, moved to the river and camped for the night on an island a short distance below the one where he had originally been contacted. By this time, many of the men were violently sick with dysentery, whose symptoms were acute diarrhea and vomiting. Lewis was virtually immobilized for a few days. The dried fish may have contained bacteria to which the Nez Perces had developed an immunity. Other possible causes were the change of diet from essentially meat to cereals and fish; the famished condition of the men and the strange food; and the drastic weather change they had recently undergone, from the intense heat of the plains to the severe cold of the mountains. Clark dispensed Rush's pills, emetics, and salts. For several days the complement was reduced almost to helplessness. If the Nez Perces had been hostile, they would have enjoyed an opportunity to destroy the Corps of Discovery.

Still, the terror of the Bitterroots had ended and the Rockies had been conquered. The men had survived starvation, freezing cold, fatigue, strange food, all sorts of medicines. They were finally on the Columbia drainage, which they hoped would carry them to the ocean. They could not be certain this river system would lead them to it or that the system could even be navigated. But hopes were high, and the future looked much brighter than it had during the past month.

On September 25 Clark and Twisted Hair set off downstream to find trees large enough to construct canoes. About 4 or 5 miles away, in a small bottom some 5 miles west of present Orofino, Idaho, on the south side of the river opposite the point where the Clearwater's north fork joined the main stream, they found pines that were suitable. The next day, the expedition moved to the site, which has come to be known as Canoe Camp. To help their comrades regain their strength, any hunters who were able to move about went to work to find food more agreeable than dried fish and camas roots. Game was scarce, but some deer were taken. One of the party's horses was also killed and eaten.

Some of the sick recovered, and all the able-bodied worked on the canoes. These were built by the easier Indian method of burning out tree trunks rather than hewing them. On October 5 two of the boats were completed; and the 38 remaining horses, which Twisted Hair agreed to care for until the expedition's return, were collected and branded.[120] The following day, the saddles and some ammunition were cached and the last three of the five canoes—four large and one small —were completed and put in the water.

DURING their brief stay with the Nez Perces, Lewis and Clark, who called the tribe "Chopunnish" or "Pierced Noses," observed that their culture was advanced. Another characteristic was their friendliness; in time, the two leaders came to feel they were the most likable and hospitable of any native group encountered. The horses were also noted to be superlative, but slight attention was paid to them at the time because of the primary interest in canoes.

Waterborne once again—navigating the Clearwater and Snake

The journey down the swift-flowing Clearwater and Snake to the Columbia consumed 9 days (October 7–16). Currents, rapids, and

Salmon was the staff of life for the inhabitants of the Columbia River basin. Until the many dams were built along its currents, Indians harvested this then abundant resource.

boulder-strewn channels made passage a trial. The friendly Nez Perces who lived in the numerous encampments along the shores, subsisting on salmon and other fish, often provided navigational help. Some of them owned dogs, bought by many of the men, who preferred well-cooked dog meat to fish, for almost no game was available. Sometimes, however, fish as well as roots had to be purchased, in addition to firewood, which was difficult to find.

The second day on the Clearwater, in rapids, rocks gashed Sergeant Gass's canoe, and it sank in waist-deep water. Only the shallowness prevented loss of life and provisions. While the latter were being dried and the canoe repaired, Old Toby and his son deserted for some reason, possibly fear of the rapids and realization they were no longer effective as guides. Some Nez Perces reported seeing them running eastward along the riverbank. They subsequently took two of the horses that Lewis and Clark had left with the Nez Perces and apparently headed back over the Lolo Trail to their own country. Because of their sudden departure, they were never paid—to the regret of the two captains. But new guides, familiar with the route, were already on hand. Twisted Hair and another chief named Teto- harsky, who had agreed to accompany the expedition to the Columbia, had joined it on October 8.

On October 10 the party entered its principal tributary, the Snake. Clark, believing it to be a western stretch of the Salmon, which he had named the Lewis River, applied the same name to the Snake.[121] The party bivouacked on its east, or north, bank near the site of Lewiston, Idaho. The following morning, the push down the canyon-lined stream resumed into present Washington. The way was still difficult. At times, canoes overturned or grounded. Supplies were damaged and a portion of the critically short trade goods were lost. Some of the men who could not swim were luckily rescued by others.

Down the broad Columbia

October 16 was a banner day. Into view came the broad Columbia —the "River of the West" that led to the "Western Ocean," or the "Great South Sea" as Clark called it. No other white men had seen it east of the Cascade Mountains. The Pacific could not be far away! Excited and triumphant though the leaders must have been, they filled their journals with unemotional and matter-of-fact observations.

Camp was established at the mouth of the Snake for 2 days, during which the Columbia was investigated for about 10 miles upstream. The men were astounded at the number of salmon in the island-dotted river. But, noting that a large percentage were dead or dying, they refrained from eating them and continued to procure dogs from the natives whenever possible.

The boats swept downstream on the 18th. The Indians remained friendly. On the 18th and 19th, councils were held with Yellept, chief of the Walla Wallas, and a delegation of tribal leaders. Yellept, specially hospitable, wanted Lewis and Clark to stay longer so that his people might visit the expedition, but the two captains excused themselves and promised to stay with him a few days on their return. Twisted Hair and Tetoharsky, understanding the languages of the river tribes, translated with signs for Lewis and Clark. The commanders assured the chiefs of the friendly disposition of the U.S. Government and distributed medals and gifts.

When Lewis & Clark saw the Columbia, it was without dams and hydro-electric stations. Pictured here in 1953, the islands in the Columbia are now under an artificial lake.

THE attitude, as well as the economy, of the natives was to change at the same time that serious navigational problems again arose. On October 23 the boats entered a dangerous but spectacular stretch of the Columbia that extended for about 55 river miles. It contained a series of four major barriers, created by the stream as it tore its way through the Cascade Range on its sudden and sharp descent to the sea. All these barriers are today inundated by dam reservoirs.

More than a week of herculean effort was expended in passing through this part of the river. In comparison, earlier nautical difficulties seemed almost like child's play. To prevent loss of life and the destruction of canoes and supplies, portages were sometimes mandatory. Eager to reach the Pacific, however, Lewis and Clark sometimes took chances and ran the boats through hazardous areas.

The first barrier, breached on October 23, was the Celilo, or Great, Falls. In this short stretch of violent, roaring cataracts, the river funneled into several narrow channels, between cliffs as high as 2,000–3,000 feet, and dropped almost 38 feet. One falls was 20 feet high and the cargo and boats had to be portaged around it. The canoes were floated the rest of the way, however, though in some places they needed to be lowered by elk skin ropes.

The second obstacle, which began about 2 miles farther downstream, was The Dalles, traversed on October 24–25. In the Short Narrows, a quarter-mile-long swirling vortex of roaring waters, the channel constricted to a mere 45 yards wide. No portage of the canoes was possible over the rocky ledges so, to the amazement of Indian spectators, the boats and much of the cargo were ridden

This pre-1915 photograph shows The Dalles-Celilo Falls area before the present dam and canal were built. This view is from the Oregon side of the river looking toward Washington.

through the narrows by everyone who could swim; the others portaged with guns, ammunition, valuable papers, and some supplies.

Below the Short Narrows was a 3-mile stretch of river that offered no special difficulty except for one bad rapids. Then, at the Long Narrows of the Lower Dalles, 3 miles or so in length, the stream narrowed to 50–100 yards wide. It was possible to run the canoes with part of their cargoes through the entire extent; again valuable articles were portaged. Once the Long Narrows were negotiated, on October 26–27 the exhausted men rested, recaulked the canoes, and dried out equipment. Further relief came the next 4 days in a quieter part of the river.

The final barrier, surmounted on November 1–2, was the Cascades, or Grand Rapids, 3 to 4 miles of boiling rapids passing through a series of chutes and falls. Portaging of equipment and boats was often necessary, and sometimes the boats had to be lowered on poles running from one rock to another.

WATER hazards were not the only ones. Beginning at Celilo Falls, the Indians changed substantially—in temperament as well as way of life. Their economy, like that of their upriver brethren, was based on salmon, which swarmed in the water by now, but it was riverine in nature. Travel and life on the Lower Columbia were centered on the river, and thick woods prevented use of horses in the hunt.

Some of the lower river Indians were friendly and cooperative, but a goodly number were thieves, vandals, devious traders, and beggars. All the men disliked them for these traits, if not for their infestation with fleas and lice, which they passed on to the expedition's complement. Particularly irksome were the natives in the Celilo Falls-Dalles-Cascades area, a center of the great Indian salmon fisheries and thus a meetingplace and focus of trade of the Northwest Indians for untold centuries. Navigational difficulties there had always given tribes in the vicinity unusual opportunities to prey on passersby, whom they often harassed or robbed. They enjoyed a bad reputation throughout early white contact.

Either Twisted Hair or Tetoharsky passed on to Lewis and Clark a rumor that one of the tribes planned to massacre the entire party. Probably only its size, superior weaponry, and special security measures prevented serious trouble. These factors were not enough to pacify Twisted Hair and Tetoharsky, who grew frightened for their

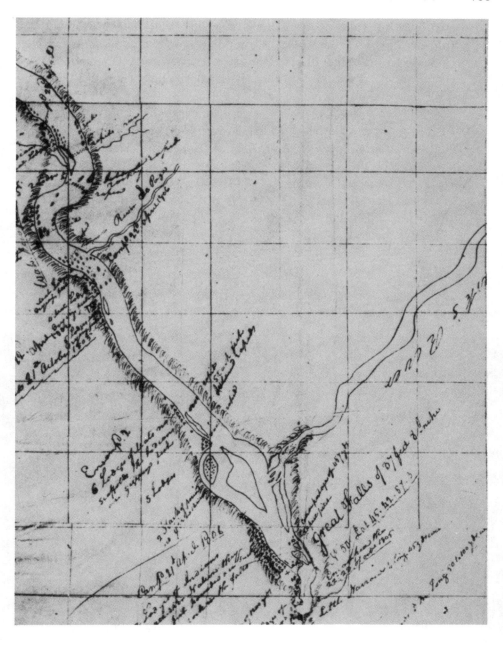

Section of one of Clark's maps showing Celilo, or Great, Falls of the Columbia.

own lives, for their people were at war with these lower river tribes. Anyway, because they could not understand the languages, they felt they could be of no further service as translators. On October 25 they purchased two horses from the local Indians, said farewell, and returned to their upriver home.

AS early as mid-October, Indians were seen wearing or possessing manufactured objects of American or European origin that could only have originated with northwest traders: guns, other weapons, beads, trinkets, wool clothing and blankets, cloth, powder flasks, and brass and copper kettles. These goods were apparently obtained in trade from tribes at the mouth of the Columbia—a cheering sign that journey's end was near.

Indian fishing for salmon below Celilo Falls some time before The Dalles Dam was built and covered the falls.

This drawing, made in the mid-1850's, shows The Dalles and Mount Hood. The landscape had not changed appreciably during the preceding 50 years. At The Dalles, the Columbia ground through great slabs and dikes of lava rock.

There were other signs that the Pacific was not far away. On October 24, Lewis and Clark saw what they thought were sea otter but later decided were seals. Emerging from the gorge of the Columbia and leaving the Cascade Mountains behind, on November 2 the explorers noted that the river broadened to more than 2 miles wide at Beacon Rock, the beginning of tidewater.

This region, covered with fir, spruce, ash, and alder, contrasted sharply with the semidesert country of the Upper Columbia and the Snake. Game again made an appearance, though dried fish and roots still had to be purchased from the Indians—new groups of whom were met daily. Large numbers of waterfowl provided a welcome dietary supplement. Fog was frequent and often thick. Nevertheless, Mount Hood, which had first been sighted to the southwest on October 18, was seen again on November 3 far back to the southeast.

Hat Rock State Park in Oregon is a great place to see the evidence of the tectonic forces which pushed this and other basalt flows to the surface around the Columbia River. The Columbia River Gorge is a remarkable area and must have been an inspiring sight for the expedition members. Hat Rock is mentioned in the Journals on October 19, 1805.

"Ocian in View! O! The Joy"

Near Pillar Rock, on November 7 Clark, seldom emotional in his journal, exclaimed, "Great joy in camp we are in *view* of the Ocian . . . this great Pacific Octean which we been so long anxious to See." But he was mistaken. He was actually viewing the open-horizoned estuary of the Columbia, whose salty waters reached up some 20 miles from its mouth.[122]

Just the day before, a violent storm had erupted. Rain persisted for 11 straight days, never ceasing for longer than 2 hours. Lightning flashes seared the sky, and thunder boomed like cannon. Day and

Beacon Rock, a lava monolith about 900 feet high on the Washington side of the Columbia today included in a State park, is one of the landmarks mentioned in the Lewis and Clark journals.

night, everyone was soaked and miserable, as well as weary from bailing water out of the boats and wringing out wet clothing, bedding, and equipment. Sacagawea and some of the men became seasick as high waves and heavy winds tossed the boats about like driftwood. Only extreme exertion prevented huge waterborne cedar, fir, and spruce trees—bigger than anyone had ever seen, some almost 200 feet long and up to 7 feet in diameter—from crushing the canoes. Hunting was impossible, but dried fish, roots, and dogs were sometimes purchased from Chinook Indians, who were encountered almost daily. Finding shelter was difficult. Fires were hard to start and maintain.

The view of the Pacific Ocean at the mouth of the Columbia is a remarkable sight even today. The photograph shows a calm and remarkably clear perspective in this location, which the Lewis & Clark Expedition found rainy, cloudy and rough during the winter of 1805-6.

Through it all, the boats inched their way along the northern side of the estuary. On November 10, when they tried to round Point Ellice, opposite present Astoria, Oreg., giant waves whipped them back. Camp had to be established along the point's more protected eastern side on a pile of drift logs. During the night, the logs were awash in the tide for awhile. Small stones from the steep nearby hillside, loosened by the driving rain, pelted the party. The next day, to prevent waves and floating tree trunks from further damaging or destroying the canoes, they were sunk with rocks. The men then moved inland a short distance to high ground. In the predawn hours of the 12th, a severe thunderstorm broke out, and continued bad weather held the group to the camp until November 15.

In the meantime, 2 days earlier, Lewis and Clark had dispatched

Colter, Willard, and Shannon in an Indian canoe, which rode the swells better than the expedition's craft, to explore the shoreline beyond Point Ellice to see if a better campsite could be found. Colter returned the next day with a favorable report. In mid-afternoon, a party of five men carried Lewis, Drouillard, Joseph and Reuben Field, and Frazer around the point in a canoe. They proceeded by land toward the mouth of the Columbia, exploring and looking for the white men the Indians had said were in the area. That day, the Pacific may have been sighted, but it is unlikely because of the stormy conditions and the few hours of daylight available.

Back at the base camp, abating weather on the morning of November 15, the day after Lewis left, made possible the refloating and reloading of the canoes. But high winds sprang up and delayed departure until 3 o'clock. Clark and his party then moved about 4 miles downstream around Point Ellice to a sandy beach Colter had earlier discovered, about a half-mile southeast of Chinook Point. There they met Shannon and five Chinook Indians. Some distance below, Shannon and Willard had met Lewis, who took the latter with him and sent the former back to await the main body. Camp was made near an abandoned Chinook village, consisting of 36 board houses, whose lumber was used in building shelters. This campsite was utilized as a main base until November 25.

Visible for the first time were Point Adams and Cape Disappointment, the whole breadth of the Columbia's mouth between those headlands, and beyond them the open sea—the glorious Pacific.[123] After many months of privation and danger, the Corps of Discovery had reached its goal!

The next day was clear with high winds. The men relaxed and lolled about, satisfied they were at journey's end. They watched mountainous waves rolling free out in the ocean and seagulls soaring dreamily about overhead. Clark estimated the distance from Camp Wood at 4,133 miles—3,096 from there to Camp Fortunate, then 379 miles overland to Canoe Camp on the Clearwater, followed by a 658-mile river trek to the mouth of the Columbia. On November 17 the Lewis party, which had proceeded to Cape Disappointment and explored the seacoast to its north for a short distance, arrived back at Chinook Point. The next day, Clark and 11 men set out.[124] Between then and the 20th, they traveled overland to Cape Disappointment and explored about 9 miles to its north.

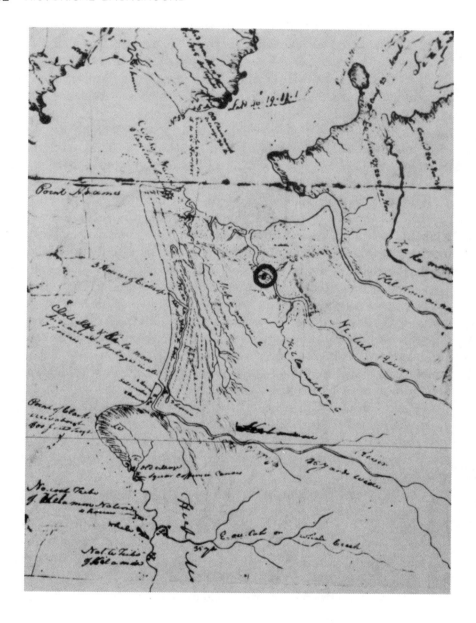

Central portion of Clark's map of the mouth of the Columbia and adjacent coastal area. A circle has been added to his symbol for Fort Clatsop.

Finding Lewis' name carved on a tree near Cape Disappointment, Clark etched on it his own, "by land," and the day, month, and year (November 18, 1805). Some of the other men carved their names, too. The next day, Clark engraved another tree. On November 23, back at the Chinook Point camp, he, Lewis, and the entire complement engaged in one more tree-carving ceremony.

Searching for a winter camp

As soon as Lewis and Clark arrived at the mouth of the Columbia, they began to consider a location for a winter camp, for they knew they could not return over the mountains until the next spring. All their reconnaissance revealed that the area north of the Columbia was unsatisfactory. Game was scarce, and living on dried fish and roots was not only an unpalatable thought but also costly, for the Indians demanded high prices. Also, the pervasive dampness rotted clothing and bedding, and hides were needed to replace them.

The Indians reported that game, particularly elk, and edible roots were in good supply on the south shore of the Columbia. Lewis and Clark decided to investigate that area and, if their informants were correct, establish winter quarters there close to the coast. The only other alternative was returning upstream some distance on the Columbia. Game was available there, but salt could not be obtained and chances of meeting any northwest traders would be practically non-existent. And the climate was colder, undesirable because of the poor condition of the clothing. Practically all the wool garments had been used up, and everyone was dressed in animal skins, especially those of deer.

Wanting their command to be satisfied with the decision during the long winter ahead, on November 24 Lewis and Clark put the matter to a vote. The men favored examination of the south side of the Columbia, and location there if hunting was good; otherwise, they chose to move upstream to a likely place. The next day, thwarted in a direct crossing of the broad mouth of the river by the high waves, the expedition worked its way upstream along the north bank and camped near where it had on November 7, in the vicinity of Pillar Rock.

Proceeding onward the following day, the 26th, about 17 miles above Tongue Point the boats crossed to the south side of the river and moved downstream. That night, camp was made some 5 miles southeast of Tongue Point. Heavy swells forced a stop on its west side on November 27, and bad weather forced the expedition to stay there until the 29th.

On that date, while the rest of the party remained behind, Lewis took five of his best men—Drouillard, Colter, Reuben Field, Shannon, and Labiche—and set out in the small canoe searching for a winter campsite. One day, Clark, awaiting Lewis' return, in shades of Mackenzie, inscribed the following on a large spruce tree: "Capt William Clark　December 3rd 1805.　By land.　U. States in 1804-1805."

By this time, everyone had begun to worry that some misadventure had befallen the Lewis party, which had not been heard from. But, 2 days later, Lewis returned with three men, having left two others behind to hunt. He reported that a suitable spot for a winter headquarters had been found on a high point of land about 10 miles distant where elk and timber were plentiful. The surrounding area consisted mainly of salt marshes and swampy lowland. It was brush-covered, dotted with hummocks, and laced with tidal creeks. The higher places were covered with a dense growth of gigantic spruce and fir.

Construction of Fort Clatsop (1805–6)

Bad weather held the expedition to its camp the next day, the 6th. The following morning, guided by Lewis, the men headed the canoes toward the winter campsite. They proceeded past the site of present Astoria, Oreg., and around the eastern end of Young's Bay until they came to the mouth of a river they called by its Indian name, the Netul (today's Lewis and Clark River). They ascended it about 3 miles to the first point of high land on its west side. In a thick growth of spruce about 200 yards back from the river, winter camp was established—home for the next 3½ months.

The next morning (December 8), Clark and five men set out directly westward to reconnoiter the shore of the ocean, whose roaring could be heard at the camp, as well as search for game and seek a site for a saltmaking camp. Clark found the going rough, though he calculated the distance at only 7 miles. Although much of it consisted of an undulating, grass-covered, prairie-like area, it was crisscrossed by several streams, lagoons, and marshy areas. Friendly Clatsop Indians helped Clark and his party across the streams in canoes. They visited a Clatsop coastal village on the 9th, and returned the next day.

Reconstructed Fort Clatsop, Oreg., commemorated as a national memorial. The fort was the expedition's 1805–6 winter quarters.

By this time, the main body was busy felling trees for a fortification, completed on December 30 and named Fort Clatsop after the local tribe. About 50 feet square, it consisted of two long, facing structures that were joined on the sides by palisaded walls. One of the latter apparently accommodated the main gate; the other, a "water gate," provided access to a fresh water spring about 30 yards distant. Between the two buildings was a "parade ground" about 48 feet long by 20 feet wide.

One of the structures was divided into three rooms, or "huts," occupied by the enlisted men. The other contained four rooms: one for the two captains, one for the Charbonneau family, an orderly room, and a meathouse. All these rooms were used before the fort was fully completed. Most of the men moved into them during a heavy rain on Christmas Eve, following a frantic effort that day to finish the roof.

Thus a touch of hominess was added to the celebration the next day. Merrymakers parading, singing, and firing a round of small arms awakened Lewis and Clark at daybreak to wish them a Merry Christmas. The commanders distributed half of the remaining tobacco to those who used it; to the seven who did not, handkerchiefs. Other gifts were exchanged among members of the party; Sacagawea gave Clark two dozen white weasel tails. Dampening the celebration was the lack of liquor and the miserable dinner fare of spoiled elk, rotting fish, and a few roots.

For 5 days following Christmas, the finishing touches were applied to the fort: completing the palisaded walls and gates, erection of chimneys in most of the rooms, and fabrication of crude furniture and bunks.

Saltmaking operations

By this time, Lewis and Clark decided they could spare three men for the vital function of setting up a saltmaking camp. Enough of this commodity would need to be produced to last until the cache at Camp Fortunate could be recovered. On December 28 Joseph Field, Bratton, and Gibson, accompanied temporarily by Willard and Wiser, left with five of the largest kettles available. Based on Clark's opinion that the direct westward route to the coast was too difficult to traverse, the group headed southwestward. As the days passed and Willard and Wiser did not come back, everyone grew concerned. Finally, on January 5, the two men arrived with some salt. They reported that 3 days earlier a suitable spot for the camp had been found about 15 miles by trail to the southwest. It was located near the mouth of the Necanicum River not far from some Killamuck lodges, at present Seaside, Oreg.

Subsequently the number of personnel at the saltmaking camp varied, though it usually consisted of three. Illness caused some of the men to be replaced, and others were rotated. They lived on game they killed or meat brought from Fort Clatsop. Boiling the ocean water was a slow and tedious operation. On February 3 a party from the camp brought to the fort about a bushel of salt, all that had been accumulated. Two weeks later, Joseph Field arrived and reported that 2 kegs, or about 3 bushels, had been obtained. This, together with what was on hand at the fort, was considered to be all that was needed. On February 19 Sergeant Ordway took six men to bring back

The National Park Service has determined the location of the salt works of the Lewis & Clark Expedition during the winter of 1805-6. In the town of Seaside, Oregon, the reconstructed salt works are open to the public year round just off the surf of the nearby Pacific Ocean.

the salt and the kettles; closing the camp, they returned 2 days later. About 3 bushels of salt were packed in two ironbound kegs for the eastward journey.

Dietary problems

Obtaining and preserving enough meat to flavor with the salt was a problem. Four or five of the best hunters were active daily. Between December 1, 1805, and March 20, 1806, they bagged 131 elk, 20 deer, a few beaver and otter, and one raccoon. These were supplemented with occasional waterfowl and fish. As game near the fort became exhausted and the animals shifted forage ground, the hunters had to range as far as 20 miles from the fort and stay out for as much as 2 days at a time. This worsened the job of transporting meat to the fort, especially when carcasses were located several miles from the nearest water transportation. Sometimes predatory animals or Indians reached them first.

Procuring the meat was hard enough. Curing and preserving it in the humid weather created extreme difficulty. Only a few days' supply could usually be maintained. Because of the lack of the large quantities of salt required to preserve the meat, it had to be smoked for long periods. Even then, it often deteriorated. To complicate matters, hardwood was scarce. Furthermore, most of the available timber was wet and only smoldered, not smoking properly.

As a result, palatable food was often scarce and the diet monotonous. Berries, roots, dried fish, and dogs continued to be purchased from the Indians. Dog meat was especially valued for the sick and the feeble. Lewis, who noted the highly beneficial effect of its consumption on the strength and health of the men, vastly preferred it to lean venison or elk. Clark could not stand it.

Other adversities

Other negative morale factors were numerous. One was the damp and chilly weather. It was much milder than it had been at Fort Mandan the winter before, but the continual rain, fog, and murky skies were depressing. From November 4, 1805, to March 25, 1806, rain fell every day except 12 and only half of those were clear. The dampness damaged the gunpowder and mildewed and rotted clothing, bedding, and trade goods, which had to be dried by the fire. Many of the men suffered from rheumatism, colds, and influenza. Fleas pestered everyone.

Another recurrent complaint was the shortage of tobacco, exhausted by the end of March, after which for a substitute chewers used crab-tree bark and smokers the bark of the red willow and *sacacommis* (bearberry). Boredom was another problem, created by the sedentary routine in the wake of months of strenuous activity and danger on the westbound journey. Homesickness was a natural concomitant. The commanders did all they could to keep everyone busy, but this was not always possible, and onerous chores were resented. This was particularly true of the task of dressing elk hides and making clothes and moccasins, which the men considered to be women's work. By March 13 about 338 pairs of moccasins had been made, an average of about 10 pairs per person, considered sufficient for the eastward trip.

Relations with coastal tribes

One coastal tribe in particular, the Chinooks, was another source of irritation. Numbering about 400, they resided on the north side of the Columbia and frequently visited Fort Clatsop. They possessed

Clark explores beach 9 miles north of Cape Disappointment

W A H K I A K U M

C L A T S O P

(Gray's Point)

Shallow's Bay (Gray's Bay)

Expedition moves upriver (Nov. 25) and crosses the next day to south side

COLUMBIA RIVER

Campsite Nov. 10-15, 1805

(Hungry Harbor)

(POINT ELLICE)

×Campsite Nov. 26, 1805

POINT WILLIAMS (TONGUE POINT)

Campsite Nov. 27-Dec. 7, 1805

(CHINOOK POINT)

Campsite Nov. 15-25, 1805

CAPE DISAPPOINTMENT

(Baker Bay)

SAND ISLAND

POINT ADAMS

(ASTORIA)

(Young's Bay)

(Young's

C L A T S O P

(Skidanon River)

P A C I F I C

P A C I F I C

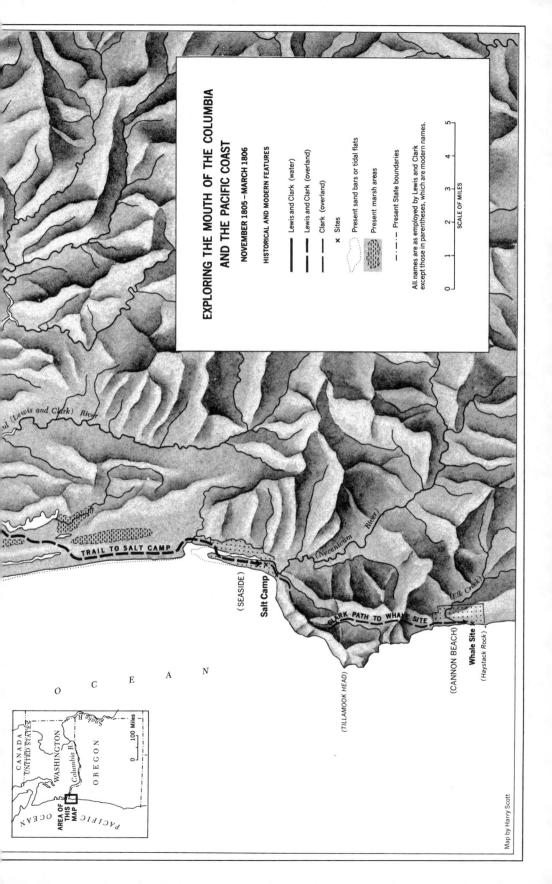

EXPLORING THE MOUTH OF THE COLUMBIA
AND THE PACIFIC COAST

NOVEMBER 1805 – MARCH 1806

HISTORICAL AND MODERN FEATURES

———— Lewis and Clark (water)

– – – – Lewis and Clark (overland)

– – – Clark (overland)

× Sites

Present sand bars or tidal flats

Present marsh areas

– · – · – Present State boundaries

All names are as employed by Lewis and Clark
except those in parentheses, which are modern names.

0   1   2   3   4   5
SCALE OF MILES

TRAIL TO SALT CAMP

ul (Lewis and Clark) River

(Necanicum River)

(SEASIDE)

Salt Camp

CLARK PATH TO WHALE SITE

(TILLAMOOK HEAD)

(Elk Creek)

(CANNON BEACH)

Whale Site
(Haystack Rock)

O C E A N

P A C I F I C   O C E A N

CANADA
UNITED STATES

WASHINGTON

Snake R.

Columbia R.

O R E G O N

AREA OF
THIS
MAP

0   100 Miles

Map by Harry Scott

many white trade goods, including sea otter robes, guns, and other arms. British and American northwest traders had brutalized and corrupted them. The women, highly promiscuous and ridden with venereal disease, considered it an honor to have the names of traders labeled on their bodies. The members of this tribe pestered the expedition's complement with petty thievery, haggling over the prices of goods and food, and hawking of the women's favors.

The Clatsops, who resided on the south side of the river, were less numerous and less corrupted than the Chinooks. Lewis and Clark considered them to be cleaner and of a higher moral caliber, and established a close friendship with a neighboring band's chief, Comowool (or Coboway). The Killamucks, or Tillamooks, who resided in the vicinity of the saltmaking camp, were friendly.

Lewis and Clark, who counciled with and made extensive observations of all the coastal tribes, found that maritime traders had debased them to varying degrees. Most engaged in thievery and were experienced traders. Like the tribes upriver to Celilo Falls, they suffered badly from fleas and lice. Most of the groups flattened their heads, lived in wooden-plank houses, demonstrated proficiency as watermen, and maintained salmon-oriented economies. They were not warlike, and did not drink liquor. Lewis and Clark communicated with them mainly in sign language, but managed to pick up a few words of the local dialects.

To protect the scant possessions from the Indians, reduce vandalism, and provide insurance against any hostilities, on January 1, 1806, the day after Fort Clatsop was completed, Lewis established a formal guard routine. The detail, consisting of a sergeant and three privates, was relieved each morning at sunrise. Sentinels were required to report the approach of any Indians. The sergeant of the guard had authority to expel them from the fort if he considered it necessary or advisable; if serious trouble threatened, he was to report it to the commanders.

On the other hand, the men were under strict orders never to strike or otherwise abuse any of the natives; they were not very hostile and the leaders wanted to keep it that way. At sunset each day, all Indians were ordinarily required to leave the fort, but on a few special occasions a visiting chief or messenger was allowed to remain inside overnight. The sergeant of the guard kept the key to the meathouse. Strict accountability was maintained for all tools, precious items,

This is possibly the earliest portrayal of a Chinook, some time prior to 1848, though artist George Catlin did not execute this painting in the tribe's home country along the Lower Columbia River. Note the technique employed to create the peculiar deformity of the Chinook head.

Cannon Beach, along the Oregon coast in the vicinity of the spot where Clark and his party in January 1806 viewed the skeleton of a whale that had washed ashore. The big monolith in the water is known as Hay Stack Rock.

which had to be turned in nightly. Only Shields, the most skilled gunsmith and blacksmith, was exempted from this order.

A trip to see a whale

One diversion for some members of the expedition was a jaunt to the coast in hopes of seeing the carcass of a whale that had washed ashore not far south of the salt camp, according to the Indians in the vicinity. Willard and Wiser brought back this report and a sample of the blubber when they returned from the camp on January 5. Great curiosity was aroused.

Clark decided to go to see the whale, and hopefully also to purchase some of the blubber as a supplement to the low food stores. Yielding to Sacagawea's entreaties to visit the whale and the "great waters" she had come so far to view, Clark allowed her, her son, and Charbonneau to join him and 11 men.[125] They set out on the 6th in two canoes. Following a circuitous route to the salt camp, they proceeded down the Netul to Young's Bay before heading southward along various creeks and streams until they had to abandon the canoes and move overland.

At the salt camp, reached on the 7th, Clark hired an Indian to show the way to the whale, located only about 8 miles to the south at the mouth of present Elk Creek. Yet the journey, made on the 7th and 8th, was a slow and arduous one over the tortuous terrain east of Tillamook Head. To everyone's disappointment, the Indians had stripped the whale of all its meat and blubber, a mere 300 pounds of which Clark was able to purchase along with a few gallons of rendered oil. He measured the skeleton and found it to be 105 feet long. Other bones of whales were seen along the shore. The group went back to the salt camp on January 9, spent the night there, and the next day followed essentially the outbound route back to Fort Clatsop.

Vain hope: contact with northwest traders

All winter long, Lewis and Clark and their men anxiously watched for English or American northwest traders, known to be active around the mouth of the Columbia. They not only offered a source of badly needed supplies and trade goods, but also possibly a mode of transportation back to the east coast. For these purposes, the two captains carried a special letter of credit from President Jefferson guaranteeing reimbursement by the U.S. Government.

But the commanders were never able to use the letter, for it was the wrong season. The majority of the traders usually arrived in April and stayed until October or November, trading with the Indians for sea otter, elk, and other pelts. The Indians knew the names and reputations of many of the skippers, as well as their expected arrival times.

Ironically, Capt. Samuel Hill, commanding the brig *Lydia* out of Boston, traded along the mouth of the Columbia for a few weeks after arriving there in November 1805, but neither he nor Lewis and Clark were aware of the other's presence. When Hill returned in the spring, after trading farther up the coast, the Indians gave his crew some of the medals the two commanders had presented to them, as well as a notice the explorers had left behind.

Had Lewis and Clark come across any of the northwest traders, they undoubtedly would have purchased supplies and trade goods to replenish their badly depleted stores, upon which they would be critically dependent on the eastbound trip. Whether or not they would have sailed on one of the ships to the east coast is a speculative matter. It would have depended on the attitude of the skipper, the size and condition of his vessel, his itinerary, and the willingness of the two captains to forgo their planned exploration of the Upper Marias and Yellowstone.

Planning the eastbound trek

Hard put though Lewis and Clark were to keep their charges occupied during the long and dreary winter, they managed to keep busy themselves. Lewis made fresh comments in his journals on botanical, zoological, meteorological, and anthropological topics involved on the journey so far and also systematized and expanded observations he had made since leaving the Mandan villages. Clark codified his geographical data and worked on a series of master maps, including one from Fort Mandan to the Pacific coast, as well as various detail maps of specific areas west of the Great Falls of the Missouri.

As they reviewed their track across the continent and poured over their notes and maps, Lewis and Clark were satisfied that the route they had followed was the best possible with one clear exception: failure to utilize the overland shortcut connecting Travelers Rest and the area west of the Great Falls that the Minitaris, Old Toby, other Shoshonis, and the Nez Perces had told them about.[126] The land-water route they had employed, via the Three Forks, Lemhi Pass, and the Lemhi-Salmon-Bitterroot Rivers, was not only needlessly long, 500 or 600 miles farther than the shortcut the captains calculated, but was also more difficult because of severe navigational problems on the Missouri above the Great Falls, especially the headwaters.

To accomplish various exploratory objectives on the eastbound journey, particularly reconnaissance of the Upper Marias and Yellowstone, Lewis and Clark decided to split the expedition into two groups at Travelers Rest in the Bitterroot Valley, the eastern terminus of the Lolo Trail. One segment, led by Lewis, would follow and investigate the shortcut eastward to the Great Falls area. Then it would probe the Upper Marias to determine for Jefferson how far north it extended.

The other group, under Clark, would move southeastward from Travelers Rest and pick up the canoes and supplies cached at Camp Fortunate. From there, it would proceed to the Three Forks of the Missouri, from which a small boat party would travel to the Great Falls to rendezvous with a detachment of the Lewis contingent and make the portage. The bulk of the Clark complement would move overland to the Yellowstone River and explore it to its mouth, as

Lewis had promised Jefferson in a letter before they had left Fort Mandan the previous spring. The two groups planned to reunite at the mouth of the Yellowstone.

Readying to depart

As winter neared an end, everyone grew restless to head home. Lewis and Clark had a special reason for wanting to make an early start—a desire to cross the Lolo Trail with the Nez Perces as soon as the deep snow subsided. The commanders were anxious to make all possible speed in reaching their villages, where they had left their horses. The chiefs had told them the previous autumn that they intended to cross to the eastern side of the mountains as soon as possible in the spring. The two captains were afraid that if the Indians did so before their arrival they would be unable to reclaim their mounts and would have difficulty in making the recrossing on their own.

A tentative departure date from Fort Clatsop of April 1 was established. Shields checked and put all the guns in order, and other preparations were carried out. One of the final acts was the writing of notices that listed the members of the expedition and briefly explained its purpose and accomplishments. Included on the back of several of them was a sketch map showing the Upper Missouri and Columbia drainage systems and delineating the group's outbound and proposed eastbound routes. The notices were given to several chiefs and one was posted in the captains' room at Fort Clatsop. It was thought that some of them might find their way into the hands of northwest traders and would constitute a record of the expedition in the event of a catastrophe on the way home.[127]

Homeward bound at last

The weather remained so wet and depressing that the planned departure was moved up from April 1 to March 20, but heavy rains caused a few more days' delay. On the 22d an advance hunting party was dispatched. That same day, Lewis and Clark said goodbye to their friend Chief Comowool and presented Fort Clatsop and its furniture to him.[128]

The following morning was so wet and cloudy—like the departure date so long ago from Camp Wood—that the start was again held up. But, as the weather cleared, the three large and two small canoes were loaded.[129] The men's spirits soared with the thought that they were finally homeward bound. At 1:00 p.m. they paddled a few miles down the river they knew as the Netul and turned up the Columbia.

Hunting remained a day-to-day affair requiring the full-time services of the best woodsmen. They shot mainly elk, but also an occasional deer; these needed to be supplemented with dogs, dried fish, and roots, purchased from the natives along the Lower Columbia. Otherwise, the latter were even more irksome than on the outbound trip. Probably only the size of the expedition prevented serious harm from befalling it.

Even rigid security and threats failed to stop Indian vandalism and the pilfering of tomahawks, tools, cutlery, and other objects. Catching one culprit in the act, the exasperated Lewis, in a rare display of temper, dealt him several severe blows and kicked him out of camp. On another occasion, Scannon was stolen and only recovered when a search party caught up with the thieves, who then abandoned him.

The weather on the lower reaches of the river was as bad as it had been the year before. Fog, mist, and overcast skies obscured visibility and prevented celestial observations. Continual rain lowered morale and dampened equipment. Gales sometimes whipped the waters into wild turbulence and created insurmountable waves. The boats often had to be hurriedly beached to avoid their destruction.

But yet there were major differences with the westbound journey. This time, the vicious current had to be fought, and spring runoff from the mountains had gorged the Columbia. This time, the boats usually hugged the south, instead of the north, bank of the Lower Columbia. This time, the Willamette River, known as the Multnomah to Lewis and Clark, which they had heard of from the Indians at Fort Clatsop and whose course they had speculated on, was explored. On the way downstream, it had been missed because islands obscured its mouth. The same thing occurred en route upstream, but Indians later told the two captains about it, and Clark retraced his steps. With seven men and an Indian guide, on April 2–3 he probed its lower reaches for about 10 miles southward to the site of the city of Portland.

Another major exception on the homeward trek up the Columbia was the use of horses, instead of boats, beginning at The Dalles. In the treacherous Cascades, on April 12, one of the large canoes was swept away and was replaced the next day by two small canoes, obtained from the Indians. Finding The Dalles, too, even more formidable than the previous fall because of the higher water, Lewis and Clark cut up some of the remaining canoes for firewood and sold others to the Indians. From this point on, horses, in scant supply in this stretch of the lower river, began to be purchased from the Indians and in at least one instance hired.[130]

On April 21 a Nez Perce, who said he knew the route to his home country, joined the expedition, as did also another Nez Perce and his family 2 days later. On the following day, Lewis and Clark broke up the last of the canoes and moved on by land. They bypassed Celilo Falls, detouring via the high land around the canyon, and pushed forward along the north bank of the river into the plains region of the Upper Columbia.

Another substantive difference on the upriver journey was the use of an overland shortcut between the Columbia and the Clearwater that eliminated practically the entire extent of the Snake and saved about 80 miles. The commanders learned of it from Walla Walla Chief Yellept, who said it ran over an extensive plain, where grass, water, and deer and antelope were plentiful.

The reunion with Yellept, on April 27, was a happy one. Two days earlier, the first of his people, who included 150 men, had begun to be encountered. The chief, whom the captains found to be as honest as he was warmhearted, not only provided firewood and food and sold them numerous dogs but also entertained them royally during their 3-day visit. He persuaded some of his upstream neighbors, the Yakimas, who were in the same language family as his tribe, to come to his village to dance. At the festivities, about 100 Yakima men, who were accompanied by a few women, danced. Some of the men in the Lewis and Clark contingent also danced for and with the Indians to the tune of Cruzatte's fiddle.

Communication with Yellept was better than on the downriver trip, when sign language had been utilized, because a Shoshoni woman prisoner was discovered who could translate from Walla Walla into Shoshoni to Sacagawea, who converted the message into Minitari and transmitted it to Charbonneau. The chief presented a fine white horse to Clark; in return, the supply of trade goods critically low, Clark gave him his sword, 100 balls and powder, and a few small articles. During the stay, Clark also ministered medically to Yellept's band.

On April 28, preparatory to taking the shortcut recommended by Yellept, the horses were swum across the Columbia at the mouth of the Walla Walla, which entered the Columbia from the east some distance downstream from the Snake. The next day, using two canoes Yellept made available, the men and the baggage crossed, along with the chief and a few of his people. The following morning, two more horses were purchased from the Indians, which brought the total to 23.

Everything in readiness, Lewis and Clark took leave of Yellept and set out over the shortcut. It consisted of a group of Indian trails that ran northeastward along the Touchet River past present Waitsburg and Dayton, Wash., then left the Touchet and ended at a point on the Snake River about 7 miles below its confluence with the Clearwater. On May 1 the Nez Perce family departed, leaving the one guide. Two days later, the day before the trek over the shortcut ended, a Nez Perce band was encountered.

Revisiting the Nez Perces—the long wait

The expedition was back again in Nez Perce country. On May 4, among some tribesmen met by chance about 3 miles up the Snake from the end of the shortcut was Chief Tetoharsky, the downriver guide. At his suggestion, with the help of three Indian canoes, a crossing was made to the north bank. He said a better road to the Nez Perce villages ran along it for about 4 miles and thence along the north side of the Clearwater. As the march proceeded, the scant supply of trade goods was used to purchase dogs, horses, and roots from the Indians. On the evening of May 5, camp was made along the mouth of a stream that Lewis and Clark called Colter's Creek (present Potlatch River) near some Nez Perce habitations.[131]

On the 7th, following the recommendation of the Nez Perce guide, the river was crossed to its south side, where he said game was more plentiful and a better road ran inland from the river to the main villages. Departing from the westbound route at a point in the vicinity of Canoe Creek about 9 miles below its Canoe Camp of the previous year, the party traveled southeastward. That day, an Indian gave Lewis and Clark two canisters of powder his dog had dug up from the cache placed at nearby Canoe Camp the preceding fall and which he had saved so that he could restore them to their rightful owners.

The next day, May 8, Lewis and Clark came across their old friend Chief Twisted Hair and a Chief Cutnose, who had been away on a war party the previous year. Twisted Hair seemed distant and cool. Apparently he had clashed with Cutnose and Broken Arm, probably the principal chief, over the horses Lewis and Clark had left in his care. Twisted Hair charged that on Cutnose's return he expressed anger because Twisted Hair had agreed to supervise the horses. Cutnose claimed he and Broken Arm had to stop the young men of Twisted Hair's band from riding and abusing the animals and had to water and care for them. In the quarrel's aftermath, they had scattered, but the Indians promised to round them up. On the 9th, when everyone proceeded to Twisted Hair's lodge, Willard, Twisted Hair, and two native boys took a packhorse and retrieved about half the saddles and some ammunition that had been cached the past year at Canoe Camp. They also collected 21 of the expedition's horses.

On the following day, a move was made to Broken Arm's village, situated in a protected valley along Lawyer's Creek. For the next few days, councils were held. Fortunately, communication was better than on the outbound trip, through the medium of a Shoshoni captive of the Nez Perces. Responding to pleas for food, the chiefs provided roots, root bread, dried fish, and two horses. Gifts were exchanged.

After having hurried from the coast to make an early crossing of the mountains over the Lolo Trail, Lewis and Clark were taken aback when they learned they could not do so yet—probably not for 3 or 4 weeks at the earliest. The Indians said that the snow was too deep in the mountains and that no forage was available for the horses. A look eastward at the towering, snow-covered Bitterroots buttressed these statements. Resigned to the need to stay awhile in the area, the two commanders decided to move to a location a few miles to the east that the chiefs recommended for its good hunting and nearby pasturage.

On May 13 the expedition set out. It moved several miles down Lawyer's Creek and then turned north along the Clearwater, at a high stage because of melting snow in the mountains. The next day, aided by the Nez Perces and one of their canoes, the explorers crossed over with their baggage and swam the horses over. There, along the river in a thickly timbered level bottom, nearly opposite the present town of Kamiah, Idaho, and within but close to the eastern boundary of the present Nez Perce Indian Reservation, they set up camp. They utilized a highly defensible site of an "ancient" Indian habitation, a circular area about 30 feet in diameter sunk about 4 feet in the ground and surrounded by a 3½-foot-high wall of earth. Around this, they erected shelters of sticks and grass facing outwards, and deposited their baggage within the sunken area under a shelter they constructed.

This camp, though nameless to Lewis and Clark, has since become known as Long Camp or Camp Chopunnish. The expedition stayed there for about a month, longer than at any place except Fort Mandan, Fort Clatsop, and Camp Wood. "Chopunnish" was one of the captains' names for the Nez Perces. The free time available allowed considerable relaxation. Footraces were run with the braves. Many dances were held, Cruzatte as usual supplying the fiddle music.

But the shortage of palatable food, acute because the salmon had not yet arrived in the river, smashed morale. Complaints were frequent about the dietary staple, roots, purchased from the Indians at a dear rate. Supplements were an occasional deer or bear. Hunting was stepped up, and trading parties were sent out to various villages to procure dried fish, roots, and root bread. Chief Broken Arm won Lewis' praise for his generosity and "civilized" spirit by telling him he could kill any of the horses running at large in the neighborhood when he needed them for food—a practice the Nez Perces themselves were sometimes forced to resort to.

As soon as the expedition arrived back among the Nez Perces, Clark found that some simple ministrations the preceding fall had gained him a reputation as a medicine man. Lewis called him the Indians' "favorite phisician." Treating chiefs, braves, women, and children alike for such ills as scrofula, ulcers, rheumatism, sore eyes, and weak limbs, he dressed sores and wounds, drained abcesses, and distributed salves, laxatives, and eyewash.

Much was learned about the tribe, which owned a wealth of horses. Its members were fine equestrians, and they loved to race their mounts. Their saddles were constructed of joined wood covered with skins and buffalo robes. On several occasions, chiefs made gifts of superb gray or white steeds to Lewis and Clark. The tribe seemed to prize white horses most of all, then the spotted breed known today as the Appaloosa.

On June 10, eager to cross the Lolo Trail as soon as possible, Lewis and Clark moved from Camp Chopunnish to a location adjacent to the trail's western terminus. They traveled northeastward about 8 miles to the southern part of Weippe Prairie. There, close to the place where they had first met the Nez Perce Indians the preceding autumn, camp was established.

Recrossing the Lolo Trail—failure and success

Anxious to head eastward, on June 13 Lewis and Clark sent out two advance hunters, and began to round up and pack the horses, which numbered about 66.[132] On June 15, after about 6 weeks among the Nez Perces, the expedition set out over the Lolo Trail—without guides. That proved to be a mistake. Once in the mountains, each mile became more difficult. The snow-covered trail was sometimes traceable only by trees from which Indians had peeled the outer bark to obtain the inner bark for food. The horses were hampered by fallen timber and brush, and often slipped on the icy steep path. Snowbanks were sometimes 12 to 15 feet deep. The frigid cold numbed feet and hands.

Finally, Drouillard, the principal tracker, expressed doubt about his ability to find the way through the mountains at that time of the year. Catastrophe was near at hand. The expedition was nearly lost, barely able to move through the deep snow, short of food for steeds and men, and running the risk of losing all the papers and baggage as well as lives. On the morning of June 17, on a high mountain to the northeast of Hungry Creek and just west of Sherman Pass, the commanders decided to turn back to Weippe Prairie—one of the few times they ever retreated from an objective.[133] Most of the baggage, some food, and the papers and instruments were cached in the trees.

The next day, their anxiety to cross the Lolo Trail surprisingly undiminished, Lewis and Clark dispatched Drouillard and Shannon back to the Nez Perce villages to try to obtain guides with instructions to offer them as much as three guns and 10 horses. During the hazardous descent of the mountains, Potts and his horse fell in swollen Hungry Creek. The current rolled them over several times among the rocks, and one of Potts' knives badly slashed a leg.

Finally out of the mountains, on June 21 the party met two Indians who were planning to move over the trail. Uncertain as to the success of Drouillard and Shannon, the captains convinced them to wait for the expedition's return and act as guides. That evening, the exhausted party arrived back at the same camp on Weippe Prairie it had set out from. Two days later, Drouillard and Shannon brought in three young Indians, who had agreed to serve as guides for the price of two guns.

The next day, the 24th, undaunted by its recent failure, the expedition set out once again with the guides. At the foot of the mountains, it met the two others who had agreed to wait and plunged into the towering heights. Two days later, the cache on the mountain to the northeast of Hungry Creek was recovered. The snow averaged about 7 feet in depth, 4 feet or so less than before, but the frozen crust supported the horses. In the evening a sixth Nez Perce, who had been following the trail of the group in the snow, caught up and joined it. A rest halt was made in the mountain depths the next day at a place where natives had piled a conical mound of stones 6 to 8 feet high and at its peak placed a pine pole 15 feet tall.[134]

On June 28 the expedition passed the point where it had climbed up the trail from the Lochsa River the preceding year. This time, it kept to the mountain trail and did not descend to the river, where Old Toby had mistakenly gone the year before. The next day, the party rejoined its westbound route, passing through Packers Meadow just to the east of Lolo Pass and entering present Montana from Idaho.

The worst of the trip was over. Seven miles farther, a stop was made at Lolo Hot Springs, on the north side of Lolo Creek, which the Indians had dammed to create a bathing pool. Most of the men bathed in the steaming waters, whose temperature Lewis found comparable to the hottest of the hot springs in Virginia. The Indian guides, to the party's amazement, alternated dips in the hot water of the springs with plunges in the ice-cold creek.

The next day, June 30, the expedition arrived back at Travelers Rest campsite. In 6 days, averaging about 26 miles daily, it had traversed the Lolo Trail, whose length Lewis and Clark estimated at 156 miles. Because the route was better known, Old Toby's detour was avoided, and the crusted snow held up under the horses, the eastbound journey was much less harrowing and was accomplished much more quickly than the westbound, which had required 11 days.

Separation at Travelers Rest

As they had done the year before, Lewis and Clark stayed at Travelers Rest for a couple of days to allow the men and horses to recuperate. Once again, after a long period, game was abundant and the hunters were busy. The captains also took advantage of the time to work out the details of the forthcoming exploration—considerably different than on the westbound phase.

According to plans laid back at Fort Clatsop, from Travelers Rest two groups would separately explore the Marias and the Yellowstone. Lewis and a small party would travel over the shortcut to the Great Falls of the Missouri and investigate the Upper Marias. Clark and the bulk of the group would proceed via Camp Fortunate and the Beaverhead and Jefferson Rivers to the Three Forks of the Missouri, from which they would move overland to explore the Yellowstone. At the point that it was found to be navigable, canoes would be built, and Sergeant Pryor and a few men would travel ahead with the horses on a special mission to the Mandan villages.

Meantime, Lewis would leave a few men to recover the cache at the upper portage camp near the Great Falls, put the equipment in order, and await a detachment of the Clark party bringing up the canoes and the supplies from the Camp Fortunate cache via the Three Forks. Together the two detachments would make the portage, pick up the white pirogue and cache that had been left near the lower portage camp, and proceed to the mouth of the Marias to rendezvous with Lewis. The Lewis and Clark segments were to reunite at the mouth of the Yellowstone.

Pryor, on his special assignment, was to carry a message, apparently drafted by Lewis and Clark at Travelers Rest, to the North West Company's Hugh Heney, who had favorably impressed them the previous year at the Mandan villages. For a specified salary and expenses, as well as the promise of consideration for a position as U.S. Indian agent among the Sioux, Heney was asked to persuade some key chiefs of that nation—especially the hostile Tetons—to accompany him and the expedition to Washington. There the power of the U.S. Government would be demonstrated to the Indians. He was authorized to use some of Pryor's horses to purchase gifts for them from the village tribes.

The message also advised Heney that the expedition had descended the Columbia to its mouth and en route had discovered and named the Marias, which it planned to explore, as well as the Yellowstone, on the return trip. Lewis and Clark probably hoped that Heney would pass this information on to his company and governmental officials in Montreal, who would thus at the earliest possible moment

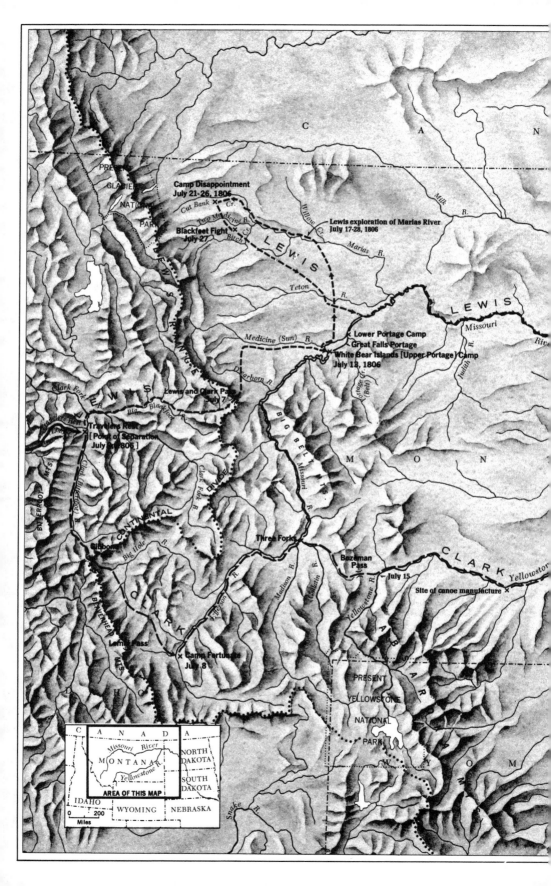

Camp Disappointment
July 21-26, 1806

Cut Bank Cr.
Two Medicine R.
Blackfeet Fight
July 27
Birch Cr.

Lewis exploration of Marias River
July 17-28, 1806

L E W I S

C   A   N   A   D   A

Milk R.

Willow Cr.

Marias R.

L E W I S

Teton R.

Missouri

Medicine (Sun) R.

Lower Portage Camp
Great Falls Portage
White Bear Islands [Upper Portage] Camp
July 13, 1806

River

Clark Fork

Dearborn R.

Indian R.

L E W I S

Lewis and Clark Pass
July 7

Big Blackfoot R.

Portage Cr. (Belt)

Traveler's Rest
[Point of Separation
July 3, 1806]

BIG BELT MTS.

B I T T E R R O O T   M T S.

Clark Fork R.

CONTINENTAL

DIVIDE

Missouri R.

M   O   N   T   A   N   A

Gibbons

Big Hole R.

Three Forks

Bozeman Pass

C L A R K

Yellowstone

July 15

Site of canoe manufacture

Lemhi Pass

Jefferson R.

Camp Fortunate
July 8

Madison R.

Gallatin R.

Yellowstone R.

C L A R K

BEAVERHEAD MTS.

I   D   A   H   O

PRESENT
YELLOWSTONE

NATIONAL

PARK

W Y O M

Snake R.

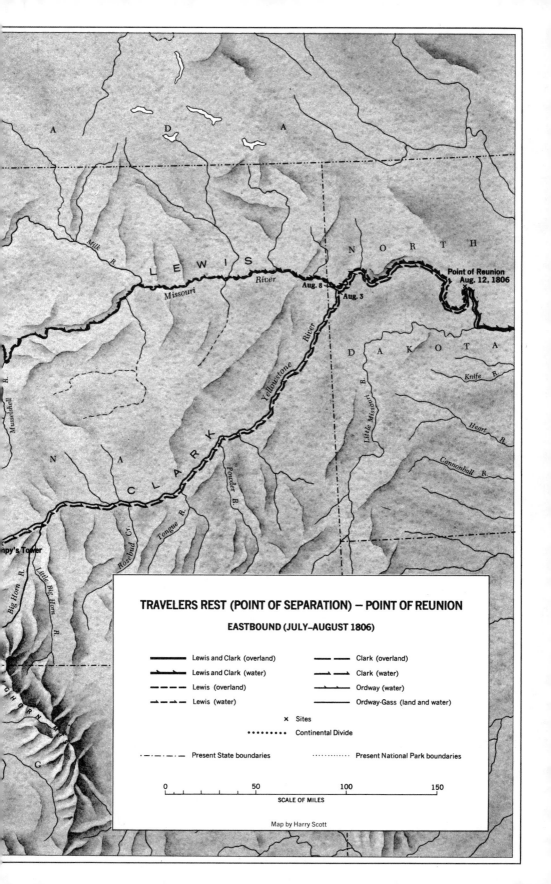

A   D   A

Milk R.

L E W I S

Missouri   *River*

Aug. 8

Aug. 3

N   O   R   T   H

Point of Reunion
Aug. 12, 1806

D   A   K   O   T   A

Knife R.

Yellowstone River

Little Missouri R.

Heart R.

Cannonball R.

Musselshell R.

N   A

C L A R K

Powder R.

Tongue R.

Rosebud Cr.

Big Horn R.

Little Big Horn R.

npy's Tower

BIGHORN MTS.

G

TRAVELERS REST (POINT OF SEPARATION) – POINT OF REUNION

EASTBOUND (JULY–AUGUST 1806)

———— Lewis and Clark (overland)	— — — Clark (overland)
—⚓— Lewis and Clark (water)	—▸—▸ Clark (water)
– – – Lewis (overland)	—▸—▸ Ordway (water)
–▸–▸ Lewis (water)	———— Ordway-Gass (land and water)

×   Sites

•••••••• Continental Divide

–·–·–·– Present State boundaries   ············· Present National Park boundaries

0   50   100   150

SCALE OF MILES

Map by Harry Scott

be informed of investigation by the United States of its northern boundary and its claim to the Columbia country. If Heney was not at the Mandan villages, according to Pryor's instructions, he was to leave some of the horses there and take the others to the British posts on the Assiniboine River in Canada in the hope of contacting Heney there. Pryor would finally rejoin the main body at the Mandan villages.

None of these arrangements were to work out precisely as planned. This was the first and only time the expedition deliberately divided in such a manner to pursue different missions. The partition of the group quashed the spirits of all the men. They realized that the Lewis party, performing the most daring exploration of the entire expedition, was vulnerable to attack by hostile Blackfeet and faced many other dangers in an unknown area.

Lewis called for volunteers. From the many who offered to serve, he chose six men: Drouillard, Sergeant Gass, the Field brothers, Frazer, and Werner. He selected Thompson, McNeal, and Goodrich for the Great Falls portage assignment.

On July 3, 1806, the two elements of the Corps of Discovery started out from Travelers Rest. They were to be separated for 40 days— until August 12.

Lewis follows the shortcut to the Great Falls

Lewis, the nine men, five Nez Perce guides, and 17 horses traveled north down along the Bitterroot River about 10 miles, moved eastward along the Missoula-Hellgate Rivers, and bivouacked that night at a point a mile or two to the east of the present city of Missoula.[135] The next day, on July 4, the guides, who considered the Hellgate area and region to the east a dangerous place because Blackfeet war parties frequented it, said they would go no farther and expressed concern for the safety of the Lewis party. They planned to ascend the Clark Fork to visit a friendly tribe and then return over the Lolo Trail to their homeland. They said the branch of the buffalo road that was being followed eastward would continue to be clearly visible and later run along the Big Blackfoot River, which they called the "River of the Road to Buffaloe." Lewis, who deeply appreciated their services, smoked the pipe with them, gave them some meat, and said goodbye.

Lewis and his men, proceeding onward, entered Hellgate Canyon,

Artist's rendition in the mid-1850's of Hellgate, the defile where the river of the same name cuts a passage through a spur of mountains near present Missoula, Mont. Lewis and his party passed through the region in July 1806 en route to the Marias River on the return from the Pacific.

followed it eastward to the Big Blackfoot River, and moved along the well-marked road. Evidences of a large Blackfeet war party and abandoned camps caused the commander to bolster security. On July 7, at a point about 45 miles northwest of present Helena, the Continental Divide was crossed and the Louisiana Territory and the United States reentered via a pass that came to be known as Lewis and Clark Pass—though Clark never saw it.

The next day, the first buffalo on the return trip were viewed. Busy pursuing them and other game, Lewis bypassed the Dearborn River route to the Missouri and detoured northward to the Sun River, which he descended to the Missouri, and on July 11 arrived opposite the upper portage camp of the year before. Some 8 days had been required to come from Travelers Rest to the Great Falls area—3 more than the Nez Perce guides had said was necessary, but the hunting detour probably accounted for the difference.

The men set to work building a round Mandan-style bull boat, stretching a buffalo hide over a timber framework, and fashioned a canoe covered with two other hides. On the evening of the 12th, the party with its baggage crossed in the boats to the south side of the Missouri, swimming the horses across. The next day, it moved to the upper portage camp.

The grizzlies, rattlers, and prickly pear in the area were found to be as abundant and troublesome as before. The grizzlies, as well as big timber, or lobo, wolves, which howled continuously day and night, feasted on buffalo. When the year-old cache at the upper portage camp was opened, it was discovered that the river had risen so high that water had entered it, destroying all the plant specimens and bearskins and dampening some of the papers and articles. A stopper had come out of one of the medicine bottles, spoiling most of the other medicines.

The next day, the 14th, the wagon wheels and the framework of the "Experiment" were dug up and found to be in fairly good condition. The following afternoon, Drouillard, who for several days had been searching on the north side of the Missouri for seven horses that had disappeared before the crossing was made to the south side, came into camp. Lewis, who had given him up as lost to a grizzly, was happy to see him again but sorry to learn that he had pursued but failed to catch the Indians who had stolen the animals.

Only 10 horses remaining, Lewis had little choice but to alter his plans for the Marias exploration. He reduced the number of men from six to three and chose the three woodsmen best equipped to meet any emergency: Drouillard and the Field brothers. They would take six horses and leave four with Sergeant Gass and his five men.[136] The latter group was to wait at the upper portage camp until the arrival of Sergeant Ordway and the nine men from Clark's party with the canoes. Then they were jointly to portage the canoes and baggage around the Great Falls, recover the white pirogue and supplies cached at the lower portage camp, and proceed downriver to the mouth of the Marias to meet Lewis. Lewis, who expected to be back there by August 5 if he did not meet some misfortune, instructed Gass to wait until September 1 before moving down to the mouth of the Yellowstone and reuniting with Clark's party.

Lewis explores the Upper Marias

On July 16 Drouillard and Reuben Field set out from the upper portage camp with the six horses, which they swam across the Missouri above the White Bear Islands to the lower side of the Sun River. Lewis and Joseph Field, transporting the baggage in the canoe, moved down the Missouri to that point. After abandoning the boat, the four men swam the mounts across the Sun, and spent the night along the Great Falls. The water was lower than the year before but the falls were still, in Lewis' words, a "sublimely grand object."

With the rising sun, the explorers pushed northward over plains resembling an ocean. They arrived the following evening, the 18th, at the Marias, well up from the mouth. They knew they were in the Blackfeet heartland and maintained a vigilant day and night watch. On the afternoon of the 21st, the river forked into a northern branch, Cut Bank Creek, and a southern one, Two Medicine River. Beginning to fear that the Marias system did not extend as far north as he had hoped, to 49° or preferably 50° latitude, Lewis moved some 28 miles up Cut Bank Creek.

On July 22 camp was made about 12 miles northeast of present Browning, Mont., in a beautiful bottom about 20 miles from the foot of the Rockies. In the distance, Lewis saw that the creek curved toward the mountains to his southwest, and knew he had reached the northernmost point of the Marias system. He decided to stay for awhile at this site, which he called Camp Disappointment, to rest the horses and men and make geographical and astronomical observations. This camp was the northernmost of the expedition and only a few miles west of the place on Cut Bank Creek that represented the northernmost point attained.

Drouillard, on his commander's instructions, the next day, the 23d, proceeded up Cut Bank Creek and confirmed Lewis' visual judgment. He brought back disquieting news. He had discovered a 10-day-old abandoned camp of 11 lodges. Blackfeet, with whom Lewis wished to "avoid an interview," must be near! For the next 2 days the weather was so rainy, windy, and cloudy that he was unable to make instrument observations and thus could not determine the latitude (48°40′ N.). The same conditions prevailing on the morning of the 26th, he decided he could wait no longer to begin the trip back to the Missouri. He and the three men struck out southward, crossed Two Medicine River to its south side, and began to follow it downstream.

Lewis clashes with Blackfeet

After lunch, Lewis and the Field brothers climbed the river bluffs while Drouillard continued down the valley to hunt. When Lewis

The "X" indicates the site of Camp Disappointment, Mont., on the south bank of Cut Bank Creek near the northernmost point reached by the explorers. Lewis and his three companions bivouacked at this place during the period July 22–26, 1806. Three local people, Edward Mathison, Robert H. Anderson, and Helen B. West, researched and located the site.

reached the top he saw, a mile or so away, also on the bluffs, several Indians and about 30 horses. He studied them with his spyglass, noted they were intently watching something below in the valley, and surmised they had discovered Drouillard. Believing him to be in danger, Lewis felt he had no alternative but to approach the natives, who had not yet seen him. With Joseph Field holding aloft a U.S. flag, brought along for just such a purpose, the three men slowly advanced toward the Indians. Soon noticing them, the latter seemed to grow confused and milled about. Because the 30 horses so inordinately outnumbered the eight Indians he had counted and half the steeds were saddled, Lewis feared that other braves were nearby out of sight.

Members of the Cut Bank, Mont., Boy Scout troop standing approximately at the spot where Lewis and the Field brothers on July 26, 1806, discovered a group of Blackfeet about 2 miles away (marked by arrow) intently watching something in the valley below. Correctly assuming it was Drouillard, who was hunting along Two Medicine River, Lewis decided to approach the Indians as friends. The Cut Bank troop, aided by Edward Mathison, Robert H. Anderson, and Helen B. West, identified the places associated with the incident and the subsequent fight with the natives.

Nevertheless, deciding that retreat might be considered a sign of weakness and would jeopardize the safety of Drouillard, Lewis moved forward. When his group was about a quarter of a mile away from the Indians, one of them mounted and rode forward at full speed. He pulled up short at about 300 feet and studied the white men, who had by this time dismounted and were walking forward, Lewis beckoning with his hand. Suddenly, the rider turned and rode back to his companions. Certain that these were Blackfeet and anticipating difficulty, Lewis resolved to resist to the last and vowed he would die before he would give up his papers, instruments, and gun. He cautioned the Field brothers to keep on the alert.

The two groups cautiously approached and greeted each other. In sign language, the Indians expressed a desire to smoke the pipe. Lewis, anxious for Drouillard's safety and needing his help in sign communication, told them he had his pipe and suggested that, because they had been watching Drouillard and knew where he was, they send a man with Reuben Field to bring him back. The Indians agreed to do so. While awaiting Drouillard's return, Lewis learned the Indians were Blackfeet. Three claimed to be chiefs, though he doubted it. He gave one a medal, another a flag, and the third a handkerchief. He observed that only two possessed guns, and the rest bows and arrows and tomahawks. By this time, too, he was certain the entire party totaled but eight. Satisfied they could be controlled if hostile, despite their 2 to 1 numerical superiority, he suggested that everyone camp together down by Two Medicine River. Drouillard, Reuben Field, and the Indian joined the group, which made its way down the 250-foot bluffs.

About 4 miles below the mouth of Badger Creek in a small bottom on the south side of the river, the Blackfeet erected a large semi-circular tent of dressed buffalo skins. Lewis and Drouillard accepted an invitation to bed down inside, and the Field brothers decided to stay outside in front of the fire.

That evening, July 26, Lewis carried on an extensive conversation with the Blackfeet through Drouillard. They claimed to be part of a large band, accompanied by a white man, that was encamped about a half day's march to the west at the foot of the Rockies on the "main branch" of the Marias. Another sizable band, they said, was hunting buffalo to the west and expected to be at the mouth of the river in a few days. The Indians said they traded at a Saskatchewan River post about 150 miles away.

Lewis told them about the purpose and accomplishments of the expedition, his plans to reunite with the rest of it at the mouth of the Marias, and the desire of the U.S. Government to establish peace between all tribes and to initiate trade with them. During the night, the four explorers, fearful the Blackfeet might steal their horses or perpetrate other treachery, took turns on watch.

At daybreak, the 27th, the fears were realized. The natives awakened and crowded around the fire. Joseph Field, on watch duty, had carelessly left his gun behind him near where his brother was sleeping. Stealthily one Indian slipped behind Joseph and grabbed both guns, while two others crept into the tent and took the guns of Drouillard and Lewis. Seeing the latter movement, Joseph turned to seize his gun, but saw the Indian running away with it as well as that of Reuben. He yelled to Reuben, who jumped up, and the two gave chase. Within 50 or 60 paces, they overtook the Indian and wrested their guns from him. Reuben plunged a knife into his heart.

Meantime, almost simultaneously Drouillard, inside the shelter, was awakened by the commotion outside and saw the Indian seizing his rifle. He sprang on him and pulled it away. This scuffle awakened Lewis, who automatically reached for his gun—only to find it gone. He drew a pistol from his holster, pursued the other Blackfoot, who was running off with his rifle, called to him, and told him to lay it down. He was in the act of doing so when the Field brothers returned and requested permission to shoot him. Lewis, who had issued standing orders not to harm any native unless one's life was in danger, noted that the Indian was subdued and denied the request, as well as a similar one from Drouillard. The brave dropped the gun and walked away.

The Blackfeet, thwarted in their disarming effort, next tried to steal the horses. To prevent this, Lewis told the men to shoot if necessary. Drouillard and the Field brothers chased most of the Indians, who were driving part of the mounts upriver, while Lewis pursued two others who were herding off another group. About 900 feet from camp, the latter two turned into a gulch. One jumped behind a rock. The other, armed with a gun, turned and at 30 paces faced Lewis, who shot him in the abdomen. He fell to his knees, partly raised himself, and returned the fire. The bareheaded Lewis felt the breeze from the bullet as it whistled over his head. His adversary then crawled behind a rock and before long undoubtedly died.

His shot pouch back at camp and unable to reload his rifle, Lewis set out to return, meeting Drouillard on the way. Leaving the Field brothers to chase the other Indians stealing the horses, the latter had come to help out after he had heard the shots. The brothers soon rode in with four of the group's six horses. Faced with the prospect of a ride for their lives, the party abandoned one of these and took four of the best Indian mounts, leaving nine behind. The

High Plains country on the north side of the Missouri River near where the Marias joins it. This jumbled, broken landscape, Blackfeet country at the time of Lewis and Clark, is now sometimes called the Marias River Breaks. The far distant bluff line in the left center marks the Missouri River trough.

Indians, who had all fled, had taken the remainder or they had scattered.

One Indian lay dead and another dead or dying, and the four men feared their erstwhile adversaries would soon come back with reinforcements. Departure was hasty. The seven horses were saddled and packed and the Indian possessions lying all around were burned, except for an Indian gun and some buffalo meat that were taken. Lewis also repossessed the flag he had given to one of the Blackfeet, but left the medal around the neck of another so that the tribe "might be informed who we were." [137]

Fearing that Blackfeet might be on their trail or ahead of them trying to cut them off, the men began a forced ride southeastward toward the Missouri en route to the mouth of the Marias to reunite with the Gass-Ordway party. By 3 o'clock in the afternoon, when he stopped the men and horses for an hour and a half to eat and rest, Lewis estimated they had covered 63 miles. Before dark, when they halted again for 2 hours and killed a buffalo for food, they made another 17 miles. The march continued at a more leisurely pace another 20 miles in the moonlight, during which many herds of buffalo were passed, until 2:00 a.m., when a stop was made to obtain some sleep and let the horses graze.

A providential meeting

So sore they could hardly stand and still deeply fatigued, at day-break of July 28 the men struggled into the saddle again with the full realization that their lives and possibly those of their companions on the river depended on their every exertion. In about 12 miles, they realized they were near the Missouri and thought they heard the sound of a gun. Eight miles farther, well above the mouth of the Marias, they unmistakably heard the "joyfull sound" of rifle fire. Running down to the riverbank, with "unspeakable satisfaction" they saw the Gass-Ordway boat party en route downriver from the Great Falls planning to meet Lewis at the mouth of the Marias.[138]

Lewis and his companions had ridden 120 miles in slightly more than 24 hours. They stripped their possessions from their horses, turned them loose, and embarked in the boats without delay shortly after 9:00 a.m. In view of the Blackfeet threat, it was fortunate that Lewis and his three men happened to encounter their comrades. The substantially increased manpower and weaponry would help stave off any attack.

THE portage of the Great Falls had been smoothly accomplished. On July 19, or 3 days after Lewis and his companions had departed from the upper portage camp, Ordway and his nine men from the Clark group had arrived and joined Sergeant Gass and his five men from the Lewis contingent. The Ordway party, bringing along the six canoes and the supplies from the cache at Camp Fortunate, had traveled down the Beaverhead and Jefferson to the Great Falls via the Three Forks, where they had separated from Clark and the land party.

At the upper portage camp, one of the six canoes, damaged and considered to be too heavy to portage, was broken up and used for firewood. The other five were placed on the wagons and loaded with the baggage and equipment Ordway had brought as well as what remained of the already-opened cache at the upper portage camp. The portage, utilizing the four horses Lewis had left behind to tow the wagons, was far easier and faster than it was the year before, though much less manpower was available. Only 8 days were consumed in contrast to 11 days the year before. At the lower portage camp, the cache and the white pirogue that had been hidden there the year before were retrieved.

On July 27 Gass and Willard crossed the Missouri with the four horses to take them overland to the mouth of the Marias, where Lewis planned to use them for hunting purposes. The rest of the party set out in the five canoes and the pirogue for the same destination, where all planned to reunite with Lewis. It was the boat party that he met so fortuitously some distance above the mouth of the Marias on July 28.

Lewis moves downstream

About noon that day, the reunited party arrived at the mouth of the Marias. After hastily investigating the area for Blackfeet, they opened the main cache and several smaller ones, all on the riverbank. The main cache had caved in and the bulk of the contents had been injured, except for most of the food. The small caches were found to be in good order. At 1:00 p.m. Sergeant Gass and Private Willard arrived with the horses from the Great Falls. Everyone then moved over to the small island at the mouth of the river where the red pirogue had been hidden. It had decayed so badly it was beyond repair, but the nails and iron parts were salvaged.

Spurred by evidence of abandoned Blackfeet camps, Lewis and his party, leaving the horses behind, moved rapidly downstream that same day, July 28. When they reached the mouth of the Yellowstone, on August 7, they were disappointed not to find Clark there. They surmised from the name "Lewis" on a piece of paper attached to a pole and the remnant of a note found at an old Clark campsite that game was so scarce and the mosquitoes so troublesome he had proceeded farther downriver to wait for them.[139]

As Lewis glided down the Missouri, each day he expected to catch up with Clark, but found him always ahead, though campsite evidence showed the distance shortening. Unable to calculate how soon they would reunite, Lewis decided to "proceed as tho' he was not before me and leave the rest to the chapter of accedents."

On August 11 Lewis was seriously wounded while hunting with Cruzatte. Separated, the two were looking for a wounded elk. Lewis found it and was about to administer the *coup de grace* when, from out of nowhere, a bullet smashed through the top rear of his left thigh. It fortunately missed the bone and artery, and ripped a gash in his right buttock. Dressed in brown leather like everyone else, he assumed his companion, one-eyed and nearsighted at that, had mistaken him for an elk. Lewis called out to him several times but received no response, though the sound of the gun had been close. Thinking then that possibly Indians had shot him, he hurriedly limped back to the boats to warn the others. A scouting party found no warriors but soon came back with a chagrined Cruzatte, who admitted he had thought Lewis was an elk. Lewis, with the assistance of Sergeant Gass, removed his clothes and dressed his wounds. He stretched out in the white pirogue, and spent a painful and feverish night.

At 8 o'clock the next morning two American independent trappers, Joseph Dickson and Forrest Hancock, were met. They said they had passed and talked to the Clark contingent the previous noon. Continuing on, Lewis reunited with it at 1 o'clock.

Clark proceeds to Camp Fortunate and the Three Forks

While Lewis had been exploring the unknown country of the Upper Marias, Clark had been investigating some new terrain himself. He, too, set out from Travelers Rest on July 3, 1806. With 18 enlisted men,[140] York, Charbonneau, Sacagawea, her baby, and 49 horses and a colt, he moved up the Bitterroot Valley. July 4 was celebrated with a "sumptious" dinner of venison and roots, but no whisky was available for the occasion.

The westbound route was employed as far as Ross's Hole. From there to Camp Fortunate, one recommended by the Flatheads was utilized that Clark estimated would save 2 days. It deviated considerably from the old one. Instead of moving through Lost Trail Pass and proceeding down the valleys of the Salmon and the Lemhi, then through Lemhi Pass, this time, on July 6, the explorers negotiated the Continental Divide at Gibbons Pass, not far to the northeast of Lost Trail Pass, and moved into the Big Hole River Valley.[141] Sacagawea, who knew the country, served as a guide. Camp Fortunate, at the forks of the Beaverhead—164 miles by Clark's estimate from Travelers Rest over an "excellent road"—was attained on the afternoon of July 8.[142]

The nicotine-starved men, who had been without real tobacco for about 3 months, were so impatient to reach the supply they knew was in the cache that they barely took time to obey Clark's order to remove the saddles from their horses first. Clark saved some of the tobacco and later sent it with Ordway to the Lewis group. All the other articles were safe but somewhat damp. Six of the seven canoes, sunk in the pond, were undamaged. One that had a hole in the side and a split bow, probably inflicted by an Indian, was cut up for firewood and paddles.

No time was lost in refloating, repairing, relaunching, and loading the six boats. Early on the morning of July 10, part of the contingent set out in them for the Three Forks while Sergeant Pryor and six men took the horses overland to the same destination. The two groups stayed close together as they moved down the Beaverhead and Jefferson. The downriver journey, aided by the current, was far more rapid than on the westbound trip despite navigational obstacles. On the third day at noon, the main party arrived at the Three Forks an hour later than Pryor.

Clark probes the Yellowstone

Clark wasted no time. He directed that all the baggage and equipment he would need for his Yellowstone exploration be removed from the canoes. After lunch, Sergeant Ordway, carrying a letter from Clark to Lewis, and nine men [143] pushed down the Missouri to rendezvous with the Gass detachment of the Lewis party at the Great Falls. Late in the afternoon, Clark and the rest of his group moved overland with the 49 horses and colt on what was to prove to be one of the easiest—almost idyllic—phases of the entire journey to the Pacific and return. With him were 12 persons: York, Charbonneau, Sacagawea, her baby, Sergeant Pryor, and seven privates.[144] The expedition was now divided into three nearly equal parts: Lewis (including the Gass detachment at the Great Falls), Ordway, and Clark.

Sacagawea, who as a young girl had often visited this part of the country during the summer with her people, knew it well and guided Clark. As the party proceeded rapidly over plains and hills up the lush Gallatin and East Gallatin Rivers, large herds of deer, elk,

Alfred Jacob Miller (1810-1874) was brought to the West by Captain William Drummond Stewart for the fur trade rendezvous of 1837. He, like George Catlin, was one of the first artists to travel into the Rocky Mountain region. His drawings and paintings are some of the best sources for learning what the West was like in the early part of the nineteenth century, especially the Rocky Mountains.

antelope, and other game were viewed on the plains and in the river bottoms, including "emence quantities of beaver" as well as otter.

Following a well-traced buffalo road, on July 15 the group crossed Bozeman Pass and dropped down to the Upper Yellowstone at a point 9 miles from the pass near present Livingston, Mont. There the river turned abruptly eastward after exiting from the rugged, snow-capped mountains of the Gallatin Range to the south, in today's Yellowstone National Park. Clark estimated the distance from Three Forks to the place he struck the Yellowstone River as 48 miles, all except the last 18 of which he noted were navigable by canoe.

Clark was disappointed that the trees along the Upper Yellowstone were not large enough for canoes that could carry any more than three people—too small for his purposes. He was also concerned as he moved downriver along the north bank at numerous signs that the Crow Indians, who frequented the area, were near and were keeping the party under observation.

On July 18 Gibson suffered a painful wound when his horse threw him. The next morning, he had to be placed on a litter carried by a gentle horse. As the day wore on, however, his agony intensified

The nimble-footed dexterity of Rocky Mountain bighorn sheep in high and dangerous spots amazed the two captains. The species was first seen near the mouth of the Yellowstone in April 1805, but large numbers were in evidence in the Missouri River Breaks region. Apparently the first to be killed were the four Clark shot while he was descending the Yellowstone in 1806.

so much that he had to be removed from the mount, and left behind with two men to rest for an hour or so. In the evening, 4 miles beyond at a point on the north side of the river about halfway between present Laurel and Columbus, Mont., Clark found some cottonwoods of the appropriate size for canoes and decided to camp there, even though Charbonneau reported seeing across the river in the distance an Indian, the first seen on the Yellowstone.

During the 5-day stay, Indians made away with 24 of the 50 horses, which had been turned out to graze. Two dugout canoes, 28 feet long, were constructed and lashed together for stability. On the morning of July 24, Sergeant Pryor, Shannon, Windsor, and Hall set out overland along the river with the remaining horses, headed for the Mandan villages with the message to Heney. Clark, his group

Pompey's Pillar is now a Bureau of Land Management Interpretive Site in Montana for the Lewis & Clark Trail along the Yellowstone River. William Clark and his returning party visited this location on July 25, 1806.

dwindled to only eight, pushed downriver in the canoes, passing the site of Billings before the sun set.[145]

The following afternoon, a stop was made on the south side of the river near a remarkable sandstone formation. It was located about 250 paces back from the river and measured some 400 paces in circumference. Clark estimated its height at 200 feet. He named it "Pompy's Tower" after Sacagawea's infant son, whom he had nicknamed "Pomp" or "Little Pomp," but today it is known as Pompeys Pillar. Clark and some of the others climbed the only accessible side, the northeast. Near a spot on the path leading to the top where Indians had etched animal and other figures in the rock, Clark inscribed his name and the date. Although somewhat altered, they are still readable today. On the grass-covered soil of the summit, the natives had piled two heaps of stones. The surrounding countryside was visible for a distance of 40 miles. The plains were alive with buffalo, elk, and wolves. Beyond, were the Rockies and other mountains.

The rest of the trip down the Yellowstone was comparatively

uneventful. Early on August 3 Clark arrived at its juncture with the Missouri, where plans called for him to meet Lewis. But conditions were miserable. The mosquitoes drove everyone crazy; Pomp's face was badly swollen from bites. No buffalo were present. Elk were plentiful, but the meat was difficult to dry in the sun, and even then it spoiled easily. Late the next afternoon, leaving a message informing Lewis of his plans, Clark pushed down the Missouri. The trouble with mosquitoes continuing on successive days, he went farther than he had originally contemplated.

On the morning of August 8, to everybody's surprise, Sergeant Pryor and his three companions came floating downriver in two Mandan-type bull boats. Pryor reported that, the second night out, Crow Indians had stolen all the horses, and prevented completion of the mission. Demonstrating their self-sufficiency and mastery of life in the raw wilderness, the unhorsed men—outdistanced more each day by the main body—kept calm. They walked to Pompy's Tower, killed some buffalo, and stretched the skins over a light wooden framework to make two circular bull boats, each about 7 feet in diameter. All four individuals rode in one; the second was a reserve in case the first sank.

The reunited party, taking along the bull boats, continued downriver. Three days later, on August 11, two trappers, Joseph Dickson and Forrest Hancock, who were on their way from the Illinois River to the Yellowstone, were met. They were the first white men anyone in the expedition had seen since mid-April 1805.

Clark and Lewis reunite

At noon of the 12th, the Lewis group finally caught up with the Clark contingent. It must have been a happy reunion, yet the two captains described it prosaically in their journals. Clark was alarmed to find Lewis, shot in the thigh, lying in the white pirogue, but was relieved to learn that the injury was not serious. Each of the five detachments—Clark, Lewis, Gass, Pryor, and Ordway—compared notes on what had happened to the others during the past 6 weeks. In view of the dangers that had been involved, the absence of personnel losses was especially heartening.

That same afternoon, Dickson and Hancock, who for some reason had temporarily abandoned their plans to travel to the Yellowstone and decided to return to the Mandan villages with the expedition, arrived in camp. Losing no time, the entire group set out that afternoon in the five canoes and the white pirogue Lewis had brought, as well as the two lashed-together canoes that Clark had built on the Upper Yellowstone. The two bull boats were left behind. Two days later, on August 14, the Mandan villages came into view.

Farewells at the Mandan villages

This time, the stay was short, only 3 days. For translator, Lewis and Clark utilized René Jessaume, still residing at the villages. Councils with the Mandan chiefs Black Cat and Sheheke ("Big White"), the Minitari Le Borgne ("One-Eye"), and others revealed that the two tribes had not kept peace with the Arikaras as they had promised the previous year. This brought a reproach from Lewis and Clark. As soon as the expedition had departed in the spring, the Minitaris had sent a war party into the Rockies and defeated a Shoshoni village, possibly that of Cameahwait. The Sioux and Arikaras had also raided the Mandans, stolen horses, and killed a few men. In addition, the latter tribe was now divided by internal quarrels.

A visit to the site of Fort Mandan, the 1804–5 winter quarters, revealed that most of it had been consumed by flames, apparently a prairie fire. All that remained was one of the rear, or side, huts and some pickets from the front palisade.

At the villages, sad farewells were said to the Charbonneau family, which maintained its home there at the Minitari villages, and to Private Colter. Agreeing that the latter could be spared for the journey to St. Louis, Lewis and Clark granted his request that he be released so he could join Dickson and Hancock on their trapping jaunt to the Yellowstone. Accounts were settled with him on August 16. He was to stay in the wilderness for 4 more years, during which time he was to experience many adventures—one of which was his discovery of present Yellowstone National Park.

On August 17 the captains paid Charbonneau the $500.33⅓ due him for his services and "the price of a horse and Lodge purchased of him for public Service." Leave was taken of him, Sacagawea, and their 19-month-old son.[146] Clark, who had become attached to Little Pomp, offered to take him with him, and raise and educate him. But, because the child had not yet been weaned, it was decided that in a year or so Charbonneau would bring him to Clark.

Lewis and Clark themselves were unable to persuade any of the Mandan and Minitari chiefs, who feared the Sioux, to come to Washington to see the Great White Father. An intermediary was successful. Jessaume, stimulated by the promise of employment as interpreter, convinced the Mandan Sheheke to make the journey, along with his wife and son. Jessaume's traveling companions were his Indian wife, son, and daughter. Two large canoes were fastened together with poles to accommodate the party.

The final downriver sweep

At 2 o'clock in the afternoon on August 17—after bidding adieu to Colter, who set out upriver with the two trappers, and the Charbonneaus—the expedition continued downstream. Four days hence, it made an overnight stop at the Arikara villages. The two captains counciled with the leaders, as well as some visiting Cheyennes, and as usual stressed intertribal peace. Present was the principal Arikara chief, Gray Eyes, who had not been on hand when the expedition passed by in 1804. None of the chiefs of either tribe would agree to make the trip to Washington. They all dreaded the Sioux, and the Arikaras were particularly concerned because Chief Ankedoucharo, who had departed with Warfington the previous year, had not yet come back.

The trek resumed on the 22d. Eight days later, a parley was held with some Tetons, who were encountered at or near present Yankton, S. Dak.—much farther downstream than on the westbound journey. But other close contact with this troublesome group was avoided. Any exchanges were limited to unpleasantries at a distance.

On September 1, near the mouth of the Niobrara River, a council was conducted with some friendly Yanktons. Three days later, Lewis and Clark and a few men, momentarily casting aside their joy as they neared journey's end, made a sad pilgrimage. Visiting Sergeant Floyd's grave, they found that the Indians had opened it and left it half-covered; they refilled it. By this time, Lewis had recovered sufficiently from his thigh wound so that he could walk again.

As the happy voyagers sped home down the Missouri—past the site of Omaha, the mouth of the Platte, the future location of Kansas City, and eastward across present Missouri—they sometimes averaged 70–80 miles a day. Almost daily they met or camped with trading parties moving upriver to trade with the Indians. The Lower Missouri was becoming a thoroughfare. Fellow Americans were a welcome sight. The delicacies they furnished—biscuits, sugar, flour, pork, chocolate, tobacco—were greedily consumed and paid for with corn or a thanks. Whisky, the first since July 4, 1805, brought a grin and a snort. Several men exchanged their leather tunics and beaver hats with traders for linen shirts and cloth hats.

Ears long attuned only to wilderness noises heard news from St. Louis and the East: Alexander Hamilton's death in a duel with Aaron Burr, the founding of Cantonment Belle Fontaine near the mouth of the Missouri, strained governmental relations with England and Spain, Gen. James Wilkinson's assumption of the governorship of Louisiana Territory, and the departure of Capt. Zebulon M. Pike to explore the Red and Arkansas Rivers. The men also learned that most people in the United States—believing rumors they had succumbed to wild animals or Indians, drowned in far-off waters, or suffered enslavement by the Spaniards—had long ago given them up as lost.[147] Yet President Jefferson, who had received no word from the expedition since the keelboat returned from Fort Mandan to St. Louis in the spring of 1805, nevertheless still entertained some hope for its return.

To the surprise and delight of Lewis and Clark, one of the trading parties they met was led by former Capt. Robert McClellan, with whom Clark had served during the 1790's in General Wayne's campaign against the Indians of Ohio and Indiana. With McClellan were Joseph Gravelines and the old Pierre Dorion, who had been associated with the upriver phase of the expedition. The former, hired as an interpreter at the Arikara villages, had returned from the Mandan villages with the keelboat; the latter, who joined as an interpreter not far upriver from St. Charles, had been left behind with the Yankton Sioux to arrange for the visit of chiefs to Washington, D.C.

The two men, under instructions from President Jefferson to make inquiries concerning Lewis and Clark, were carrying messages and gifts from him to the Indians. Gravelines was charged with the difficult task of expressing regret to the Arikaras for the death at Washington, D.C., in April 1806, of Chief Ankedoucharo, whom he had been escorting, and with instructing them in agriculture. Dorion was to help Gravelines pass safely by the hostile Teton Sioux and try to influence some of the chiefs of that tribe to visit President Jefferson.

Another chance occurred to renew an old friendship. John McClallan, also a onetime Army captain and an acquaintance of Lewis, headed another party. He was pursuing a plan that foreshadowed the Santa Fe trade. He intended to travel to the Spanish settlements on the Rio Grande via the Platte River, where he hoped to inveigle some Otos and Pawnees into guiding him to Santa Fe. There he expected that large gifts would convince Spanish officials to establish a route and fix rendezvous points in the Louisiana Territory for trade, which he planned to conduct with packhorse trains.

On the morning of September 20, the two lashed-together canoes that Clark had built on the Upper Yellowstone were set adrift and the party consolidated in the other craft. This was necessary because the eyes of a few of the men had become swollen and inflamed, apparently caused by looking into reflections of the sun on the water, and they were unable to row.

That afternoon, the sight of cows on the bank near La Charette brought enthusiastic shouts. As the voyagers landed at the village, three rounds of small arms fire were returned by nearby trading boats. In the evening, the citizens, whose homes many of the men visited, provided food and entertainment. Dancing with or watching the ladies, the first nonnative women the party had seen in more than 2 years, was a favorite pastime. Departure time in the morning, Sunday, was 7:30 a.m.

Sighting St. Charles late in the afternoon, the boatsmen "plyed thear ores with great dexterity" Clark said, and saluted the enthusiastic and hospitable villagers lining the banks with three rounds from a blunderbuss and small arms fire. Old friends renewed acquaintances during another evening of merriment. Celebration was the new way of life. Cannon boomed a welcome the following night, September 22, at Cantonment Belle Fontaine, on the south bank of the Missouri 3 miles above its mouth. General Wilkinson had established this post in the spring of 1805, the year after the expedition had left Camp Wood, and artillery under Col. Thomas Hunt now occupied it.

Journey's end—the triumphant arrival at St. Louis

Dawn of September 23, 1806, brought the last day of the epic voyage. After traversing the last few miles of the river that had borne them so long and they knew so well, the men crossed the Mississippi

Ending of Sgt. John Ordway's journal, dated September 23, 1806, recording the arrival at St. Louis. The entry reads as follows: "...the Town and landed oppocit the center of the Town. the people gathred on the Shore and Huzzared three cheers. we unloaded the canoes and carried the baggage all up to a store house in Town drew out the canoes. then the party all considerable much rejoiced that we have the Expedition Completed and now we look for boarding in Town and wait for our Settlement and then we entend to return to our native homes to See our parents once more as we have been so long from them —— finis."

and briefly visited Camp Wood, the departure point that rainy day 2 years, 4 months, and 10 days before. The boats then swept downstream to St. Louis and docked at noon. Just about everybody in town, hearkening to advance word from St. Charles or Cantonment Belle Fontaine of the arrival of the group, lined the riverfront cheering.

LONG given up for dead, the men of the expedition must have resembled Robinson Crusoes. These strangers to roofs and beds, with a far-off look in their eyes, the first U.S. citizens to cross the continent, were a special breed. Until the day they died, no matter what fate might inflict or where it might scatter them, they would always stand apart from other men—united in memory with their old comrades of the 7,000-mile trip to the Pacific that no one else could ever share.

THE long and momentous "voyage of discovery" had ended. Its manifold consequences were yet to unfold.

EPILOGUE

TO celebrate the return of the explorers, the leading citizens of St. Louis held a gala dinner and ball in their honor on the evening of September 25 at Christy's Inn.[148] Wined and dined and partaking of dainties they had not tasted in more than 2 years, they heard innumerable toasts to their courage and resourcefulness.

Disbanding the expedition

Closing out the expedition's affairs detained Lewis and Clark in the city longer than they had anticipated—for about a month. On October 10 they settled accounts with Drouillard and discharged all the enlisted men,[149] who the next day received the pay and clothing arrearages due them. At an unknown date, the two captains sold at public auction all the weapons, ammunition, supplies, equipment, and likely the canoes.[150] The sale yielded $408.62. Lewis and Clark also visited with old friends in the area and worked on reports and correspondence.

The eastward jaunt

Probably in late October, Lewis and Clark set out eastward overland. In their party were: York; Ordway; Labiche; probably Frazer; Mandan Chief Sheheke, with his wife and son; his escòrt-interpreter Jessaume, his Indian wife, and their two children; Pierre Chouteau, Osage Indian agent, as well as various chiefs of that tribe he was escorting to Washington; and likely Pierre Provenchere and others from St. Louis.[151] Packhorses apparently carried botanical and zoological specimens the expedition had acquired since leaving Fort Mandan in April 1805, including sea otter and other skins, skeletons of various quadrupeds and birds, and a plant and seed collection.

The group arrived in Louisville on November 5, 1806.[152] Everyone, including the Indians in their finery, attended a grand ball given especially for them. Lewis and Clark undoubtedly visited George Rogers and Jonathan Clark, and paid a call on Lucy (Clark) Croghan at Locust Grove.[153] Gass, who had been waiting at Vincennes to meet Lewis, came to Louisville when he learned the latter had deleted a planned stop at Vincennes.[154]

William Clark and York stayed behind at Louisville. The former planned to spend some time with his relatives and then proceed to Fincastle, Va., to court Julia ("Judith") Hancock, after whom he had named the Judith River in Montana. About mid-November Lewis and the rest of the party headed east.[155] At Frankfort, Ky., Chouteau and his Osages separated from the rest; and traveled via Lexington, Ky., to Washington, D.C., where they arrived sometime before December 24, a few days ahead of Lewis. Meantime, moving from Frankfort over the Wilderness Road through Cumberland Gap into Virginia, Lewis reached Locust Hill estate, his birthplace along Ivy Creek, in plenty of time to spend Christmas with his mother, Mrs. Lucy Marks. While there, as Jefferson had probably requested, he took Sheheke and his party to see Mandan and other Indian artifacts that had been assembled at Monticello.

Lewis' stay in Washington

Lewis and his party arrived in Washington on December 28.[156] He and his Indian charges, objects of special attention along with

Chouteau's Osages, were quickly swept up in a social whirl. The Indians received personal audiences with President Jefferson, and he honored them with a New Year's Day levee at the White House.[157] Lewis, and Clark *in absentia*, were feted on January 14 at a banquet presided over by Maj. Robert Brent and attended by prominent Washington residents, Congressmen, Government officials, Sheheke, Chouteau, and Provenchere.[158] This celebration had been postponed from an earlier date in the hope that Clark could be present, but he did not make an appearance in the city until a few days afterwards.[159]

Clark visits the Capital City

Clark spent about 7 weeks in Washington. He visited with Lewis and probably called on President Jefferson. About the time Clark left town, Congress affirmed his appointment by Jefferson as Superintendent of Indian Affairs for Louisiana Territory and his nomination by Secretary of War Dearborn as brigadier general of militia for the Territory.[160]

Clark goes back to St. Louis

On March 10, 1807, Clark set out for St. Louis, where he faced the task of sending Sheheke back to his people. After a stop at Fincastle to see his sweetheart once again, he proceeded to Louisville, where he paused for a time before pushing on to his destination. He arrived there at the end of June or early in July 1807 to take up his new duties.

Clark attempts to send Sheheke home

Clark assigned the task of returning Sheheke to Ens. Nathaniel H. Pryor, who had been a sergeant with the Lewis and Clark Expedition. In the summer of 1807, he led a detachment of 13 soldiers, which included the expedition's George Shannon and probably George Gibson. Accompanying the detachment were Pierre Chouteau and a trading party of 32 men. But the Arikaras, who resented the death of their chief, Ankedoucharo, in Washington, D.C., in 1806, and some Sioux allies attacked and turned back the group. Four men in Pryor's party died and nine suffered wounds, one of whom was Shannon. By the time the expedition could return home, his wounded leg had become gangrenous. At Camp Belle Fontaine, where Sheheke and his family were also left, an Army surgeon amputated the leg

Philadelphia artist C. B. J. Fevret de Saint Mémin executed this sketch of Sheheke, or Big White, apparently while the Mandan chief was visiting the city in the spring of 1807. Lewis likely commissioned the work for his proposed history of the exploration, which never saw the light of day.

just above the knee. For a time Shannon was near death, but he eventually recovered.

Lewis lays publication plans

Meantime Lewis, detained in Washington by various business, had been appointed as Governor of Louisiana Territory.[161] Many matters relating to the governorship needed to be discussed with Jefferson and other officials. Another task, urged by Jefferson, was launching a history of the expedition. Also stimulating Lewis in this endeavor was news that some of the enlisted men who had kept journals were proceeding with publishing plans.[162] Already, in October 1806, Frazer had issued with Lewis' approval a prospectus for a history, to be published by subscription, but the project ultimately came to naught.

Lewis was particularly irritated when he learned of unauthorized plans to issue the Gass journal, which David McKeehan, a Pittsburgh bookseller, had purchased and was preparing for publication. Lewis responded with a scathing attack on the quality of any publications based on enlisted men's journals—particularly their treatment of geographic and scientific topics.[163] Announcing at the same time plans to produce his own official and authoritative three-volume work, he stated he had approved only Frazer's book and denounced all others. McKeehan countered with a scurrilous letter to Lewis dated April 1. Five days before, the former had issued his prospectus in the *Pittsburgh Gazette.*

Late in March 1807, Lewis, substituting action for rhetoric, proceeded to Philadelphia. He quickly found a publisher, C. and A. Conrad and Company. About April 1 it issued a prospectus outlining a three-volume project plus a large map of North America that would sell for a total of $31. Lewis persuaded some of the foremost natural history authorities in the United States, who resided in the city, to undertake technical descriptions and drawings of botanical and zoological specimens procured by the expedition for use in volume three, which was to be devoted exclusively to scientific topics.[164]

Meantime, McKeehan had been busy at Pittsburgh. His efforts were more fruitful. On July 7, about the time Lewis returned to Washington, McKeehan published his work, the first of those based on the journals of members of the expedition. The book consisted of a rewriting of the Gass journal in polished prose, a capability Gass did not possess, and the addition of annotations.

Despite the many pressing problems awaiting Lewis at St. Louis in his gubernatorial capacity, of which both he and Jefferson were well aware, Lewis for some reason stayed in Washington after his return from Philadelphia through the winter of 1807–8. During this time, he probably was busy handling some matters for Jefferson relating to Aaron Burr's trial for treason at Richmond in August–September 1807 and its aftermath. Not until the next March, after stopping en route in Kentucky to examine some family land claims, did Lewis arrive in St. Louis.

Lewis becomes Governor of Louisiana Territory

The "dangers" of civilization were to prove to be more formidable than any Lewis had faced in the wilderness. Partly because his previous experience had been limited to the command of small military units, he found himself unprepared to cope with the problems of a Territorial official. Such a position required political acumen, administrative ability, and social grace rather than courage and ingenuity —the qualities he had demonstrated as a frontier Army officer and commander of a major exploring expedition. Even his perseverance and conscientiousness were not sufficient to surmount the burdens of the new office.

Louisiana Territory was plagued with problems, which had all mounted during Lewis' long absence: a sudden influx of population; contention between ambitious Government officials and scheming businessmen; administration of the Indian population; keen rivalry for trading licenses with the tribes; difficulties in controlling traders; confused land titles and trading rights, created by obscure Spanish and French antecedents; and the intrusion of white squatters and hunters on Government and Indian lands.

Lewis might have been able to handle the complicated situation better had he enjoyed the cooperation of his second-in-command, Territorial Secretary Frederick Bates, a lawyer and fellow Virginian who had directed the Territory while Lewis was in Washington and still exercised much power. Seeming friendliness on Bates' part quickly turned to hostility and surreptitious efforts to undermine Lewis' position, and ultimately to open enmity. Bates also continually embarrassed Lewis socially. The two men became so estranged that, had Lewis lived, only a duel might have resolved their differences.

The lack of cooperation even extended to Washington. Under

Jefferson's patronage, Lewis had enjoyed a virtual Presidential *carte blanche* to spend as much money as he needed. When Madison assumed the Presidency in 1809, his administration protested through the Secretary of War some of Lewis' drafts on various departments in Washington.[165]

Lewis arranges for Sheheke's return

Ironically, some of the protested drafts were associated with one of Lewis' major achievements as Territorial Governor: the return of Sheheke to his people in the fall of 1809, which Ensign Pryor had been unable to accomplish 2 years earlier. Lewis probably later regretted the means he chose. He entered into a contract on behalf of the U.S. Government with the St. Louis Missouri Fur Company, which Manuel Lisa had organized only a few months before, in March 1809.

Although encouraged by the profitability of his expedition up the Missouri and Yellowstone in 1807–8, Lisa realized that better organization and greater capital were needed for proper exploitation of the trade in the northern Rockies. He had gained a good knowledge of it and its potentialities, as well as experience in conducting it. He convinced other entrepreneurs that only large companies could operate successfully there; the long trips necessary to reach the hunting grounds were costlier than individual traders or small companies could finance, and hostile Indians would likely prevent the passage of small parties.

The Chouteaus and other traders joined forces with Lisa in the trade of the Upper Missouri because they realized it was the most effective way to share in it; any attempt to break his hold would require a long and costly operation. Officers of the new company were: William Clark, Pierre Chouteau, Sr., Auguste Chouteau, Jr., Meriwether Lewis' brother Reuben, Benjamin Wilkinson, and Sylvestre Labbadie, all of St. Louis; Pierre Menard and William Morrison of Kaskaskia; Andrew Henry of Louisiana; and Dennis Fitzhugh of Kentucky.

Lewis' logic in assigning the Sheheke mission to the company was unassailable. By this time the chief had been away from his tribe for 2½ years, and his expeditious return had become a matter of urgent political necessity. The company was planning to send a major trading expedition up the Missouri. There seemed to be no other way to recruit or finance such a large force to accomplish the mission.

Despite this fact, Lewis' detractors and some others questioned the propriety of his action. The company's profits would be shared by his brother, Reuben; his friend Clark, whose participation in the company while Superintendent of Indian Affairs was ethically questionable anyway; and Fitzhugh, who was related to Clark through marriage.

Under the arrangement, the company, which guaranteed Sheheke's safety, was to recruit a number of men to guard the party, led by Pierre Chouteau and including Reuben Lewis. If the company succeeded in returning the chief to his people, it would receive $7,000. After 101 days in transit and a major display of force while passing by the Arikaras and Sioux, on September 24, 1809, he was delivered to his village.

Lewis clashes with the War Department

New Secretary of War William Eustis, far less cooperative than Dearborn, refused to honor a draft of $500 that Lewis had signed on May 13, 1809, in favor of Chouteau for goods intended for distribution among the Indians through whom the expedition needed to pass. Another rejected draft, in the amount of $440 and dated May 15, was also associated with the project.

The Government's refusal to honor these drafts, as well as some others, created a crisis in Lewis' personal, as well as public, life. Under the circumstances, he became personally accountable for payment of the drafts. This in itself would not have been too serious, but his credit was already strained to the limit. He had borrowed heavily for some unwise speculation in land and for investment in at least one mining venture, along the Arkansas River. Lewis stood on the brink of insolvency, though he still held the land warrant for 1,600 acres he had received as a reward for his part in the Lewis and Clark Expedition. His creditors, suspecting his imminent financial ruin, reacted quickly and demanded immediate satisfaction.

Realizing that other protests would undoubtedly follow and anxious to justify his choice of the St. Louis Missouri Fur Company for the Sheheke assignment, Lewis decided to return to Washington, plead his case in person, and defend his honor and reputation. He also apparently decided to take advantage of the opportunity to further his history of the expedition, for which neither he nor Clark had been able to write a line, though the work had been announced to the public. This was another source of embarrassment.

Lewis heads for Washington

After granting Clark and two other close friends the power of attorney to dispose of his property to pay off his debts, on September 4, 1809, Lewis and his free mulatto servant, John Pernier, set out down the Mississippi by boat, intending to travel to the East by sea from New Orleans. Apparently Lewis planned to raise money en route, for he had sent ahead to New Orleans his 1,600-acre land warrant to be sold if possible at $1 per acre. Besides official papers concerning the protested drafts, Lewis carried with him the Lewis and Clark journals and other documents relating to the expedition for use in his publication project. On September 11, for some reason, he prepared his last will and testament.

Omens of tragedy

Four days later, on Lewis' arrival at Fort Pickering, at the Chickasaw Bluffs (present Memphis), the post commander, Maj. Gilbert C. Russell, found him to be in a "state of mental derangement." Also learning that the boat crew had been watching Lewis closely because he had twice tried to commit suicide and once nearly succeeded, Russell temporarily took possession of his papers and detained him. Within about a week, he apparently recovered and before long seemed able to resume his journey.

Hearing rumors of imminent war between Britain and the United States and fearing that the papers dealing with the expedition might fall into British hands at sea, Lewis decided to proceed overland to Washington via Nashville, through Tennessee and Virginia, instead of by sea from New Orleans. On September 29, or exactly 2 weeks after his arrival at the fort, he and Maj. James Neelly, the Chickasaw Indian agent and newly found traveling companion he had met at the fort, their two servants, and some Chickasaw chiefs, set out. They first traveled southeastward to the Chickasaw Agency, near present Houston, Miss., where the chiefs apparently remained. Lewis, Neelly, and their servants rested at the agency for 2 days, during which Neelly noticed evidences of relapse. Nevertheless, they left there on October 6, moving northeastward along the Natchez Trace.

Lewis' demise

During the night of October 9–10, at a camp near present Collinwood, Tenn., two of the packhorses escaped. At Lewis' request, in the morning Neelly remained behind to search for them. Lewis, promising Neelly he would halt at the next white habitation, and the two servants continued along the trace. That night they stopped at a backwoods inn, or "stand," Grinder's Stand. Arriving there the next morning, Neelly found Lewis dead from two gunshot wounds, and buried him beside the trace near the inn; the gravesite is today part of Meriwether Lewis Park (Natchez Trace Parkway).

One week later, Neelly, writing to Jefferson from Nashville to inform him that Lewis had taken his life, reconstructed the events based on the accounts of Mrs. Robert Grinder and the two servants. Apparently, after Lewis arrived at the inn, on October 10, Mrs. Grinder, noting his aberrant behavior and frightened because her husband was away, moved with her children into a small detached kitchen building to spend the night. The two servants slept in the stable.

About 3:00 a.m., awakened by the sound of two pistol shots from the direction of the inn, Mrs. Grinder aroused the servants. They rushed to Lewis' room, where they found him wounded in the head and just below the breast. Exclaiming to Pernier, according to Neelly's later account, "I have done the business my good Servant give me some water," he died within a few hours. Thus his career ended tragically at the age of 35, only 3 years after his triumphant return to St. Louis as commander of an epochal exploration. Unmarried, he left neither widow nor child to lament his death.

Except for some members of the Lewis family, apparently none of his contemporaries doubted his suicide. Years later, rumors that he had been murdered, either for political reasons or while being robbed, began to spread among residents along the trace. By the 1880's, the murder theory was well embedded in local folklore. During the next decade the theory began to appear in print and in time gained wide circulation. Some historians and journalists accepted it and others did not; the debate continues to this day.

Yet, not a single bit of contemporary evidence points to foul play.[166] Indeed, most of the evidence, though circumstantial in nature, strongly indicates suicide. It is unlikely that any of the people directly involved, Neelly, the servants. or Mrs. Grinder—though the latter subsequently elaborated upon the event and gave some contradictory information—had any reasons to hide the truth.

Jefferson, who substantiated Neelly's account by personally interviewing Pernier, never seems to have doubted that Lewis committed suicide. In a preface to Biddle's history of the expedition (1814) entitled "Life of Captain Lewis," Jefferson stated that Lewis from early life had been subject to "hypochondriac affections" inherited from his father and other family members and that while serving as his private secretary had at times demonstrated "sensible depressions of mind." But after Lewis took up his duties in St. Louis following the expedition, Jefferson said, the symptoms returned "with redoubled vigour, and began seriously to alarm his friends." Clark, his most intimate friend, upon hearing of the death, exclaimed, "I fear O! I fear the weight of his mind has overcome him."

Other major factors pointing to suicide are Lewis' serious difficulties as Governor of Louisiana Territory, personal financial troubles, the preparation of a will shortly after leaving St. Louis, and reports of his mental instability all along his final journey.

Clark's later career

Clark's post-expedition public career and personal life were as filled with success and individual fulfillment as those of Lewis were with disappointment and tragedy. Fortune deserted the one; it stayed with the other. A prominent resident of St. Louis for 31 years, Clark lived to a ripe old age, his interest in all western matters never dimming. He corresponded with or was visited by princes, politicians, scientists, authors, travelers, Army officers, businessmen, and traders.

DURING these years, while profiting in the fur trade and in real estate investments in St. Louis and environs, Clark held numerous key offices, sometime holding more than one concurrently. He apparently served as Superintendent of Indian Affairs almost continuously from 1807 until his death in 1838.[167] Also, on July 1, 1813, President James Madison appointed Clark as the first Governor of newly created Missouri Territory; he was reappointed three times, holding the office until Missouri became a State in 1821. Although a candidate for the office of Governor that same year, he failed to win election. In 1824–25 he served as Surveyor-General of the States of Illinois and Missouri and Arkansas Territory.

AS Superintendent of Indian Affairs, Clark worked through a network of Indian agents, many of them former Army officers, who lived
at their agencies with their tribes. Clark participated in treaty matters, tried to prevent tribal wars, negotiated disputes among tribes,
drove white squatters off Indian lands, and kept the natives from
returning to lands they had already sold or ceded.[168] In this role, he
broadened the base of goodwill the Lewis and Clark Expedition had
established, and probably did more to help the Indians than any of his
successors. Their friend, protector, and advocate, who always tried to
obtain as much justice as possible for them, he was fondly known to
many of them as the "Red-Headed Chief." Tribal delegations visiting
St. Louis called on him; and, as a means of protection, Government
or fur trading expeditions sought messages and greetings from him
to the natives.

Clark's deft handling of the Indians insured relative peace in the
area. While brigadier general in the militia of Louisiana Territory
(1807–13), when troubles arose—most often with the Winnebagoes,
Foxes, and Sauks up the Mississippi, under the influence of British
traders—he raised units to quell them. During the War of 1812, he
spared the Upper Mississippi Valley from anything more than stray
raids by winning over to the American side hostile tribes, especially
the Sioux, whom the British in Canada tried to incite.

OVER the years, Clark made numerous trips to the East on official
or personal business, always stopping on the way to visit his family
in Louisville.[169] On the first of these, in 1807–8, at Fincastle, Va., on
January 5, 1808, he married 16-year-old Julia Hancock. She was to
have five children.[170] In 1821, the year following her death, Clark
married Mrs. Harriet Kennerly Radford, her first cousin and close
friend and a widow with three children. She was to bear him two
sons.[171]

IN 1809–10 Clark had made his second trip to the East.[172] Accompanied by his wife, his infant son Meriwether Lewis Clark, and two
black servants, he set out on September 21, or only 17 days after
Lewis had begun his tragic journey. While conducting official business in Washington, Clark likely also hoped to defend the propriety
of his participation in the St. Louis Missouri Fur Company.

Apparently between Louisville and Lexington, Ky., where the

night was spent with George Shannon, Clark learned of Lewis' death from a newspaper. This changed Clark's plans considerably. He would now need to close out Lewis' affairs, rescue the papers pertaining to the expedition, and arrange for publication of the history. Instead of spending a few weeks in the East as earlier planned, he would need to stay many months; he would not return to St. Louis until July 1, 1810.

Clark left his wife and son behind at Fincastle, Va., and proceeded alone. He did not find Lewis' mother, Mrs. Marks, at her home near Charlottesville, but spent the night with the family. He had better luck at Monticello, where he passed some time with Jefferson. Among other subjects, they talked about the death of Lewis and the problems it created. At Jefferson's suggestion, Clark journeyed to Richmond. He met the Governor and sat in at a meeting of the Assembly. He also discussed with William Wirt, a jurist and writer, the possibility of his preparing a history of the expedition, but nothing ever came of the meeting.

In Washington the Secretary of War assured Clark that Lewis had not lost the confidence of the Government despite the protested drafts —though it was too late to benefit Lewis. Clark also removed from Lewis' trunks, which had been forwarded to the Capital City, the papers relating to the expedition and carried them to Philadelphia to show to the prospective publisher of the proposed volume.[173]

While there, Clark persuaded scientist Benjamin S. Barton to finish writing the botanical and zoological descriptions for the scientific part of the book. Nicholas Biddle, prominent literary figure and lawyer, at first declined but later agreed to write the general narrative. In April 1810 he spent several days with Clark at Fincastle and interviewed him in depth about the expedition, after which he carried the Lewis and Clark journals back to Philadelphia. As further aids, Clark provided Biddle with Ordway's journal; hired Shannon to travel from Lexington to Philadelphia to provide direct assistance; corresponded regularly with Biddle; and paid at least one visit to him in Philadelphia, in March 1813. Biddle, who refused to accept any money for his effort, also utilized the journal of Patrick Gass and completed a rough draft within a year. He then turned it over for final polishing to Paul Allen, a journalist. Barton, a busy man, never completed his part of the history.

In 1812 C. and A. Conrad and Company went bankrupt, and Bid-

The Lewis & Clark Expedition returned to the St. Louis Riverfront on Tuesday, September 23, 1806. The whole village turned out at noon that day to give the explorers a resounding welcome.

dle arranged with the Bradford and Inskeep Company to print the book. They did so in 1814, in two volumes, with the title page credit going to Allen rather than Biddle. But, before distribution could be made, Bradford and Inskeep also went out of business. As a result, Clark never saw a copy of the book until many years later.

AT the age of 68, after an 8-day illness, on September 1, 1838, Clark died at the home of his eldest son, Meriwether Lewis Clark.[174] Besides Meriwether Lewis, the other surviving sons were George Rogers and Jefferson K. William Clark was buried on September 3 with Masonic and military honors on the farm of his nephew Col. John O'Fallon, on the edge of St. Louis; the gravesite is today part of Bellefontaine Cemetery. The funeral procession, the largest in the history of St. Louis until that time, was about a mile in length.[175]

The fate of other members of the expedition

What of the others? Of the sergeants? Of the other enlisted men? Of the interpreters? Of Sacagawea and her baby? Of York?

MOST of the enlisted men soon passed into obscurity. They are by and large a group of forgotten men. Little is known about their subsequent careers, few monuments mark the known graves, and only a handful of them left reasonably full records of their lives. A few selected and occupied the 320-acre plots in surveyed public lands west of the Mississippi that Congress granted them in 1807, at the same time it awarded them double pay.[176]

Most of them, however, apparently sold their land warrants, sometimes to other members of the expedition, and settled down east of the Mississippi. Among those who lived in the East, some are known at one time or another to have resided in present Illinois, Indiana, Kentucky, Virginia, West Virginia, and Wisconsin; and in the West, in California, Missouri, and Oklahoma. Some married, raised families, and prospered. A considerable number became farmers. A few of those who remained out of the Army experienced difficulty in adjusting to civilian life. They took to drink, turned into drifters, got into scrapes with the law, and sank into debt.

A substantial group reenlisted in the Army, some for short terms and others for life: Sergeants Gass and Pryor; Privates Bratton,

Shannon, and Willard; and likely Privates Gibson, Howard, McNeal, and Windsor. Of these, Gass, Pryor, Bratton, and Willard, and possibly others, served in the War of 1812. Pryor rose to the rank of captain.

Colter and Drouillard played epic roles in the early history of the organized fur trade that grew in the wake of the Lewis and Clark Expedition. Also taking part in it were Potts, Wiser, and possibly Collins.[177] Colter remained continuously longer in the wilderness of the Upper Missouri and the Rocky Mountains than any other white man of his day. After leaving Camp Wood in the spring of 1804, he did not return to "civilization" until May 1810. During that time, he experienced many adventures with the Indians.

After his fur trading days were over, in 1810 Colter married an Indian woman named Sally and settled on a farm close to that of Daniel Boone near La Charette, Mo., but died 3 years later.[178] Potts and Drouillard succumbed at the hands of the Blackfeet in the Three Forks of the Missouri area, in 1808 and 1810 respectively.[179]

Subsequent to his discharge from the Army in 1815, Pryor lived and traded among the Osages, especially the Clermont band, in present northeastern Oklahoma; married one of them, who bore him a family; and represented the tribe in negotiations with the military at nearby Forts Smith and Gibson. In 1830 Clark appointed Pryor temporarily as subagent for the Clermont Osages, but he died the next year at his subagency southeast of present Pryor, Okla., which was named after him. Willard worked as a Government blacksmith for some time among the Sauk, Fox, Shawnee, and Delaware tribes.

Shannon probably had the most successful post-expedition career of the group. After the loss of his leg in 1807, except for his trip to Philadelphia in 1810 to help Biddle, he resided for some years in Lexington, Ky., where he read law at Transylvania University. There he became acquainted with Henry Clay, who befriended him. After completing his studies, he entered into practice and married. In the early 1820's he served in the Kentucky legislature. He later moved to Missouri, where he practiced law and became a State senator and U.S. attorney. He passed away in 1838.

Likely the first of the enlisted men to die was Joseph Field, about a year after the expedition returned; the last, in 1870, was Gass, who lived to be 99 years of age, the oldest of any of the men. Willard died in 1865 at the age of 88, and Bratton lived to be 63.

Patrick Gass was one of the sergeants of the Lewis & Clark Expedition.   He is here shown as an elderly man; he had lost the vision of his left eye in 1813 while still in the Army.

AFTER the expedition, Clark freed all his slaves, including York in 1811, though he was ever afterwards interested in his welfare. Clark gave him a six-horse team and wagon, which he used for a freighting business between Nashville and Richmond. But he proved to be a poor manager and his commercial venture failed, after which he turned from one odd job to another. He was apparently on his way back to join Clark in St. Louis when he fell ill with cholera and died at an unknown date somewhere in Tennessee.

SACAGAWEA and Charbonneau apparently resided at the Minitari villages at the mouth of the Knife River from 1806 until late 1809 or 1810. At that time, responding to Clark's long-standing invitation to visit him and recognizing his interest in educating their 4-year-old son, Jean Baptiste ("Pomp"), they traveled to St. Louis. Sacagawea and Charbonneau apparently stayed there with him until the spring of 1811, when they returned to the Minitari villages. Clark became the youngster's guardian and educated him. In August 1812 Sacagawea gave birth to a daughter, named Lizette.[180] That same summer, Sacagawea left the Minitari villages and joined Charbonneau, who was employed by Lisa at newly established Fort Manuel, just below the present North Dakota-South Dakota boundary. She apparently died there that December.[181]

Charbonneau outlived Sacagawea by about 28 years, residing most of the time among the Mandans and Minitaris. For the last years of his life, Clark employed him as an interpreter for those tribes. In 1833 Charbonneau worked for Prince Maximilian of Wied, a visitor to the Upper Missouri. In 1839, the year after Clark's death, Charbonneau visited St. Louis. That year, or the next, aged about 80, he died, probably in one of the Mandan or Minitari villages.

AND how about the final years of the youngest member of the expedition, Jean Baptiste?[182] By 1816, after spending some time with Clark in St. Louis, he was back among the Indians. In 1824 he met young Prince Paul of Württemberg, who was making a trip up the Missouri, at a traders' village at the mouth of the Kansas River and, with Clark's consent, accompanied him to Germany. Jean Baptiste lived abroad for 5 years, learned several languages, and then returned to the United States.

For many years thereafter, Jean Baptiste lived the life of a mountain man, traveling the mountain ranges from New Mexico to Oregon. He also served many Army officers and explorers as an interpreter and guide. In 1846 he guided Philip St. George Cooke and his Mormon Battalion to California and apparently took up residence there. In 1866 he left his home near Auburn, in the mining country, with two companions and headed toward the goldfields of Montana. On the way, aged 61, he died of pneumonia and was buried in the Jordan Valley near the present community of Danner, Oreg.

TIME and circumstances separated the members of the expedition, but to the end of their days they shared vivid memories of their trip across the Continent. Memories of an awesome new world to the west. Of adventure, trial, and danger. Of drudgery and fatigue. Of boredom and excitement. Of sickness and sundry aches and pains. Of eating horses, dogs, and roots. Of numbing cold, pelting rain, and baking sun. Of deadly rattlers, bellowing buffalo herds, and yowling wolves. Of ferocious grizzlies and pesky mosquitoes and gnats. Of endless days on foot, horse, and boat. Of their fallen comrade Floyd. Of encounters with strange Indian bands. Of spectacular mountains, surging rivers—and the shores of the western ocean.

PART TWO

Lewis and Clark:
Survey of Historic Sites
and Buildings

THE passage of some 170 years and the emergence of an industrial-technological America have wrought vast changes along the route of Lewis and Clark—changes they could never possibly have envisioned. Although not even the most enthusiastic preservationist would expect the land to remain totally unchanged, the scarcity of sites associated with the expedition is astonishing.

That the rampaging Missouri River Lewis and Clark knew would be tamed, that many of their campsites would be submerged, that most of the native trails they traversed would disappear from the plains and mountains, that the majestic Great Falls of the Missouri would be reduced to a trickle—all would seem unbelievable to the two captains. That the vast herds of buffalo, elk, and antelope, as well as the numerous grizzly, would be all but extinct, except where sanctuary exists, would seem equally as preposterous. The disappearance of the great falls of the Columbia would be beyond comprehension.

Yet, all this has come to pass—and more. As a matter of fact, were Lewis and Clark alive today, they would be unable to recognize many parts of their route and the raw wilderness they encountered. Where once were swirling and dangerous rapids, in many places today water skiers glide over glassy waters; where once salmon and other fish swarmed in the crystal-clear rivers or wildlife thrived along their banks, are often polluted streams and semibarren land; where once powerful currents lashed at riverbanks, are frequently huge levees; where once were dense forests and fertile soil, are sometimes scarred, depleted, and eroded areas.

THE greatest alteration to the Lewis and Clark route—primarily a watercourse along the Missouri and Columbia River drainages—has been made by the dams constructed by the Army Corps of Engineers, the U.S. Bureau of Reclamation, and private power companies. In the process of remaking the river systems, they have provided industry with energy, brought payrolls, furnished irrigation water and electricity to farmers and ranchers, controlled floods and erosion, and enhanced recreational facilities. Regrettably, losses have occurred from the archeological and historical points of view.

Only relatively short stretches of the Missouri and the Columbia remain in an unharnessed state, and in other places the worst bends have been sliced away to improve navigation and reduce erosion. The Middle Missouri has been transformed. Beginning at a point just above Yankton, on the South Dakota-Nebraska border, six Corps of Engineers dams have converted the once-rugged stream into a string of placid lakes—sometimes known as the "Great Lakes of the Missouri." Extending from Nebraska across both Dakotas and into Montana, in order upriver these dams (reservoirs in parentheses) are: Gavins Point (Lewis and Clark Lake), Fort Randall (Lake Francis Case), Big Bend (Lake Sharpe), Oahe (Oahe Reservoir), Garrison (Lake Sakakawea), and Fort Peck (Fort Peck Reservoir).

The tail waters of each of these reservoirs practically laps at the face of the next. They have impounded thousands of square miles of water, inundated thousands of acres of river valley, and obliterated many prehistoric and historic places—not only those related to the Lewis and Clark Expedition, but also those of Indian villages and hunting grounds, fur trading posts, missions, battlefields, and emigrant routes.

Oahe Reservoir covers the Corson County, S. Dak., sites of the three Arikara villages that the expedition visited in 1804 and 1806 and that of Fort Manuel, the apparent location of Sacagawea's death and possibly that of her grave. Point of Reunion (Mountrail County), N. Dak., where the two Lewis and Clark elements reunited on the return trip after separating at Travelers Rest, Mont., lies beneath Lake Sakakawea.

Fortunately, just before the dam construction occurred, in 1946, the Missouri Basin Project, part of the River Basin Surveys of the Inter-Agency Archeological Salvage Program, began to investigate sites scheduled for inundation by the Corps of Engineers and the Bureau of Reclamation. Within rigid budgetary and time limitations and using both governmental and private funds, the National Park Service, Smithsonian Institution, and various universities and historical societies surveyed, investigated, excavated, and researched

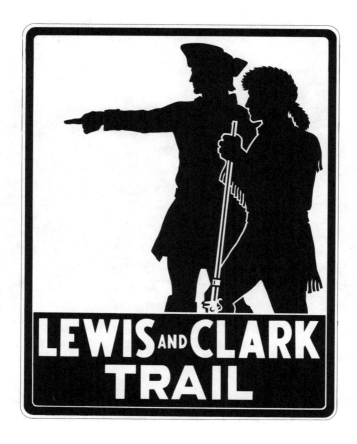

Official emblem of the Lewis and Clark Trail Commission.
This symbol, slightly modified, highlights the trail
throughout the West.

scores of paleontological, prehistoric, and historic sites. Photographs were taken, artifacts collected, data recorded, and many of the results published.

Farther upriver, at the Great Falls of the Missouri extensive hydro-electric development has been carried out by the Montana Power Company along a 9-mile stretch of the Missouri near the city of Great Falls. Five dams utilize the power generated by the several falls.

Beginning another 84 miles upstream are the Montana Power Company's Holter (Holter Lake) and Hauser (Hauser Lake and Lake Helena) Dams, as well as the U.S. Bureau of Reclamation's Canyon Ferry Dam and Reservoir, which extends as far as Town-

Modern America has left its mark along the Lewis and Clark route. Pictured here are grain elevators at Wallula Gap, Wash. Lewis and Clark met the Walla Walla Indians in this area.

send, Mont. The river is submerged at one place in the area to a depth of nearly 100 feet. Included is the spectacular gash in the 1,200-foot granite heights known to Lewis and Clark as the "Gates of the Rocky Mountains." But the sheer rock walls still tower above the gorge so overpoweringly that the only perceptible difference is the still water that has replaced the once-powerful current.

The U.S. Bureau of Reclamation's Clark Canyon Dam (Hap Hawkins Lake), on the Upper Beaverhead River, has eradicated a major Lewis and Clark site, Camp Fortunate (Beaverhead County), Mont. It was the scene of many key events, especially on the westbound journey.

From Clarkston, Wash., and Lewiston, Idaho, at the mouth of the Clearwater, a chain of reservoirs on the Snake and Columbia reaches 320 river miles to Bonneville Dam, only 145 miles from the Pacific, and have immeasurably changed the streams. Dams on the Snake include (east to west) Little Goose, Lower Monumental, and Ice Harbor, all operated by the Corps of Engineers.

Various Corps of Engineer dams are located on the Lower Columbia: McNary, John Day, The Dalles, and Bonneville. The latter two have inundated Celilo Falls, The Dalles (including the Short Narrows), Long Narrows of the Lower Dalles, and the Cascades (Grand Rapids)—a 55-mile stretch of treacherous falls, rapids, narrows, and chutes that were a severe problem to the Lewis and Clark Expedition. Now they all lie quiet and unseen beneath huge artificial lakes; churning white water and leaping salmon can no longer be seen.

IF man has destroyed and defaced many Lewis and Clark locales, so too has nature. The rivers themselves have capriciously meandered in places and swept away or altered sites. Because of a gross change in the Mississippi channel near St. Louis, the site of Camp Wood, once on the south bank of the Wood River in Illinois, is now on the Missouri side of the Mississippi. Another example is the Council

Celilo Falls at some unknown date prior to construction of The Dalles Dam, which covered the great falls. To the men of the expedition, they were not only a major obstacle, but also provided a breathtaking view.

Bluffs, Nebr., location, where the two captains held their first council with the Indians. Now, instead of being at stream's edge, it is 3 miles away from the river, which is not even visible from the spot. The wandering of the Missouri has obscured the site of Fort Mandan, N. Dak., the 1804–5 winter camp, and marred the nearby environment of the Mandan-Minitari-Amahami villages.

Nature has also altered the landscape. In some areas, major changes in vegetation have occurred. For example, above the mouth of the Platte, the hills and bluffs along the Missouri were for the most part bare of trees and shrubs in 1804–6. Today, the growth is so dense that one cannot see the river from the crests. The paintings and drawings of such artists as George Catlin and Karl Bodmer in the 1830's clearly show the difference.

DESPITE all the damage, in places the route of Lewis and Clark remains much as it was. Providentially, one of the most spectacular parts of the Missouri River has not only been spared, but also in the region man's imprint is slight. This is the 180-mile length of free-flowing, almost pristine waters lying between the upper reaches of the Fort Peck Reservoir and the Montana Power Company's Morony Dam, near the eastern end of the expedition's Great Falls portage. Within this span, east of the city of Fort Benton, is the picturesque badlands known as the Missouri River Breaks. Particularly notable is its western part, the 55-mile-long White Cliffs section, where nature-sculpted forms rise hundreds of feet in the eroded bluffs above the serpentine stream.

Beyond the city of Great Falls, the 84 miles of undisturbed terrain to Holter Dam is a delightful reach of river, canyon, plain, and mountain. Highway I-15 never runs far from the stream, and in places immediately alongside it. In this area, one can follow the nautical progress of the expedition—but on wheels. At the Three Forks of the Missouri, Mont., not far south of the Holter-Hauser-Canyon Ferry dam complex, manmade and natural changes have been minimal, both in the river course and the surrounding vicinity.

Another relatively virginal expanse is the high Bitterroot Range country of Idaho along the Lolo Trail. There, modern visitors can still see the western wilderness through the explorers' eyes. Lemhi Pass is also still essentially unspoiled, as are various other sites such as Travelers Rest and Lewis and Clark Pass. Unurbanized and non-

Example of excavation accomplished by the Missouri River Basin Survey before much of the Middle Missouri River Valley was inundated by dam construction in the 1960's. This photograph shows Nightwalker's Butte in the Bull Pasture Site (32ML39), Lake Sakakawea (Garrison Reservoir), N. Dak. This was an early 19th-century earthlodge village, located atop a small, high butte, that was surrounded by a fortification palisade. The small black dots are post holes indicating outlines of houses.

industrialized sections of the Lower Missouri and the Lower Columbia below Bonneville Dam, as well as other rivers in the Columbia and Missouri drainage systems, occasionally offer vistas that Lewis and Clark might recognize.

The Yellowstone River Valley, though various cities, towns, ranches, farms, railroads, and highways are scattered along it, has not yet been unduly affected by modern development. The stream itself is essentially wild and is unobstructed by dams. Pompeys Pillar, along the river about 28 miles east of Billings, is as much a landmark in this day as when Clark climbed it on July 25, 1806, and carved his name and date on its eastern face. That inscription, though once partly disfigured and twice deepened, is still readable.

THUS, only in a few places can a modern American see the western wilderness for any considerable distance in essence as Lewis and Clark saw it. But even some of the few remaining areas remindful of one of America's greatest explorations are threatened.

Historic preservationists and environmentalists, with the support of Congress, have recently headed off a plan to construct the High Cow Creek Dam, which would flood the Missouri River Breaks. The Yellowstone River Valley is imperiled by the recent growth of strip mining among the huge low-sulphur coal deposits in eastern Montana and northern Wyoming. In this "Ruhr of the Northwest," as it is already being called, a giant generating complex that would utilize new dams on the Yellowstone, Bighorn, and Tongue Rivers has been proposed.

Conservationists hope that Congress will declare the Missouri River Breaks, the Yellowstone, and other similarly endangered streams or parts of streams as "wild" or "scenic" rivers so that posterity may enjoy them.

NUMEROUS governmental and private agencies, as well as individuals, are engaged in commemorating Lewis and Clark sites. An exemplary program was that of the congressionally authorized Lewis and Clark Trail Commission (1964–69). The 28-man body, chaired by Sherry R. Fisher, prominent Des Moines banker, consisted of representatives of Illinois, Missouri, Kansas, Iowa, Nebraska, South and North Dakota, Montana, Idaho, Washington, and Oregon; 4 U.S. Representatives; 4 Senators; representatives of the Interior, Agriculture, Defense, Health-Education-Welfare, and Commerce Departments; and 4 from the J. N. "Ding" Darling Foundation. The latter had been the catalyst that spurred the entire movement in 1962 by recommending a "Lewis and Clark Trail" to the Secretary of the Interior. The Bureau of Outdoor Recreation immediately began work with the appropriate States and various other governmental units to give life to the concept.

In 1961 J. N. ("Ding") Darling, cartoonist-conservationist for the *Des Moines Register* and for many years a director of the Izaak Walton League, had conceived a plan to create the trail and to improve, establish, and link up historical, recreational, and conservationist sites along it. Following his death soon thereafter, friends and associates founded the J. N. "Ding" Darling Foundation to advance

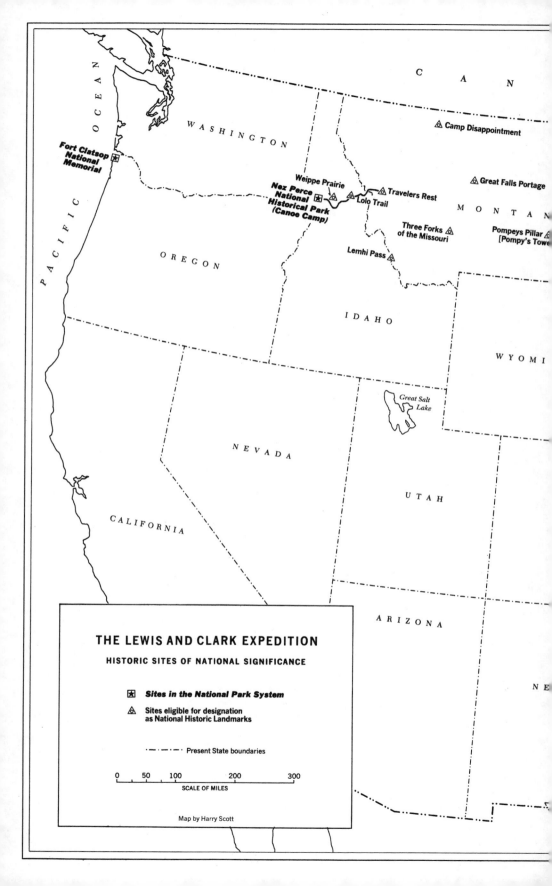

THE LEWIS AND CLARK EXPEDITION

HISTORIC SITES OF NATIONAL SIGNIFICANCE

⊞ **Sites in the National Park System**

△ Sites eligible for designation
   as National Historic Landmarks

—··—··— Present State boundaries

0   50   100   200   300
SCALE OF MILES

Map by Harry Scott

Fort Clatsop
National
Memorial

Nez Perce
National
Historical Park
(Canoe Camp)

Weippe Prairie

Lolo Trail

Travelers Rest

Three Forks
of the Missouri

Lemhi Pass

Camp Disappointment

Great Falls Portage

Pompeys Pillar
[Pompy's Tower]

Great Salt
Lake

PACIFIC OCEAN

WASHINGTON

OREGON

CALIFORNIA

NEVADA

IDAHO

UTAH

C A N

M O N T A N

WYOMI

ARIZONA

N E

the conservation principles he had espoused. The foundation chose the Lewis and Clark proposal as one of its first projects.

The accomplishments of the Lewis and Clark Trail Commission were extensive. To mark the trail highways, it devised a distinctive emblem that consisted of the standing silhouettes of the two explorers over the words "Lewis and Clark Trail." Among its many activities, the commission also aided the States in founding Lewis and Clark Trail Committees; and collected and disseminated information on Federal, State, county, municipal, corporate, and private plans and programs along the route. These included the surveying, identification, marking, and preservation of pertinent sites; sponsorship and production of publications, movies, and television and slide presentations dealing with the expedition; and improvement and construction of parks, recreational areas, and roads and trails.

When the commission expired in 1969, its functions were continued by the Lewis and Clark Trail Heritage Foundation, Inc., a private, nonprofit organization. It was organized in 1968 by the State Committee of the Lewis and Clark Trail Commission and included many of the latter's members and supporters. Most of the State Lewis and Clark Trail Committees, which had operated under the commission, remained in existence.

Also active in interpreting the Lewis and Clark Expedition to the public, in addition to the National Park Service, are the Department of the Interior's Bureau of Outdoor Recreation and Bureau of Sport Fisheries and Wildlife, the Army Corps of Engineers of the Department of Defense, and the Department of Agriculture's U.S. Forest Service, plus various State and local agencies and historical societies. They all rely principally on markers, publications, lectures, and other audiovisual programs.

HOMAGE has also been paid to the explorers by the placenames that dot the West, such as those of cities, counties, streets, highways, parks, recreational areas, lakes, reservoirs, and bridges—not to mention business establishments and civic organizations. Of particular note are the twin cities of Lewiston, Idaho, and Clarkston, Wash.; Lewis and Clark College, Portland, Oreg.; Lewis and Clark National Forest, Mont.; Lewis and Clark Lake (Gavins Point Dam reservoir), S. Dak.; Clark Fork of the Columbia River; and the Lewis and Clark River. Honoring others on the expedition are Lake Sakakawea (Garrison

Dam reservoir), N. Dak., nearby Sakakawea State Park, and Sacagawea Peak, Mont.; Charbonneau Park, Wash. (Federal); Gass Recreation Site, Idaho (proposed Federal); and Montana's Pryor Mountains,
Pryor Creek, and Pompeys Pillar.

DESCRIBED in the following pages are the principal extant sites
associated with the Lewis and Clark Expedition. In the National Park
System are Jefferson National Expansion Memorial, Mo.; Nez Perce
National Historical Park, Idaho; Fort Clatsop National Memorial,
Oreg.; and Meriwether Lewis Park (Natchez Trace Parkway), Tenn.
National Historic Landmarks number 11. Except for Meriwether
Lewis Park, where Lewis is buried, all sites are located in the trans-
Mississippi West.

Several others in the Eastern United States, however, have perti-
nence to Lewis and Clark, though they contain no remains that have
any significant relationship with the two explorers and are therefore
not included in this volume. Most of these sites are generally discussed in various other volumes in this series. In the National Park
System is Harpers Ferry National Historical Park, Md.-W. Va., where
Lewis procured Army rifles and other equipment. National Historic
Landmarks include the Forks of the Ohio, Pa., at Pittsburgh, where
he made final logistical arrangements before setting out down the
Ohio; and Monticello, Va., and the White House, D.C., where he
lived with Jefferson just before setting out on the expedition.

Among places in the Other Sites Considered category (see following
section) in the Eastern United States, also excluded from this work,
are the Clarksville, Ind.-Louisville, Ky. area; two other key stops in
Illinois on the Pittsburgh-St. Louis segment of the journey, Fort
Massac and Fort Kaskaskia, now both State parks; the city of
Cahokia, Ill., visited by Lewis and other members of the complement
while it was in the St. Louis area; the town of Fincastle, Va., today a
historic district, the place Clark returned to after the expedition and
where, in the still-standing Col. George Hancock Mansion ("Santillane"), he married his first wife in 1808; and Locust Grove, Ky., the
estate in Louisville that Lewis and Clark visited to call on Clark's
sister on their eastbound journey and possibly also on the westbound.

Lewis' birthplace, Locust Hill, no longer stands, but the site, in
Albemarle County, Va., is near the hamlet of Ivy, not far west of
Charlottesville. The exact location of Clark's birthplace, in Caroline
County, Va., has not been ascertained. Also, except for Monticello,

the White House, "Santillane," and Locust Grove, no extant residences can be associated with the two men, nor any other members of the expedition.

THE following descriptions are comprised of three categories: National Park Service Areas, National Historic Landmarks, and Other Sites Considered.

The principal aim of the National Survey of Historic Sites and Buildings is to identify nationally important sites that are not *National Park Service Areas*, but no survey of historic places would be complete without including them. This is particularly true because many of them were designated as National Historic Landmarks before they became part of the National Park System. Further information about a particular area may be obtained by writing directly to the park superintendent at the address listed immediately following the location.

National Historic Landmarks are those sites judged by the Advisory Board on National Parks, Historic Sites, Buildings, and Monuments to meet the criteria of national significance in commemorating the history of the United States (pp. 382–383). They have been declared by the Secretary of the Interior to be eligible for designation as National Historic Landmarks. Final designation occurs when the owners apply for such status. They receive certificates and bronze plaques attesting to the distinction.

Other Sites Considered consist of those sites deemed by the Advisory Board to possess noteworthy historical value but not national significance. The list of those included in this category does not purport to be exhaustive; it is merely a representative sampling, all that is possible because of space limitations.

Many sites in the Other Sites Considered category in all phases of history are listed on the National Register of Historic Places, maintained by the National Park Service's Office of Archeology and Historic Preservation. The register consists not only of sites in the National Park System and National Historic Landmarks, but also those of State and local significance, nominated through appropriate channels by the various States. It is published biennially and distributed by the Superintendent of Documents, U.S. Government Printing Office, Washington, D.C., 20402. The latest volume is *The National Register of Historic Places, Supplement, 1974*, price $9.45.

For the convenience of users of this volume, sites and buildings are listed alphabetically by State. The following code indicates site categories:

Site Categories

★ NATIONAL PARK SERVICE AREAS
⚠ NATIONAL HISTORIC LANDMARKS
⊗ OTHER SITES CONSIDERED

NOTE: *The following descriptions indicate sites that are open to the public. Before visiting any of them, inquiry should be made to the owners or custodians concerning dates and hours of access and admission costs, usually nominal. Special permission should be obtained to visit privately owned sites.*

Cameahwait's Village, Idaho ⊗

Location (approximate): The village was located at two different places, both in present Lemhi County, while the Lewis and Clark Expedition was in the area. The first site was about 7 miles north of present Tendoy on the east bank of the Lemhi River, probably just north of the point where present Sandy Creek flows into it from the east. The second location was about 3 miles to the south and upstream on the same bank of the Lemhi, likely at or near the mouth of Kenney Creek, some 4 miles north of Tendoy. Both sites, which are situated about one-quarter mile west of a secondary road that follows the east bank of the Lemhi, are accessible only on foot. The secondary road branches off Idaho 28, which runs along the west bank of the Lemhi, about 3¼ miles north of Tendoy.

Because of the inundation of the site of Camp Fortunate, Mont., by a dam reservoir, the sites of Cameahwait's Village are all that remain, except for the Lemhi Pass area, to mark the crucial meeting of the expedition with the Shoshonis, a major highlight of the westbound journey.[183]

From the time the two captains left the Mandan-Minitari villages, in present North Dakota, in the spring of 1805, their principal goal was contacting the Shoshonis, whom the Minitaris had told them about. From the former tribe, Lewis and Clark hoped to obtain horses, food, and guides to cross the Bitterroot Mountains. Upon leaving the Great Falls of the Missouri, the search for the Shoshonis intensified and concern mounted, especially when they were not found in the

Lemhi River Valley, looking westward, near Tendoy, Idaho. The road in the right foreground leads to Lemhi Pass.

Valley of Trail Creek as seen from the summit of Lemhi Pass looking eastward.

Three Forks area, where the Minitaris said they would be. If the expedition did not soon meet the tribe, it could not cross the mountains to the west before winter set in.

Lewis and an advance party of three men encountered some Shoshonis on August 13, 1805, in the Lemhi River Valley after crossing Lemhi Pass. The tribesmen entertained the explorers for 2 days at their village (first location). On the 15th and 16th, the Lewis group, along with Chief Cameahwait and some of his people, returned back through Lemhi Pass to what has come to be known as Camp Fortunate, located on the south bank of the Beaverhead River where it is formed by Horse Prairie Creek and the Red Rock River. The next day, Clark and the main body joined them there. Sacagawea was delighted to find that Cameahwait was her brother, whom she had not seen in years. The following day, the 18th, Clark and part of the expedition, accompanied by Cameahwait and most of his people, set out for the Shoshoni village, reached on the 20th. Meanwhile, Lewis had remained behind with a small group at Camp Fortunate, where he maintained a base camp until the 24th.

Until August 30, when the expedition headed northward to cross the Lolo Trail, many major activities were associated with the Shoshoni village. Probably by the time of Clark's first visit there on August 20, and definitely by the time of Lewis' second visit, on August 26, it had moved about 3 miles southward (second location) from its original site.

The village was the base for the Clark group's reconnaissance (August 20–29, 1805) of the Salmon River, a westward-flowing stream. As the natives had said, its waters were found to be impassable by boat and its shores by foot or horse. Also, game was scarce along the river and no timber was available for making canoes. Clark reunited with Lewis at the Shoshoni village on August 29, the day before the expedition moved north. The two captains also purchased food and horses for the trek across the Lolo Trail, which the Indians told them about, and recruited Old Toby as a guide. Neither the Clark nor Lewis contingents contacted Cameahwait on their return trip from the Pacific.

The two unmarked sites of Cameahwait's Village are located in flat bottom land, used for agricultural purposes. Vegetation is sparse except for sagebrush and a few scattered trees.

Camp Chopunnish, Idaho ⊗

Location: Idaho County, along the north, or east, bank of the Clearwater River, on the eastern edge of the Nez Perce Indian Reservation, about 1½ miles downstream, or northwest, from the bridge over U.S. 12 that crosses the river at Kamiah, and some 2 miles below the mouth of Lawyer's Creek. The site is accessible by a secondary road running off U.S. 12.

Arriving back among the Nez Perces on May 3, 1806, far too early to cross the Lolo Trail, the homeward-bound expedition was forced to spend several weeks with the tribe while waiting for the snow to recede in the Bitterroot Mountains. Most of this period, almost a month (May 14–June 10), was spent at what has come to be known variously as Camp Chopunnish, after the two captains' name for the

Nez Perces; Long Camp, because of the duration of the stay; and Camp Kamiah, for its location. The Indians had recommended the site for the availability of pasturage and the good hunting nearby.

Mingling with the Nez Perces, the men used the time to relax. Their commanders counciled with the chiefs and learned much about the tribe. Practically all the horses that had been left with it the year before were recovered. Because of the food shortage, a problem shared with the Indians, the hunters were busy, not only to satisfy immediate needs but also to lay in a supply of food for the crossing of the Bitterroots.

On June 10 the explorers moved northeastward from Camp Chopunnish about 8 miles to the southern part of Weippe Prairie to be near the starting point of the Lolo Trail, which was crossed the last week in June after the failure of an earlier attempt.

In 1902, when historian Olin D. Wheeler visited the site, he could still see the sunken circular ring where Lewis and Clark had established their camp. Since that time, however, the integrity of the site has been destroyed. A large sawmill now covers it, and numerous other buildings are located in the vicinity. The area may be viewed from an unmarked turnout on U.S. 12 along the opposite, or south, side of the river.

Lemhi Pass, Idaho-Montana ⚠

Location: On the Continental Divide in Lemhi County, Idaho, and Beaverhead County, Mont. Along a rough, dirt road that extends east from Idaho 28 just south of Tendoy, Idaho, some 12 miles to the summit of the pass and then continues almost the same distance to its junction with Mont. 324. The junction occurs at a ranch on Trail Creek where the latter road switches from a general north-south to west-east direction about 22 miles west of I-15.

Probably no other area on the westbound route of the expedition is associated with so many events crucial to its success as is Lemhi Pass and vicinity. Moving through the pass in August 1805, the party crossed the Continental Divide, the first U.S. citizens on record to do so. At the same time, while passing from the upper reaches of the eastward-flowing waters of the Missouri drainage to the Pacific slope of the Rockies and the westward-wending waters of the Columbia system, the explorers also traversed the boundary of newly acquired

View from south to north across the shallow saddle of Lemhi Pass. The fence separates Montana, on the right, from Idaho, on the left, and traces the Continental Divide at this point.

Louisiana Territory and thus moved from the United States into a region claimed by various European powers.

Also, in the pass area, Lewis and Clark encountered the Shoshonis, the objective ever since leaving the Mandan villages, in present North Dakota, and upon whom all hopes of crossing the Bitterroot Mountains depended. Fortuitously, the chief of the band was Cameahwait, Sacagawea's brother, whom she reunited with at Camp Fortunate, Mont., east of Lemhi Pass; his village lay to its west. On August 30 the expedition, utilizing Indian guides, horses, and food, pushed northward from the Shoshoni village toward the Lolo Trail. On the return from the Pacific, neither the Lewis nor Clark elements of the expedition crossed Lemhi Pass.

Unlike passes to the north and south that are traversed by improved roads and have accordingly been much changed by the hand of man, providentially Lemhi Pass (8,000 feet elevation), in a remote section of the Beaverhead Range, has remained almost in a pristine condition—all but unknown except to U.S. Forest Service employees, prospectors, ranchers, and an occasional student of the Lewis and Clark Expedition. From the summit, the same wild and majestic scenes that Lewis and Clark beheld still meet the eyes to the east and west.

The only noticeable change is that, instead of the Indian trail they followed, the route is delineated by the narrow, dirt access road. At the crest of the pass itself, grassy, rolling slopes predominate, and visible in all directions are deep valleys and heavily timbered uplands. In the distance to the west and northwest, even in July, the snow-covered peaks of the Bitterroot and Salmon River Ranges glisten in the sky.

The eastern side of the pass is in Beaverhead National Forest, Mont.; the western, in Salmon National Forest, Idaho. Some of the land in the area is privately held or is claimed by miners and is used for ranching and prospecting. The eastern approach to the pass climbs a rather moderate slope; the western, via Agency Creek, a considerably steeper grade through frequent high canyon walls and an occasional narrow meadow.

The pass is unmarked, but the U.S. Forest Service has installed interpretive markers at the heads of the streams on the east and west sides of it that Lewis and Clark thought were the beginnings of the Missouri and Columbia Rivers. The Forest Service plans to reconstruct the dirt road from Tendoy, Idaho, to the pass to meet modern standards.

Lolo Trail, Idaho-Montana ⚠

Location: Clearwater and Idaho Counties, Idaho, and Missoula County, Mont. Extends 155–165 miles in a northeast-southwest direction. The eastern terminus is the confluence of Lolo Creek with the Bitterroot River near the village of Lolo, Mont., which is about 11 miles south of Missoula at the junction of U.S. 12 and U.S. 93. The western terminus is Weippe Prairie, in Idaho.

Ever a dim track through a primeval land, this rugged trail across the backbone of the Bitterroot Mountains is still essentially in wilderness country and is little changed from the days when the Lewis and Clark Expedition passed over it both en route to and returning from the Pacific. Since long before that time, the Nez Perce Indians had been traversing the trail annually as they passed back and forth from their homeland along the Clearwater River in north-central Idaho to their buffalo hunting grounds in Montana. And in 1877, during the Nez Perce War, the nontreaty faction of the tribe, pursued by Gen. Oliver O. Howard's troops, utilized the route in its epic retreat from Idaho into Montana.

The trail is sometimes known as the Nez Perce Buffalo Road because of the early Indian use, though it was only the main branch of the road. At the eastern end, it forked into two main branches. One led southeastward to hunting grounds on Deer Lodge Prairie, between present Missoula and Butte; the other ran northeastward toward the Sun River-Great Falls of the Missouri area, another grounds. Only in the 1850's did a variation of the main section of the route come to be known as the Lolo Trail; to the Nez Perces it was apparently nameless, and Lewis and Clark called it only "the road."

Rugged landscape in the Bitterroot Mountains of Idaho along the Lolo Trail. The crest of the ridge in the left center of the picture, about 2 miles away, indicates the location of the trail in the vicinity of Indian Post Office.

Section of the Lolo Trail, which is visible beyond and to the left of the marker. This photograph was taken on the crest of the high mountain ridge north of the Lochsa River where the U.S. Forest Service's Jerry Johnson Trail reaches the crest.

Finding the mountains that separated them from the Pacific impenetrable via the Salmon River, in August 1805 the two captains decided to head northward from the Shoshoni village in the Lemhi Valley to the difficult Nez Perce trail over the Bitterroots that the Shoshonis had told them about. From the latter, the explorers acquired as many horses as possible—for food as well as for riding and packing. Between August 30 and September 9, guided by Old Toby, the expedition moved overland via the Lemhi and Salmon Rivers and likely through Lost Trail Pass to the Bitterroot River and thence to Travelers Rest campsite, near the eastern terminus of the Lolo Trail.

The explorers took 11 agonizing days (September 11–22, 1805) to traverse the trail—the most arduous stretch in their entire journey to the Pacific. Battling rain, sleet, and deep snow, as well as hunger and dangerous mountain terrain, often hacking their way through dense underbrush and around fallen timber, gasping for breath in the rarefied mountain air, and eating some of their horses for sustenance, the half-frozen and thoroughly exhausted men trudged wearily onward. For some time, it appeared they might be stranded in the mountains or forced to turn back. To add to their woes, Old Toby, who had passed over the trail only once years before, strayed from the main branch along the high ridges and descended to the Lochsa River, a detour that added at least a day of travel.

The situation finally became so critical that on September 18 the expedition separated to get out of the mountains. Two days later, Clark and a small advance party reached trail's end and met the Nez Perces at Weippe Prairie, where the main body arrived in another 2 days. The explorers, after resting and recovering, built canoes and on October 7 moved down the Clearwater River.

The eastbound crossing of the trail, which took only 6 days, was much easier. The route was better known, and this time the crusted snow supported the horses. Nevertheless, the first attempt to traverse the trail on June 15–21, 1806, was not successful because of heavy snow and the failure to utilize Nez Perce guides. A successful, guided crossing was made on June 24–30.

Another dramatic incident associated with the trail occurred in 1877. At that time, about 700 nontreaty Nez Perces—men, women, and children—crossed it after the Battle of the Clearwater, Idaho. Resisting confinement to a reservation and seeking refuge, they moved into Montana to escape General Howard's slow-moving troops. The Indians were finally vanquished in September-October at the Battle of Bear Paw Mountains, Mont. Both the Nez Perces and the soldiers, in the Weippe Prairie-Lolo Pass segment of the route, passed over sections of it that had been converted into a crude wagon road by private contractors a decade or so earlier, in 1866–67. This never-completed project was carried out as part of a U.S. Government program to improve communications between western mining towns.

After the Nez Perce War, the trail fell into disuse and gradually tended to lose its identification. But, threading through a jumble of ridges, ravines, mountains, thickets, and gorges, it had never been well defined and changed slightly from year to year as trees blocked certain pathways or as better local variations were discovered. To this day, many parts of the route have never been precisely located.

The longest section of the Lewis and Clark pathway that can still be indisputably identified, though considerable woodsman skill is necessary to locate it, is one about 6 miles in length, running in a southwest to northeast direction, between Rocky Point Lookout and Packers Meadow, which is a mile or so east of Lolo Pass.

For most of its distance, the trail passes along the high backbone of the mountain mass between the north fork of the Clearwater River and its middle fork, the Lochsa. Along the stream courses, cascades and rapids make the river gorges impassable by boat, and the steep rock walls of the gorges prevent the establishment of practical foot and horse trails. The eastern part of the route is in Lolo National Forest, Idaho-Mont., and the middle and western parts in Clearwater National Forest, Idaho.

What is called the Lolo Trail today is a steep, dirt fire-access road, constructed by the U.S. Forest Service in the 1930's that generally follows a large portion of the historic trail. Steep, narrow, twisting, and blocked by snow except for parts of July and during August, the road is ordinarily suitable only for trucks and four-wheel-drive vehicles. It runs from the vicinity of Powell Ranger Station, Idaho, on U.S. 12 about 12 miles southwest of Lolo Pass, to Pierce, Idaho. Its western portion runs north of the old trail, but its central and eastern portions closely conform to it. Many of the Lewis and Clark sites that lie off the road can be reached only on foot or horseback.

U.S. 12, called the Lewis and Clark Highway, today parallels the historic trail, but for the most part runs south of it. From Travelers Rest wayside near its eastern end, the highway closely follows the Lewis and Clark route up Lolo Creek, passes the Hot Springs, crosses Lolo Pass, and just west, or south, of the pass skirts Packers Meadow. The explorers' route is picked up again at Powell Ranger Station and traced downstream for about 4 miles, where the two captains and their men climbed out of the Lochsa gorge by a spur ridge (Wendover Ridge) of the main mountain mass.

From this point in the Lochsa gorge, the highway runs along the river down to Kooskia, Kamiah, and Orofino, Idaho. Then it generally conforms with the Lewis and Clark route on to Canoe Camp and thence along the bank of the Clearwater River to its junction with the Snake at Lewiston. An interesting feature along the highway is the Bernard de Voto Memorial Grove of Cedars, on Crooked Creek about 5 miles east of the Powell Ranger Station. This memorial commemorates the author of various works on the Lewis and Clark Expedition.

The U.S. Forest Service, which interprets the trail under a cooperative agreement with the National Park Service as part of the Nez Perce National Historical Park, has placed markers at various points dealing with Nez Perce prehistory, the Lewis and Clark Expedition, and the Nez Perce War.

Nez Perce National Historical Park, Idaho ★

Location: Clearwater, Idaho, Lewis, and Nez Perce Counties; headquarters at the Spalding park unit, in Nez Perce County, about 10 miles east of Lewiston; address: P.O. Box 93, Spalding, Idaho 83551.

Situated in the ruggedly beautiful Nez Perce country, which encompasses 12,000 square miles of northern Idaho, this new and unique park allows today's traveler to see the land as Lewis and Clark described it more than a century and a half ago. The park, much of which is located within the boundaries of the historic Nez Perce Indian Reservation, is the scene of many significant events in the history of the Rocky Mountain frontier. It interprets not only the Lewis and Clark Expedition, but also the prehistory, history, culture, and religion of the Nez Perces; missionary efforts among them; the invasion of fur traders, miners, and settlers; and the Nez Perce War (1877).

Lewis and Clark, on their westward journey in 1805, were the first nonnatives to contact the hospitable Nez Perces. In 1811 the tribe also aided a small group of Astorians, a section of the overland party, who passed through the area on their way to found a fur post, Fort Astoria, near the mouth of the Columbia River. The next year, personnel from the fort established trade relations with the Nez Perces, and other American and British traders soon visited them.

In 1836 the Reverend and Mrs. Henry H. (Eliza) Spalding, the first U.S. missionaries to the Nez Perces, arrived and began a program that lasted many decades. Relations between the Americans and the tribe remained good until the 1860's, when miners and settlers poured into its ancestral homeland of north-central Idaho, northeastern Oregon, and southeastern Washington. This led in time to the Nez Perce War (1877), caused by the refusal of the nontreaty Nez Perces to accept assignment to the reservation their fellow tribesmen had occupied. [The history of the missionary movement and the Nez Perce War and their relation to Nez Perce National Historical Park, along with pertinent sites, are treated in detail in *Soldier and Brave*, New Edition, Volume XII in this series.]

Nez Perce National Historical Park, authorized by Congress in 1965 and still in the initial phase of development, represents a new concept in a national park. It is a joint venture of the National Park Service, other governmental agencies, the State of Idaho, the Nez Perce Tribal Executive Committee, private organizations, and individuals. Of the 24 sites involved, 20 will remain in the hands of their present owners or under a protective scenic easement. Folders available to visitors at National Park Service units give exact locations of all sites and routing information.

The Service administers four major sites: Spalding; East Kamiah; White Bird Battlefield; and Canoe Camp, which is associated with the Lewis and Clark Expedition. This camp, now a 3-acre roadside park, was the approximate location of a key Lewis and Clark campsite, occupied on the westbound journey during the period September 26–October 7, 1805. In Clearwater County along U.S. 12 and about 5 miles west of Orofino, it is situated along the south bank of the Clearwater River opposite the junction of the north fork of the river with the main stream.

This site derives its name and importance from the construction there of the five dugout canoes the expedition used to resume its water journey on the Columbia River system to the Pacific after the difficult crossing of the Bitterroot Mountains from Montana into present Idaho over the Lolo Trail. That arduous trek had debilitated the entire party, which was exhausted and half-starved.

Fortunately, the Nez Perces, first encountered by the advance party on Weippe Prairie at the western end of the trail on September 20, provided a friendly reception. But probably the strange food— camas roots and dried fish—that they furnished the group caused an outbreak of dysentery, which further weakened the men. Anxious nevertheless to continue their trip, they soon moved a few miles westward to the Clearwater, aided and accompanied by many Nez Perces. On September 25 Clark and Chief Twisted Hair found along the river a clump of trees—apparently yellow pine, known today as Ponderosa —that were large enough for the building of canoes. The next day, the main body came up to what has become known as Canoe Camp.

All the men who were able set to work. Instead of hewing the wood, they burned out the tree trunks, the faster and easier Indian method. Before leaving, the explorers branded their 38 horses and left them in Twisted Hair's care over the winter so they could be recovered on the return trip. Nearby, the saddles and some ammunition were cached.

Most of the camp area, narrow and triangular in shape and situated between the river and U.S. 12, is covered with lawn grass, but a few pine trees are scattered about. Unfortunately, modern intrusions are

Site of the expedition's Canoe Camp, on the south bank of the Clearwater River about 5 miles west of present Orofino, Idaho, on Highway U.S. 12. The camp was across and close to the river in the copse of 12 to 15 trees along the bank in the right center of the photograph. While staying there from September 26 to October 7, 1805, the explorers constructed five dugout canoes to carry them to the Pacific.

numerous, because level plots along the Clearwater are few, and those that exist are at a premium for building sites. A filling station and several houses are immediately adjacent to the park area. Construction of the Dworshak Dam on the north fork of the Clearwater has resulted in landscape changes and scars on the north bank of the Clearwater, opposite the Canoe Camp site. An exhibit at the site consists of a modern dugout canoe, covered by an open-sided wooden shelter, as well as an interpretive marker.

Two of the 20 sites among the non-Park Service group have major associations with the Lewis and Clark Expedition: Weippe Prairie and the Lolo Trail. These are National Historic Landmarks and are described separately in this volume. The other 18 sites are related to Nez Perce culture, legend, and mythology; the Nez Perce War; military and missionary relations with the tribe; and the mining rush to Idaho in the 1860's.

Weippe Prairie, Idaho ⚠

Location: Clearwater County, adjacent to Idaho 11, along the southern edge of the town of Weippe. The part of the prairie north of the town bears no special relevance to the Lewis and Clark Expedition.

On this prairie, the western terminus of the Lolo Trail over the Bitterroot Mountains, Lewis and Clark first encountered the Nez Perces on their westbound journey in 1805 and camped there the following year just prior to recrossing the trail. In both instances, the friendly Nez Perces, who had never seen white men before, provided valuable assistance. The cordial relations the explorers established with them remained unbroken for more than seven decades, until the encroachment of white settlers on their lands led to the Nez Perce War (1877).

Leaving behind mountains and forest and entering the southeastern corner of the elevated, open prairie, which had earlier been sighted in the distance, on September 20, 1805, Clark and an advance party of six men proceeded about 5 miles to a Nez Perce village. Just before then, they had met the first tribesmen. The next day, Clark and his group moved to another village about 2 miles to the northwest. From there, they sent back Reuben Field and an Indian with food for Lewis and the main party, which arrived at the easternmost village on September 22. The two captains called the prairie the "camas flats," "quawmash flats," or "quawmash grounds." The Nez Perces obtained from it an important part of their food supply—camas, or quawmash, roots.

The Indians helped the famished and weary explorers recover from the ordeal of the Lolo Trail, particularly by giving them camas roots, dried fish, and berries from their own small supply. The tribesmen also provided some encouraging news: the Clearwater River was navigable and led to the Pacific via the Snake and Columbia Rivers. On September 24, leaving the prairie, the party moved a few miles northwestward to the Clearwater at what has come to be known as Canoe Camp (described in Nez Perce National Historical Park). There, the Nez Perces helped locate trees that were large enough for the construction of canoes. And, on October 7, after about 2½ weeks among the tribe, the expeditioners left their horses behind for safekeeping with the tribe and moved downriver.

On the return trip the next year, the explorers stayed much longer among the Nez Perces, some 7 weeks, while waiting for the snow in the Bitterroots to melt sufficiently to permit a crossing. Most of the

Weippe Prairie, looking to the northwestward toward the city of Weippe, Idaho. On this upland prairie, western terminus of the Lolo Trail and long a camas-digging ground of the Nez Perces, Clark and his advance party met the first tribesmen in September 1805.

horses that had been left with the tribe the year before were recovered. The last camp prior to recrossing the Bitterroots was on Weippe Prairie, roughly a mile southeast of the easternmost of the two villages where the Nez Perces had first been encountered the previous year. On June 10 Lewis and Clark moved up to the camp from Camp Chopunnish. On June 15 they made their first attempt to cross the Lolo Trail but were driven back to their base camp on June 21 by deep snow and frigid cold. On June 24 they set out once again and this time successfully crossed the trail, in 6 days.

Weippe Prairie, interpreted to the public today as part of Nez Perce National Historical Park, is still a beautiful upland prairie, bordered by pine forests. Looming against the sky in the distance to the east are the dark Bitterroots. Although a few farmhouses and some fencing are present, enough open area remains to suggest the unspoiled prairie that Lewis and Clark visited. The property in the area is privately owned or held by the town of Weippe.

The site of the westernmost of the two villages visited by the expedition in 1805 is about a mile southwest of the town; the easternmost, about 2 miles southeast of the other village. The expedition's 1806 campsite was located approximately a mile farther east, or about 2 miles southeast of the town of Weippe, between two branches of Jim Ford Creek.

Sergeant Floyd Monument, Iowa △

Location: Woodbury County, overlooking the Missouri River at the summit of Floyd's Bluff, on the southern edge of Sioux City. Along a gravel road that extends southwestward from the corner of Glenn Avenue and Lewis Road (U.S. 75), between the latter and I-29, which follows the river but does not provide access to the monument.

This 100-foot-high obelisk of yellow sandstone, looming over the Missouri, commemorates Sgt. Charles Floyd, the only member of the expedition to die on the transcontinental journey. He was also the first U.S. soldier to succumb west of the Mississippi and in the newly acquired Louisiana Purchase area.

Floyd was one of seven men recruited by Clark and one of the nine civilians inducted into the Army in the Louisville area. He was promoted to sergeant at Camp Wood. When he passed away near present Sioux City, Iowa, on August 20, 1804, undoubtedly from a ruptured appendix, his comrades carried his body to a high bluff about a mile east of the river, buried it with the honors of war, and marked the site with a red cedar post. As further memorialization, Lewis and Clark named the bluff and a small stream about a mile to the north after him. His replacement as sergeant was Patrick Gass, who was elevated to that rank from private.

The members of the expedition, returning from the Pacific in September 1806, visited the grave and found that some Indians had apparently opened it and left it partially uncovered. It was refilled. In the following decades, many travelers on the Missouri visited the site, whose cedar post served as a landmark to navigators. Included were such notables as Henry M. Brackenridge in 1811; George Catlin, who painted a picture of the bluff, in 1832; Maximilian, Prince of Wied, the following year; and John Audubon, in 1843.

During the 1850's, the Missouri River encroached on the bluff, and in 1857 a spring flood carried away a large portion of it. According to local tradition, not long afterwards someone noticed bones protruding from the face of the bluff. Realizing they must be those of Floyd, a committee of Sioux City residents decided to rescue them. One member, lowered on a rope, retrieved them. In May 1857, amid impressive ceremonies, they were reinterred in a coffin about 200 yards back from the face of the bluff. But the new grave was unmarked, and cattle and horses grazed over it.

Other changes took place. In 1877 a railroad built into Sioux City and ran its track along the base of the bluff. Dirt from the construction was dumped near the gravesite. Gradually its location was forgotten. In 1895 the *Sioux City Journal* agitated for its identification. As many people as possible who had witnessed the 1857 burial were assembled at the site. Excavation at the spot they selected yielded a coffin, containing a skull and some other bones.

About the same time, the Floyd Memorial Association was formed to raise funds to commemorate the 91st anniversary of Floyd's death, on August 20, 1895. On that ceremonious occasion, his bones were removed from the casket, placed in an urn, and reburied. The association also inaugurated a movement to erect a memorial. In May 1899 it purchased a tract of about 22 acres that included the gravesite. In addition, funds were raised to construct a monument. The Federal Government appropriated $5,000; the State of Iowa, $5,000; and the city of Sioux City, Woodbury County, and popular subscription provided $10,000 more. Subsequently, the Floyd Memorial Association

Sergeant Floyd Monument. Floyd was the only member of the expedition to die during the transcontinental trek.

deeded the tract to Sioux City, which continues to administer it as a city park.

The U.S. Corps of Engineers drew plans for the monument, and in 1899 construction began, later under the supervision of Capt. Hiram M. Chittenden. On August 20, 1900, exactly 96 years after Floyd's death, his remains were placed in the concrete foundation and the cornerstone laid. The dedication occurred on May 30, 1901.

Plaques have been affixed to each of the four sides of the monument. Three memorialize, respectively, Floyd; the late John H. Charles, who as president of the Floyd Memorial Association was instrumental in establishing the memorial; and the Louisiana Purchase, the Lewis and Clark Expedition, and the soldiers and pioneers who tamed and settled the trans-Mississippi West. On the fourth side is the National Historic Landmark plaque, the first ever awarded.

The monument, which is surrounded by an iron fence and illuminated at night, is situated in the midst of an area of rugged terrain. Unfortunately, adjacent to the park are many modern intrusions, including a maze of telephone and power lines. A small town, Sergeant Bluff, a few miles to the south, is named in honor of Floyd.

Although the site of Floyd's original burial is no longer extant and the vicinity has changed immeasurably since that day in 1804 when his comrades sadly laid him to rest on a quiet prairie bluff, one can still stand on it, look downstream, and take in the stretch of river where he died.

Camp Wood, Missouri ⊗

Location (approximate): St. Charles County, along the west bank of the Mississippi River, about 2¼ miles north of the present north bank of the Missouri River at its mouth. No road leads to the site; the nearest one is Mo. 99-140, about 5 miles to the west.

During some 170 years of changing river channels in the vicinity, the site of Camp Wood has shifted from the south bank of the Wood River at its junction with the Mississippi River, in Madison County, Ill., to the opposite bank of the Mississippi (see "Location of Camp Wood (Dubois)" map). The Missouri at its mouth has pushed southward; the Mississippi has moved eastward; and a new channel has been dredged for the Wood River.

Confluence of the Missouri and Mississippi, looking upstream to the northeast. The former enters from left center. The original site of Camp Wood is apparently across from the city of Hartford, Ill., visible on the east bank of the Mississippi's big bend, and somewhere on the northeastern corner of the point of land between the two streams that is known locally as Missouri Point. At the time of Lewis and Clark, the Missouri emptied into the Mississippi about 4 miles upstream from its present mouth.

Camp Wood was the expedition's base camp and its home for slightly more than 5 months—between December 12, 1803, and May 14, 1804. Clark established it and directed operations there during the winter while Lewis procured supplies and gathered intelligence data in the St. Louis area—though he paid occasional visits to the camp, as did Clark to St. Louis and Cahokia. But for most of the winter, despite his frequent sickness, the latter labored at selecting, organizing, training, and disciplining the complement; receiving and packing supplies; modifying the keelboat; and providing it and the two pirogues with armament. Lighter moments were provided by shooting matches with local settlers and visits with passing Indians and traders.

On the return trip from the Pacific, on September 23, 1806, just a short time before it arrived in St. Louis, the expedition revisited the Camp Wood site.

The complexities created by the gross changes in the channels of the three rivers render identification of the Camp Wood site extremely difficult, and it is only possible to achieve through a careful examina-

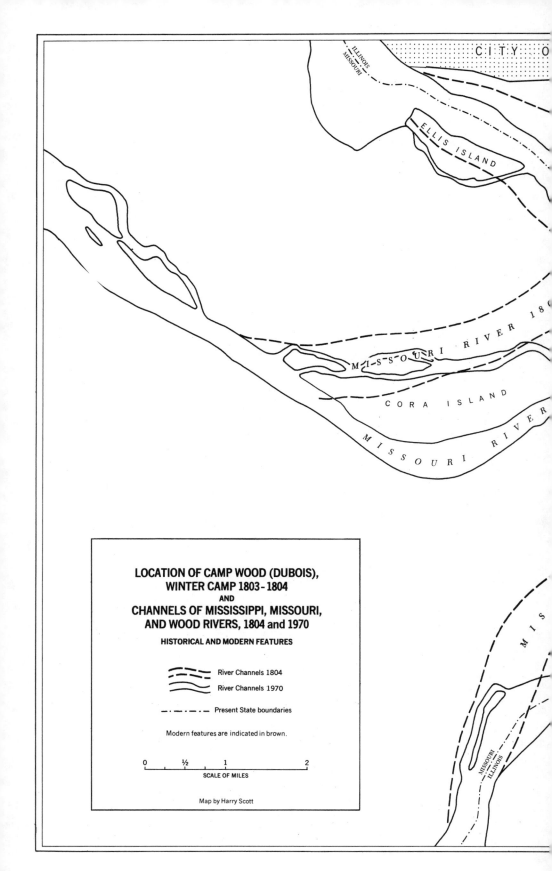

ILLINOIS
MISSOURI

C I T Y · O

E L L I S   I S L A N D

M · I - S - S - O - U - R · I   R I V E R   18

C O R A   I S L A N D

M · I · S · S · O · U · R · I   R I V E R

M I S

MISSOURI
ILLINOIS

**LOCATION OF CAMP WOOD (DUBOIS),
WINTER CAMP 1803-1804
AND
CHANNELS OF MISSISSIPPI, MISSOURI,
AND WOOD RIVERS, 1804 and 1970**

HISTORICAL AND MODERN FEATURES

River Channels 1804

River Channels 1970

Present State boundaries

Modern features are indicated in brown.

0   ½   1   2
SCALE OF MILES

Map by Harry Scott

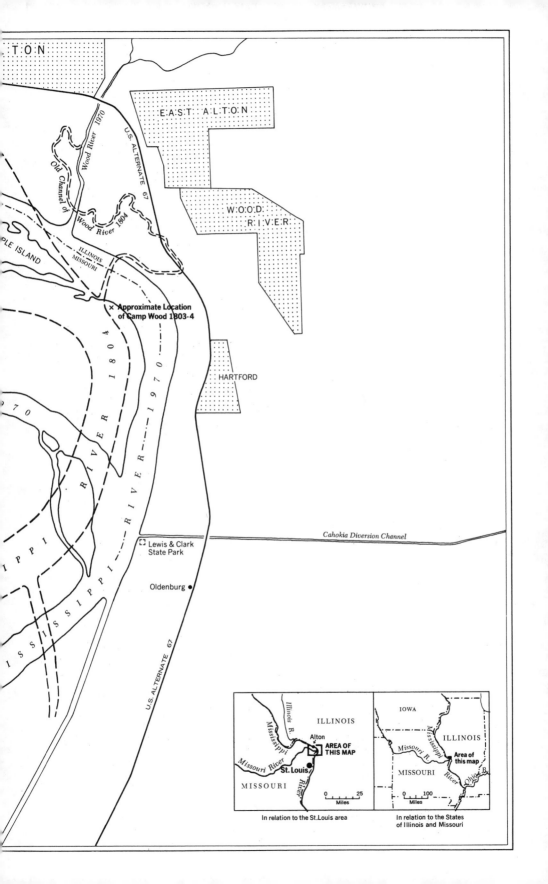

.T.O.N

E.A.S.T A.L.T.O.N

W.O.O.D R.I.V.E.R

Wood River 1970

Old Channel of

Wood River 1804

U.S. ALTERNATE 67

PLE ISLAND

ILLINOIS
MISSOURI

× Approximate Location
of Camp Wood 1803-4

HARTFORD

RIVER 1804

RIVER 1970

970

S S I P P I

I S S I S S I P P I

Cahokia Diversion Channel

⌞⌝ Lewis & Clark
State Park

Oldenburg ●

U.S. ALTERNATE 67

Illinois R.

Mississippi

ILLINOIS

Alton

AREA OF
THIS MAP

Missouri River

St.Louis

River

MISSOURI

0   25
Miles

In relation to the St.Louis area

IOWA

Mississippi

ILLINOIS

Missouri R.

Area of
this map

MISSOURI

River

Ohio R.

0   100
Miles

In relation to the States
of Illinois and Missouri

Upstream view along the north bank of the 1804 channel of the Wood River, in Illinois. Its mouth, which an oil company keeps dredged for a short distance to provide its operations with a water supply from Mississippi backup, is about 100 feet to the right out of the picture where it joins the Mississippi; some ways upstream, the 1804 channel is a dry bed. The present Wood River, running in a newly dredged channel, empties into the Mississippi upstream from the 1804 course. Because of a major change in the channel of the Mississippi, the site of Camp Wood is now on its west side in the State of Missouri.

tion of historical sources and maps. Since the time of Lewis and Clark, the bed of the Missouri, where it debouches into the Mississippi, has moved about 3½ air miles, or some 4½ river miles, along the bend of the Mississippi channel, to the southeast. During the same period, the Mississippi has moved eastward about three-quarters of a mile, eroding away the outside of a great sweeping curve on the Illinois side; as a result, what was river channel in 1804 is now Missouri soil and what was dry land on the Illinois side is inundated by the Mississippi or in Missouri.

This change in the course of the Mississippi has cut off the lower three-quarters of a mile of the Wood River. The lower part of the river channel that remains, which meanders widely and is today a dry bed except for stagnant pools of water in wet weather, can be traced on the ground between the cities of East Alton and Wood River and the Mississippi. Because of the meandering and in the interest of improving its property in the vicinity, about 1917 the Standard Oil Company of Indiana dredged a new channel for the lower extremity of the Wood River that cuts off about 3 miles of the 1804 channel and empties into the Mississippi about three-fifths of a mile north of the remaining old channel. The Standard Oil Company keeps its lower end dredged to accommodate backup waters of the Mississippi that provide a water supply for its operations.

The State of Illinois has erected a monument commemorating the site of Camp Wood, but it is opposite the present mouth of the Missouri, or about 3 miles southeast of the actual campsite. The monument is situated in a small park on the east bank of the Mississippi just south of the point where the Cahokia Diversion Channel empties into the Mississippi about three-quarters of a mile northwest of the village of Oldenburg. U.S. Alternate 67 runs along the river bottom land about three-quarters of a mile east of the monument.

Clark Gravesite and Monument, Missouri ⊗

Location: Bellefontaine Cemetery, bounded by Broadway, W. Florissant, and Calvary Avenues and I-70, St. Louis.

Atop a hill overlooking the Mississippi River in Bellefontaine Cemetery rises an impressive stone monument marking the gravesite of William Clark. A prominent citizen of St. Louis in the years following the expedition, he served there for about three decades as a U.S. Government official. On September 1, 1838, at the age of 69, he died at the home of his eldest son, Meriwether Lewis Clark. Burial, with military and Masonic honors, occurred 2 days later on the farm of the elder Clark's nephew Col. John O'Fallon. Bellefontaine Cemetery later absorbed the gravesite.

Jefferson K. Clark, who died in St. Louis in 1902, then William Clark's only surviving son, bequeathed money for the monument and his widow supervised its construction. Unveiled in 1904, it consists of a tall obelisk on a pedestal. At its base stands a bust of Clark inscribed with the following epitaph: "William Clark—Born in Virginia August 1, 1770—Entered Into Life Eternal September 1, 1838 —Soldier, Explorer, Statesman, and Patriot—His Life Is Written in the History of His Country."

The memorial is located in the northern part of the cemetery above Meadow Lane near the Broadway Avenue entrance. The 333½-acre burial ground also contains the graves of such noted personalities as

Clark Gravesite and Monument, in Bellefontaine Cemetery, St. Louis.

Gens. B. L. E. Bonneville, Stephen W. Kearny, and Sterling Price; fur traders Manuel Lisa, William Sublette, and Robert Campbell; Senator Thomas H. Benton; physiologist Dr. William Beaumont; and engineer James B. Eads.

Fort Osage, Missouri ⚠

Location: Jackson County, northern edge of Sibley.

Although this fort was primarily significant as a fur trading post and one of the first military outposts in the trans-Mississippi West, it also had associations with the Lewis and Clark Expedition and the later career of Clark. On their westbound journey, in June 1804 the two explorers noted that the site, on the south bank of the Missouri overlooking a river bend, would be an ideal one for a fort and fur trading post. Four years later, while serving as a militia general and Superintendent of Indian Affairs at St. Louis, Clark, supported by Volunteer and Regular troops, founded there a "factory" and Army post. That same year, U.S. Government officials signed a treaty at the fort with the Osages, who ceded most of their lands in present Missouri and the northern part of Arkansas.

Fort Osage, sometimes called Fort Clark, was one of the most successful of the 28 Government factories. The ill-fated factory system, inaugurated among the Indians in 1795, sought to win their good will by supplying them with goods from official trading posts, strengthen military policy, promote peace on the frontier, prevent the exploitation of the Indians by private traders, and offset British and Spanish influence over the natives.

Both the Army and the factor abandoned the post during the War of 1812, but returned a year or so later. The Army remained until 1819; the factor until 1822, the year the Government abolished the complicated and idealistic factory system, which had never been very successful. After that time, Fort Osage served as a Government storehouse and stopping point for Santa Fe Trail traders.

No remains of the original log post are extant. In 1941 the County Court of Jackson County, Mo., acquired the site. Between 1948 and 1961, based on extensive archeological excavation and historical research, the Jackson County Park Department, with the technical assistance of the Native Sons of Kansas City (Mo.), reconstructed the fort. It includes five blockhouses, the main one containing exhibits and cannon; officers' quarters; barracks; the factory, which is furnished with period pieces and has a museum on the second floor featuring exhibits on the factory system and military artifacts; an interpreter's house; blacksmith shop; well; and "Little Osage Village."

Jefferson National Expansion Memorial, Missouri ⊠

Location: St. Louis, downtown; address: 11 North Fourth Street, St. Louis, Mo. 63102.

This memorial celebrates the vision of President Jefferson, sponsor of the Lewis and Clark Expedition and architect of westward expansion, as well as all aspects of that vital national movement—in which St. Louis, the "gateway to the West," played a key role. The expedition set out from nearby Camp Wood, and Lewis made many of the final arrangements at St. Louis, the return destination.

Founded in 1764 by Frenchmen from New Orleans, St. Louis evolved as a center of French culture and Spanish governmental control. In 1803 the United States acquired it as part of the Louisiana Purchase, an area soon traversed by Lewis and Clark. Conveniently located in relation to the mouths of the Ohio, Missouri, and other Mississippi tributaries, St. Louis became the hub of midcontinental commerce, transportation, and culture—the point where East met West and jumping-off place to the wilderness beyond. A base of operations for traders, travelers, scientists, explorers, military leaders, Indian agents, and missionaries, it was also headquarters of the western fur trade and focus of scientific and political thought in the West.

Along the waterfront, hulking steamboats from the East and South met the river boats that served the frontier communities and outposts on the upper Mississippi and Missouri Rivers. At this major transfer point, a small but teeming city, mercantile establishments, boatyards, saloons, and lodginghouses accommodated and supplied the westbound settlers and other frontiersmen who congregated there before setting out across the Plains. Oregon and California pioneers and gold seekers bought tools, wagons, guns, and supplies; lumbermen, planters, farmers, and fur dealers sold their products; and artisans fashioned Newell & Sutton plows, Murphy wagons for the Santa Fe trade, Grimsley dragoon saddles, Hawken "plains" rifles, and the cast-iron stoves of Filley, and Bridge & Beach.

Lewis and Clark had been in the vanguard of that westward surge. In 1803–4 their expedition wintered at Camp Wood, then in present Illinois and now in Missouri, about 18 miles north of St. Louis at the mouth of the Wood River on the east bank of the Mississippi. While Clark directed operations at Camp Wood, Lewis spent most of his time in St. Louis, Kaskaskia, and Cahokia recruiting men, obtaining supplies, and acquiring information. At St. Louis, capital of Upper Louisiana and still in Spanish possession despite the cession of Louisiana back to France in 1800, he established relatively amicable relations with governmental authorities and gathered all possible knowledge about Louisiana. On March 9–10, 1804, he witnessed the ceremonies transferring Upper Louisiana from France to the United States; similar ceremonies about 3 months earlier in New Orleans had marked the transfer of Lower Louisiana.

On May 14, while Lewis was still in St. Louis, Clark and the rest of the expedition started up the Missouri from Camp Wood and 2 days later arrived at St. Charles. Lewis joined them there on May 20, and the next day the westward trek resumed. More than 2 years

Gateway Arch at Jefferson National Expansion Memorial, Mo. It commemorates President Jefferson, the Louisiana Purchase, and U.S. expansion to the Pacific. On September 23, 1806, the returning Lewis and Clark Expedition landed at a point that is now within the national memorial, built on the site of old St. Louis.

and 4 months later, on September 23, 1806, Lewis and Clark triumphantly returned to St. Louis, where they disbanded the expedition.

Clark returned to St. Louis from the East the next year and established his residence there. For most of the period until his death in 1838, he held the office of Superintendent of Indian Affairs, but also served at various times as a general in the militia and as Governor of Missouri Territory. Lewis also resided in the city, in 1808–9, while Governor of Louisiana Territory. He apparently committed suicide in Tennessee in the latter year while returning to Washington, D.C., on official business.

To dramatize westward expansion and the rich cultural, political, and economic benefits accruing from the Louisiana Purchase of 1803, an extensive development program for the memorial is being undertaken by the National Park Service and the Jefferson National Expansion Memorial Association, a nonprofit organization of public-spirited citizens. Obsolescent industrial buildings occupying about 40 city blocks have been cleared away as part of a broad urban renewal program. The area of the memorial, which comprises about 85 1/2 acres along the Mississippi waterfront in the heart of downtown St. Louis on the site of the original village, is bounded on the south by Poplar Street, on the north by Washington Avenue, on the east by the Mississippi River, and on the west by the I-70 expressway, except for two blocks extending westward that contain the Old Courthouse.

The dominant feature of the memorial is a 630-foot-high stainless steel arch, designed by the noted architect Eero Saarinen and completed in 1965. Rising from the west bank of the Mississippi River, it symbolizes the historic role of St. Louis as gateway to the West. It contains a special elevator system enabling the visitor to reach an observatory at the top. Scaled to the heroic dimensions of such structures as the Washington Monument, the Eiffel Tower, and the Statue of Liberty, the arch ranks with them in size and grandeur.

The underground George B. Hartzog, Jr., Visitor Center, features the Museum of Westward Expansion, the second largest museum among the national parks. This museum presents the story of the western heritage of the United States, including an extensive section on Lewis and Clark.

Two historic buildings are preserved at the memorial. One is the Old Courthouse, constructed ruing the period 1839-64. It was the scene of the first trial in the Dred Scott case and the dominant architectural feature of the town during the years St. Louis was the "emporium of the West." Its rotunda resounded with the oratory of Senator Thomas H. Benton and other famed speakers of the 19th century. At the courthouse, Benton delivered his well-known oration, using as his theme Bishop Berkeley's poetic phrase "Westward the course of empire." The second historic structure is the Old Cathedral, built during the years 1831-34 on Catholic church property set aside at the time of the founding of St. Louis. At one time the seat of the archdiocese, it is still a shrine and place of worship.

In the general vicinity of the Gateway Arch are the sites of several structures once owned or occupied by William Clark, as well as many others related to early St. Louis history. These sites, which by now have all been obliterated or buried, include those of various Clark residences, which he purchased or constructed; his museum of Indian curiosities, which attracted many visitors to St. Louis; storehouses, offices, and council houses he utilized in dealing with the Indians; and properties he rented to others. In his later years, he lived mainly at his farm, on Bellefontaine Road about 3½ miles north of the city, until his death at the downtown home of his son Meriwether Lewis Clark.

St. Charles Historic District, Missouri ⊗

Location: St. Charles County. The historic district encompasses an area 8½ blocks long and 1½ blocks wide that fronts on the north bank of the Missouri River and is surrounded on three sides by the modern city of St. Charles and on the fourth, or eastern, side by the river. South Main Street, running in a north-south direction, forms the long axis of the historic district, whose northern boundary is the south line of Madison Street.

Although Camp Wood was the base camp and winter quarters (1803–4) for the expedition and the place from which the bulk of the main body set out, St. Charles was the final embarkation point. There, on May 20, 1804, Lewis and the last few members of the complement came on board, the boat loading was adjusted, and last-minute supplies were obtained. Clark and his group, which had departed from Camp Wood on May 14, arrived at St. Charles 2 days later. Scattered along the riverbank they found about 100 homes, whose 450 inhabitants were mostly of French origin. On the afternoon of May 21, everything in readiness, the explorers set out upriver. Returning from the Pacific, on September 21–22, 1806, they stopped at the village overnight.

Originally called "Les Petites Côtes" ("The Little Hills") because of the nature of the surrounding terrain, St. Charles was founded as a fur trading post in 1769 by Louis Blanchette, a French-Canadian hunter. It was the first permanent white settlement on the Missouri River and one of the earliest in the present State. The original settlers were primarily French traders, hunters, and farmers. The Spaniards, who ruled Louisiana Territory in the period 1762–1804,

St. Charles, Mo., final embarkation point of the expedition. It was also once the capital of Missouri and still shows evidence of early French settlement.

made little effort to colonize St. Charles or the surrounding area. In 1791 Don Manuel Peréz, Lieutenant Governor of Upper Louisiana, gave the city its present name, which is translated from the Spanish.

Following the assumption of control of Upper Louisiana by the United States in 1804, the year after the Louisiana Purchase, the influence of the town increased. Located near the confluence of the Mississippi and Missouri Rivers, it became an outfitting station for both land and water transportation routes to the West. In addition to its role as a river port, St. Charles was the eastern terminus of the Boonslick Road. Originally blazed to serve the Boone brothers in their salt manufacturing works in Howard County, the road quickly became the route to Arrow Rock, at which point the Boonslick route joined the Santa Fe Trail. In 1821–26 St. Charles served as the first State capital, on a temporary basis until it moved to its permanent location, Jefferson City.

Fire and deterioration have already removed from the scene a large number of structures once present in the historic district. About 60 of the approximate 102 that remain are noteworthy and 10 warrant further study to determine their importance. The condition of the extant buildings varies, but a high proportion of those that are exemplary are either being restored or are restorable. The various structures are used for private residences, commercial and industrial purposes, or are publicly owned. Houses closely resembling those in the district are scattered throughout the modern city.

Taken as a whole, the historic district retains the layout of the original town plan and provides an example of town planning and development in the Midwest at the turn of the 19th century. Most of the buildings were erected of handmade brick, quarried limestone, and hewn timber. Similar construction occurred elsewhere in the Midwest, but was frequently supplanted by successive waves of building.

Besides various interesting structures and features pertinent to later phases of 19th-century history and architectural development, the district contains a large concentration of early 19th-century buildings that are little altered from their original appearance. None of them can be directly associated with the Lewis and Clark Expedition, but possibly some of them were standing when it passed through. If not, they were soon thereafter and thus represent the architecture of the period.

Tavern Cave, Missouri ⊗

Location: Franklin County, along the track of the Chicago, Rock Island, and Pacific Railroad about a mile from the nearest secondary road, some 2 miles northeast of St. Albans.

On May 23, 1804, or 2 days after leaving St. Charles on their westward trek, Clark and probably some other members of the expedition visited this large cave, located on the south bank of the Missouri at the base of a huge sandstone bluff called Tavern Rock. On the homeward trip, the explorers passed it on September 21, 1806.

Although they were the first men known to describe it, since long before their time, perhaps as early as the late 1770's, it had been a well-known landmark and had been utilized by French and Spanish trappers and traders as a shelter. Because they called it the "Taverne" (cafe or restaurant), some form of a rest stop or inn may have existed there to provide for the comforts of river travelers.

American fur traders visited the cave until the 1840's, as did also such notable Missouri River voyagers as John Bradbury (1809), Henry M. Brackenridge (1811), Surgeon John Gale (1818), and Prince Maximilian of Wied (1832). From the earliest times, many visitors etched into the sandstone walls their names, dates, and other still-visible inscriptions. None of them, however, can be associated with any member of the Lewis and Clark Expedition.

The cave is now located about 250 feet from the Missouri, whereas at the beginning of the 19th century it was right at its edge. Today is is also about 20 feet less wide than in the early days because of the accumulation of land fill at the north and south ends. This fill apparently consists of debris from the present railroad bed, which is located about 60 feet above the level of the cave. An intermittent stream flows from its east wall. At the mouth of the cave is a huge mound. This likely resulted from repeated floodings of the Missouri and the dumping of refuse from the railroad bed.

The area directly surrounding the cave's entrance is covered with brush and trees. Beyond to the river is swampland, apparently created by periodic river floodings and poor drainage. Tavern Rock once rose to a height of 300 feet, but blasting in modern times to form the railroad bed has transformed the bluff's configuration. The Chicago, Rock Island, and Pacific Railroad owns the cave site.

Beaverhead Rock, Montana ⊗

Location: Madison County at the edge of the Beaverhead County line, on the north, or west, bank of the Beaverhead River, along Mont. 41, about 12 miles southwest of the city of Twin Bridges and 14 miles northeast of Dillon. Direct access to the rock is possible only by a rough, ranch-type road.

Always a locally prominent landmark, this massive stone outcrop was a major milestone to the Lewis and Clark Expedition, as it had long been to the Shoshonis. A flurry of anticipation passed through the expedition on August 8, 1805, when Sacagawea recognized it in the distance and said that the summer retreat of her people, the Sho-shonis, was not far to the west. By this time, the explorers were worn out from navigating the troublesome Jefferson-Beaverhead River. Even worse, they were virtually lost and were anxiously seeking the

Beaverhead Rock, Mont. Sacagawea's recognition of this landmark assured the expedition that the Shoshonis, her people, would probably soon be encountered.

tribe, from which they hoped to obtain horses and guides to cross the mountains to the Pacific.

That night, camp was made about 7 miles northeast of the rock. The next morning, Lewis and three men set out overland in search of the Indians, left the river, and traveled behind the rock. On the next day, the 10th, the main, or boat, party, under Clark, passed the rock on its river side. Three days later, on the 13th, Lewis and the advance party made contact with the Shoshonis. Because of the separation of the expedition at Travelers Rest, Mont., on the return trip, only the Clark segment passed Beaverhead Rock, in July 1806.

Considerable confusion exists about the identity of Beaverhead Rock because some writers and the local populace have given the name to what Lewis and Clark called Rattlesnake Cliffs, about 25 miles to the southwest, and have designated Beaverhead Rock as "Point of Rocks." To further complicate the matter, Rattlesnake Cliffs bear a closer resemblance to a beaver's head than does Beaverhead Rock. The cliffs, in contrast to the rock, are closer to the river, are almost perpendicular, and extend along both sides of the stream.

Mont. 41 crosses from the south to the north side of the Beaverhead River close to the rock and skirts its eastern side. Part of the property in the vicinity is administered by the Bureau of Land Management, and the remainder is held by private owners. Unfortunately, recent rock and gravel removal operations by one of the latter at the base of Beaverhead Rock have threatened its integrity. The surrounding area, however, has changed little since the days of Lewis and Clark.

Bozeman Pass, Montana ⊗
Location: Gallatin County, along I-90 (U.S. 10-191), about 13 miles east of Bozeman.

Like the city just to its west, this pass was named after John M. Bozeman, who in 1863–66 brought prospectors and emigrants through it northward from the Platte Valley route of the California-Oregon Trail to the Montana gold mines and settlements. The pass might more aptly have been named after Sacagawea, for on July 15, 1806, on the return journey from the Pacific, she had guided the Clark contingent across it from the Gallatin to the Yellowstone River Valley. There, the group built canoes and proceeded downriver to the Missouri, where a reuniting with the Lewis party took place.

Besides Clark and Sacagawea, the detachment consisted of her infant son, Pomp; her mate, Charbonneau; York; Sergeant Pryor; and seven privates. The nine soldiers, Charbonneau, and York apparently were the first nonnatives to see and traverse the pass. Two days earlier, at the Three Forks of the Missouri, Sergeant Ordway and nine men had taken the canoes recovered at Camp Fortunate, Mont., and headed down the Missouri to meet part of the Lewis complement at the Great Falls; at the same time, the Clark party, with 50 horses, pushed overland toward the Yellowstone River.

Since Indian days, the pass has always been a thoroughfare and accommodated some sort of road or trail. In the 1880's the Northern Pacific Railroad built its main line up the Yellowstone Valley. Until a tunnel could be built through and below the pass, which has an elevation of 5,712 feet, the line utilized a switchback. Later, in 1910, the railroad dug a new tunnel and vacated the old one. Although

Sacagawea was not honored in the name of the pass, in 1903 the U.S. Geological Survey named the Bridger Range's highest peak after her. Rocky and rising to a height of 9,665 feet, it is 18 miles northwest of Bozeman Pass.

Buffalo Jump, Montana ⊗

Location: Chouteau County, about 1¼ miles downstream from the mouth of Arrow Creek on the opposite, or north, bank of the Missouri River and approximately 9 miles by river upstream, or west, from the mouth of the Judith River. A boat provides the best means of access. Mont. 236, about 10 air miles to the north and east, is the nearest improved road; the closest unimproved one comes within a mile of the site, on the north. Make local inquiry.

At this site, in the beautiful White Cliffs section of the Missouri Breaks, discussed elsewhere in this volume, the members of the Lewis and Clark Expedition were probably the first U.S. citizens to see and record a buffalo jump site where the dead animals were still in place.

Before the advent of the steel-tipped arrow and lance and the rifle-musket, it was difficult for Indians to kill buffalo. A particularly fruitful method in the high Plains country was mass killing by the use of "jumps." These were located where buttes, eroded cliffs, and river gorges provided sufficient drop to kill or maim the beasts. The Indians enticed a herd within a short distance of the jump, and then started a stampede that carried the animals to the brink. There, the pressure of those behind forced those in front over the edge.

On May 29, 1805, on the westbound journey, the Lewis and Clark Expedition came upon such a jump. It was on the north side of the Missouri along the base of a 120-foot-high cliff that came almost to the water's edge. The men observed and smelled the carcasses of more than 100 dead and rotting buffalo, which wolves were devouring. Likely, some Blackfeet Indians, whose 2-week-old campsite had been discovered near the mouth of the Judith earlier that day, had conducted the jump. The explorers later appropriately named modern Arrow Creek, a little more than a mile to the west and flowing in from the south, as "Slaughter Creek."

The site was identified in 1963 as 24CH240 by a team from the Missouri Basin Inter-Agency Archeological Salvage Program, which surveyed sites in this part of the river. Even at the time Lewis and Clark passed by, the waters were eroding away the dead buffalo at the stream's edge. In the intervening 170 years or so, floods and erosional action have removed nearly all archeological evidence of the jump. The salvage team found only two pieces of bone fragments, some others of which the private owner had also observed.

Camp Disappointment, Montana ⛫

Location (approximate): Glacier County, on the Blackfeet Indian Reservation, along the south bank of Cut Bank Creek just above the junction of Trail Coulee, about 12 miles northeast of Browning and some 6 miles due north of the Great Northern Railroad and U.S. 2. Access is only possible from the latter by a primitive road that runs northward at the point just west of a monument to Lewis and Clark. The monument is about 22 miles west of the city of Cut Bank and is situated several hundred yards north of the highway. Make local inquiry.

One of the key sites associated with the Lewis contingent on the eastbound journey, during which it investigated the northern extent of the Missouri River drainage at the behest of President Jefferson, this was the northernmost camp established by the expedition and was not far west of the point on Cut Bank Creek that was the most northerly point attained. Lewis, Drouillard, and the Field brothers bivouacked at this place in the period July 22–26, 1806. Lewis apparently named the camp to express his discouragement over the cloudy and overcast weather that prevailed throughout the stay and prevented him from obtaining a good astronomical fix to determine the exact location—though he remained longer than he intended and considered safe.

Lewis had planned to take along six men on the Marias River exploration, but the theft of seven horses by Indians near the Great Falls of the Missouri required him to reduce the number to three, who consisted of the best woodsmen of the expedition. This group took six steeds and left four with Sergeant Gass and his five men, who were later to unite at the falls with Sergeant Ordway and his nine personnel from Clark's party, make the portage around the falls, and set out to meet Lewis at the mouth of the Marias.

On July 16 Lewis and his three companions, ever on the alert,

Monument to Meriwether Lewis, along Highway U.S. 2 about 22 miles west of Cut Bank, Mont. The northernmost point reached by the expedition lies a few miles farther north. The mountains in the background are in Glacier National Park.

set out from the falls into the Blackfeet heartland. Two days later, they arrived at the Marias about 60 miles from its mouth. Finding on July 21 that the river forked into Cut Bank Creek on the north and Two Medicine River on the south, Lewis moved about 28 miles up Cut Bank Creek. The next day at 48°40′ N. he established Camp Disappointment in a clump of large cottonwood trees on a spacious and beautiful bottom. Reconnaissance indicated that the northernmost reaches of the Marias system had been attained and that Blackfeet were in the area. Rainy and cloudy weather prevented any astronomical observations.

The group broke camp on the morning of the 26th to return to the Missouri. The next day, the party encountered eight Blackfeet and camped overnight with them. The following morning, the Indians jumped Lewis and his men, who killed two of their adversaries and managed to escape, later meeting the Gass-Ordway party along the Missouri.

The site of Camp Disappointment, on privately owned land in the Blackfeet Reservation, is in an area that is still almost as primitive as when Lewis and his companions saw it. The terrain consists of rough and broken country, of coulees and plain; the only trees are located along creeks and rivers. An occasional small ranch building, some grazing, and jeep and dirt roads are the only evidence of human activity. The Rockies are visible about 20 miles to the west.

Confluence of the Marias and Missouri, Montana ⊗
Location: Chouteau County, just off a secondary road leading from U.S. 87, about one-half mile southwest of the village of Loma.

Had Lewis and Clark not made the right decision as to what stream to follow at the juncture of the Marias and Missouri and proceeded up the former, the expedition might have failed. The lost time would have seriously reduced the limited food supply; probably have prevented a crossing of the mountains ahead before winter set in; and might have resulted in a disastrous meeting with hostile Blackfeet, whose homeland was along the Marias.

Well aware of most of the implications of the wrong choice of route, the two captains bivouacked at the rivers' junction from June 2, 1805, until June 11–12. Lewis named the Marias as "Maria's River" after Maria Wood, a cousin in Virginia. At the confluence of the two streams, the commanders were confronted with their first major geographical dilemma. They were particularly puzzled because they had earlier decided that the Milk River was the one flowing in from the north that the Minitaris had described. To determine which of the rivers was the Missouri, the route to the Rockies and the Shoshonis, the cautious leaders with small parties separately reconnoitered a considerable distance up each stream.

Most of the command believed the Missouri was the northwestern fork, which was muddy like the Missouri so far and discharged an almost equal volume of water. Lewis and Clark, in a fine example of geographic insight and analysis, decided the Missouri was the somewhat larger southwestern fork. It flowed from the expected direction and possessed the characteristics of a stream originating in nearby mountains: swift current, clear water, and a rocky bed.

Knowing that the Great Falls of the Missouri would be not far ahead if their decision was correct, on July 11 Lewis and four men moved ahead overland to find them. The next day, Clark and the boat party followed. Left behind was the red pirogue, which was hidden on a small island at the mouth of the Marias. Some supplies were also cached along the riverbank.

On the eastbound trip, the Lewis contingent of the expedition, consisting of the commander, Sergeants Gass and Ordway, and 17 enlisted men, spent only part of a day, July 28, 1806, at the juncture of the Marias and Missouri. Fearing an encounter with Blackfeet, the party hurriedly recovered the cache but left the badly decayed red pirogue and four horses. The group then headed downriver in five canoes and the white pirogue to reunite with the Clark element.

Since 1805–6, the junction of the Marias and Missouri has changed several times and is now impossible to locate as it was in the days of Lewis and Clark except in a general way. At that time, it was probably about 2½ miles downstream from the present confluence. The bluffs and bottom lands of both rivers define the limits within which the two streams might then have strayed. The bluff lines of both of them are now high and well defined; the country back from their channels is rough where the drainage cuts down to them from the upland plains. One of the more recent superseded channels of the Marias now is a dry bed running nearly parallel to the Missouri for 2–3 miles and finally angling into it in a willow and cottonwood thicket. Even today, the surrounding land, a rough, brown, almost treeless expanse, is little changed from the Lewis and Clark era except for the village of Loma. It is almost lost to view in the cottonwood and willow bottom near the mouth of the Marias. Most of the land in the vicinity is privately owned.

Gates of the Rocky Mountains, Montana ⊗

Location: Lewis and Clark County. A stretch of the Missouri River about 5¾ miles long in Holter Lake, roughly equidistant between Holter and Hauser Dams, along the northwestern tip of the Helena National Forest. Accessible only by boat. A secondary road, however, runs a little more than 3 miles to the northeast from I-15 (U.S. 91-287), at a point about 15 miles north of Helena, to Lewis and Clark Landing. The landing is on the western bank of Holter Lake not far above the upstream, or southern, end of the gates area. All other parts of the area are inaccessible by road.

Although the expedition had actually entered the Rocky Mountains at the Great Falls of the Missouri, Lewis named this stretch of river the "Gates of the Rocky Mountains," today usually called "Gates of the Mountains."

On July 19, 1805, not long after leaving the Great Falls of the Missouri and shortly before arriving at the Three Forks of the Missouri, the main body of the expedition, in eight canoes under the command of Lewis, passed through the gates—a cliff-walled, claustrophobic, gloomy expanse of river. The day before, Clark, Joseph Field, Potts, and York had set out overland to seek the Shoshonis, so they did not see it. Returning from the Pacific, on July 16, 1806, Ordway and nine men passed through the gates. They were en route from the Three Forks, where they had left the Clark group, to the Great Falls to join the Sergeant Gass detachment of the Lewis party.

Today, Holter Dam, two more dams above it, and their reservoirs create an almost continuous 70-mile-long lake that has drastically changed the Missouri in a region originally comprising some of its most spectacular scenery. No one will ever again see this sight as the Lewis and Ordway parties saw it. The Montana Power Company's Holter Dam, a few miles below the northern exit of the gates, backs up 26½ miles of water in Holter Lake reservoir to the same company's Hauser Dam. The latter creates 16½-mile-long Hauser Lake and Lake Helena in the Helena Valley. Finally, the Canyon Ferry

Photograph of the east entrance of the Gates of the Mountains area as it looks today. Holter Dam, further up the Missouri River, has raised the level of the water about 100 feet above where it was when Lewis & Clark passed through.

Photograph of the west entrance of the Gates of the Mountains as it looks today from Lewis Lake. Formed by Holter Dam, this lake, near Helena, Montana, now has excursion craft which take visitors into the canyon of the Gates of the Mountains.

Dam, erected by the U.S. Bureau of Reclamation, makes 25-mile-long Canyon Ferry Reservoir, which extends to Townsend, Mont.

Yet, despite the greatly elevated water level in the gates area, the spectacular cliffs and sheer rock walls are still so high that the effect of the change is diminished. The only really perceptible difference is the stream's current, which is now placid instead of swift. During the summer months, a cruise boat named *Sacajawea II* takes visitors on daily trips through the gates from Lewis and Clark Landing.

To the north of the gates, from their downriver, or northern, end to a point about 30 road miles southwest of Great Falls where I-15 leaves the Missouri, the river passes through beautiful mountain scenery and threads its way through several closely confined canyons.

The highway parallels the stream on its west side, avoiding many of its widest loops, but running alongside it at many places and affording a fine opportunity to see the Missouri in intermountain plain and mountain canyon. This area, as well as that north of it to the city of Great Falls, is much like it was in the time of Lewis and Clark. At the southern, or upstream, end of the gates is located a ranch, at which point the surrounding land bellies out into a pleasant wide mountain cove. This stretch of river is not visible from I-15 nor accessible by road.

Great Falls Portage, Montana ⚠

Location: Cascade and Chouteau Counties, south of the Missouri River to the east and south of the city of Great Falls. U.S. 87-89 intersects the portage route at the southeastern edge of the city.

Except possibly for the Bitterroot Range and the falls-cascades area of the Middle Columbia, no other physical obstacle challenged the ingenuity and endurance of the Lewis and Clark Expedition as much as the portage around the Great Falls of the Missouri. There, at the beginning of the Rocky Mountains, within a few miles the river suddenly dropped hundreds of feet in seething, foamy torrents over five falls and through a series of rapids—insurmountable barriers to navigation.

The time consumed in making the westbound portage threatened the success of the entire venture, for the summer season was advancing, the Shoshonis had not yet been contacted, and the mountains to the west would need to be crossed before the advent of winter. During the month spent in the Great Falls area, several specific adventures also befell the explorers. For all these reasons, it enjoys a preeminence rivaled by few other sites along their route. Unfortunately, extensive hydroelectric development in the vicinity of the city of Great Falls has obliterated the sublime spectacle at the falls that Lewis and Clark viewed. Yet the general setting—the expansive, beautiful upland rimmed by snow-tipped mountains in all directions except on the north—is unchanged.

From the time Lewis and the four men in his overland party arrived at the falls on June 13, 1805, until the expedition moved upriver on July 13, days of backbreaking labor were expended making

The Great Falls of the Missouri have changed substantially from their appearance when Lewis and Clark came through this area. Depending on the flow of water, however, as this picture shows, the falls can take on some of their former vitality. Down river from Great Falls, at the Bureau of Land Management Interpretive Center in Fort Benton, Montana, arrangements can be made to go into the Missouri Breaks, perhaps the only stretch of the Missouri still much as it was when Lewis and Clark saw it. This piece of the Missouri River is part of the Wild and Scenic Rivers program of the federal government. The Missouri Breaks is under the management of the Bureau of Land Management and well worth the two or three day canoe trip or one day excursion craft outing it takes to enjoy it.

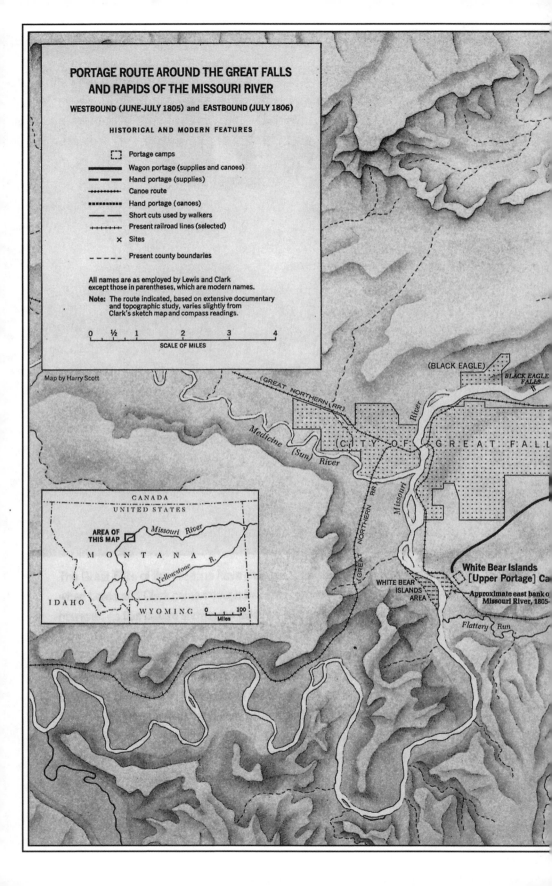

PORTAGE ROUTE AROUND THE GREAT FALLS
AND RAPIDS OF THE MISSOURI RIVER

WESTBOUND (JUNE-JULY 1805) and EASTBOUND (JULY 1806)

HISTORICAL AND MODERN FEATURES

⊡	Portage camps
▬▬▬	Wagon portage (supplies and canoes)
▬ ▬ ▬	Hand portage (supplies)
+++++++	Canoe route
▪▪▪▪▪▪▪	Hand portage (canoes)
── ──	Short cuts used by walkers
++++++	Present railroad lines (selected)
×	Sites
─ ─ ─ ─	Present county boundaries

All names are as employed by Lewis and Clark
except those in parentheses, which are modern names.

Note: The route indicated, based on extensive documentary
and topographic study, varies slightly from
Clark's sketch map and compass readings.

```
0    ½    1         2         3         4
            SCALE OF MILES
```

Map by Harry Scott

(GREAT NORTHERN RR)

(BLACK EAGLE)

BLACK EAGLE FALLS

Medicine (Sun) River

(C I T Y   O F)   G R E A T   F A L L

River

Missouri

GREAT NORTHERN RR

CANADA
UNITED STATES

AREA OF
THIS MAP   Missouri River

M O N T A N A

Yellowstone R.

IDAHO   WYOMING

```
0        100
   Miles
```

WHITE BEAR
ISLANDS
AREA

White Bear Islands
[Upper Portage] Ca

Approximate east bank o
Missouri River, 1805-

Flattery Run

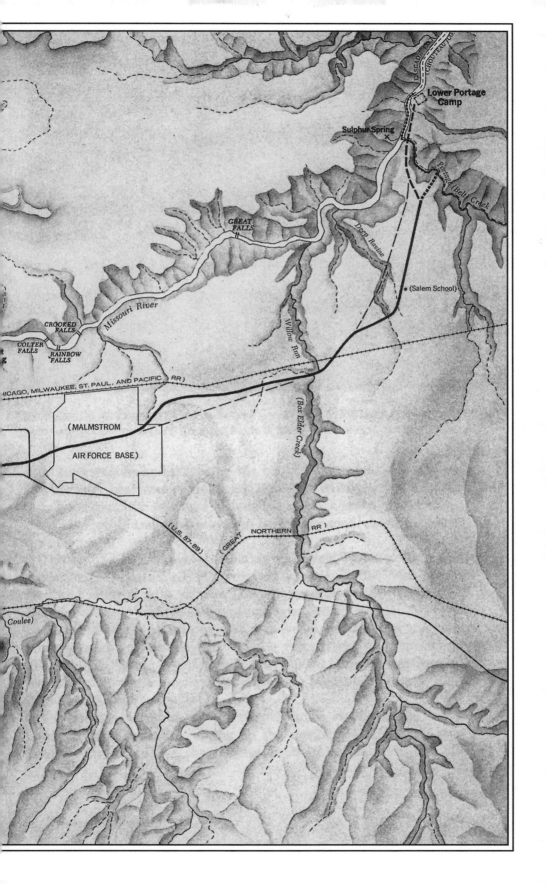

Ryan Dam, in the center, sits just above the Great Falls. To the right, farther upstream, is Cochrane Dam. Irrigated fields in the distance stripe the landscape.

two crude wagons and portaging the boats, equipment, and supplies. The summer heat was oppressive. Close calls with grizzlies and rattlers were common. During a violent rainstorm, Clark, York, Sacagawea, her baby, and Charbonneau barely escaped drowning along the riverbank.

The failure of improvised caulking materials to keep out water rendered the iron-framed "Experiment" useless. It had been assembled and covered with skins at the upper portage, or White Bear Islands, camp to replace the white pirogue, which was too heavy to portage and was hidden along with a cache of supplies near the lower portage camp for possible use on the return trip. To replace the "Experiment," more valuable time then had to be spent constructing two canoes at a place some distance above the upper portage camp where the timber was suitable.

But some occurrences at the Great Falls were favorable. Water obtained from a sulphur spring on the north side of the Missouri near the lower end of the portage route miraculously cured the deathly ill Sacagawea, without whom subsequent relations with her people, the Shoshonis, might not have been as smooth as they proved to be. And, at the falls, the plentiful buffalo provided a good food supply.

To affirm that the correct stream had been selected at the mouth of the Marias, Lewis and the advance party had set out from there to locate the Great Falls, of which the Minitaris had told them. Knowing that Clark and the main party would be anxious to learn the news, at sunrise on June 14, the day after he reached the falls, Lewis sent back Joseph Field to advise them. They arrived at the site of the lower portage camp on the evening of June 15, and the next afternoon reunited with Lewis and his comrades. Once a route was staked out, the portage was conducted between June 21 and July 2. Then, after other preparations were made, on July 14 the whole complement pushed upriver.

Because of the separation of the expedition into two major elements under Lewis and Clark, on the eastbound trip, in July 1806, only part of the overall command made the portage: Sergeant Ordway and nine men from the Clark group, and Sergeant Gass and five men from the Lewis party. Despite less manpower, but aided this time by four horses to pull the wagons, they accomplished the portage in only 8 days, in contrast to 11 on the outbound journey. The Gass-Ordway element then proceeded downriver to rendezvous with Lewis and his three companions, who had been exploring the Upper Marias River.

No signs of the portage route are discernible today, but documentary and cartographic research, coupled with terrain study, has made possible its approximate delineation in the map in this volume entitled "Portage Route Around the Great Falls and Rapids of the Missouri River." It also includes key sites, camps, portage methods, and modern features.

From the lower camp, for most of the way the portage route lay 2–3 miles south of and generally paralleled the Missouri, and reached the river again only at the upper camp. Except at the eastern extremity, for the greater part of the distance the route, finally reduced to 17¾ miles in length from 18¼, ran nearly straight in a northeast-southwest direction across a plain that was level in parts and semilevel in others. Then, near the upper camp, the track descended a gradual slope to an open level cove at the river. Except for a segment of the portage route that crosses Malmstrom Air Force

When little water is released by Ryan Dam, in the background, the Great Falls dwindles to a trickle.

Base and those few places where Federal, State, and county roads and the track of the Milwaukee Road (Chicago, Milwaukee, St. Paul, and Pacific Railroad) intersect or run along it, it is located on private property.

Lower portage camp, on the south, or east, bank of the Missouri, marked the eastern terminus of the portage. About a mile to the south of its site, Belt Creek (called Portage Creek by Lewis and Clark) empties into the Missouri from the south side. Except for livestock grazing, the lower portage camp site, the rocky, gorge-like Belt Creek channel, the rapids of the Missouri at the point where the creek comes into the river, and the bluffs on both sides of the stream are free from modern intrusions—one of the few unspoiled areas prominently associated with the Lewis and Clark Expedition.

At this point, the Missouri flows between high and, in most places, precipitous banks. The area at the mouth of the creek is virtually treeless. Brush and low shrubs grow in drainage rivulets. High native grass covers the benchland; prickly pear cactus dot the ground. The terrain in the area about a mile up the creek where the canoes were hand-carried up the steep bluff to the plain is treacherous and is in a state of nature except for limited pasturage of livestock and the presence of a dirt road that crosses the creek.

The Montana Power Company owns the land on both sides of Belt

Creek for a distance of about 1,000 feet upstream from its mouth. The remainder in the vicinity is privately owned ranch land. The lower Belt Creek area can be best reached by a dirt-gravel county road, but local inquiry is necessary. The lower portage camp site is unmarked and is accessible only on foot or by boat.

The portage route from the edge of the plain above Belt Creek to Malmstrom Air Force Base, about 8 miles in extent, is mainly open farmland. The route then intersects approximately 2 miles of the runway section of the air force base, south of the major buildings and hangars; and, just after crossing U.S. 87-89, traverses the southeastern edge of the city of Great Falls, which is progressively making inroads into the area to its east toward the base. The final 3 miles to the site of the upper portage camp is mainly farmland, though here again the city is encroaching.

The present appearance of the White Bear Islands area and the upper portage camp site has changed considerably since 1805-6. Because the river channel has changed, the three islands have all but disappeared. The two westernmost have become a part of the north, or west, bank of the Missouri, but a heavy growth of cottonwood, willow, and brush still marks the low-lying area. What was the easternmost island has been joined, in effect, to the east bank of the river. A surfaced highway, River Drive (Route 226), out of Great Falls, comes onto the old island area by a short fill, runs its full length, and then crosses over a short causeway back to the old bank. The track of the Burlington Northern, formerly Great Northern, Railroad loops around what was probably the edge of the old riverbank. The latter is separated from the highway only by a water-filled slough that apparently was originally part of the river channel separating the island from the mainland.

Just east of the remnant of the old eastern island, across the railroad track, is apparently the upper portage camp site, which is unmarked. It is in the northern end of a level area, which is nearly a mile in extent north and south along the river and about half a mile wide from the river back to a low benchland. The presumed campsite is about three-quarters of a mile north of Sand Coulee, which bounds the level area on the south and flows into the Missouri River not far above the White Bear Islands area. Great Falls suburban development is taking place along the coulee near its mouth and on the bench above the river bottom. But this has not yet spread to the

Sulphur Spring, whose waters cured Sacagawea of a serious illness. The outlet stream pours into the Missouri about 300 yards away, near the tree in the upper left.

presumed campsite, which remains open ground and is privately owned.

No one will ever again see the 9-mile stretch of river encompassing the five great falls and rapids, with its sunken, trench-like channel formed by 200-foot-high, precipitous stone walls, as the explorers saw it. It was inevitable that a growing industrial United States would utilize the downpouring flood at the great falls and that a major city, Great Falls, the largest in Montana, would grow near them. This urban center has pushed over onto the north, or west, bank along the mouth of the Sun River. On the bluff behind the town of Black Eagle, on the north bank of the Missouri opposite the city of Great Falls, rises the huge, 506-foot-high smelter stack of the Anaconda Copper Company.

The two captains named only the first two falls downstream: Great Falls, the easternmost, and Crooked Falls. The other falls, in order from east to west, were later called Rainbow Falls, Colter Falls, and Black Eagle Falls. Clark calculated their heights at 87, 19, 47, 6, and 26 feet, respectively. Four of the five shelves of rock, excepting Colter Falls, are still visible in their jagged and massive grandeur, though they are deprived of their mantle of white, churning water.

The only time of much flow is in the spring runoff season and during heavy rainfall; in the dry period, only Rainbow Falls shows a sizable drop of water, at its southern edge.

The Montana Power Company has built a series of five dam-powerplants in the area; in order going upstream, they are named Morony, Ryan, Cochrane, Rainbow, and Black Eagle. Three of them have been built just upstream from three of the falls: Ryan Dam near Great Falls, and Rainbow and Black Eagle Dams close to the falls of the same name. Morony Dam is about 4½ river miles below the Great Falls and some 1¼ miles above Belt Creek, and Cochrane Dam a little less than 2 miles above them. Colter Falls, the smallest of the five, is inundated in the reservoir back of Rainbow Dam.

The Montana Power Company owns most of the riverbank on both sides of the Missouri and for varying depths inland from the Black Eagle Dam to a point some distance below the Morony Dam. But, along this stretch of river, some property is privately owned and the city of Great Falls holds title to a few tracts.

Along the north bank of the Missouri, various roads lead to Black Eagle Dam, which is adjacent to its namesake town; Rainbow Dam Road runs from the town to Rainbow Dam; and Ryan Dam Road, beginning off U.S. 87 some 3 miles northeast of town, extends to Ryan Dam and offers access to Morony Dam. At the Great Falls, just below Ryan Dam, the Montana Power Company maintains a free picnic area on an island, which is connected by a bridge to the north bank. On the south side of the river, River Drive (Bypass U.S. 87) passes Black Eagle Dam and runs eastward from the city of Great Falls to connect with a secondary road that leads to Rainbow Dam before turning south toward Malmstrom Air Force Base. Only horse trails and footpaths give access to the river downstream from Rainbow Falls to Belt Creek on the south side of the river.

Two specific features along the stream that are associated with Lewis and Clark, Giant Spring and Sulphur Spring, are little changed. On June 18, 1805, Clark discovered the former, a tremendous spring of fresh, cold water, along the south bank of the Missouri about a mile above Rainbow Falls. Lewis visited the spring later, on June 29. It was about 25 yards from the river, into which it fell over steep, irregular rocks and at one point dropped 6 feet.

Giant Spring, in a city park just off the secondary road leading from Bypass U.S. 87 to Rainbow Dam, remains much like it was then. To this day, it pours forth a gush of 388,800,000 gallons of water daily, out of and over granite rocks; and it still flows into the Missouri, which is immediately adjacent. In fact, at first glance the spring seems to be a part of the river. The only separation today between the two is a low rock shelf, over which the water rushes into the river. A concrete walkway surrounds the spring, whose water is utilized by a nearby Montana fish hatchery.

The Sulphur Spring, whose water probably saved Sacagawea's life, is located opposite the mouth of Belt Creek about 300 yards from the north bank of the Missouri on a sloping grass shelf. The spring is about 30 feet in diameter, and the rivulet it creates drops in a fine little waterfall over a high rock shelf into the Missouri. The spring, which is unmarked and privately owned, is situated in a remote area. Except for a rickety wire fence that keeps out livestock, the environment is virginal. Access, which is extremely difficult, is provided by U.S. 87, Ryan Dam Road, and circuitous travel over unimproved roads and trails; local inquiry is mandatory.

Lewis and Clark Pass, Montana ⊗

Location: Lewis and Clark County, in the Helena National Forest, about 17 miles northeast of Lincoln, Mont., on the Continental Divide at the heads of Alice Creek, on the west, and Green Creek, on the east. The best approach is from the west side of the divide. About 8 miles east of Lincoln on Mont. 200, a marker points up Alice Creek to Lewis and Clark Pass. A passable road extends northward along the creek for about 15 miles to the Alice Creek Ranger Station (Helena National Forest). From there, a 1-mile jeep trail leads to the crest of the pass.

Over this pass—subsequently misnamed Lewis and Clark Pass because Clark never saw or traversed it—on July 7, 1806, Lewis and his nine-man party recrossed the Continental Divide and reentered U.S. territory. Clark and his much larger contingent, which had separated from the rest of the expedition at Travelers Rest, Mont., passed over the divide via Gibbons Pass.

When Lewis crossed Lewis and Clark Pass, he was following an overland Indian shortcut between Travelers Rest and the Missouri just above the Great Falls that the explorers had missed on their westbound journey and which would have saved them almost 50 days and the tribulations of the land-water route they had utilized. The two missions of the Lewis group were investigation of the shortcut and exploration of the Upper Marias. The traverse of the shortcut to the Great Falls, utilizing 17 horses, required 8 days. After crossing Lewis and Clark Pass, Lewis, pursuing buffalo and other game, pushed north beyond the Dearborn River route to the Missouri until he reached the Sun River, which he followed downstream to the Great Falls area.

Remote Lewis and Clark Pass (6,421 feet) is all but forgotten today and does not even appear on most highway maps. The major reason for this is the routing of Mont. 200 over the divide via Rogers Pass (5,610 feet), about 6 air miles to the southeast, instead of by Lewis and Clark Pass or Cadotte Pass (6,040 feet), situated midway between the two other passes. Mont. 200, which runs from the Sun River Valley to Missoula, generally follows the old Indian trail traveled by Lewis and his men.

Over the years, Lewis and Clark Pass has changed little. To the west, where the ascent is easy, is a mixture of forest and open glade land; to the east, where the ascent is rocky and steep, rising 1,400 feet in the last 2 miles, lies barren and broken country. This leads down from the divide to the great game plains at the foot of the mountains—where enormous buffalo herds roamed in the time of Lewis and Clark.

Lewis' Fight with the Blackfeet Site, Montana ⊗

Location (approximate): Pondera County, on the Blackfeet Indian Reservation, along the south side of Two Medicine River about 4 miles below the mouth of Badger Creek and 1½ miles south of the Glacier-Pondera County line, some 14 air miles southwest of the town of Cut Bank. Ranch trails come close to the site. These trails lead from the secondary road to the village of Valier that runs south from U.S. 2 about 3 miles west of the town of Cut Bank. The site is about 4½ miles west of the point where the secondary road crosses Two Medicine River. Make local inquiry.

While reconnoitering the Marias River area on the return from the Pacific in 1806, at this site the Lewis party killed two Blackfeet Indians, the only Indian fatalities inflicted by the expedition. Indeed, the fight with the Blackfeet and the acrimonious clash with the Teton

The circle marks the approximate place where Lewis and three companions camped with eight Blackfeet Indians on the evening of July 26, 1806, along Two Medicine River. The next morning, a fight erupted when the natives tried to seize the explorers' rifles and run off with their horses. In the ensuing melee, two Indians died. Edward Mathison, Robert H. Anderson, and Helen B. West identified this site in 1963–64.

Sioux were the only major examples of bad relations with the natives on the entire journey.

On July 26, 1806, Lewis and his three companions were moving southward from Camp Disappointment, Mont., heading back to the Missouri to rendezvous with the rest of their party. Along Two Medicine River, eight Blackfeet were encountered. Although wary of hostilities, the explorers camped overnight with them along the south side of the river. At dawn, the Indians jumped the white men and tried to steal their horses. In the clash, during which Lewis narrowly missed being shot, two of the Blackfeet died and the rest fled with part of the white men's horses, but left some of theirs behind. The prospect of meeting a large band of Blackfeet, known to be in the area, spurred the four men to make a forced ride to the Missouri, where they reunited with the main body of their group on July 28.

The site, a small bottom surmounted by 250-foot-high bluffs, is still almost untouched by man. It is in private ownership within the Blackfeet Indian Reservation.

Missouri River Breaks, Montana ⊗

Location: Chouteau, Fergus, Phillips, and Blaine Counties. A stretch of about 140 river, or 100 air, miles along the Missouri River from Ryan Island, near the upper, or western, end of the Fort Peck Reservoir to the city of Fort Benton. A section of about 55 river, or 40 air, miles west of the Judith and running almost to the Marias is called the White Cliffs. Below this area for roughly an equal distance extends what is known as the Missouri River Badlands. Various roads provide access to specific parts of the Missouri River Breaks.

Nowhere along the route of the expedition is there such a long stretch of country so unspoiled since 1805–6 as is this picturesque area of the Missouri River—a twisting ribbon of water through eroded land in the high Plains. The scenic splendors that enthralled Lewis and Clark and their command are as apparent now as then, though the bighorn sheep, elk, buffalo, and deer they saw are now rarely viewed.

On the westbound journey, the explorers passed through the area in late May and the first half of June 1805. On the eastbound phase, the Lewis contingent, separated from Clark's group, passed through it in late July and the first few days of August 1806—more quickly this time because the current was favorable and a long stop at the Marias was not necessary. On the westward trek, in the breaks area, the explorers saw their first Indian buffalo jump and spent more than a week at the junction of the Marias and Missouri trying to determine which stream to follow. Both of these sites are described separately in this volume. Also, during this period, Lewis and Clark named the Marias and Judith Rivers and encountered evidence of Blackfeet camps.

The most spectacular portion of the breaks area is the White Cliffs section, where perpendicular cliffs rise 200 to 300 feet. The white sandstone is sufficiently soft to erode easily. Water and wind

Toadstool area near the Hole-in-the-Wall, White Rocks Section, Missouri River Breaks.

have created thousands of fancy and grotesque figures, sometimes specked with browns and reds—visionary enchantment appearing in such forms as buildings, cities, pillars, spires, gargoyles, and castles. Along this area, in 1833 the Swiss artist Karl Bodmer, who was accompanying Prince Maximilian of Wied, sketched and painted several views that can still be identified today.

The Missouri River Breaks has been spared from many modern intrusions by the inhospitality of the surrounding land to use by man, except mainly for limited ranching and farming. Another factor is the absence of dams that have so altered the river from Fort Peck downstream, around the Great Falls area, and farther upstream between the Gates of the Mountains and the Three Forks. Probably no more than 5,000 acres of land are under cultivation along the

140-mile stretch of river bottom. For these reasons, population is sparse. The two largest villages in the area are Loma and Virgelle, which are located at its western end near the city of Fort Benton. Only one highway bridge and three little-used ferries traverse the river. The bridge conveys U.S. 191, which crosses the river in a north-south direction on the eastern edge of the breaks.

The Missouri River Breaks are essentially a primitive wilderness. The eroded bluffs along the river vary from 2 to 10 miles in width. The relatively flat upland plains that border them, used primarily for ranching today, are usually from 500 to 1,000 feet above the river channel, along which the bottom land is narrow. The stream drops about 3 feet to the mile on the average. For about 100 miles below Fort Benton, numerous rapids exist, just about as Lewis and Clark encountered them. Most are from 20 to 30 inches deep. Rocks carried into the river by tributary streams and gullies, and pushed into masses by ice, form frequent shoals.

The U.S. Bureau of Land Management owns more than half the land contiguous to the river below Arrow Creek, and most of the remainder is in private ownership; above the creek, most of the land along the stream is privately owned.

When this volume went to press, Congress was considering various proposals to establish the Missouri Breaks National River, and the Department of Interior's Bureau of Land Management and Bureau of Outdoor Recreation were making studies of the area under the provisions of the National Wild and Scenic Rivers Act (1968). Steps to insure preservation of the area will offer future generations the opportunity to see it in essentially the same condition as did Lewis and Clark.

Pompeys Pillar [Pompy's Tower], Montana △

Location: Yellowstone County, on the south bank of the Yellowstone River, approximately one-half mile north of I-94 (U.S. 10), between the villages of Nibbe and Pompeys Pillar and some 28 miles northeast of Billings.

William Clark's inscription of his name and the date on the north-eastern face of this huge rock formation is the only surviving physical evidence known to remain along the route of the explorers that was left by them and can be indisputably associated with the expedi-

Clark's inscription on Pompeys Pillar, protected by shatterproof glass and a bronze frame.

tion. Possibly two others in the party also etched their names, but this cannot be proven.

On the afternoon of July 25, 1806, while separated from the Lewis group on the return trip from the Pacific and proceeding down the Yellowstone River, Clark, York, Sacagawea, her infant son, Charbonneau, and four privates stopped at the river landmark. Some of them climbed it, and viewed the surrounding panorama of mountain plains and wildlife. Clark carved his name and the date near some Indian pictographs, which are not extant today. He apparently named the rock as "Pompy's Tower" after the infant, whom he called "Pomp" or "Little Pomp." But either Nicholas Biddle, the author, or Paul Allen, the editor, of a history of the expedition issued in 1814, renamed the rock as "Pompey's pillar."

After the stop there, the Clark party moved down to the Missouri. It reunited first, on August 8, with Sergeant Pryor and three men who had left the Clark group earlier and had been unable to complete a special mission; and later, on August 12, with the Lewis contingent.

Although Clark was the first white man to carve his name in the soft light sandstone of the massive formation, he was not the first to visit it. The year before, in September 1805, the Frenchman François Antoine Larocque paid a call while on a trapping expedition with some Crow Indians who had come to trade at the Mandan villages. Lewis and Clark had met him there during the winter of 1804–5.

Subsequently, other explorers, trappers, soldiers, gold seekers, railroad surveyors, and steamboat crews passed or stopped at the well-known landmark. Many of them inscribed their calling cards. In 1876 Lt. James Bradley, chief of scouts for Col. John Gibbon's column in the campaign that climaxed in the Battle of the Little Bighorn, Mont., complained that one of his soldiers had carved his name across the "k" in Clark's name. Apparently he did not cut it deeply, however, for time has obscured the alteration.

In 1873 Lt. Col. George A. Custer camped near the rock with part of his 7th Cavalry while guarding a Northern Pacific survey party. A group of hostile Sioux fired on the cavalrymen from the opposite bank of the river. In later times, railroad passengers could readily see the landmark from train windows, as they still can today.

In the far distant geological past, the pillar was obviously part of the same formations now exposed in the bluffs a few hundred yards north across the river, but the stream eroded through a protruding headland and isolated the landmark that is seen today. As viewed from the west and south, the stone face of the pillar juts vertically above the level valley floor, more than a mile across at this point, sparsely populated and in agricultural use. The northeastern, or river, side of the rock gradually slopes downward to ground level. Contrary to most written descriptions, the overall height of the pillar, including its cap of earth, is probably not more than 120 feet above its base. The diameter of the long axis, running east to west, is about 350 feet. A strip of land 300 feet wide separates the rock from the riverbank.

The Clark etching, in script, reads as follows:

Wm Clark

July 25   1806

Along with various other inscriptions, it is located on the eastern face on an overhanging wall of rock just below the top. The wall is about 7 feet above a short path running along the wall's base. The site is easily reached from one of several trails leading up the sloping northeastern face.

The Northern Pacific Railroad deserves major credit for preservation of the inscription. In 1882, when the line was building up the Yellowstone Valley, its officials noted that vandalism was rapidly effacing the etching and they installed over it a heavy double iron screen, or grating. Without this action, it likely would have been destroyed. The screen, however, did not impede weathering and erosion. It also made the inscription difficult to read and impossible to photograph effectively. On a visit in 1900, historian Olin D. Wheeler found that it had been scratched over and that various names had been cut all around it and just over and below some of the letters of Clark's name. All this had apparently been done before the screen was put in place. In 1926, responding to the interest of the Daughters of the American Revolution in deepening and freshening the inscription, the Northern Pacific hired a Billings marble and granite firm to deepen it.

In 1956, the year after a new private owner acquired the rock and surrounding land to preserve it as a historic monument, the iron grating was replaced with a heavy bullet- and shatter-proof glass, edged in bronze. This left the inscription fully visible but protected it from the elements. Other steps later taken to enhance the area were the construction of a road from the highway, the grading of trails up the pillar, and installation of some steps and railings, as well as interpretive markers. The site, now owned by the widow of the 1955 purchaser, is open to the public at nominal cost.

Rattlesnake Cliffs, Montana ⊗

Location: Beaverhead County, on both banks of the Beaverhead River, along I-15 (U.S. 91), about 10 miles southwest of Dillon adjacent to the hamlet of Barretts.

On August 10, 1805, Lewis and three companions, heading overland to seek the Shoshonis, stopped at and named these cliffs because of the large number of rattlers in the vicinity. Five days later, Clark's boat party passed by. On the return from the Pacific in 1806, the Clark element went by the cliffs. Today they are known locally as

Beaverhead Rock. In 1963, as part of the Clark Canyon Reclamation Project, a diversion dam was built in the river along the cliffs. Most of the land in the immediate vicinity is federally owned.

Rattlesnake Cliffs from the land side. Union Pacific tracks are in the foreground. Similar cliffs rise on the opposite bank of the Jefferson River.

Ross's Hole, Montana ⊗

Location: Ravalli County, in Sula State Forest, along U.S. 93 in the vicinity of the hamlet of Sula.

In the southwestern corner of this beautiful mountain cove at the junction of Camp Creek and the east fork of the Bitterroot River, en route from the Lemhi Valley to the Lolo Trail, on September 4, 1805, the westbound expedition encountered a village of Flathead Indians and spent 2 days with them. From the friendly tribe, the explorers obtained badly needed horses. Charles M. Russell's huge 12 by 26 foot painting (1912) of the event, commissioned by the State of Montana, hangs behind the Speaker's desk in the capitol

Corner of the intermountain valley known today as Ross's Hole. At this place, the explorers encountered some Flathead Indians and obtained from them a number of badly needed horses.

at Helena. On the return trek from the Pacific, the Clark contingent stopped at the hole on the night of July 5–6, 1806.

Later, the cove was named Ross's Hole after Alexander Ross, leader of a Hudson's Bay Company trapping brigade, who camped there in 1824.

The shape of the hill- and mountain-enclosed valley resembles a Christmas tree, whose base is at the south, where the valley is about 4 miles wide. It extends northward about 8 miles, gradually tapering to a point. Except for the small community of Sula, a few ranch-houses, and highway U.S. 93, which skirts the southwestern corner of the hole, where Lewis and Clark met the Flatheads, modern intrusions in the cove are negligible. Various unimproved roads provide access to the northern part of the valley. Between Salmon, Idaho, and Lolo, Mont., U.S. 93 closely follows most of the Lewis and Clark route.

Three Forks of the Missouri, Montana ⚠

Location: Broadwater and Gallatin Counties, about 3 miles north of U.S. 10 along Route 286, some 4 miles northeast of the town of Three Forks.

This lush and beautiful area, lying on the northern edge of a vast, mountain-rimmed basin, is one of the key sites in western history, particularly in the fields of Indian intertribal relations, exploration, and the fur trade. Notable figures who were prominently associated with the place include Lewis, Clark, Sacagawea, John Colter, George Drouillard, and Cols. Pierre Menard and Andrew Henry. At this "essential point in the geography of this western part of the Continent," as Lewis termed it, the Gallatin flows into the Jefferson-Madison to form the Missouri approximately one-half mile northeast of the juncture of the Jefferson and the Madison.

Lewis and Clark, the first white men to visit the locale, found it teeming with otter, beaver, and other wildlife. For this reason, it was a meetingplace and disputed hunting ground—often a dark and bloody no man's land—for various Indian tribes. In this region, the Blackfeet and Minitaris raided the Shoshonis and Flatheads when they ventured eastward over the mountains to hunt. As a matter of fact, Sacagawea's village of Shoshonis had been camped at the same place as the expedition, near the confluence of the Jefferson and Madison, about 5 years earlier when she was about 12 years old. The Minitaris attacked the village and captured her about 4 miles farther up the Jefferson.

The Lewis and Clark Expedition, eagerly seeking the Shoshonis, who could help in crossing the mountains to the west, arrived at the Three Forks not long after completing the arduous portage of the Great Falls of the Missouri. Clark and an advance element of four men reached the forks on July 25, 1805, and explored the lower 32 and 20 miles, respectively, of the Jefferson and Madison. The boat party made its appearance 2 days later, set up a base camp on the south bank of the Jefferson a short distance from its juncture with the Madison, and reunited with the Clark group. The next day, some men probed a ways up the Gallatin. Nursing the ailing Clark and trying to decide which of the three streams led westward, the expedition stayed at the forks until July 30. The crucial decision was rather easily reached to follow the Jefferson, which the commanders named as well as the other two rivers.

On the return trip from the Pacific, the Clark contingent arrived

View to the northwest from the south bank of the Gallatin a few hundred yards from where it joins the Jefferson-Madison to form the Missouri. Lewis, when he arrived at the Three Forks on July 27, 1805, climbed the limestone cliff at the right.

at the Three Forks on July 13, 1806. That same day, Sergeant Ordway and nine men headed down the Missouri to join Sergeant Gass and his detachment of the Lewis party at the Great Falls; and Clark and the 12 people in his group headed eastward overland to explore the Yellowstone River.

IN the spate of fur trade activity that occurred in the years immediately following the expedition's return to St. Louis, the Three Forks area was heavily trapped. Three of the participants were erstwhile members of the Lewis and Clark Expedition: John Colter, George Drouillard, and John Potts. They all experienced some hair-raising adventures with the Blackfeet, which resulted in the death of the latter two.

Probably in 1808, a few months after he had become the white discoverer of the present Yellowstone National Park while on another venture, Colter was wounded in a battle in the Gallatin Valley near the Three Forks between a large party of Crows and Flatheads and hundreds of Blackfeet. The latter were repulsed. Colter, who was leading the Crows and Flatheads to trade at Manuel Lisa's Fort Raymond, on the Yellowstone River at the mouth of the Bighorn, had no choice but to join them in the fight. Nevertheless, his participation was apparently one of the major reasons for subsequent Blackfeet hatred of American traders and trappers.

No sooner had Colter recovered from his wounds than he and John Potts, operating out of Fort Raymond, were trapping on a creek flowing into the Jefferson River a short distance from the Three Forks when a band of Blackfeet surprised them and ordered them to bring their canoes to shore. Colter complied; Potts died when he refused, but not before he killed one of his adversaries.

The Indian chief decided to give his young warriors the sport of running Colter down on the prickly pear cactus-studded plain. He was stripped of his clothes and moccasins and given a hundred or so yards head start. Outdistancing the braves, who were in hot pursuit, though he was bleeding from the nose and mouth because of his exertion, Colter managed to reach the Madison fork, about 5 miles distant, killing one of his pursuers en route. Diving under a pile of drift logs and brush in the stream and finding a place where he could keep his head above water, through an opening he watched the Indians search for him and, on several occasions, walk over the driftwood. After dark, he swam downstream, crept to the bank, and started overland for Fort Raymond, about 200 miles eastward. Exhausted and almost starved, he made it in 11 days.

Back again at the Three Forks that winter, Colter once more almost lost his life, this time on the Gallatin fork, when Blackfeet nearly surprised him in his camp one night. But by another herculean effort he escaped to Lisa's post.

Colter made his last visit to the Three Forks in the spring of 1810, guiding there from Fort Raymond a party of 32 French, American, and Indian trappers under Col. Pierre Menard. Included in this group or in reinforcements who soon arrived and brought the total to some 80 men was George Drouillard. On April 3 the trappers began erecting a palisaded fort, either on a 2-acre or so elevated, rock-capped area between the Gallatin and Madison Rivers, or at the point of land at the juncture of the Madison and Jefferson not far from the Lewis and Clark campsite.

On April 12 a group of 18 men, Colter among them, who were trapping along the Jefferson, scattered from their base camp when Blackfeet discovered it. The Indians killed two men and three others were never found. Colter and the other trappers escaped back to the stockade at the Three Forks. After this episode, Colter apparently decided he had exhausted his luck with the natives. On April 22 he and two others set out eastward, but once again Colter foiled an Indian attack. He went back to St. Louis and never returned to the mountains.

In May, only a short time after Colter's departure from the Three Forks, Drouillard died along with two Shawnee Indian companions in an ambush while trapping along the Jefferson with a group of 21 hunters. His decapitated and mutilated body was buried at some unknown spot in the Three Forks area.

The continual Blackfeet threat, as well as trouble with grizzlies, caused Menard to abandon the post later that same year. He led part of his group back to the Yellowstone River. His second in command, Col. Andrew Henry, led the larger part of the trappers westward across the mountains to a point outside the range of the Blackfeet. He erected a small post on present Henrys Fork of the Snake River in Idaho, the first American fur trading establishment on the western side of the Continental Divide.

FEW modern intrusions mar the Three Forks area, an oasis-like delta. The drainage pattern is essentially as it was in the days of Lewis and Clark. And, unlike so many other parts of the route, dams do not obstruct the streams in the vicinity. The town of Three Forks, situated about 4 miles southwest of the river forks amidst the trees of the delta area, is unobtrusive and all but lost in the vastness of the scene. Other modern features include a bridge over the Gallatin near its mouth on the access road (Route 286) running to the forks; the Milwaukee Road, whose track follows the west bank of the Missouri to a point a short distance southwest of the juncture of the Gallatin with the Jefferson-Madison; and the Northern Pacific, whose line follows the other bank of the Missouri and proceeds along the Gallatin a ways before bending eastward.

All the property in the Three Forks area is in private ownership except for 9 acres of the 10-acre Missouri Headwaters State Monument; a cement company, whose plant is at Trident, a hamlet a few miles northeast of the Three Forks, owns 1 acre of the park. An overlook provides a panoramic view of the area, and interpretive trails give access to key points. A prominent physical landmark visible from the overlook, across the Gallatin River and about half a mile from its junction with the Jefferson-Madison, is the limestone bluff that Lewis climbed when his boat party first arrived at the Three Forks.

Travelers Rest, Montana ⚠

Location (approximate): Missoula County, along U.S. 93 just south of the village of Lolo, about 2 miles upstream from the Bitterroot River on the south side of Lolo Creek, some 11 miles southwest of Missoula.

As the eastern terminus of the Lolo Trail, this site in the Bitterroot Valley was a pivotal one on both the westbound and eastbound phases of the Lewis and Clark Expedition. On their way to the Pacific, the explorers paused at this place for 2 days, September 9–11, 1805, to rest and prepare for the ordeal they knew they would face in crossing the trail. They also took advantage of the excellent weather to make celestial observations. Unfortunately, hunting was poor and added little to the scant larder.

On the positive side, the commanders learned two important facts. Their guide, Old Toby, told them of a fine overland shortcut used by the Indians between the site and the Missouri in the Great Falls vicinity. The Minitaris had told Lewis and Clark of this route, but they had passed the Sun and Dearborn Rivers without recognizing that these streams provided access to it. Secondly, one of three Flathead Indians encountered at Travelers Rest explained that a related tribe lived over the mountains to the west along the Columbia River, which was navigable to the sea.

On the eastward trip, the expedition stayed at Travelers Rest from June 30 to July 3, 1806, while recuperating from its trek over the Lolo Trail and making final plans to separate. On departure from the camp, the Lewis group explored the shortcut Old Toby had delineated as well as the dangerous Upper Marias River area, which Blackfeet were known to frequent. The Clark contingent recovered the cache and boats on the Beaverhead River at Camp Fortunate, Mont., before probing the Yellowstone, below the mouth of which the two elements reunited on the Missouri.

Aside from the small village of Lolo, agricultural activity, and modern highways in the vicinity, the Travelers Rest area has little felt the impress of the hand of man since the time of Lewis and Clark. New channels for the Bitterroot River and Lolo Creek have been

Travelers Rest in the mid-1850's, drawn by Gustav Sohon. This view is from the Bitterroot River Valley looking to the northwest. The Bitterroot River is off the sketch to the right. Lolo Creek runs along the thin strip of timber in the middle distance that extends across the right side of the sketch. The Bitterroot Mountains are to the west and northwest.

The same scene today. Intrusions are few in the Travelers Rest area.

dredged in the locality. U.S. 93, extending north to south along the Bitterroot River, passes the campsite, which is used for farming today and is privately owned. A plaque erected about one-half mile north of the site by the Daughters of the American Revolution, as well as one placed by the Montana Highway Department, identify it. From Lolo, U.S. 12 (Lewis and Clark Highway) follows up Lolo Creek and generally parallels the Lolo Trail across the Bitterroot Mountains.

Blackbird Hill, Nebraska ⊗

Location: Thurston County, on the Winnebago-Omaha Indian Reservation, about 7 miles north of Decatur, along an unimproved road about 1 mile east of U.S. 73 at a point some 3 miles south of the hamlet of Macy. Make local inquiry.

This 300-foot-high promontory on the west side of the Missouri River in present northeastern Nebraska was once a prominent river landmark. Obscured by timber growth, today it is all but forgotten and difficult to locate, though it is the highest point along the stream for many miles.

On August 11, 1804, Lewis and Clark and 10 men climbed the hill to visit the well-marked grave of Omaha Chief Blackbird, who had been buried there 4 years earlier when he died during a smallpox epidemic that decimated his once-powerful tribe. His ruthlessness with other Indians and traders from St. Louis had gained him widespread notoriety. Many 19th-century travelers visited the grave, including artist George Catlin, who in 1832 painted the hill.

No road markers in the vicinity point to the location of Blackbird Hill and the gravesite, both of which are unmarked. An airplane beacon is situated on the grass-covered crest, which is privately owned and surrounded by cornfields. Heavy timber and scrub growth that drops off toward the river from the point of the bluff and replaces the semi-open grass slopes depicted in Catlin's painting have obscured the once-magnificent view up and down the river and at the same time rendered the hill invisible from it. The only views of the promontory in the area are at a high point on U.S. 73 about 2 miles north of Macy, and from an unimproved road along the bottom land in the network east and south of the village.

Blackbird Hill is the high point of the river bluff in the middle distance about 3 miles away to the south. The Missouri River bottom land is at the left.

The great village of the Omahas was located about 20 miles north of Blackbird Hill in the broad and fertile valley where Omaha Creek joined the Missouri from the west and where the river bluff almost receded from view. This site is now either skirted or traversed by U.S. 87 about 1 mile north of Homer, Nebr., and 6½ miles south of Dakota City.

Calumet Bluff, Nebraska ⊗

Location (approximate): Cedar County, on the south, or west, bank of the Missouri, just off Nebr. 121 about 1 mile west of the village of Aten, some 2 miles below Gavins Point Dam and a few miles upstream and across from Yankton, S. Dak.

At this campsite, where the expedition stayed during the period August 28–September 1, 1804, the first council was held with the Sioux, some friendly Yanktons, on August 30–31.

For some days before, Lewis and Clark had been expecting to meet the Sioux. On August 25, to no avail, the explorers had set fire to the prairie as a signal for the tribe to come to the river. Two days later, near the mouth of the James River, three Yanktons were encountered. They said their village was not far away, about 9 miles up the James. That same day, Sergeant Pryor, Old Dorion, and a French boatman set out to invite tribal representatives to a council.

The next day, August 28, awaiting their arrival, the boat party camped along the south bank of the Missouri on a plain just below Calumet Bluff. It was one of a series of bluffs, lining the river on both sides, that were generally higher on the south side. The bluff, 170 to 180 feet in height, was "composed of a yellowish red, and brownish clay as hard as chalk, which it much resembles."

Late the following day, Sergeant Pryor's group arrived on the opposite bank with five chiefs and 70 men and boys, as well as Old Dorion's son, who lived with the Yanktons. The next morning, they were brought across in one of the expedition's pirogues. The council, for which Old Dorion served as translator, began at noon and continued throughout that day and all the next. On September 1 the expedition departed. Old Dorion stayed behind to negotiate peace among tribes in the area and to try to persuade some of the Yankton chiefs to visit Washington, D.C.

On the return trip from the Pacific, on August 30, 1806, Lewis and Clark counciled warily with some Teton Sioux somewhere in the Calumet Bluff vicinity—the only dealings on the eastbound trek with that tribe, which had been hostile on the westbound journey.

The precise location of the Lewis and Clark camp near the landmark they called Calumet Bluff is impossible to ascertain and may even be inundated by the tail waters of the Gavins Point Dam and be in Knox County, but a careful study of the various sources indicates that it probably was about 1 mile west of Aten, in Cedar County. That area is typical Missouri River bottom land and is about 10 to 15 feet above the river below the bluff line. The privately owned site is cultivated.

Council Bluffs, Nebraska ⊗

Location (approximate): Washington County, about 15 miles north of downtown Omaha, just east of the site of Fort Atkinson. The latter is accessible via a secondary road that runs east from U.S. 73 about 1 mile west of the fort site at the town of Fort Calhoun.

This site, which bears no relationship to the city of Council Bluffs, on the Iowa side of the Missouri River some miles downstream, is significant as the place where Lewis and Clark conducted their first council with Indians. From July 30 to August 3, 1804, the explorers camped at this location, along the bottom land at the edge of some high bluffs on the west bank of the Missouri.

Responding to an invitation from an emissary the commanders had sent out on July 29, a group of Oto and Missouri Indians arrived late on August 2. The council began early the following morning, and at its conclusion later in the day the expedition departed. On the eastbound journey, on September 8, 1806, a brief stop was made at the Council Bluffs.

In 1819 the War Department, confirming the judgment of Lewis and Clark that the site was ideal for a fort and trading post to deal with the tribes in the area, established Fort Atkinson and an associated Indian Agency on the bluffs back of the expedition's campsite. The second post to be established on the "Permanent Indian Frontier," it was one of the first activated west of the Mississippi, and the first west of the Missouri. It served as an important outpost in Indian country and as a base for explorers and trappers until the Army abandoned it in 1827. To afford better protection of the Santa Fe Trail, Fort Leavenworth, farther down the Missouri, replaced it. Nothing remains of Fort Atkinson, but the site, today a National Historic Landmark, is commemorated by 147-acre Fort Atkinson State Historical Park.

The many changes wrought by the Missouri have substantially altered the appearance of the river bottom area, most of which is now committed to agricultural use. The bluffs no longer afford a fine view up and down the river. Indeed, because of intervening timber growth and the shifting of the channel over the years, some 3 miles to the eastward, the river is not even visible from the vicinity of the council site. The site of the fort, the closest identifiable spot to the campsite, is on the level plain just back from the edge of the 60-foot-high river bluffs. Scrub trees and brush growth cover the face of the bluffs. A township road runs down over them to the widened bottom land, where evidences of the old channel are apparent among the cornfields. Neither the exact location of the Lewis and Clark campsite, nor that of Cantonment Missouri, the temporary predecessor of Fort Atkinson, also established in the bottom lands, can be determined.

Fort Mandan, ⊗ Big Hidatsa (Minitari) Village, ⌂ and Other Minitari-Mandan Village Sites, ⊗ North Dakota

Location: McLean and Mercer Counties, in the vicinity of the village of Stanton. For location of individual sites, see the following description.

This complex of interrelated sites in central North Dakota possesses major archeological significance and has important associations with

View from the Missouri River bluffs, along the north side of the river, looking to the southeast over the site of Fort Mandan. The cottonwood forest below the bluffs stretches away toward the Missouri, which is vaguely recognizable in the right top distance. The fort site, lost before 1833 because of the changing river channel in the area, cannot be precisely identified but it was probably somewhere in the bottom land shown here.

the Lewis and Clark Expedition. Fort Mandan, the 1804–5 winter quarters, was erected on the north bank of the Missouri River near the lowest of five Indian villages scattered along the Missouri and Lower Knife Rivers. See map entitled "Fort Mandan (Winter Camp, 1804–1805) and Nearby . . . Indian Villages."

White traders, Frenchmen, probably first contacted the Minitaris (Hidatsas) shortly after the tribe moved northward about 60 miles from near the junction of the Heart and Missouri Rivers to the mouth of the Knife River, where they were living by about 1740. About three decades later, the Mandans, with whom they shared many cultural traits and had lived in close proximity on the Heart, joined them and established their villages nearby, on the Missouri. Immediately prior to this, the Mandans had resided for a time at a site about 20 miles to the south of the Knife River following their departure from the Heart River.

Even before the direct relationship with traders, the two tribes apparently had served as middlemen in the Northern Plains trade involving white trade goods. The Assiniboin and Cree, who were in direct contact with the French, bartered the goods to the Mandans and Minitaris for corn, which they had grown, and buffalo robes,

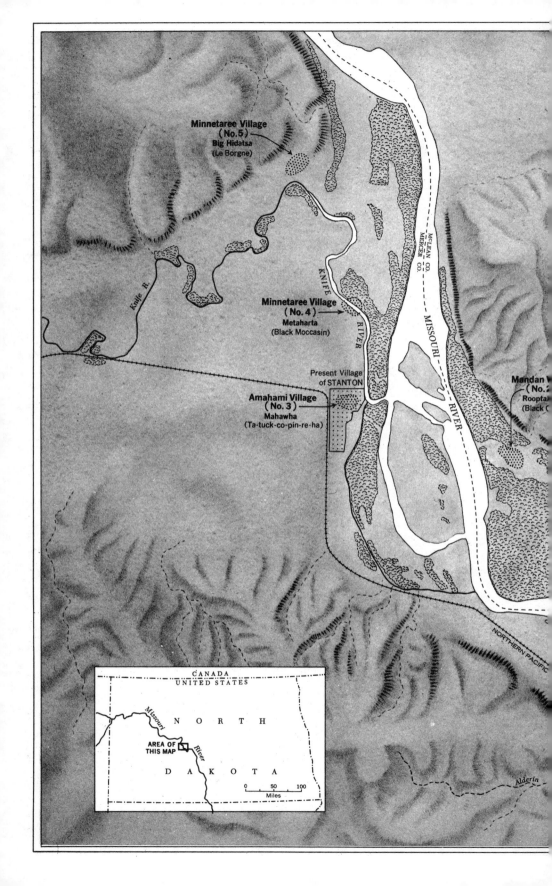

Minnetaree Village
(No.5)
Big Hidatsa
(Le Borgne)

Minnetaree Village
(No. 4)
Metaharta
(Black Moccasin)

KNIFE RIVER

McLEAN CO.
MERCER CO.

Knife R.

MISSOURI   RIVER

Present Village
of STANTON

Amahami Village
(No. 3)
Mahawha
(Ta-tuck-co-pin-re-ha)

Mandan V
(No.
Rooptal
(Black

NORTHERN PACIFIC

CANADA
UNITED STATES

Missouri

N O R T H

AREA OF
THIS MAP

River

D A K O T A

Alderin

0   50   100
Miles

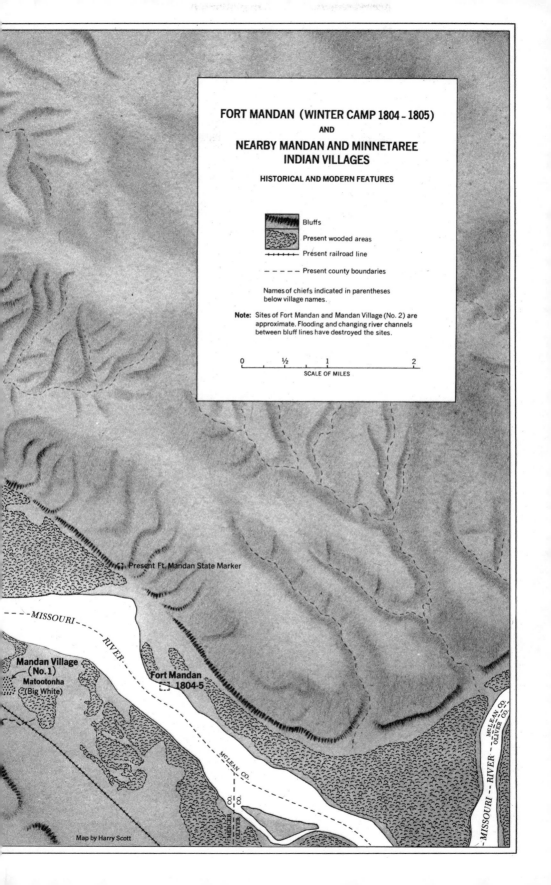

FORT MANDAN (WINTER CAMP 1804 - 1805)

AND

NEARBY MANDAN AND MINNETAREE INDIAN VILLAGES

HISTORICAL AND MODERN FEATURES

Bluffs

Present wooded areas

Present railroad line

Present county boundaries

Names of chiefs indicated in parentheses below village names.

Note: Sites of Fort Mandan and Mandan Village (No. 2) are approximate. Flooding and changing river channels between bluff lines have destroyed the sites.

0   ½   1   2

SCALE OF MILES

Present Ft. Mandan State Marker

MISSOURI

RIVER

Mandan Village
(No.1)
Matootonha
(Big White)

Fort Mandan
1804-5

MCLEAN CO.

MCLEAN CO.
OLIVER CO.

MERCER CO.
OLIVER CO.

MISSOURI — RIVER

Map by Harry Scott

LaBarge Rock is one of the major landmarks along the Missouri Breaks in
Montana, a piece of geology festooned with landmarks.

furs, and meat they had obtained from the Crow, Cheyenne, Arapaho,
Kiowa, and other nomadic western tribes. In return, the latter tribes
received corn and limited quantities of trade goods.

By the end of the French and Indian War, in 1763, Mandan-Minitari trade with the French had virtually ceased, but the British fur
companies that replaced the French traders in present Canada
resumed the commerce in 1766 even though France had ceded Western Louisiana, in which the villages were located, to Spain 4 years
earlier. Spanish traders who visited them in the 1790's were unable
to gain a foothold in the fur trade or to expel the Britishers, who were
still there when Lewis and Clark arrived late in 1804 despite the
U.S. purchase of Louisiana Territory the previous year.

The two captains found the Mandans occupying the two lower

villages, on the Missouri; the Minitaris, two others a few miles up the Knife; and the Amahamis, one at its mouth. The latter consisted of various fragments of Indian groups that had been displaced by the tribal wars in the region or had dwindled because of disease and had gathered there under the protection of the Minitaris. Over the years, intermarriage and merger had taken place. This was the most powerful Indian complex on the Missouri River at the time. No other permanent villages were located on it all the way west to the mountains, and the Minitaris hunted and raided westward all the way to the Continental Divide. The less warlike Mandans were essentially an agricultural people.

During the explorers' long stay at the villages, from October 26, 1804, until April 7, 1805, they constructed and occupied Fort Mandan; counciled with the Mandans and Minitaris and learned all they could about the country to the west; recruited Baptiste Lepage and Toussaint Charbonneau, who would be accompanied by his Indian wife Sacagawea and their infant son Baptiste; held conferences with the resident British traders of the North West and Hudson's Bay Companies; readied reports and specimens for dispatch to President Jefferson on the keelboat, which was to go back to St. Louis in the spring; and made preparations for the westward trek.

On the return from the Pacific, a stop was made at the villages on August 14–17, 1806. It was found that a prairie fire had destroyed most of the fort; goodbyes were said to Charbonneau, Sacagawea, and their son, as well as John Colter, who was released so that he could go trapping; and Mandan Chief Sheheke (Big White) was persuaded to accompany Lewis to Washington.

In the period 1832–34, artists George Catlin and Karl Bodmer, as well as Prince Maximilian of Wied, visited the villages. Maximilian and Catlin described the Big Hidatsa (Minitari) Village in their journals, and the artists sketched it. Maximilian reported that no traces remained of Fort Mandan and that its site had been inundated or relocated to the south bank by river meandering. Tragically, a smallpox epidemic in 1837 almost wiped out the Mandans; seriously weakened the Minitaris and Amahamis; and killed many Arikaras, who were by then living adjacent to the lower Mandan village near Fort Clark, a fur trading post close to the west bank of the Missouri.

In 1845 the surviving Minitaris and the remnant of Mandans moved about 60 river miles up the Missouri. That same year, the American

Big Hidatsa Village Site is situated just to the left of the farm buildings at the right. The Knife River is marked by the closer tree line just beyond the buildings; the Missouri, by the heavy tree line in the distance. The bluffs are on the east side of the Missouri.

Fur Company began erecting Fort Berthold nearby. In 1861, when fire destroyed Fort Clark, the Arikaras also moved upstream and joined the Mandans and Minitaris. Descendants of these three great tribes, which figured so prominently in the Lewis and Clark Expedition, continue to live on the relocated Fort Berthold Reservation, though Garrison Dam has inundated their historic village sites.

Although the *Fort Mandan site* lies in the river bottom land or under the waters of the Missouri, the area may be viewed from Fort Mandan State Park, consisting of about 35 acres. The park is in McLean County on a semilevel bench on the bluff along the north, or east, side of the river just above, or north, of the point where it bends abruptly from a southeast-northwest to east-west direction. The approximate fort site lies about 1¾ miles to the south and slightly east of the park marker placed by the State of North Dakota near the edge of the river bluff. County Route 17, which runs westward from U.S. 83 one-half mile north of Washburn, provides access to the park.

The McLean County Historical Society, using local funds entirely, has erected a generalized replica of Fort Mandan, based on a model in the possession of the State Historical Society. The replica, dedicated in June 1972, is in the river bottom land about 10 miles downstream from the actual site and 4 miles west of Washburn along County Route 17.

Archeologists and historians have numbered the village sites from 1 to 5, running from southeast to northwest. *Village No. 1 (Lower Mandan Village)* is situated in present Mercer County on the south, or west, bank of the Missouri. Sheheke was the chief of this community, which at the time of Lewis and Clark numbered 40 to 50 earthlodges and was the closest to Fort Mandan, then only 2 miles directly east across the river. The privately owned and unmarked site is probably near the old Deapolis Post Office.

Village No. 2 (Upper Mandan Village) was the larger of the two Mandan villages. It was on the same side of the river as Fort Mandan but about 4½ air miles to the northwest. Lewis and Clark considered Black Cat, the chief, to be the most influential in his tribe and the most intelligent of all the Indians they dealt with during the winter. The exact site of Village No. 2, in McLean County, has not been determined but was probably about a mile downstream from the village of Stanton, on the opposite bank. Archeological evidence has probably been covered with river silt or carried away in the course of many channel changes and floodings. This privately owned site is not accessible by road.

Village No. 3 (Amahami Village) was the smallest and least important of the five. It was on the south bank of the Knife River at its junction with the Missouri. The town of Stanton, seat of Mercer County, has grown up on the site and nothing remains of the latter today except for one lodge ring in the yard of the Mercer County Courthouse.

Village No. 4 (Lower Minitari Village), the smaller and more southerly of the two Minitari villages near the mouth of the Knife River, is in Mercer County about 1 air mile north of present Stanton and the mouth of the Knife. A dirt-gravel road running upstream

This farm lane, in the environs of Stanton, N. Dak., leads to the half-eroded site of one of the 1804–5 Minitari villages near the mouth of the Knife River. The stream runs along the near edge of the tree line and joins the Missouri about a mile away downstream and out of the picture at the right. The bluffs in the background are on the far side of the Missouri. Fort Mandan was a few miles to the southeast of this picture on the other side of the river.

from Stanton along the Knife, which nearly parallels the Missouri at this point, passes within .3 of a mile of the site, on privately owned farmland. The Missouri River, obscured by a heavy growth of cotton-woods, lies about one-half mile to the east.

The Knife River, whose banks are 25 to 30 feet high at this point, has already eroded away about half of the village site. The remaining earthlodge circles, averaging about 60 feet in diameter and marked by depressions 2 to 3 feet deep, are readily distinguishable; the north-eastern part of the site is covered with cottonwood trees. The ground is white with bone fragments.

In 1804–5 Black Moccasin was the principal chief of the village, in which Toussaint Charbonneau and Sacagawea were probably residing when they joined the Lewis and Clark Expedition. And their son,

Baptiste, whom she carried with her, was either born at this place, or, more likely, at the interpreters' camp outside Fort Mandan.

Village No. 5 (Upper Minitari Village) (Big Hidatsa Village Site), also known as the Olds Site, is a National Historic Landmark primarily because of its archeological status. It is in Mercer County approximately 2 air miles northwest of the lower Minitari village along the north side of the Knife on a terrace about a quarter mile from the river. This village site is accessible via the same dirt-gravel road that passes Village No. 4.

The site is in private ownership. Although barns and other outbuildings cover a small part of its 15-acre extent, most of it has never been cultivated and is exceptionally well preserved. Clearly distinguishable earthlodge rings, the largest averaging 60 feet in diameter, are crowded closely together and number more than 100. Also visible are several fortification trenches. The black soil is flecked white by enormous quantities of bone fragments of buffalo and other animals. Powerful Chief Le Borgne ("One-Eye"), feared by Indians and traders alike, ruled this village in the days of Lewis and Clark.

Slant (Mandan) Indian Village, North Dakota ⊗

Location: Morton County, along the west, or south, bank of the Missouri River, in Fort Lincoln State Park, just off N. Dak. 6, nearly opposite Bismarck and about 5 miles south of Mandan.

Fort Lincoln State Park, on the Missouri River near the mouth of the Heart River, primarily commemorates the sites of Fort Abraham Lincoln (1872–91), an Army post during the Indian wars, and its predecessor, Fort McKean (1872), about 5 miles to the north. An interesting subsidiary feature in the park, however, are five replicas of Mandan earthlodges. They are located on the 6 to 8 acre site of an abandoned village, just above which the Lewis and Clark Expedition camped on the night of October 20–21, 1804. While returning from the Pacific, on August 18–19, 1806, it bivouacked across the Missouri on its east bank. Probably because of its location on the side of a hill, the village on the west bank has been called Slant Indian Village. The explorers noted vacated settlements along both sides of the river.

In 1738 the French trader-explorer Pierre Gaultier de Varennes,

Reconstructed Mandan earthlodges at Fort Abraham Lincoln State Park.

Sieur de la Vérendrye, and his two sons had visited the place. By that time, the Minitaris, who had resided with the Mandans, had likely moved away; by 1740 they were living along the mouth of the Knife River, around 60 river miles to the north. About 1764, apparently pressured by encroaching Sioux, the Mandans moved upriver about 40 miles and stayed there for awhile. By 1770 they had pushed another 20 miles up the Missouri and established two villages along that stream near the Minitari Knife River settlements. It was at these locations that Lewis and Clark first encountered the two tribes.

The mounded, circular earthlodges in Fort Lincoln State Park are the only full-sized replicas extant on an original site. Construction materials and techniques were based on archeological excavations and documentary sources, including the Lewis and Clark journals. Besides the earthlodges, the park includes the sites of the two forts. Locations of various buildings have been marked, and three blockhouses of Fort McKean have been reconstructed. A museum interprets the history of the forts and the Mandans.

Fort Clatsop National Memorial, Oregon ★

Location: Clatsop County, just south of U.S. 101 about 4½ miles southwest of Astoria; address: Route 3, P.O. Box 604-FC, Astoria, Oreg. 97103.

Fort Clatsop, the 1805–6 winter camp of the Lewis and Clark Expedition, was its home for more than 3½ months. When the explorers first arrived at the estuary of the Columbia in November 1806, they followed its north bank. But their camps were exposed to ocean gales and hunting was poor. Aware that a location near the ocean would be convenient for making much-needed salt and learning from the Indians that elk were more plentiful on the south side of the river, the men voted to seek a suitable wintering spot there. Rough water made it necessary to move back upstream several miles before making the crossing.

From a temporary camp established late in the month near Tongue Point, just east of present Astoria, Lewis and five men set out and found a suitable site. Located about 3 miles up the present Lewis and Clark River on the west bank, it was near good hunting in the lowlands, where elk wintered in large numbers; stood 30 feet above the river high-water mark; and was close enough to the coast to facilitate contact with any visiting northwest traders. Timber suitable for construction and fresh-water springs were also at hand, and the forest cover and hills provided shelter from the winter gales that lashed the open estuary of the Columbia. The seashore was only a little more than 3 air miles to the west.

Construction of Fort Clatsop, named after a local Indian tribe, began soon after the party arrived on December 7. Although the finishing touches were not completed until December 30, everyone was under roof by Christmas—celebrated in the lonely outpost at the western extremity of a vast wilderness. The fort, about 50 feet square, consisted of two long facing buildings joined on the sides by palisades, which created a small "parade ground" between the structures.

During the winter, a saltmaking camp was set up about 15 miles by trail to the southwest at present Seaside, Oreg. Other activities of the complement included: reconnoitering the surrounding area, hunting, servicing of weapons and equipment, making elk hide clothing and moccasins, and completing other preparations for the eastbound trek.

Lewis and Clark reworked their earlier journals; recorded ethnological, zoological, and botanical observations; collected specimens of flora and fauna; and planned the eastward journey. As usual, Lewis concentrated on the accumulation of scientific data, and Clark on cartographic matters. They were disappointed that they encountered no northwest traders, who would have offered a source of supplies

Visitors touring Fort Clatsop National Memorial.

and trade goods and possibly even a mode of transportation back to the east coast.

One unusual highlight of the winter was the trip Clark, Sacagawea, her son, Charbonneau, and 11 men made from Fort Clatsop on January 6–10, 1806, to the site of the present city of Cannon Beach, Oreg., at the mouth of what they called Ecola (modern Elk) Creek. It was about 8 miles below the salt camp and the southernmost point on the Pacific reached by the expedition. The lure was an Indian report that a whale had washed ashore at that place. But, by the time the group arrived, Killamuck Indians had stripped all the flesh off the skeleton. Clark was able to purchase only 300 pounds of blubber and some oil.

Except for this diversion, life at the fort was usually monotonous and depressing. Because of the almost constant rain, the men suffered from colds, influenza, and other ailments. The dampness damaged equipment and supplies. Fleas were a major nuisance. Worst of all, a chronic food shortage existed, and the diet was rarely balanced. Procuring and transporting enough meat, especially as the hunters had to travel farther and farther afield, was problem enough. Much of it quickly spoiled. Dry wood was almost impossible to find for smoking the meat, and wet timber was hardly suitable for the purpose. As a result, the scarce trade goods had to be used to purchase dog meat, roots, berries, and fish from the Indians as dietary supplements.

Dugout canoe, similar to those the explorers employed in reaching the Pacific, on display at Fort Clatsop National Memorial. Some 31½ feet long, it was hewn and burned out of a large red cedar trunk by Quinault Indians/and copied from an old canoe in the Sacagawea Museum at Spalding, Wash., said to date from the Lewis and Clark period.

For all these reasons, departure on March 23, 1806, was a joyous occasion. As a goodbye present, Lewis and Clark presented Fort Clatsop and its furnishings to Chief Comowool, a friendly Clatsop. He probably used the fort as a hunting lodge for a few years during the autumn and winter seasons. Over the years, the structure decayed, and had almost completely disappeared by the time U.S. settlers entered the area about 1850. Subsequently, all traces of it vanished.

In 1901 the Oregon Historical Society acquired the Fort Clatsop site. During the Lewis and Clark Sesquicentennial celebration in 1955, local business, civic, patriotic, and historical groups erected a replica of the fort. It faithfully followed the floorplan and room separations as drawn by Clark on the elk hide cover of his field notebook. But in all other respects, in the absence of any contemporary drawing, the reconstruction was generalized to conform with similar structures of the period.

In 1958 the National Park Service acquired the replica, along with 125 acres of surrounding land, and 4 years later established Fort

Clatsop National Memorial. Since that time, some repairs and minor changes have been made to the structure to bring it closer to authenticity, and it has been furnished to resemble its 1805–6 appearance. In the 1950's and 1960's National Park Service archeologists dug test trenches in the vicinity, but found no evidence of the original building. They may have missed the exact site, or the construction of several houses in the area during the 19th century may have obliterated any traces that once remained. Yet, all the documentary evidence indicates that the replica is on the site of the original fort or close to it.

A museum in the visitor center of the national memorial interprets the Lewis and Clark Expedition. Trails corresponding to those used by its members lead to the canoe landing, the camp spring, and in the direction of the seacoast. Deer and elk still graze in the park area, as they did in the time of Lewis and Clark.

For major sites and routes of the expedition along the Columbia estuary, see map entitled "Exploring the Mouth of the Columbia and the Pacific Coast."

Part of the route the Clark party followed to the whale site, over lofty Tillamook Head, passes through Ecola State Park, north of Elk Creek. A State highway marker is at a high point on U.S. 101 about a mile from and overlooking the whale site.

Saltmaking Camp, Oregon ⊗

Location: Clatsop County, on the southern end of the ocean-front promenade at Q Street, in the city of Seaside.

To augment their low supply of salt upon arrival at the Pacific coast, Lewis and Clark assigned high priority to the task of producing this commodity. On January 2, 1806, Privates Joseph Field, Bratton, and Gibson established a saltmaking camp about 10 air miles southwest of Fort Clatsop near the mouth of the Necanicum River, which provided fresh drinking water. The camp operated until February 21. Usually at least three men were assigned there, though the number varied and personnel were rotated. Salt was obtained by laboriously boiling sea water in five large kettles. About 3 of the approximately 4 bushels produced at the camp were packed in kegs and carried eastward from Fort Clatsop with the expedition on March 23.

Bonneville (top), The Dalles (middle), and John Day (bottom) Dams convert the powerful waters of the Columbia into electrical energy for the homes and factories of Oregon and Washington. Mount Hood, Oregon's highest peak, 36 miles distant, graces the skyline behind The Dalles Dam.

This view from the east bank of the Missouri looks westward across the river. The Confrontation with the Teton Sioux Site, S. Dak., was situated somewhere in the bottom land along the west bank of the river.

Parts of the trail running from the camp to Fort Clatsop may still be traced today. In 1900 the Oregon Historical Society authenticated the site of the saltmaking camp, known today as the salt cairn. It is owned by the society and administered by the city of Seaside. The cairn, originally constructed of boulders cemented together with native clay, was rebuilt in 1955 and five kettles placed on it. The area is now enclosed with an iron fence, and a plaque describes its significance.

Confrontation with the Teton Sioux Site, South Dakota ⊗

Location (approximate): Stanley County, along County Route 514, on the west, or south, bank of the Missouri River, about 4 miles north of the city of Fort Pierre and 2 miles south of Oahe Dam.

The confrontation with the Teton Sioux late in September 1804, one of the few incidents on the entire journey involving hostile Indians, represented the Lewis and Clark Expedition's first major test. The initial council with chiefs of the tribe occurred on a sandbar at the mouth of the Bad River on September 25, and ensuing ones about 5 miles farther upriver at an Indian village (present site) on September 26–27. The councils were amicable enough, but the Tetons demonstrated hostility on several other occasions, including the departure of the expedition on September 28. For this reason, all its members were on the alert for an attack. Had it not been for a show of firmness and astute handling of some delicate situations, Lewis and Clark, as well as their command, might have been killed or captured.

The site of the meeting on September 25 is apparently lost in the mouth of the Bad. The unmarked second site is probably situated in the bottom land upstream about 5 miles and is either traversed or closely approached by County Route 514, which runs north from U.S. 14 near the city of Fort Pierre. The area is privately owned farmland, but is partly covered with native grass. The river bottom at this point is about a mile wide, a width that is rather uniform from just above the mouth of the Bad nearly to Oahe Dam, a distance of about 7 miles. Across from the confrontation site, the east side of the river is lined by high bluffs. Viewed from them, the west river bottom and bluffs have a tawny brown-light green appearance and must look much like they did in 1804.

Aerial view looking southwestward over the site of Fort Manuel, S. Dak., before Oahe Reservoir inundated it. Sacagawea probably died at the fort in 1812 and was undoubtedly buried nearby. Archeological excavations, completed before water obscured the site in 1966, are noticeable on the bluff edge just beyond the rising reservoir waters in the foreground, which are covering the cottonwood-forested Missouri River bottom land.

Spirit Mound, South Dakota ⊗

Location: Clay County, just west of S. Dak. 19, about 8 miles north of Vermillion.

On a stiflingly hot day, August 25, 1804, Lewis and Clark and nine other men, thirsty and tired, trudged northward a few miles from the Missouri to visit this distinctive conical mound. The Indians in the vicinity, who never visited the place themselves, said it was the residence of devils—18-inch-high dwarves with extraordinarily large heads, who were armed with sharp arrows they used to kill any intruders.

The explorers encountered no dwarves or other spirits, but from the top of the hill they beheld what Clark termed a "most butifull landscape." Visible in all directions were herds of buffalo and timberless plains, which extended on the north as far as the eye could see.

The site, in an agricultural area, is privately owned. Cattle, instead of buffalo, now graze on the plains.

Meriwether Lewis Park (Natchez Trace Parkway), Tennessee ★

Location: Lewis County, just northwest of the junction of the Natchez Trace Parkway and Tenn. 20, about 7 miles southeast of Hohenwald.

This park, a unit of Natchez Trace Parkway, contains the site of the frontier inn where Meriwether Lewis died and his grave—far from that of his partner in discovery, Clark. The parkway, a scenic road now about two-thirds completed, generally follows the route of the old Natchez Trace, which extended from Natchez to Nashville. Originally a prehistoric Indian trail and later used by the Spaniards, French, British, and Americans, the trace was for several centuries an important trade and emigrant road in the old Southwest.

On October 10, 1809, Lewis was traveling along the trace en route from St. Louis to Washington, D.C., where he hoped to straighten out his affairs as Governor of Louisiana Territory and conduct other business. That morning, his traveling companion, Maj. James Neelly, had remained behind to look for two lost packhorses. Lewis and the two servants accompanying him stopped for the night at an inn named Grinder's Stand. In the early hours of the morning, Lewis died of two gunshot wounds, apparently self-inflicted. Neelly, arriving later that morning, buried his body nearby.

Monument to Lewis at his gravesite, in Meriwether Lewis Park, Natchez Trace Parkway. The broken column is symbolic of his untimely death.

Although some writers have contended Lewis was assassinated for political reasons or murdered, possibly while being robbed, his agitated mental state during most of the trip, reflected in two previous attempts to kill himself, and the recorded circumstances of his death stress the probability of suicide. Also, before he left St. Louis, he had granted to three of his friends power of attorney so they could dispose of his property to satisfy his creditors. And, en route, on September 11, he prepared a last will and testament. Whatever the facts surrounding his death, his sudden and tragic demise at an obscure place in a remote wilderness ended the career of one of the Nation's most noted explorers.

Except for a "post fence" built in 1810, the gravesite remained unmarked until 1848. That year, the State of Tennessee erected a broken column, symbolizing Lewis' untimely death at the age of 35. On its east side is the following inscription:

> In the language of Mr. Jefferson:— "His courage was undaunted; his firmness and perseverance yielded to nothing but impossibilities; a rigid disciplinarian yet tender as a father of those committed to his charge; honest, disinterested, liberal, with a sound understanding and a scupulous fidelity to truth."

Five years before construction of the monument, the State had also created a new county, Lewis County, which included the area of the gravesite.

In 1925 President Calvin Coolidge designated the site as Meriwether Lewis National Monument, and in 1961 it was redesignated as Meriwether Lewis Park and became a unit of the Natchez Trace

Parkway. In addition to the monument and gravesite, an interpretive marker on the foundation site of Grinder's Stand, in a well-maintained grass area about 700 feet from the grave, outlines the building's dimensions. A small museum displays exhibits commemorating Lewis' career. Depressions and old road remains mark the route of the trace in the vicinity.

Cape Disappointment, Washington ⊗

Location: Pacific County, in Fort Canby State Park, about 2 miles southwest of Ilwaco, accessible via U.S. 101 and Wash. 12.

Although some of the members of the Lewis and Clark Expedition in November 1805 were the first men of record to stand on this bold northern headland at the mouth of the Columbia River, it had been seen and named by explorers of other nations, as were many other landmarks along the Lower Columbia.

Three decades before Lewis and Clark, on August 17, 1775, the Spanish navigator Bruno Heceta had sighted the cape, which he called "Cape San Roque." He named the large, sheltered bay behind it, which he did not enter, as "Assumption Bay" (present Baker Bay). Noting the strong current, he conjectured that he was at the mouth of a great river. More than a decade later, on June 6, 1788, a British sea captain and fur trader, John Meares, tried to confirm Heceta's suspicion. But, fooled by the big breakers that closed off the bay, Meares called it "Deception" and its northern headland Cape Disappointment.

Four years later, in the period May 11–20, Capt. Robert Gray, an American trader out of Boston in the *Columbia Rediviva*, was the first white man to cross the bar and explore the mouth of the river, which he named the "Columbia" after his ship. Five months hence, Capt. George Vancouver of the British Navy, seeking the Northwest Passage, appeared off the Columbia's mouth to investigate a report he had received from the Spanish commandant at Nootka that Gray had discovered a major river near "Deception Bay." Deeming it unsafe to cross the bar with his ship, the *Discovery*, he sent the brig *Chatham*, commanded by Lt. William R. Broughton, into the mouth of the river. Broughton anchored his vessel in Gray's Bay, along the northern side of the estuary, and penetrated with some of his men in small

Looking northwest from Fort Stevens, Oreg., on Point Adams along the south bank of the Columbia, across its mouth to Cape Disappointment, which is visible in the right middle. Spanish explorer Bruno Heceta discovered the cape in 1775, but Lewis and members of his party were the first nonnatives to stand on it, on November 14, 1805.

boats some 100 miles upstream, almost to the impassable Cascades. This was the state of knowledge and exploration of the Lower Columbia when the Lewis and Clark Expedition arrived there in November 1805.

On the 14th Lewis and four men, after being carried around Point Ellice west of their campsite by some of their comrades in a canoe, set out overland to visit the ocean; en route, one man from an advance party of three joined them. On November 17, having probed as far as Cape Disappointment and a few miles to the north, the party returned to the Chinook Point camp, which Clark and the main body had established 2 days earlier. From that base, between November 18 and 20, Clark and 11 men traveled overland to Cape Disappointment and explored some 9 miles to its north.

In 1852 the War Department created a military reservation at the cape for the purpose of accommodating a coastal fortification to protect the mouth of the Columbia, but construction did not begin until August 1863. The post, named Fort Cape Disappointment, was completed and occupied by troops the following April. For their permanent shelter, that year and the next several frame garrison buildings were erected. The fortifications, at the southernmost tip of the cape, consisted of three earthwork batteries. In 1875 the base was redesignated as Fort Canby.

Between 1896 and 1908, after a long period of neglect during which the fort and its armament had become obsolete, the Army completely renovated them. New barracks and other buildings were constructed, and two batteries with a total of five rifled guns in concrete emplacements were installed. In 1911 a new mortar battery of four guns was added. Further modernization occurred during World War II. In 1947 the fort was deactivated. Present surviving structures date from the World War II period.

Subsequently, the State of Washington acquired 791 acres of the military reservation, which are now included in Fort Canby State Park. The U.S. Coast Guard retains Cape Disappointment Light House and other facilities at the cape. Further changes in its appearance have been caused by the accumulation of considerable masses of sand by the jetties the Corps of Engineers has constructed to stabilize the mouth of the Columbia.

Chinook Point Campsite, Washington ⊗

Location: Pacific County, along U.S. 101 in a 1-acre State roadside park adjacent to Fort Columbia State Park, just west of McGowan and 2 miles west of the Astoria Bridge.

Two small advance parties that set out from the Point Ellice campsite on November 13 and 14 may possibly have seen the Pacific, but it is certain that Clark and the main body of the expedition first viewed it from this site along the north bank of the Columbia on November 15. Of course, 8 days earlier, from Pillar Rock, a landmark in the river some 25 miles from its mouth near present Altoona, Wash., Clark had erroneously believed he had sighted the ocean, when he was actually viewing the open-horizoned estuary of the Columbia.

The Chinook Point campsite, established by Clark and the bulk of the complement about 4 miles west of the Point Ellice site, was the

Locale of the campsite at Chinook Point, occupied November 15–25, 1805. From here, the explorers first saw the Pacific Ocean, in the left distance.

main base during the period November 15–25. Just southeast of Chinook Point, the site was located near an abandoned Chinook Indian village, whose boards were utilized for the construction of shelters. Lewis and his small group, which had set out from Point Ellice on November 14 and probed overland as far west as Cape Disappointment, returned to the Chinook Point camp on November 17. The next day, Clark and 11 men set out. Between then and the 20th, they proceeded to the cape and explored about 9 miles to its north before returning to their base.

During all this reconnaissance, no favorable site was found for a winter camp and game was discovered to be scarce. Indians told the explorers that hunting was better on the south side of the river. On November 24 the complement voted to search there for a permanent base. The following day, in clear but windy weather, the boats cast off from Chinook Point. Because the swells were too high to permit a crossing near the mouth of the river, the craft followed the north bank upstream. Camp that night was made near Pillar Rock. The next day, November 26, at a point some 17 miles above Tongue Point, the boats crossed to the south side of the river. There, they renewed their search for a winter encampment that ended with the establishment on December 7 of a base at the Fort Clatsop site, in Oregon.

The Chinook Point campsite, designated by a State marker, is little

Lower Monumental (top) and Little Goose (bottom) Dams, Snake River, Wash.

changed from the days of Lewis and Clark. A small museum in a barracks building at nearby Fort Columbia State Park contains exhibits relating to the early exploration of the coast and to regional history.

Chinook Point, the overall geographical feature as distinct from the Lewis and Clark campsite, has been accorded National Historic Landmark status because of its associations with the era of discovery in the Pacific Northwest.

Point Ellice, Wash., on the north bank of the Columbia about 10 miles from the Pacific and directly opposite Astoria, Oreg. One of the most disagreeable campsites (November 10–15, 1805), because of rain and high winds, was located at this 500-foot-high rocky promontory.

Point Ellice Campsite, Washington ⊗

Location (approximate): Pacific County, along Wash. 401, about 1 mile east of the Astoria Bridge, at Hungry Harbor.

Of all the campsites utilized by the expedition, this one on the east side of Point Ellice—called by Clark the "blustering point" or "Point Distress"—was probably the most unpleasant.

As the explorers neared the mouth of the Columbia, beginning on November 6, 1805, and lasting through the 14th, severe rainstorms and high winds buffeted them almost continuously. On November 10 giant waves prevented the five tiny craft from rounding Point Ellice, a 500-foot-high rocky promontory on the north bank of the river. That night, a miserable one, camp was made on a pile of drift logs that for awhile were whipped about by the tide in the raging waters. For the next 4 days, until the weather abated, the cold, drenched, and hungry men took shelter inland on adjacent high ground. On November 15 the group moved ahead to a better location on Chinook Point.

The Point Ellice campsite is unmarked.

Notes

1. Except where otherwise indicated, documentation for this volume, including quotations, is provided by the works cited and annotated in Suggested Reading. Sources indicated in the notes by authors' names in all capital letters are fully identified in Suggested Reading. For the reader's convenience, throughout this book modern names of geographical features, Indian tribes, and animal species are usually employed.

2. The Northwest Passage was not discovered, through remote and rarely passable Arctic waters, until the mid-19th century by British explorers; it was not navigated until 1903–6, by Norwegian explorer Roald Amundsen.

3. Lewis and Clark did not discover any of the mineral resources that were later to spur the westward movement even more than the furs did originally. The two explorers did make limited observations and brought back a few specimens, but they had neither the time nor the equipment for a meaningful mineralogical survey.

4. Because Lewis' projected history of the expedition never saw the light of day, Nicholas Biddle's work in 1814 (see BIDDLE) omitted most of the natural history data, and the Lewis and Clark journals were not published until 1904–5 (see THWAITES), the two captains were late in receiving full credit for their scientific contributions.

5. See Carl I. Wheat, *Mapping the Trans-Mississippi West, 1540–1861* (5 vols., San Francisco: Institute of Historical Cartography, 1957–63), II, 1958 (From Lewis and Clark to Fremont, 1804–1845), pp. 1–15, 31–68; and Herman R. Friis, "Cartographic and Geographical Activities of the Lewis and Clark Expedition," in the *Journal of the Washington [D.C.] Academy of Sciences,* Vol. 44, No. 11 (Nov. 1954), pp. 338–351.

6. The first of these maps was sent back to the War Department from the Mandan villages, in present North Dakota, in April 1805; cartographer Nicholas King prepared versions of it in 1805 and 1806 [see Note 85]. The second Clark map was brought back by Lewis to Washington, D.C., late in 1806, and King utilized it or Lewis and Clark notes to prepare a third map (1806); the present whereabouts of the former map is unknown and the latter is preserved in the Boston Athenaeum. The third Clark map (ca. 1809), today in the Western Americana Collection of Yale University, was one he prepared in St. Louis. In addition to recording the expedition's trek, it includes data later brought back to St. Louis by trappers and others. In 1810 Clark sent this map or a copy of it to Nicholas Biddle in Philadelphia for use in his account of the exploration, which came off the press in 1814 (see ALLEN). The published rendition of the map was copied by Samuel Lewis and engraved by Samuel Harrison.

7. Most of the separate detail maps are presently in the Western Americana Collection of Yale University. The others are found in the Lewis and Clark

journals, held by the American Philosophical Society. All were reproduced in THWAITES.

8. These specimens found their way to Jefferson's collection at Monticello, to Clark's assemblage at St. Louis, and to Charles Willson Peale's museum at Philadelphia. Most of the items that survive today were in Peale's museum. When its collections were dispersed in 1848, about half of those originating with Lewis and Clark went to showman P. T. Barnum. This part perished in 1865 when fire destroyed his American Museum at New York City. Moses Kimball, a friend of Barnum's who ran his own museum in Boston, acquired the other half of the Lewis and Clark specimens from Peale. Kimball ultimately donated them to the Peabody Museum of Harvard University, where they remain today. Included are a decorated Mandan buffalo robe; and, from various tribes, items of women's apparel, an otterskin tobacco pouch, an elk antler bow, and an ornamental device of raven skins. Now in the University of Pennsylvania Museum at Philadelphia are fragments of two Mandan pots. For the shipment and disposition of ethnological specimens sent back from Fort Mandan, see Note 82.

9. CUTRIGHT provides the latest and best treatment of the natural history aspects of the expedition. Earlier works on the subject were prepared by Velva E. Rudd and Raymond D. Burroughs. See Rudd's "Botanical Contributions of the Lewis and Clark Expedition," *Journal of the Washington [D.C.] Academy of Sciences,* Vol. 44, No. 11 (Nov. 1954), pp. 351–356; and Burroughs, ed., *The Natural History of the Lewis and Clark Expedition* (East Lansing, Mich.: Michigan State University Press, 1961). The latter work, based on the journals, confines itself to zoological topics.

10. More botanical specimens survive than of any other kind procured by the expedition. The major existing collection of these, more than 200 in number, is at the Lewis and Clark Herbarium of the Academy of Natural Sciences of Philadelphia. Most of the zoological specimens have been lost, including some that Jefferson personally retained. He sent the bulk of the remainder to Charles Willson Peale for his museum in Philadelphia. In 1848 P. T. Barnum bought Peale's specimens from his heirs for his New York museum, but fire destroyed it in 1865. A few bird specimens are still extant at the Smithsonian Institution's Museum of Natural History in Washington, D.C., Vassar College, and the Academy of Natural Sciences of Philadelphia.

11. Ironically enough, Tarleton was the brother of Frederick, who some years later in St. Louis was to become a bitter enemy of Lewis and cause him extreme anguish. Tarleton had also received from Jefferson for delivery with the Lewis letter one for Gen. James Wilkinson, commanding general of the U.S. Army, that requested Lewis' release. But Wilkinson had returned to Washington, so Bates forwarded the letter to him.

12. Most biographies of Lewis, as well as Clark, including the most recent ones, leave much to be desired; none are definitive. For biographies of Lewis, see BAKELESS and Richard H. Dillon, *Meriwether Lewis* (New York: Coward-McCann, 1965).

13. The best source on Ledyard's career is Helen Augur, *Passage to Glory: John Ledyard's America* (Garden City, N.Y.: Doubleday, 1946).

14. John Ledyard, *A Journal of Captain Cook's Last Voyage: to the Pacific Ocean, and in Quest of a North-West Passage Between Asia and America; Performed in the Years 1776, 1777, 1778 and 1779* (Hartford: Nathaniel Patten, 1783).

15. No direct evidence exists that Jefferson knew of this highly secret Army plan, but because of his high position in the Government he likely did.

16. For a biography of George Rogers Clark, see John Bakeless, *Background to Glory: the Life of George Rogers Clark* (New York: J. B. Lippincott, 1957).

17. On this subject, see NASATIR.

18. Mackay, a Scotsman, had earlier been a trader in Canada and in 1787 had visited the Mandans. Evans was a Welshman who had come to America in 1792 on what proved to be a futile search for the legendary "Welsh Indians," thought by many to be the Mandans.

19. To expedite congressional approval, the estimate was probably kept as low as possible. In any event, the $2,500 was far below actual costs. Because of major variables, these cannot be determined with any degree of accuracy, but are probably in the $35,000–50,000 range. The figure $38,722.25, based on the drafts Lewis submitted to the War Department, is often quoted. It does, however, include a few costs only indirectly associated with the expedition and those incurred in sending some Indian delegates to Washington, D.C.; and excludes the sum of $71,000 appropriated by Congress for double pay and an estimated $26,880 (based on $2 an acre) for land allotments for the expedition's personnel after their return, as well as the approximate $10,000 cost involved in sending Mandan Chief Sheheke back to his people. On the other hand, as an example of some of the major variables, the $38,722.25 figure could be substantially reduced by eliminating the salaries and other costs associated with all the soldiers who would have needed to be paid and supported by their old organizations anyway and therefore did not really represent an additional expense to the Government.

20. Jefferson apparently originally intended to include his request for a special appropriation in his regular message to Congress on December 15, 1802, but did not do so on the recommendation of Secretary of the Treasury Albert Gallatin. He suggested confidentiality because the exploration was "out of our territory."

21. This short, .54 calibre weapon, though modified several times in the following years, was long the Army's official rifle.

22. Like a B-B gun, this weapon operated by air pressure, but it discharged larger shots with more power. It is not known whether the gun carried on the expedition was the bell- or recessed-chamber type. On this weapon, see Eldon G. Wolff, *Air Guns* (Milwaukee: Milwaukee Public Museum, 1958).

23. These medals were known as the Washington Indian Peace and Season Medal (1796) and the Jefferson Peace and Friendship Medal (1801). For full information on this subject, see Bauman L. Belden, *Indian Peace Medals Issued in the United States* (New Milford, Conn.: N. Flayderman, 1966); and Francis P. Prucha, *Indian Peace Medals in American History* (Madison: Wisconsin Historical Society, 1971). Several of the Jefferson medals, probably issued by Lewis and Clark, have been discovered in the West, two recently by archeologists at Indian sites. One of these, apparently originally given to a Sioux chief, is in the possession of the Henry E. Huntington Library and Art Gallery, San Marino, Calif. Another, found at a Nez Perce site, is now owned by Washington State University, Pullman, Wash. A third is at the American Museum of Natural History, in New York City.

24. Some doubt exists about who first suggested Clark for the position and when the decision to recruit him occurred, though Lewis and Jefferson had

undoubtedly discussed it earlier. Writing about the matter a decade later, Jefferson stated that Lewis had suggested Clark. But, in a letter dated December 12, 1802, George Rogers Clark, writing to Jefferson from the Falls of the Ohio, had suggested to him that he hire William in some capacity. Possibly Jefferson casually suggested the selection of Clark to Lewis, who later made it a definite proposal.

25. No evidence exists that the cipher, now in the Jefferson Papers, Library of Congress, was ever employed. Lewis' copy of the letter of credit, dated July 4, 1803, is in the Missouri Historical Society.

26. Alexander Mackenzie, *Voyages from Montreal, on the River St. Lawrence, Through the Continent of North America* . . . (2 vols., London: various publishers, 1801), Toronto 1911 edition, II, pp. 281–282.

27. Jefferson and Lewis, on the basis of dispatches from the U.S. diplomats involved, probably knew informally of the action by late June. Representatives of the two countries signed the treaty, dated April 30, on May 2, 1803. Early newspaper reports of the purchase included those of the *Boston Chronicle*, June 30, and the *National Intelligencer* (Washington, D.C.), July 4. On July 14 Jefferson received a copy of the treaty. The next day, by letter, he so advised Lewis at Pittsburgh; Lewis received the communication on July 22. The Senate ratified the treaty on October 20; 5 days later, the House approved it.

28. This was the area known as Western Louisiana. Eastern Louisiana, a large block of land just east of the Mississippi, had been ceded by France to England in 1763, at the end of the French and Indian War. The United States acquired this territory two decades later, at the conclusion of the War for Independence.

29. The complex boundary question was only to be settled over the course of time by a series of treaties and conventions concluded among Spain, England, Russia, and the United States.

30. On July 26 Lewis wrote Jefferson requesting approval of the proposal. Secretary of War Henry Dearborn approved the assignment on August 3.

31. On July 24 Clark also wrote to Jefferson expressing appreciation for the opportunity to join the expedition.

32. On this subject, see Leland D. Baldwin, *The Keelboat Age on Western Waters* (Pittsburgh: University of Pittsburgh Press, 1941).

33. The exact nature and features of the boat at the time of construction, as contrasted with modifications that were to be made at Camp Wood, cannot be determined from the sources.

34. Although the correct date is undoubtedly August 31, a slight question exists as to whether it was August 30, August 31, or September 1. Lewis' journal, started at Pittsburgh on August 30, contains no entry for the 31st, so he likely meant the last day of the month. Also, in later letters to Jefferson and Clark he gives the date as August 31. On the other hand, Lieutenant Hooke, in a letter dated September 2 at Pittsburgh, said that Lewis had departed the previous day.

35. The sources only refer to use of the keelboat sail, but the builder supplied oars and poles, and they were undoubtedly available for the pirogues and canoes.

36. The keelboat that was to be used to ascend the Missouri was undoubtedly the one constructed in Pittsburgh. After the purchase of the second pirogue, Lewis referred to all the boats except the keelboat as "canoes." This may mean that the pirogues were comparatively small ones; this type of vessel ranged in size from one-man types to large six to eight men craft. It is possible the two pirogues are those later referred to at Camp Wood as the "red" and "white"

pirogues, which were to be used on the Missouri. The Upper Ohio was the center of pirogue, as well as keelboat, construction at the time, though of course used pirogues could be purchased at other places.

37. For some unexplained reason, Lewis did not keep his journal, or it has not survived, for the 54-day period from September 19 to November 10, 1803 (from about 235 miles west of Pittsburgh to Fort Massac, in present Illinois), including the two important stops at Cincinnati and Clarksville. The only sort of illumination on this period is provided by a few extant letters and items in Kentucky newspapers.

38. If Shannon had not come on board at Pittsburgh, he undoubtedly had done so by the time of arrival at Cincinnati. He was a native of Pennsylvania, but in 1800 his family moved to Belmont County, Ohio.

39. The specimens were lost en route. Later, in 1807, on Jefferson's instructions, Clark, on his way from Washington to St. Louis to assume his duties as Superintendent of Indian Affairs, employed a crew of men to excavate the site and provided Jefferson with specimens and a lengthy report.

40. For a description of the falls, see Edmund Flagg, *The Far West* (2 vols., New York: Harper, 1838), I, Appendix, pp. 255–257.

41. *Kentucky Gazette* (Lexington), Nov. 1, 1803.

42. Possibly, as they did on their return trip in 1806, Lewis and Clark visited the latter's sister Lucy, who was married to Maj. William Croghan and lived at Locust Grove estate, about 5 miles northeast of Louisville. A call may also have been made on Gen. Jonathan Clark or the other brothers.

43. The site, which has not been identified, is in the southwestern corner of Caroline County near the Spotsylvania County line. See Marshall Wingfield, *A History of Caroline County, Virginia* (Richmond: Trevett Christian, 1924), pp. 177–179. For a biography of Clark, see BAKELESS.

44. These individuals are known in the Lewis and Clark literature as the "nine young men from Kentucky" on the basis of Nicholas Biddle's use of the term in his 1814 history of the expedition (see BIDDLE). He did not name the men. If his basis of reference to Kentucky is as the place where the men were recruited, it is relatively accurate, for enlistment occurred in the Louisville area, though likely in Clarksville, Indiana Territory. On the other hand, if Biddle's reference is to the residence of the men, his term is a misnomer. Two of them at least, Colter and Shannon, were not residents of Kentucky.

45. Of the group, Floyd and the Field brothers were probably the first that Clark recruited. On July 24 he wrote Lewis saying he had engaged some men. These may have been the three above-named individuals. Although they were not officially inducted into the Army by Lewis until his arrival at Clarksville, in a later document their date of enlistment is given as August 1, 1803. The date specified for Colter is October 15, the same day apparently that Lewis arrived at Clarksville. The enlistment dates for the other five of the "nine young men from Kentucky" are either October 19 or 20.

46. Photostatic copy of Gen. Jonathan Clark's manuscript diary, p. 716, in the possession of the Filson Club, Louisville.

47. "Interpreter" was a special rank and those who held it earned $25, considerably more than enlisted men in the infantry and artillery (sergeants $8, corporals $7, and privates $5) but somewhat less than most officers (captains $40, first lieutenants $30, and second lieutenants $25). The other official interpreter on the expedition was to be Charbonneau, who was officially hired at the

Mandan villages on April 7, 1805, though he had served in that capacity there since the previous November. Although Pierre Cruzatte and François Labiche were also occasionally to perform the function of interpreters, they only held the rank of privates.

48. In the various sources, wide variations occur in the spelling of some names. In no case is this more true than for Drouillard, though he is most often referred to as "Drewyer." For the reader's convenience, in this volume all name spellings are standardized.

49. Pierre, at one time a captain in the British service at Detroit, specialized in relations with the Indians and exercised great influence over them.

50. South West Point, founded in 1794, was about 250 air miles southeast of Fort Massac along the Tennessee River at the site of the city of Kingston, Tenn.

51. Noel M. Loomis and Abraham P. Nasatir, *Pedro Vial and the Roads to Santa Fe* (Norman: University of Oklahoma Press, 1967), pp. 197–199, 210 ff., 427–440.

52. Because of subsequent changes in the channel of the Mississippi, this site is now on its west side, in Missouri instead of Illinois. Since 1803 the mouth of the Missouri has also shifted considerably and is presently some miles farther to the south.

53. Bratton, Colter, the Field brothers, Floyd, Gibson, Pryor, Shannon, and Shields.

54. The company of origin cannot be determined for all of the 32 enlisted men assigned to the party at Camp Wood. Included in the eight from Campbell's company were Cpl. Richard Warfington and Pvts. Hugh Hall, Thomas P. Howard, and John Potts; the other unidentified four men were to be rejected. From Daniel Bissell's company were: Pvts. John Newman and Joseph Whitehouse; from Russell Bissell's: Sgt. John Ordway, Pvt. Patrick Gass, and likely Pvt. John Boley; and probably from Stoddard's: Pvts. John Dame, John G. Robertson, Ebenezer Tuttle, Isaac White, and Alexander H. Willard. The nine men from Clarksville were newly inducted into the Army and thus had never been assigned to units. Not ascertainable are the organizations, if indeed they had previously belonged to any, of the remaining nine soldiers: Pvts. John Collins, Robert Frazer, Silas Goodrich, Hugh McNeal, Moses B. Reed, John B. Thompson, William Werner, Richard Windsor, and Peter M. Wiser.

55. In a later document, Drouillard's date of appointment is listed as January 1, 1804.

56. The only indication of the size of the cannon is Sergeant Ordway's statement on September 20, 1804, that it was loaded with 16 musket balls.

57. Evans had died in 1799, but Mackay lived in the St. Charles area and Lewis possibly received the journals directly from him.

58. Based on his relatively reliable data for the Lower Missouri, Clark estimated the distance to the Mandan villages at 1,500 miles; it turned out to be 1,600. His estimate of the total distance to the Pacific was 3,050 miles, about 1,000 miles short of the actual mileage traveled on the westward leg (3,958). Considering the great bends in the Missouri and the failure of the expedition to take the shortcut recommended by the Minitari Indians between the Great Falls of the Missouri and Travelers Rest, neither of which Clark could have foreseen at Camp Wood, his estimate was relatively accurate.

59. Lower Louisiana had been formally transferred from France to the United States by Spanish authorities at New Orleans on December 20, 1803.

Earlier, on November 30, a French official had accepted the formal transfer of jurisdiction of that region from Spain to France in accordance with the Treaty of San Ildefonso (1800).

60. Carl P. Russell, *Firearms, Traps, and Tools of the Mountain Men* (New York: Knopf, 1967), pp. 34–51, provides an excellent discussion of the expedition's arms.

61. It is possible that some of the French boatmen temporarily assigned to the party carried "fusees," lightweight muskets often used by their group. This same type of weapon was also to be carried by a few of the permanent party that set out westward from the Mandan villages.

62. The commission was effective March 26, 1804. On January 31, 1806, Clark was to be promoted to first lieutenant.

63. For a discussion of the number of French boatmen in the party from Camp Wood to the Mandan villages, see the following note.

64. Because of innumerable discrepancies in the various sources, the precise total number and names of all personnel assigned to the expedition between Camp Wood and the Mandan villages cannot be ascertained. [For an exact list of the complement departing from the Mandan villages, in April 1805, see Note 92.] There is almost no question about the makeup of the permanent party leaving Camp Wood; the major problems concern Cpl. Richard Warfington's detachment and especially the party of French boatmen, both of which returned from the Mandan villages.

The journals of Floyd, Ordway, Gass, and Whitehouse all state that three sergeants and 38 "working hands" set out from Camp Wood with Clark, but do not specify whether or not the latter figure includes Clark's servant York, who did depart from the camp but may not have been counted as a "working hand," and Drouillard. Drouillard was away on an errand at the time and did not rejoin the main body until it arrived at St. Charles. Thus, if it is assumed that the total figure of 41 (three sergeants plus 38 "working hands") is correct and does not incorporate York and Drouillard, the number departing from Camp Wood with Clark would likely be 42, including York. The other 41 personnel would consist of three sergeants and 22 privates of the permanent party, Warfington and six privates in his special detachment, and nine French boatmen.

Of the 42, the permanent party undoubtedly numbered 26 and included York; three sergeants: Floyd, Ordway, and Pryor; and 22 privates: Bratton, Collins, Colter, the Field brothers, Gass, Gibson, Goodrich, Hall, Howard, McNeal, Newman, Potts, Reed, Shannon, Shields, Thompson, Werner, Whitehouse, Willard, Windsor, and Wiser.

Some doubt exists about the members of Warfington's detachment, but the following six privates apparently were assigned to it when it left Camp Wood: Boley, Dame, Frazer, Robertson, Tuttle, and White.

It is impossible to determine with any degree of accuracy the number or names of all the French boatmen at any point en route to or returning from the Mandan villages. The leader, or patroon, was clearly Baptiste Deschamps, but any list of his crew must be highly speculative. Various sources list the following men, one or more of whom probably did not join the party until St. Charles: Joseph Collin, Charles Hébert, La Liberté (Joseph Barter), Baptiste La Jeunesse, Etienne Malboeuf, Peter Pinaut (or Pineau), Paul Primaut (or Primeau), François Rivet, Pierre Roi, Charles Cougee, "Rokey" [Rocque?], and others. Complicating the whole matter, expedition members compiling journals experienced difficulty anglicizing French names and spelled them in a variety of ways.

If 42 men left Camp Wood with Clark, probably nine of them were French boatmen. Exactly who the eight were of those listed above, in addition to Deschamps, cannot be established. If the nine figure is accepted, one nameless boatman, or possibly more, joined the main group later, probably at St. Charles [see Note 66].

The most useful of the sources cited in the Bibliography concerning personnel are JACKSON and OSGOOD. A recent volume on the subject is Charles G. Clarke, *The Men of the Lewis and Clark Expedition: A Biographical Roster of the Fifty-one Members and a Composite Diary of Their Activities From All Known Sources* (Vol. XIV, Western Frontiersmen Series) (Glendale, Calif.: Arthur H. Clark, 1970).

65. On the boatmen, see Notes 64 and 66.

66. For the reasons indicated in Note 64, the exact number and names of all personnel leaving St. Charles cannot be determined accurately any more than at any other point between Camp Wood and the Mandan villages. If it is speculated that only one temporary French boatman joined the expedition at St. Charles and it is assumed that the group aggregated 10, the total complement, in addition to Lewis and Clark, was 46 men (the 42 that set out from Camp Wood plus Drouillard, new privates Cruzatte and Labiche, and the boatman). More than one boatman, however, may have come on board at St. Charles.

As from Camp Wood, the number and names of the permanent party departing from St. Charles are quite firm. Totaling 29, in addition to the leaders, it consisted of York; Sergeants Floyd, Ordway, and Pryor; and the 22 privates— all of whom had come up from Camp Wood [Note 64]—plus Labiche, Cruzatte, and Drouillard. No change apparently occurred in Warfington's detachment at St. Charles.

67. The site of this village, located near present Marthasville, Mo., has long since been inundated by the Missouri River.

68. The only source for this fact is Whitehouse's journal, which does not make it clear whether the man departed of his own volition or was discharged. He may have been recruited initially from Captain Stoddard's artillery company.

69. Setting poles, as long as 20 feet, usually contained knobs at the upper end that fitted the hollow of the shoulder. When one man, pushing a pole, reached the stern he would recover it and return to the bow, where he started again. Except for a reference by Lewis in a letter dated September 28, 1803, to Clark from Cincinnati about being provided by the Pittsburgh boatbuilder with poles (and oars) and a mention in the journals to the use of a setting pole by the sergeant assigned to the bow, who helped the bowsman and probably used the pole to fend off objects in the water, none of the sources discuss the use of setting poles. Nevertheless, they might have been employed on the way up the Missouri and would have been helpful not only in locomotion, but also in pushing off from sandbars and warding away obstructions in the water. The catwalks, or *passe-avants,* provided by the tops of the lockers, offered a place for polers to stand and walk. On the other hand, it is possible that the keelboat was too large for the use of poles to be very effective going up the Missouri, in contrast to the Ohio, where the poles were available and probably used. Also, French boatmen, such as those on the expedition, did not originally employ them, for their use originated in the Eastern United States.

70. This site, on the Nebraska side of the Missouri, should not be confused with the present city of Council Bluffs, about 15 miles to the south on the Iowa side.

71. On October 8, 1804, Robert Frazer was to be shifted from Warfington's detachment to the permanent party to replace Reed.

72. Unlike Privates Reed and Newman, discharged for disciplinary reasons en route to the Mandan villages, Gass was never replaced as a private.

73. Despite the friendliness of the Arikaras to the Lewis and Clark Expedition, for some reason they were exceedingly hostile to later Americans. At least part of this hostility can be attributed to the death at Washington, D.C., in April 1806, of one of their chiefs, named Ankedoucharo, who had returned from the Mandan villages to St. Louis with Corporal Warfington in the spring of 1805. They treated Joseph Gravelines badly when he brought news of the death of their chief in the spring of 1807. That September, they stopped Ens. Nathaniel H. Pryor's party, escorting Sheheke ("Big White"), a Mandan chief returning home from his visit to St. Louis and Washington, D.C., and inflicted 13 casualties. In September 1809 a group under Pierre Chouteau, who threatened the Arikaras with reprisal unless they cooperated, managed to pass the Arikara villages with Sheheke. The Arikaras were also hostile to U.S. fur traders, and in 1823 turned back an Army expedition from Fort Atkinson, Nebr., led by Col. Henry Leavenworth, that sought to avenge an Arikara attack on William H. Ashley's fur brigade.

74. Baptiste Lepage was to be recruited on November 3, 1804, at the Mandan villages to replace Newman.

75. One of the gifts to the Mandans was an iron corn mill. Their use of it was a far cry from its intended purpose. Two years later, the Canadian trader Alexander Henry found that the "foolish" Mandans had made arrow points of part of the mill and the remainder, the largest part that they could not break up, was fixed to a wooden handle and used to pound marrow bone to make grease. The other iron corn mill, carried along as trade goods, had earlier been given to the Arikaras. A third mill, reserved for the expedition's use, was later to be cached at the mouth of the Marias.

76. When Charbonneau joined, he became the oldest man in the party.

77. One of these boatmen, La Liberté, had deserted at the Oto villages. The exact names and number of all persons in this category cannot be determined at any point, as indicated in Note 64.

78. The sources disagree widely on the number who departed and stayed.

79. Charbonneau also had a third wife. Sacagawea is a Minitari name meaning "Bird Woman." Alternate spellings include "Sacajawea" and "Sakakawea."

80. Apparently another violinist in the group was George Gibson, but none of the sources mention his playing.

81. This was the only major en route shipment made to Jefferson. Lewis carried with him, all the way to Washington, the collection of artifacts and specimens obtained from Fort Mandan to the Pacific and on the return to St. Louis.

82. In August 1805 Jefferson received most of this shipment, repacked en route, via Captain Stoddard at St. Louis and the Collectors of the Ports of New Orleans and Baltimore, and thence overland to Washington, D.C. Jefferson retained some of the specimens and material, even personally experimentally planting some of the corn. He distributed the rest of the shipment to Charles Willson Peale for his museum in Independence Hall, Philadelphia; the Ameri-

can Philosophical Society; and to various scholars and specialists. Of the live animals, only the prairie dog and one of the four magpies survived the trip to Washington; the two creatures were subsequently displayed at Peale's museum. One of the decorated Mandan robes, once in Peale's museum in Philadelphia, is now at the Peabody Museum, Harvard University. Most of the botanical specimens sent back from Fort Mandan are located today at the Lewis and Clark Herbarium in the Academy of Natural Sciences of Philadelphia.

83. These were all apparently received on July 13, 1805.

84. This table today is in the possession of the American Philosophical Society, in Philadelphia. President Jefferson codified and tabulated its data into a section of his Message to Congress (February 19, 1806) entitled "A statistical view of the Indian nations inhabiting the Territory of Louisiana and the countries adjacent to its northern and western boundaries."

85. The original of this map has never been found. Jefferson, who likely received it from Secretary of War Henry Dearborn in July 1805, turned it over to his friend the cartographer Nicholas King, surveyor for the city of Washington, D.C. He used it in drawing up maps of the present western United States and southern Canada he prepared in 1805 and 1806. It cannot be determined under whose auspices, if any, the 1805 map was produced; the copy that the State Department retained for a number of years has been lost, but a photostatic copy is retained by the Geography and Map Division of the Library of Congress. The 1806 map was done for the War Department; the Cartographic Records Branch of the National Archives possesses a copy.

86. By this time, Warfington's detachment apparently consisted of two less men than when it had departed from Camp Wood. Robert Frazer had joined the permanent party on October 8, 1804, to replace Moses B. Reed, who was discharged from the expedition. As indicated in the text and Note 68, John G. Robertson had apparently gone back to St. Louis on June 12, 1804, with the Loisel party.

87. See Note 64.

88. All sources disagree widely as to the number of French or French-Canadians on the keelboat.

89. These chiefs, as well as Ankedoucharo, joined others from the Middle West who were being assembled by Pierre Chouteau in St. Louis. Suffering from the heat, dysentery, and homesickness, they spent a troubled summer there and some returned to their tribes. In October 1805 the rest went East, visited President Jefferson, traveled to various Eastern cities, and came back to St. Louis in the spring of 1806. Unfortunately, Ankedoucharo died in Washington, D.C., in April 1806.

90. On the other hand, Lewis was relatively accurate in his prediction to Jefferson in the letter, as well as in one to his mother, that he would arrive back in Virginia during September 1806. He actually reached there in December. Clark was somewhat more optimistic than Lewis. In a letter from Fort Mandan to his brother-in-law in Kentucky, he stated that he hoped to return "not sooner" than about June or July 1806.

91. This is the first point in the expedition where scholars have been able to determine the precise number of personnel and their names. From this point on, until the return to St. Louis, the exact complement is known.

92. Bratton, Collins, Colter, Cruzatte (boatman-interpreter), Joseph Field, Reuben Field, Frazer, Gibson, Goodrich, Hall, Howard, Labiche (boatman-

interpreter), Lepage, McNeal, Potts, Shannon, Shields, Thompson, Werner, Whitehouse, Willard, Windsor, and Wiser. Twenty-four privates had left St. Charles, consisting of the 22 from Camp Wood plus Labiche and Cruzatte [see Note 66]. Frazer from Corporal Warfington's detachment replaced Reed, and at the Mandan villages new recruit Lepage filled Newman's position. But because Private Gass took Floyd's place as sergeant and no one filled his position as private, the privates numbered one less than on the departure from St. Charles.

93. The only two men with Lewis who can be identified are Ordway and Joseph Field.

94. The skin, horns, and bones of a bighorn shipped in April 1805 from Fort Mandan to President Jefferson must have been obtained from the Mandans or Minitaris.

95. According to Jean Baptiste Truteau, French fur trader-explorer, the three individuals were a man named Menard, on several occasions prior to 1796; and Charles Le Raye and one Pardo, in 1802–3. See NASATIR, I, p. 110; II, pp. 376–385. See also "The Journal of Charles LeRaye," in *South Dakota Historical Collections,* IV, pp. 150–180. Some authorities question the authenticity of Le Raye's journal.

96. The American Fur Company was to found Fort Union there in 1829.

97. The journals contain few references to moose. On June 2, 1806, Lewis mentioned that the Nez Perce Indians informed him they were common on the Salmon River. On July 7, the same year, in present Montana, he recorded that Reuben Field wounded one. Because the journals do not mention killing any of the species, the antlers displayed today in the entrance hall at Monticello, Va., Jefferson's home, and attributed to the expedition must have been obtained from some other source.

98. It is possible also that Lewis' complete journal, if he kept one, for the upriver journey from the time of his departure from St. Louis in May 1804 until March 1805 was lost at this time. The principal existing record for this phase is Clark's journal, supplemented by occasional Lewis entries, but the former hints that Lewis was keeping his own full journal. Ordway's journal provides good coverage for this part of the trip.

99. They were possibly viewing today's Bear Paws to the north and the Highwoods to the southwest. Some ranges Clark had reported viewing on May 19 were perhaps the Little Rockies and the Judith Mountains.

100. "Blackfeet" is the modern designation for the tribe Lewis and Clark knew by its Shoshoni name, "Minnetarees of Fort de Prarie" (variously spelled in the journals). In historical literature, the tribe is sometimes referred to as "Minitari of the North" to distinguish it from the "Minitari of the South" (the Hidatsas or Gros Ventres—Big Bellies—of the Missouri), who resided along the Knife River. All the Blackfeet the expedition encountered or saw traces of likely were Piegans, the southernmost of three subtribes, the others being the Bloods and Northern Blackfeet. The three subtribes ranged over the area running from the North Saskatchewan River in Canada to southern Montana and west-east in the present United States from the eastern base of the Rocky Mountains in western Montana over as far as the eastern part of the State. The Blackfeet proper are to be distinguished from a Sioux subtribe called the "Blackfeet Sioux." See John R. Swanton, *The Indian Tribes of North America* (Smithsonian Institution, Bureau of American Ethnology, Bulletin 145) (Wash-

ington: Government Printing Office, 1952), pp. 395–398; and John C. Ewers, *The Blackfeet: Raiders on the Northwestern Plains* (Vol. 49, Civilization of the American Indian Series) (Norman: University of Oklahoma Press, 1958).

101. The complement consisted of Cruzatte, Drouillard, Lepage, Pryor, Shields, and Windsor.

102. In Clark's group were Gass, the Field brothers, Shannon, and York.

103. Including the original keelboat cannon, which had likely been mounted on one of the pirogues since Fort Mandan. On the return trip, in the summer of 1806 it was to be recovered and subsequently presented as a gift to the Mandans on arrival at their villages. Canadian fur traders later stated that they saw the Indians cut it up for its metal.

104. The only men in this group who can be identified are Colter and Willard.

105. The Gallatin flows into the Jefferson-Madison about one-half mile northeast of the point where the Madison joins the Jefferson.

106. In 1810 a party under Col. Pierre Menard, representative of trader Manuel Lisa and the St. Louis Missouri Fur Company, was to establish a post at the Three Forks, but Blackfeet hostility forced its abandonment that same year.

107. Modern authorities contend that the source of the Missouri is the head of the Red Rock River rather than the Horse Prairie Creek drainage.

108. Other Shoshoni groups farther south had made contact with the Spanish.

109. Sacagawea subsequently learned that all her family was dead except for two brothers, one of whom was absent, and a young son of her eldest sister, whom she immediately "adopted."

110. It is also known as the Nez Perce Buffalo Road. Although Lewis and Clark usually referred to it only as "the road," for the reader's convenience the term "Lolo Trail" will henceforth be employed in this volume. The Lolo Trail was actually the main branch of the Nez Perce Buffalo Road; east of Travelers Rest, various subbranches led into present Montana.

111. Including Sergeants Gass and Pryor and Privates Collins, Colter, Cruzatte, Shannon, and Windsor. The remaining four men cannot be identified.

112. Apparently by this time the village had moved 3 miles upstream, or south, from where it was located when Lewis had first visited it, on August 13. It had definitely moved by the time Lewis later visited it, on August 26.

113. Clark later also applied the Lewis name to the lower stretch of the Snake [see Note 121].

114. Lewis noted that the village, which he said consisted of 32 brush lodges, was still located on the east bank but 3 miles south, or upstream, from its site when he had first visited it.

115. Most sources disagree as to the exact number of horses and mules at this point.

116. Most sources disagree as to the exact number of horses and mules at this point.

117. In modern terms, this route runs from Lolo Creek 10 miles north along the Bitterroot River to the junction of the Missoula River; eastward along the Missoula, Hellgate, and Blackfoot Rivers; and then across the Continental Divide via the Lewis Range by any one of several passes (Rogers and Mullan Passes, the best known today, as well as Cadotte's and Lewis and Clark Passes) to the headwaters of the Dearborn River, which empties into the Missouri about 20 air miles north of the Gates of the Mountains. A variant in the eastern part of this

route, not mentioned by Old Toby, that Lewis and part of the expedition was to follow on their eastward journey from the Pacific involved use of, instead of the Dearborn River, the more northerly Sun, which entered the Missouri just upstream, or west, of the Great Falls, or a short distance downstream from the expedition's White Bear Islands, or upper portage, camp.

Although use of the shortcut would have saved the explorers some 49 days in time, had they done so they would not have encountered the Shoshonis. Without the help of this tribe in the form of horses, food, and a guide, the crossing of the Lolo Trail over the Bitterroot Mountains would probably have been impossible.

118. The length of the Lolo Trail can only be estimated because its course cannot always be delineated precisely. Westbound, when Lewis and Clark made a needless detour of roughly 7 miles, they estimated the distance at 170 miles. Eastbound, following a direct route, they calculated it at 156.

119. The Lewis and Clark journals do not mention these cairns, which were undoubtedly there at the time.

120. The branding iron, made by one of the blacksmiths, probably Shields, and carrying the marking "U.S. Capt. M. Lewis" was found in 1892 on an island in the Columbia River 3-1/2 miles above The Dalles, Oreg. One of the few authenticated original objects associated with the Lewis and Clark Expedition known to survive, it is now in the museum of the Oregon Historical Society, at Portland. See also Note 150.

121. The Salmon merged with the Snake about 50 miles above the mouth of the Clearwater. According to Indian information, on which Clark based his deductions at this time, the Snake upstream from its junction with the Salmon was a smaller stream than the latter. Clark thus assumed that the upstream Snake was another river, or tributary, of the one he had named the Lewis River (Salmon-Snake). On the eastbound journey, the two captains were to learn from an Indian the true status of the streams and their relationship.

122. Clark also reported hearing the sound of breakers on the ocean shore. This was conceivable during the heavy storm prevailing at the time.

The late Burnby M. Bell, once park historian at Fort Clatsop National Memorial, Oreg., and an expert in Lewis and Clark site locations and history on the Lower Columbia and the Pacific Ocean, rendered valuable help in the preparation of this volume.

123. Had bad weather not obscured the view, the men could have seen this panorama from high ground in the vicinity of their Point Ellice campsite (November 10–15).

124. Sergeants Ordway and Pryor; Privates Bratton, Colter, Joseph and Reuben Field, Labiche, Shannon, and Wiser; and Charbonneau and York.

125. All the 11 men cannot be identified, but they apparently included Sergeant Pryor and Privates Frazer, McNeal, and Werner. Clark was to leave Werner at the salt camp and take Bratton along.

126. See Note 117.

127. When Captain Hill in the *Lydia* arrived back at the Columbia's mouth in the spring of 1806, the Indians gave him one of the notices. He apparently carried it to Canton, where he presented it to a friend, who sent it to someone in Philadelphia with a letter dated January 1807—months after the expedition had already returned to St. Louis.

128. For several years thereafter, he apparently occupied it during the autumn-winter hunting season.

129. This was the same number of canoes as on arrival at Fort Clatsop, but at that time they consisted of one small and four large ones that had been built at Canoe Camp on the Clearwater. During the winter, some of these had been damaged beyond repair or lost while hunting or in the tide. Lewis and Clark definitely procured two canoes from the Indians at the mouth of the Columbia for the return trip. Three of the five used then may have been the same ones employed on the outbound trip.

130. Between April 17, when the first four horses were purchased, and April 30, by which time the herd definitely numbered 23, the exact number on hand at any one time cannot be determined precisely. Some escaped and Indians stole others. Apparently, too, all purchases were not recorded in the journals because the totals listed at various points do not correlate with individual purchases specified.

131. The following route of the expedition in the Clearwater River country, from May 5–14, 1806, in addition to the journals, is based on articles by Ralph S. Space, dated December 29, 1963, and January 5, 1964, in the Lewiston (Idaho) *Morning Tribune*. Space, a native of Weippe, Idaho, and now a resident of Orofino, was formerly supervisor of Clearwater National Forest. Intimately acquainted with the terrain, he has carefully studied the Lewis and Clark route in the Clearwater River country.

132. These apparently included all 38 of the mounts that had been left with the Nez Perces the previous year except for the two taken by Old Toby and his son, as well as those brought to the Nez Perce villages and gifts received after arriving there.

133. The mountain was probably the one known locally today as Willow Mountain.

134. These stone cairns, or piles, may have had some religious significance or marked spots along the trail for specific Indian purposes. For example, at this point parties traveling the trail often went down to the Lochsa River to fish. Several of the cairns still remain along the Lolo Trail. Probably the best known, because they are adjacent to the Forest Service truck trail, are the two at what is today called Indian Post Office. Neither of these, however, is likely the one referred to by Lewis and Clark in their journals of June 27, 1806. Ralph S. Space, an expert on the Lewis and Clark route along the Lolo Trail, believes the cairn they mentioned is the one that still stands on the mountaintop about a mile south of Indian Grave Peak, some 9 air miles southwest of Indian Post Office. Letter, Space to Appleman, March 3, 1964.

135. For some reason, one of the Nez Perce guides had left at Travelers Rest.

136. Privates Frazer, Goodrich, McNeal, Thompson, and Werner.

137. Many historians have attributed subsequent Blackfeet hostility toward American trappers and traders to Lewis' encounter with the tribe, but it is more likely traceable in part to the participation of American trappers, particularly John Colter, in a major battle they had in 1808 with the Crows and Flatheads; and more broadly to Blackfeet resentment at the furnishing of arms to their enemies by American and Canadian traders. See Hiram M. Chittenden, *The American Fur Trade of the Far West* (2 vols., New York: Press of the Pioneers, Inc., 1935), II, pp. 705–711; and Richard E. Oglesby, *Manuel Lisa and the Opening of the Missouri Fur Trade* (Norman: University of Oklahoma Press, 1963), pp. 56–58.

138. This party totaled 14 men: five (Privates Frazer, Goodrich, McNeal,

Thompson, and Werner) from the Lewis contingent and nine (Sergeant Ordway and Privates Collins, Colter, Cruzatte, Howard, Lepage, Potts, Whitehouse, and Wiser) from the Clark group. Traveling separately with the horses were Sergeant Gass, from the Lewis party, and Willard from the Clark.

139. Sergeant Pryor and three men, detached from Clark's group and trying to catch up with it, had arrived there earlier. They figured Lewis had already passed by, and removed Clark's note to Lewis from the pole.

140. Sergeants Ordway and Pryor and Privates Bratton, Collins, Colter, Cruzatte, Gibson, Hall, Howard, Labiche, Lepage, Potts, Shannon, Shields, Whitehouse, Willard, Windsor, and Wiser.

141. The camp that night, July 6, was near the spot where in 1877 the non-treaty Nez Perces, following their retreat from Idaho over the Lolo Trail and through Gibbons Pass—the same route utilized by Clark—were to fight the Battle of the Big Hole with Army troops.

142. Earlier that day, the Clark group, in following Grasshopper Creek (Clark named it Willard's Creek) for a while, passed near the place where in 1862 gold was to be discovered and the town of Bannack, Mont., founded. Bannack was later the Territorial capital.

143. Privates Collins, Colter, Cruzatte, Howard, Lepage, Potts, Whitehouse, Willard, and Wiser.

144. Bratton, Gibson, Hall, Labiche, Shannon, Shields, and Windsor.

145. Accompanying Clark were York; Charbonneau and Sacagawea and their son; and Privates Bratton, Gibson, Labiche, and Shields.

146. At this point, except for the loss of Colter and the three members of the Charbonneau family, the personnel was the same as at the time of departure from Fort Mandan in April 1805 [see Note 92].

147. Because of the secrecy surrounding the expedition, public knowledge about it and its schedule was probably quite limited, particularly in the East.

148. Washington (D.C.) *National Intelligencer,* Nov. 14, 1806.

149. Including the official discharge of Private Colter, who had been released at the Mandan villages. The other dischargees consisted of Sergeants Gass, Ordway, and Pryor; and Privates Bratton, Collins, Cruzatte, Joseph and Reuben Field, Frazer, Gibson, Goodrich, Hall, Howard, Labiche, Lepage, McNeal, Potts, Shannon, Shields, Thompson, Werner, Whitehouse, Willard, Windsor, and Wiser. On the same date, October 10, Clark, apparently still piqued at not receiving the promised captaincy, submitted his resignation to Secretary of War Dearborn. It was not acted on until February 27, 1807, when it became effective.

150. This scattering of the weapons and paraphernalia of the expedition explains why so few of them have survived. The Missouri Historical Society possesses various objects once used by Lewis and Clark, including a silver watch and English telescope that the former likely carried with him on the expedition. A compass and leather carrying case probably used by Clark on the epic journey is in the Smithsonian Institution, Washington, D.C. See also Note 120.

151. Labiche served as Lewis' interpreter, and Ordway was en route to New Hampshire to visit his family. Frazer was in Virginia and the District of Columbia area early in 1807 and may have accompanied Lewis there, though this cannot be documented.

152. Gen. Jonathan Clark Diary (photostatic copy), entry for Nov. 5, 1806, in the Filson Club, Louisville.

153. Gen. Jonathan Clark Diary, entry for Nov. 8, 1806. From the spring of 1809 until his death in 1818, George Rogers Clark resided at Locust Grove.

154. John G. Jacobs, *The Life and Times of Patrick Gass* (Wellsburg, Va.: Jacob G. Smith, 1859), pp. 108–109.

155. Undoubtedly including Gass. From Washington he returned to Wellsburg, Va. (present W. Va.). It is not clear at what point Labiche, Ordway, and Frazer (if he was in the party) left Lewis, but it was probably at Washington.

156. *National Intelligencer,* Dec. 31, 1806.

157. For other activities of the Indians in Washington, D.C., and coverage of their subsequent visits to other eastern cities, see Katherine C. Turner, *Red Men Calling on the Great White Father* (Norman: University of Oklahoma Press, 1951).

158. *National Intelligencer,* Jan. 16, 1807.

159. *National Intelligencer,* Jan. 9, 21, 1807.

160. Originally exempted from the scope of Clark's superintendency of Indian affairs were the Great and Little Osage Indians, who had previously been entrusted to Pierre Chouteau.

161. On February 28, 1807, Jefferson had sent the nomination to the Senate; on March 4, the same date Lewis' resignation from the Army became official, the *National Intelligencer* announced his appointment as Governor.

162. Enlisted men who had definitely written journals were Sergeants Floyd, Gass, and Ordway; and Privates Frazer and Whitehouse. Others, especially Sergeant Pryor and possibly two other privates, likely also kept them, though none has ever been found. In April 1805 Lewis stated in his journal that seven men other than Clark and himself were maintaining journals. On other occasions he reported all the sergeants were doing so, as they had been directed, and stated that all the privates had been encouraged to do the same.

After utilizing the Lewis and Clark journals for his 1814 history of the expedition (see BIDDLE), in 1818 Biddle turned them over to the American Philosophical Society in Philadelphia. They lay in the files of that institution until 1892–93, when Elliott Coues received permission to use them at his home in preparing his history of the expedition; in the process, he marred them. Since that time, except for certain portions held by the Missouri Historical Society, they have remained at the American Philosophical Society, though in 1904–5 they were published in THWAITES. That they were not printed until that time, a century after the expedition, is one of the great inexplicable disappointments of the entire project.

The Floyd and Whitehouse journals were also not printed until 1904–5, in the same work. The Floyd document is now in the State Historical Society of Wisconsin. Apparently in the fall of 1806 or later, Whitehouse expanded and revised his journal, which is today in the possession of the Newberry Library, Chicago. The revised version has recently been discovered and is now also in the hands of the library, which apparently plans to publish it. The Gass journal was published in an extensively rewritten form in 1807 (see GASS). Biddle also used the Gass journal, later lost. Lewis and Clark, apparently in 1806 or 1807, purchased that of Ordway for $300, dividing the cost equally between them. Biddle utilized it; it was found in his family papers when the Library of Congress acquired them in 1913; it was printed 3 years later in QUAIFE; and is held today by the American Philosophical Society. The original Frazer journal has never come to light.

163. *National Intelligencer,* Mar. 18, Mar. 23, Mar. 27, Mar. 30, Apr. 1, 1807.

164. While in Philadelphia, Lewis sat for a portrait by Charles Willson Peale. Earlier, while Sheheke and his wife were visiting the city, artist C. B. J. Fevret de St. Mémin, apparently on the basis of a commission mailed him by Lewis from Washington, made paintings of them for Lewis' proposed book.

165. One of these protested drafts, as well as a list of all those protested, is now held by the Montana Historical Society.

166. The best account of Lewis' death and the controversy surrounding it is Dawson A. Phelps, "The Tragic Death of Meriwether Lewis," in *The William and Mary Quarterly,* Third Series, Vol. XIII, No. 3 (July 1956), pp. 305–318.

167. For Louisiana Territory, while also holding the rank of brigadier general in the militia, 1807–13; for Missouri Territory, created out of Louisiana Territory, in an *ex-officio* capacity while serving as Governor, 1813–21; and, "for the northern and western tribes," under Presidential appointment, 1822–38.

168. Apparently Clark had almost no dealings with the "factories," or Government-Indian trading posts, in his area. They were abolished in 1822. The factors obtained trade goods and scheduled shipments of Indian furs with the Office of Indian Affairs, under the Secretary of War.

169. During the 6-year period June 1807–June 1813, Clark was absent from his post in St. Louis at least 30 months.

170. Four sons and a daughter; the daughter (Mary Margaret) and two sons (William Preston and John Julius) died in childhood. The eldest surviving son was named Meriwether Lewis (d. 1881); the other, George Rogers (d. 1858).

171. Jefferson K. (d. 1902) and Edmund, the latter dying as an infant.

172. Clark described this trip in a memorandum book, which is now in the Breckinridge Collection at the State Historical Society of Missouri. Besides the detailed route and methods of transportation employed, the volume provides some interesting sidelights on travel in the early 19th century. The memorandum book is summarized in Donald Jackson, "A Footnote to the Lewis and Clark Expedition," in *Manuscripts,* Vol. 24 (1972), pp. 3–21.

173. On this visit to Philadelphia, Clark sat for a portrait by Charles Willson Peale.

174. Uncaptioned article, dated Sept. 3, in the *St. Louis Missouri Argus,* Sept. 6, 1838.

175. Uncaptioned article, dated Sept. 4, in the *St. Louis Missouri Argus,* Sept. 6, 1838.

176. Personnel awarded double pay and land allocations, based on Lewis' recommendations, were: Sergeants Ordway, Floyd (heirs), Gass, and Pryor (the latter three parttime as privates); interpreters Charbonneau and Drouillard; Corporal Warfington; and Privates Bratton, Collins, Colter, Cruzatte, Joseph Field, Reuben Field, Frazer, Gibson, Goodrich, Hall, Howard, Labiche, Lepage, McNeal, Newman, Potts, Shannon, Shields, Thompson, Werner, Willard, Whitehouse, Windsor, and Wiser. Lewis felt that both Newman, who was discharged for insubordination but who later made amends, and Warfington, who had remained with the expedition after his term expired and commanded the keelboat on its return from Fort Mandan to St. Louis, in the spring of 1805, deserved the extra compensation. Lewis and Clark each also received double pay and land allotments of 1,600 acres.

177. Drouillard, Potts, and Wiser accompanied Manuel Lisa from St. Louis in 1807 when he led an expedition numbering about 50 men, in two keelboats, up the Missouri and Yellowstone. Colter, who had earlier separated from Dickson and Hancock and was on his way toward St. Louis alone, joined and turned back to the wilderness with the Lisa party near the mouth of the Platte.

178. For biographies of Colter, see Stallo Vinton, *John Colter, Discoverer of Yellowstone National Park* (New York: E. Eberstadt, 1926) and Burton Harris, *John Colter: His Years in the Rocky Mountains* (New York: Scribner's, 1952).

179. The dearth of extant historical data on Drouillard has precluded the preparation of a suitable biography. M. O. Skarsten, *George Drouillard . . .* (Glendale, Calif.: Arthur H. Clark, 1964) presents some material.

180. Later, Clark served as Lizette's guardian and had a hand in raising her. Clark also helped educate and rear Toussaint, a third child of Charbonneau by his other Shoshoni wife.

181. Most of the historical evidence refutes the theory that Sacagawea died in 1884, nearly 100 years old, at the Wind River Indian Reservation in Wyoming.

182. Ann W. Hafen, "Jean Baptiste Charbonneau," in Leroy R. Hafen, ed., *The Mountain Men and the Fur Trade of the Far West* (10 vols., Glendale, Calif.: Arthur H. Clark, 1965–72), I (1965), pp. 205–224.

Although Baptiste, as well as Gass and Willard, lived after the discovery of photography, the only photographs known to exist of any members of the expedition are one of Willard with his wife, Eleanor, and one or possibly more of Gass.

183. In addition to the sources listed in the Bibliography of this volume, the files of the Historic Sites Survey, National Park Service, Washington, D.C., contain extensive documentation for all the sites described herein.

Suggested Reading

ALLEN, PAUL, ed., see BIDDLE, NICHOLAS

BAKELESS, JOHN. *Lewis and Clark: Partners in Discovery*. New York: William Morrow, 1947. A popularized joint biography, including coverage of the expedition. Separate, definitive biographies of the two men have not yet been written.

[BIDDLE, NICHOLAS]. *History of the Expedition Under the Command of Captains Lewis and Clark . . .* , ed. by Paul Allen. 2 vols., Philadelphia: Bradford and Inskeep, 1814; various domestic reprints and foreign translations. The first account of the exploration to be published based on its two leaders' journals. Biddle also studied those of John Ordway and Patrick Gass, and enjoyed the personal assistance of Clark and George Shannon. Excludes most of the natural history and other scientific data. Thomas Jefferson's special introduction is entitled "Life of Captain Lewis."

COUES, ELLIOTT, ed. *History of the Expedition Under the Command of Lewis and Clark . . . A New Edition . . . .* 4 vols., New York: Francis P. Harper, 1893; reprint, 3 vols., New York: Dover, 1965. A rewrite-editing of BIDDLE, but the author also utilized the Lewis and Clark journals. The principal value of this work lies in its lengthy notes, which are enriched by Coues' travel over a large portion of the route and his extensive knowledge of the natural history of the Missouri Valley. Includes meteorological and natural history data.

CUTRIGHT, PAUL R. *Lewis and Clark: Pioneering Naturalists*. Urbana: University of Illinois Press, 1969. The most recent and comprehensive study dealing with natural history aspects of the expedition. The author is a well-known botanist, who has surveyed much of the trail. Analyzes basic source materials, and discusses condition and present locations of surviving zoological-botanical specimens brought back by Lewis and Clark.

DeVOTO, BERNARD. *The Course of Empire*. Boston: Houghton Mifflin, 1952. The last two chapters, "Westward the Course of Empire" and "The Passage to India," ably summarize the experiences and accomplishments of the Lewis and Clark Expedition. The rest of the book provides useful background data.

DeVOTO, BERNARD, ed. *The Journals of Lewis and Clark*. Boston: Houghton Mifflin, 1953. An excellent, one-volume abridgement of the Lewis and Clark journals (see THWAITES), but also incorporates some passages from BIDDLE; from the Whitehouse, Ordway, and Floyd journals; and from McKeehan's rendition of that of Gass (see GASS). The introduction and notes are contributions in their own right.

EIDE, INGVARD H. *American Odyssey: The Journey of Lewis and Clark*. Chicago, New York, and San Francisco: Rand McNally, 1969. This photographic collection presents many fine modern views of sites, among which are interspersed quotations from the journals.

GASS, PATRICK. *A Journal of the Voyages and Travels of a Corps of Discovery, Under the Command of Capt. Lewis and Capt. Clarke* .... Pittsburgh: David McKeehan, 1807; various domestic reprints and foreign translations. Consists of McKeehan's rewriting of the journal of Gass in formal English, a capability the latter never possessed.

JACKSON, DONALD, ed. *Letters of the Lewis and Clark Expedition with Related Documents, 1783–1854*. Urbana: University of Illinois Press, 1962. Next to the various journals, this work is probably the most important source on the expedition—especially on such matters as its genesis, diplomatic and other background, personages involved, and financial and logistical arrangements. More than half of the 428 letters and documents reproduced have never previously appeared in print. Most of the others have been scattered in assorted publications, and have not always been reprinted without errors in transcription. The annotations and bibliography are valuable, and the index is outstanding.

McKEEHAN, DAVID, see GASS, PATRICK

NASATIR, A. P., ed. *Before Lewis and Clark: Documents Illustrating the History of the Missouri, 1785–1804*. 2 vols., St. Louis: St. Louis Historical Documents Foundation, 1952. Essentially a collection and translation of French and Spanish documents from the archives of Mexico, Spain, Canada, and France, though some are from U.S. repositories and a handful are in English. Clarifies the history of Upper Louisiana and the Missouri River Basin.

OSGOOD, ERNEST S., ed. *The Field Notes of Captain William Clark, 1803–1805* (Vol. V, Yale Western Americana Series). New Haven: Yale University Press, 1964. This thoroughly annotated book, which features an excellent introduction, provides a major addition to the basic sources. Consists of the text and reproduction of Clark's rough field notes for the period December 13, 1803, the day after arrival at the site of Camp Wood, to April 3, 1805, or 4 days before leaving Fort Mandan, N. Dak. Clark utilized the May 14, 1804 to April 3, 1805 segment of these notes, others of which may still be extant for the remainder of the journey, to prepare his formal notebook journals (see THWAITES). Before the discovery of the field notes in a St. Paul attic in 1953, described by Osgood, little was known about day-to-day activities at Camp Wood. Thus, publication of these notes represented the last link in a reasonably complete account of the expedition from the time Lewis left Pittsburgh until the return to St. Louis. The original field notes are now in the Western Americana Collection at Yale University.

QUAIFE, MILO M., ed. *The Journals of Captain Meriwether Lewis and Sergeant John Ordway, Kept on the Expedition of Western Exploration, 1803–1806* (Vol. XXII, Wisconsin Historical Society Collections). Madison: State Historical Society of Wisconsin, 1916; reprint, 1965. Along with the THWAITES volumes, this is a key source. Prior to the discovery of Lewis' Ohio River Journal in late 1913 or early 1914 and its publication in this book, there was virtually no knowledge of the trip down that river and up the Mississippi to Camp Wood. Ordway's journal, like the Ohio River journal, was found in the Biddle family papers; quite complete chronologically, it is second in value as a source only to the journals of Lewis and Clark themselves and provides data not found in any other place. Both documents are now at the American Philosophical Society.

THWAITES, REUBEN G., ed. *Original Journals of the Lewis and Clark Expedition, 1804–1806.* 8 vols., New York: Dodd, Mead, 1904–5; reprint, limited edition, New York: Antiquarian Press, Ltd., 1959. The basic published source on the expedition, this monumental work contains the extant formal notebook journals of Lewis and Clark (as compared to the field notes; see OSGOOD), as well as those of Floyd and Whitehouse. Also presents scientific data, an atlas of the expedition maps, and various appendices. The introduction, bibliographical analysis, and extensive annotations are highly useful.

WHEELER, OLIN D. *The Trail of Lewis and Clark, 1804–1904.* 2 vols., New York and London: G. P. Putnam's Sons, 1904; 2d ed., 1926. Although this book is outdated and contains some inaccurate site data, it is still worthwhile. At the beginning of the present century, when large parts of the trail were still little changed, the author traveled on horseback over many sections.

Criteria for Selection of Historic Sites of National Significance

A. National significance is ascribed to buildings, sites, objects, or districts which possess exceptional value or quality in illustrating or interpreting the historical (history and archeology) heritage of our Nation, such as:

1. Structures or sites at which events occurred that have made a significant contribution to, and are identified prominently with, or which outstandingly represent, the broad cultural, political, economic, military, or social history of the Nation, and from which an understanding and appreciation of the larger patterns of our American heritage may be gained.

2. Structures or sites associated importantly with the lives of persons nationally significant in the history of the United States.

3. Structures or sites associated significantly with an important event that outstandingly represents some great idea or ideal of the American people.

4. Structures that embody the distinguishing characteristics of an architectural type specimen, exceptionally valuable for a study of a period, style, or method of construction; or a notable structure representing the work of a master builder, designer, or architect.

5. Objects that figured prominently in nationally significant events; or that were prominently associated with nationally significant persons; or that outstandingly represent some great idea or ideal of the American people; or that embody distinguishing characteristics of a type specimen, exceptionally valuable for a study of a period, style, or method of construction; or that are notable as representations of the work of master workers or designers.

6. Archeological sites that have produced information of a major scientific importance by revealing new cultures, or by shedding light upon periods of occupation over large areas of the United States. Such sites are those which have produced, or which may reasonably be expected to produce, data affecting theories, concepts, and ideas to a major degree.

7. When preserved or restored as integral parts of the environment, historic buildings not sufficiently significant individually by reason of historical association or architectural merit to warrant recognition may collectively compose a "historic district" that is of historical significance to the Nation in commemorating or illustrating a way of life in its developing culture.

B. To possess national significance, a historic or prehistoric structure, district, site, or object must possess integrity. For a historic or prehistoric *site,* integrity requires original location and intangible elements of feeling and association. The site of a structure no longer standing may possess national significance if the person or event associated with the structure was of transcendent importance in the Nation's history and the association consequential.

For a historic or prehistoric *structure,* integrity is a composite quality derived from original workmanship, original location, and intangible elements of feeling and association. A structure no longer on the original site may possess national significance if the person or event associated with it was of transcendent importance in the Nation's history and the association consequential.

For a historic *district,* integrity is a composite quality derived from original workmanship, original location, and intangible elements of feeling and association inherent in an ensemble of historic buildings having visual architectural unity.

For a historic *object,* integrity requires basic original workmanship.

C. Structures or sites which are primarily of significance in the field of religion or to religious bodies but are not of national importance in other fields of the history of the United States, such as political, military, or architectural history, will not be eligible for consideration.

D. Birthplaces, graves, burials, and cemeteries, as a general rule, are not eligible for consideration and recognition except in cases of historical figures of transcendent importance. Historic sites associated with the actual careers and contributions of outstanding historical personages usually are more important than their birthplaces and burial places.

E. Structures, sites, and objects achieving historical importance within the past 50 years will not as a general rule be considered unless associated with persons or events of transcendent significance.

Acknowledgments

*Advisory Board on National Parks, Historic Sites,
Buildings, and Monuments*

E. Y. Berry, *Rapid City, S. Dak.*
Mrs. Lyndon B. Johnson, *Stonewall, Tex.*
Laurence W. Lane, Jr., *Menlo Park, Calif.*
A. Starker Leopold, *University of California, Berkeley.*
Peter C. Murphy, Jr., *Springfield, Oreg.*
Melvin M. Payne, *National Geographic Society.*
Linden C. Pettys, *Ludington, Mich.*
Steven Rose, *Arcadia, Calif.*
Walter M. Schirra, Jr., *Englewood, Colo.*
Douglas W. Schwartz, *School of American Research.*
William G. Shade, *Lehigh University.*

*Consulting Committee for the National Survey
of Historic Sites and Buildings*

James Biddle, *National Trust for Historic Preservation.*
John O. Brew, *Harvard University.*
Walter L. Creese, *University of Illinois.*
Richard H. Howland, *Smithsonian Institution.*
John W. Huston, *U.S. Naval Academy.*
Herbert E. Kahler, *Alexandria, Va.*
Charles E. Lee, *South Carolina Department of Archives and History.*
Henry A. Millon, *Massachusetts Institute of Technology.*
Frederick D. Nichols, *University of Virginia.*
Dorothy B. Porter, *Moorland Foundation, Howard University.*

National Park Service

Edwin C. Bearss, *Historian, Historic Preservation Project (East), Denver
   Service Center.*
Burnby M. Bell (deceased), *former Historian, Fort Clatsop National
   Memorial, Oreg.*
Frederick R. Bell, *Picture Librarian, Office of Information.*

John A. Burns, *Architect, Historic American Buildings Survey, Division of Historic and Architectural Surveys.*

Paul Goeldner, *Architect, Historic Sites Survey, Division of Historic and Architectural Surveys.*

David K. Hansen, *Historian, Historic Sites Survey, Division of Historic and Architectural Surveys.*

Herbert E. Kahler, *Chief (retired), Division of History and Archeology.*

Warren A. McCullough, *Public Affairs Specialist, Independence National Historical Park, Pa.*

John D. McDermott, *Assistant Executive Secretary, Advisory Council on Historic Preservation.*

R. Alan Mebane, *Chief Naturalist, Yellowstone National Park, Wyo.-Mont.-Idaho.*

Christine L. St. Lawrence, *Writer-Editor, Historic American Buildings Survey, Division of Historic and Architectural Surveys.*

Charles W. Snell, *Historian, Historic Preservation Project (East), Denver Service Center.*

Hilda E. Staubs, *Museum Technician, Harpers Ferry National Historical Park, Md.-W. Va.*

Robert M. Utley, *Assistant Director, Park Historic Preservation.*

Other Individuals

Carey S. Bliss, *Curator of Rare Books, Henry E. Huntington Library and Art Gallery.*

Beatrice Boone, *Visual Information Specialist, Bureau of Sport Fisheries and Wildlife, U.S. Department of the Interior.*

Helen Clark, *Head, Photograph Sales, The National Gallery of Canada.*

Paul R. Cutright, *Jenkintown, Pa.*

Josephine M. D'Orsi, *Division of Photography, American Museum of Natural History.*

Mrs. John G. Dotzman, *Missouri Historical Society.*

Richard H. Engeman, *Photographs and Maps Librarian, Oregon Historical Society.*

John C. Ewers, *Senior Ethnologist, Department of Anthropology, Smithsonian Institution.*

Larry Gill, *Great Falls, Mont.*

Mildred Goosman, *Curator, Western Collection, Joslyn Art Museum.*

Gail Guidry, *Curator of Pictorial History, Missouri Historical Society.*

Aubrey L. Haines, *Bozeman, Mont.*

Gertrude D. Hess, *Associate Librarian, American Philosophical Society Library.*

Donald D. Jackson, *Professor of History, University of Virginia.*

Michael S. Kennedy, *former Director, Montana Historical Society.*

Howard L. Levin, *Bettmann Archive, Inc.*

R. J. McCaig, *Montana Power Company, Great Falls.*

James H. Maroney, *Head of American Painting, Sotheby Parke Bernet, Inc.*

Charles S. Marshall, *Executive Secretary, Eastern National Park and Monument Association.*

Lory J. Morrow, *Photo Archivist, Montana Historical Society.*

Ralph S. Space, *Orofino, Idaho.*

Frances H. Stadler, *Archivist, Missouri Historical Society.*

Keith M. Thompson, *Forest Supervisor, Clearwater National Forest, Idaho.*

Helen B. West, *Archives Assistant, Museum of the Plains Indian.*

Oliver Willcox, *Staff Photographer, Thomas Gilcrease Institute of American History and Art.*

Art and Picture Credits

The National Park Service, The Lewis & Clark Trail Foundation, and Jefferson National Expansion Historical Association gratefully acknowledge the assistance of agencies and individuals furnishing illustrations and granting permission to reproduce them. Where available, names of photographers and dates of photographs are indicated in parentheses following credits.

Page

53 Drawing: Fur Trade Illustration Project, 1945-48. National Park Service.
59 National Park Service, Jefferson National Expansion Memorial.
63 National Park Service (Roy E. Appleman, 1965).
66 National Park Service, Jefferson National Expansion Memorial.
67 U.S. Army.
68 U.S. Army.
71 Drawing: Fur Trade Illustration Project, 1945-48. National Park Service.
75 Smithsonian Institution and National Park Service.
76 National Park Service.
78 American Philosophical Society.
79 National Park Service, Jefferson National Expansion Memorial.
82 Smithsonian Institution.
84 American Philosophical Society.
85 American Philosophical Society.
87 Jefferson National Expansion Historical Association (Breun, 1991).
88 Jefferson National Expansion Historical Association (Breun, 1991).
91 National Park Service, Jefferson National Expansion Memorial.
94 Oil by Catlin. National Museum of American Art, Smithsonian Institution, Gift of Mrs. Joseph Harrison, Jr.
95 Oil by Catlin. National Museum of American Art, Smithsonian Institution, Gift of Mrs. Joseph Harrison, Jr.
97 Bureau of Sport Fisheries and Wildlife, U.S. Department of Interior (E.P. Haddon)
99 Bureau of Sport Fisheries and Wildlife (Haddon).
100 Bureau of Sport Fisheries and Wildlife (E.R. Kalmbach).
102 Yellowstone National Park
103 Bureau of Sport Fisheries and Wildlife (Haddon).
105 Oil by Catlin. National Museum of American Art, Smithsonian Institution, Gift of Mrs. Joseph Harrison, Jr.
107 Jefferson National Expansion Historical Association (Breun, 1989).
108 National Park Service, Jefferson National Expansion Memorial.
110 Oil by Catlin. National Museum of American Art, Smithsonian Institution, Gift of Mrs. Joseph Harrison, Jr.
111 Drawing: Fur Trade Illustration Project, 1945-48. National Park Service.
113 Oil by Catlin. National Museum of American Art, Smithsonian Institution, Gift of Mrs. Joseph Harrison, Jr.

Page

Page

174 National Park Service (Everhart, 1958).
175 Bureau of Outdoor Recreation (Blair, 1964).
176 National Park Service (Everhart, 1958).
177 National Park Service (Mattison, 1958).
178 National Park Service (Mattison, 1958).
180 Lewis & Clark Trail Heritage Foundation, Great Falls, Montana.
182 Lewis & Clark Trail Heritage Foundation, Great Falls, Montana.
183 U.S. Army Corps of Engineers.
185 THWAITES, VIII, Map 32, Part I. National Park Service, Jefferson National Expansion Memorial.
186 U.S. Army Corps of Engineers.
187 Lithography by Sarony, Major & Knapp from a sketch by Stanley in *U.S. Pacific Railroad Surveys*, XII, Plate XLIII.
188 Jefferson National Expansion Historical Association (Breun, 1991).
189 Bureau of Outdoor Recreation (Blair, 1964).
190 Lewis & Clark Trail Heritage Foundation, Great Falls, Montana.
192 THWAITES, VIII, Map 32, Part III. National Park Service, Jefferson National Expansion Memorial.
195 National Park Service (1964).
197 Lewis & Clark Trail Heritage Foundation, Great Falls, Montana.
200 Oil by Catlin. National Museum of American Art, Smithsonian Institution, Gift of Mrs. Joseph Harrison, Jr.
201 Bureau of Outdoor Recreation (Blair, 1964).
214 Lithography by Sarony, Major & Knapp from a sketch by Stanley in *U.S. Pacific Railroad Surveys*, XII, Plate LXIV.
217 Helen B. West (Edward Mathison, 1963).
218 Helen B. West (Mathison, 1963).
221 National Park Service (Appleman, 1964).
226 Drawing: Fur Trade Illustration Project, 1945-48. National Park Service.
227 Bureau of Sport Fisheries and Wildlife (Joe Mazzoni).
228 Lewis & Clark Trail Heritage Foundation, Great Falls, Montana.
234 American Philosophical Society.
238 Crayon drawing by C.B.J. Fevret de Saint Memin. American Philosophical Society.
248 National Park Service, Jefferson National Expansion Memorial.
251 Lewis & Clark Trail Heritage Foundation, Great Falls, Montana.
259 Bureau of Outdoor Recreation.
260 Bureau of Outdoor Recreation.

Page

261 U.S. Army Corps of Engineers.
263 River Basin Surveys, Smithsonian Institution.
270 National Park Service.
271 National Park Service (Grant, 1951).
274 National Park Service (Mattison, 1958).
276 National Park Service (Mattison, 1958).
277 National Park Service (Everhart, 1958).
282 National Park Service (Mattison, 1958).
284 National Park Service (Mattison, 1958).
286 Bureau of Outdoor Recreation (Blair, 1964).
288 Lewis & Clark Trail Heritage Foundation, Great Falls, Montana.
289 National Park Service (Appleman, 1965).
291 Bureau of Outdoor Recreation (Blair, 1964).
294 National Park Service.
297 Bureau or Outdoor Recreation (Blair, 1964).
300 National Park Service (Grant, 1952).
304 National Park Service (Mattison, 1958).
307 Jefferson National Expansion Historical Association (Breun, 1991).
308 Jefferson National Expansion Historical Association (Breun, 1991).
310 Jefferson National Expansion Historical Association (Breun, 1989).
311 Bureau of Outdoor Recreation (Blair, 1964).
313 National Park Service (Appleman, 1964).
315 National Park Service (Appleman, 1964).
319 Helen B. West and Edward Mathison.
321 U.S. Army Corps of Engineers.
323 National Park Service (Thomas K. Garry, 1965).
326 National Park Service (Mattison, 1958).
327 National Park Service (Mattison, 1958).
329 National Park Service (Mattison, 1958).
333 Top, lithograph by Sarony, Major & Knapp from a Sketch by Gustav
    Sohon, in *U.S. Pacific Railroad Surveys*, XII, Plate LVII; bottom,
    National Park Service (Mattison, 1958).
335 National Park Service (Mattison, 1953).
338 National Park Service (Appleman, 1964).
339 Jefferson National Expansion Historical Association (Breun, 1991).
341 National Park Service (Appleman, 1964).
343 National Park Service (Mattison, 1961).
345 Bureau of Outdoor Recreation (Blair, 1964).
347 Bureau of Outdoor Recreation (Blair, 1964).

Page

348 Bureau of Outdoor Recreation (Blair, 1964).
350 All U.S. Army Corps of Engineers.
351 National Park Service (Appleman, 1964).
352 River Basin Surveys, Smithsonian Institution (1966).
354 National Park Service.
356 National Park Service (1960).
358 National Park Service (Mattison, 1958).
359 Both U.S. Army Corps of Engineers.
360 National Park Service (Mattison, 1958).

Index

"A statistical view of the Indian nations inhabiting the Territory of Louisiana and the countries adjacent to its northern and western boundaries," 122, 370

Absence-without-leave (AWOL), *see* Discipline

Academy of Natural Sciences of Philadelphia, 362, 370

Accidents, *see* Calamities

Advance parties, special detachments, and reconnaissances of expedition, 34, 47, 50, 57–58, 61, 62, 77, 79, 80, 81, 82, 83, 90, 92, 93, 96, 128, 132, 135–136, 137–138, 145, 147, 148, 149, 151, 152–160, 164–167, 175–178, 181, 190–193, 194, 196–197, 201–202, 203–204, 205, 210, 212–229, 271, 272, 278, 281, 283, 284, 293, 296, 298, 300, 303–304, 305–306, 307, 309, 312, 325, 328, 334, 336, 346, 347, 349–351, 353, 356, 357, 358

Adventure and adventurers, 6–7, 20, 55, 230, 250, 253, 309, 329. *See also* Calamities.

Advisory Board on National Parks, Historic Sites, Buildings, and Monuments, 267, 384

Africa, 6, 21

Age of expedition members, at various times, compared, 52, 54, 56, 64, 94, 152, 162, 250, 252, 328, 369

Agencies, governmental, *see specific agencies, especially following* United States

Agency Creek (Idaho), 275

Agents and agencies, Indian, *see* Indian agents and agencies

Agriculture, *see* Farms; Ranches; United States Department of Agriculture

Air gun, 33, 75, 92, 101, 107, 162, 363

Alabama (State), *see* Natchez Trace

Albemarle County, Va., 15, 16, 266

Alcohol, *see* Whisky

Allen, Paul, journalist and editor, 247, 249, 323, 379

Allotments of land, *see* Land warrants

Altoona, Wash., 357

Amahami Indians and Amahami villages, 109, 110, 262, 340, 342

America and Americans, *see* United States; *and appropriate topics throughout this index*

"American bottom," 61

American Fur Company, 371

American Museum, N.Y., 362

American Museum of Natural History, N.Y., 363

American Numismatic Society, 91

American Philosophical Society, 21, 23, 84, 85, 362, 369–370, 376, 377, 381

American Revolution, Daughters of the, 325, 334

Ammunition, *see* Guns

Amundsen, Roald, explorer, 361

Amusements, *see* Leisure-time and social activities

Anaconda Copper Company, 315

Anatomy and anatomists, 30–31

Anderson, Robert H., historian, 217, 218

Anglicization of foreign names, 366–368

Animals, *see* Extinction of animals; Zoological observations; *and individual species*

Ankedoucharo, Arikara chief, 124, 231, 232, 237, 369, 370

Annapolis, Md., 17

Antecedents and background of expedition, *see under* Lewis and Clark Expedition

Antelope (pronghorn), 14, 98, 102, 118, 126, 159, 206, 225–226, 257

Anthropology, 203. *See also* Archeologists.

Appaloosa horses, *see* Horses

Appendicitis, 94–96

Appleman, Roy, historian, 157

Arabian-Spanish horses, *see* Horses

Arapaho Indians, 339

Archeologists, archeological excavation, and prehistoric period, 17, 43, 51, 91, 203, 208–209, 228, 236, 258–259, 263,

Climate and weather, adverse or unique, 35, 77, 80, 82, 83, 86, 88, 131, 134, 141, 143, 144, 168, 178, 187, 188–191, 193, 194, 195, 197, 198, 204, 205, 216, 277, 303, 304, 311, 316, 346, 347, 360, 373. *See also specific seasons.*

Clothing: of expedition, 31, 69, 92, 96, 97, 118, 131–132, 144–145, 189, 193, 198, 224, 232, 235, 253, 346; of Indians, 35, 92, 96, 133, 186, 362

Coal and charcoal, 120, 145, 264

Coboway, Clatsop chief, *see* Comowool

Cochrane Dam, Mont., 311, 316

Colic, bilious, *see* Bilious colic

Colleges, *see* Universities

Collin, Joseph, expedition boatman, 367

Collins, Pvt. John, expedition member, 62, 80, 89, 194, 250, 366, 367, 370, 372, 375, 377

Collinwood, Tenn., 244

Colorado River, 34, 35

Colter, Pvt. John, expedition member and trapper, 51, 56, 57, 62, 65, 83, 97, 100, 166, 167, 171, 191, 230, 231, 250, 328, 329–331, 340, 365, 366, 367, 370, 372, 373, 374, 375, 377, 378

Colter Falls, Mont., 315

"Colter's Creek," *see* Potlatch River

Colts, *see* Horses

Columbia Basin and Columbia River Valley, *see* Columbia River

Columbia Rediviva (ship), 355

Columbia River ("Great River of the West"; "Oregan River"; "Oregon River"; "River of the West"): and Cascade Range, 182; and Clearwater River, 206; and expedition, 34, 52, 126, 152, 156, 159, 168, 179, *181–207*, 213, 257, 273, 275, 281, 283, 355–356; and Missouri River, 11, 21, 25, 34–35, 40, 115; and "Tacoutche Tesse" River, 41; as fur trade artery, 41; as key to hinterland, 38; Cascades of, *see* Cascades of the Columbia; current of, 205, 355; dams on, 260–261; discovered and named, 25, 38, 39, 41; early knowledge about, 25; estuary of, 38, 188, 190, 346, 355, 357; explored, 355–356 (*and see individual explorers*); forts along, 356–357; fur post near mouth of, 280; gorge of, 187; Great Falls of, *see* Celilo Falls; headland at mouth of, *see* Cape Disappointment; headwaters of, 152; history of, 373; Indians along, 12, 14, 120, 171, 184–187, 194, 195, 198–204, 205–207, 332, 374 (*and see specific tribes*); islands in, *see* Islands; landmarks along, 355, 357; mapped, 192, 204; navigability of,

11, 25, 159, 171, 179, 182–184, 205–206, 258, 332; northwest traders at mouth of, 202–203, 373; sources of, 25; south fork of, hypothesized, 120; terrain and scenery along, 182, 187, 188, 190, 356, 360; The Dalles of, *see* The Dalles (falls); tributaries of, 25, 164, 172, 179, 181, 207, 263; U.S. and other powers claim and explore area of, 38, 39, 40–41; wild stretches of, 258. *See also appropriate topics throughout this index.*

Columbia River Basin and Columbia River Valley, *see* Columbia River

Columbus, Christopher, navigator, 124

Columbus, Mont., 227

Commerce and trade: and Clark, 241–242, 245, 246; and expedition and expedition members, 3, 6–7, 26, 28, 29, 34, 35, 37, 38, 40, 193, 202, 209, 257–265, 288; and French, 298; and fur trade, *see* Fur trade; and northwest trade, *see* Northwest trade; and York, 252; among Indians, *see under* Indians; in various places, 15, 31, 59, 72–73, 188, 240, 247–249, 264, 265, 292, 293, 295, 298, 315, 348, 353. *See also* United States Department of Commerce; *specific businesses and businessmen; and individual companies.*

Commissions, in Army, and commissioned officers, *see* Rank; *and specific officers*

Comowool (Coboway), Clatsop chief, 199, 204, 348

Companies: in fur trade, *see* Fur trade; in other fields, *see* Commerce

Compasses, 22, 31, 35, 82, 92, 143–144, 375. *See also* Celestial navigation; Dead reckoning.

Confederation, U.S., 18

Conferences, with Indians, *see* Councils

Confluence of the Marias and Missouri, Mont., *see* Marias River

Confrontation with the Teton Sioux Site, S. Dak., *see* Teton Sioux Indians

Congress, U.S., *see* United States Congress

Connecticut (State), 18, 19

Conner, John, interpreter, 30

Conrad, C. & A., and Company, 239, 247

Conservation and conservationists, 257–265, *rear end paper. See also specific sites.*

Constitution, U.S., 22, 26

Continental Army, 15

Continental Congress, 17

Continental Divide, 3, 25–26, 43, 120, 126, 147, 155, 156, 158, 163, 214, 224, 273, 274, 317, 331, 340, 372

Oto Indians, 81, 89–90, 92–93, 95, 124, 233, 336, 369
Otter, land, *see* Fur trade
Otter, sea, *see* Northwest trade
Oxen, 50, 51

Paca (animal), 21
Pacific coast, *see* Pacific Ocean
Pacific Northwest, *see* Northwestern United States
Pacific Ocean ("Great South Sea"; "South Sea"; "Western Ocean"): and Columbia River, 25; and explorers, *see particular explorers;* and Northwest Passage, *see* Northwest Passage; and Northwest trade, *see* Northwest trade; and Rocky Mountains, 26; as terminus of expedition, *passim;* expedition explores coast of, 191–204, 345–351, 355–360, 373; mapped, *see* Maps; river route to, 40; rivers flowing to, 164; Spain seeks route to and proposes string of fur posts to, 24; U.S. expansion to, *see* Trans-Appalachian West *and* Trans-Mississippi West
Pack Creek (Idaho), 172
Packers Meadow (glade) (Idaho), 172, 174, 211, 279
Packhorses, *see* Horses
Packing of supplies, *see* Supplies
Painters and paintings, *see* Art
Painting of bodies, by Indians, 158, 159
Paleontological sites, *see* Archeologists
Palisades and pickets, *see* Log cabins and log construction
Pallas, Peter Simon, scientist, 19
Papers, important, of expedition, 131, 146, 184, 210, 215, 219, 243, 247. *See also* Lewis and Clark journals.
Parades, *see* Councils
Pardo, ——, fur trader, 371
Paris, France, 17, 18–19, 43, 46, 121
Parks: national, *see* National parks; State, 265, 266
Parleys, *see* Councils
Parties, *see* Dinners, parties, and balls
Partisan, The, Sioux chief, *see* The Partisan
"Passe-avants," *see* Boats
Passports, British and French, Lewis carries, 34, 59, 114
Patterson, Dr. William E., and expedition, 51
Patterson, Robert, mathematician, 30–31, 51
Paul of Württemberg, *see* Prince Paul of Württemberg
Pawnee Indians, 81, 89–90, 233

Pay: of Army personnel, 365; of expedition boatmen, 115; of expedition members, 230, 235, 249, 363, 365, 377; of Heney, 212; of Indian guides for expedition, 181. *See also* Land warrants.
Peabody Museum, Mass., 123, 362, 370
Peace medals, expedition gives to Indians, 33, 91, 92, 114, 162, 168, 177, 181, 202, 219, 221, 363
Peace-pipe smoking, *see* Councils
Peale, Charles Willson, museum proprietor and artist, 5, 8, 9, 32, 362, 369, 370, 377
Peale, Rembrandt, artist, 248
Pelts, *see* Fur trade; Zoological observations
Pemmican, 104, 145
Pennsylvania (region and State), 11, 16, 29–34 *passim,* 47, 50, 57, 64, 74, 266, 362, 365, 369, 370
"Pennsylvania" rifles, *see* Guns
Peréz, Don Manuel, Spanish official, 297
Peritonitis, 94–96
"Permanent Indian frontier," 337
Permanent party, on expedition, *see* Personnel
Pernier, John, servant of Lewis, 243–245
Perogues, *see* Boats
Personnel on expedition: recruitment, selection, training, utilization, and discharge of, 30, 33, 34, 47–49, 50, 51, 52, 56, 57–58, 61–65, 70, 77, 79, 80, 93–94, 114–116, 124, 125–126, 147, 196, 198, 215, 223, 224, 225, 227–228, 229, 235, 288, 293, 296, 312, 340, 365–368, 369, 370, 371, 373, 374–375, 376. *See also* Discipline; *and specific individuals.*
Peru, 21
Philadelphia, Pa., 11, 23, 29, 30–33, 34, 47, 51, 69, 174, 238, 239, 240, 247, 248, 250, 361, 362, 369, 370, 373, 377. *See also* American Philosophical Society.
Philippine Insurrection *(1899–1902),* 67
Photographs and photographers, 258–259, 325, 378, 380. *See also specific photographs throughout this volume.*
Physical evidence surviving from expedition, *see* Objects
Physical sciences, *see* Science
Physicians, *see* Sickness
Physiologists, 291. *See also* Sickness.
Picket enclosures, *see* Log cabins and log construction
Pictographs, Indian, *see* Archeologists
Piegan Indians, *see* Blackfeet Indians
Pierce, Idaho, 279
"Pierced Noses," *see* Nez Perce Indians
Pierre, S. Dak., 101

Anyone wishing to order books about the Expedition, texts of the Journals of Lewis and Clark, or lists of books about Westward Expansion, should contact:

Jefferson National Parks Association
10 S. Broadway, Suite 1540
St. Louis, MO 63102-1728
1-800-537-7962
www.jnpa.com

Cover Picture Information

Oil portrait of Willliam Clark (1810) by Charles Willson Peale. Independence National Historic Park Collection. Oil portrait of Meriwether Lewis (1810) by Charles Willson Peale. Independence National Historic Park Collection. Lewis and Clark Map of the Great Falls of the Columbia. American Philosophical Society.

As the Nation's principal conservation agency, the Department of the Interior has basic responsibilities for water, fish, wildlife, mineral, land, park, and recreational resources. Indian and Territorial affairs are other major concerns of America's "Department of Natural Resources." The Department works to assure the wisest choice in managing all our resources so each will make its full contribution to a better United States-now and in the future.